india's middle class

Cities and the Urban Imperative

Series Editor: Sujata Patel, Professor, Department of Sociology, University of Hyderabad

This series introduces a holistic approach to studying cities, the urban experience, and its imaginations. It assesses what is distinctive of the urban phenomenon in India, as also delineates the characteristic uniqueness of particular cities as they embrace change and create ways of experiencing modernities.

Taking an interdisciplinary route, the series evaluates the many facets of urbanisation and city formation, and explores the challenges faced in relation to regional, national and global processes.

The books in this series present the changing trends in macro and micro urban processes; the nature of demographic patterns of migration and natural growth therein; spatial reorganisation and segregation in urban areas; uneven economic development of manufacturing and services in cities; unequal access to power in the context of formal citizenship; increasing everyday violence and declining organised protest; breakdown of urban family life in juxtaposition with the reconstitution of community. They trace how new forms of socialities are replacing old forms of trust and solidarity, and how these are being institutionalised in distinct and diverse ways within South Asia.

Also in this Series

Growing up in the Knowledge Society: Living the IT Dream in Bangalore
Nicholas Nisbett
ISBN 978-0-415-55146-5

Governing India's Metropolises: Case Studies of Four Cities
Editors: Joël Ruet and Stephanie Tawa Lama-Rewal
ISBN 978-0-415-55148-9

India's Middle Class: New Forms of Urban Leisure, Consumption and Prosperity
Christiane Brosius
ISBN 978-0-415-54453-5

Urban Navigations: Politics, Space and the City in South Asia
Editors: Jonathan Shapiro Anjaria and Colin McFarlane
ISBN 978-0-415-61760-4

Participolis: Consent and Contention in Neoliberal Urban India
Editors: Karen Coelho, Lalitha Kamath and M. Vijayabaskar
ISBN 978-0-415-81193-4

Dharavi: From Mega-Slum to Urban Paradigm
Marie-Caroline Saglio-Yatzimirsky
ISBN 978-0-415-81252-8

india's middle class

*new forms of urban leisure,
consumption and prosperity*

Christiane Brosius

Routledge
Taylor & Francis Group
LONDON NEW YORK NEW DELHI

First published 2010 in India
by Routledge
912 Tolstoy House, 15–17 Tolstoy Marg, Connaught Place, New Delhi 110 001

Simultaneously published in the UK
by Routledge
2 Park Square, Milton Park, Abingdon, Oxon OX14 4RN

Routledge is an imprint of the Taylor & Francis Group, an informa business

Paperback edition published 2014

Typeset by
Star Compugraphics Private Limited
D–156, Second Floor
Sector 7, Noida 201 301

Printed and bound in India by
Avantika Printers Private Limited
194/2, Ramesh Market, Garhi, East of Kailash
New Delhi 110 065

British Library Cataloguing-in-Publication Data
A catalogue record of this book is available from the British Library

ISBN 978-1-138-02038-2

CONTENTS

ॐ

part III
'Masti! Masti!' Managing Love, Romance and Beauty

PLATES

༅

All photographs courtesy of the author, unless mentioned otherwise.

ABBREVIATIONS

ॐ

ACC	Akshardham Cultural Complex
AOL	Art of Living
BAPS	Bochasanwasi Shri Akshar Purushottam Swaminarayan Sanstha
BJP	Bharatiya Janata Party
BPO	Business Process Outsourcing
CBI	Central Bureau of Investigation (USA)
CCTV	Closed Circuit Television
CEO	Chief Executive Officer
CP	Connaught Place
DDA	Delhi Development Authority
FICCI	Federation of Indian Chambers of Commerce and Industry
HUDCO	Housing and Urban Development Corporation
INR	Indian Rupees
ISKCON	International Society for Krishna Consciousness
MCD	Municipal Corporation of Delhi
MNC	Multinational Corporation
NCAER	National Council for Applied Economic Research
NCR	National Capital Region
NRI	Non-Resident Indian
PBD	Pravasi Bharatiya Divas (Day of Overseas Indians)
PIO	Person of Indian Origin
PSM	Pramukh Swami Maharaj
VHP	Vishwa Hindu Parishad
VLCC	Vandana Luthra Curls and Curves (Beauty and Slimming Institute)

PREFACE

🍂

This book is the result of a very personal investigation that began in New Delhi more than 10 years ago, when I conducted research on the ways in which various individual and collective agents within the Hindu Right produced and circulated audio-visual material through which they sought to advertise their ideological beliefs and religio-political interests (Brosius 2005). Most of the ethnographic field research was undertaken in New Delhi, a nodal point of political power and of television and video production. While living in this vibrant city I developed an interest in the different, partly overlapping, spatial topographies that shaped the urban space and the experience of it. Events, institutions, people and sites created a net of more or less stable points of reference, an urban sensorium that still accompanies me when I return to Delhi, thinking or writing about, and exploring the city. It is the people of Delhi, friends, informants, strangers, who give Delhi the unique and yet ever changing character it has for me. Even though I discovered some of the places on my own, my knowledge of the existence of others was conveyed through those people who would take me along, or guide me towards, a new place. This was often accompanied by their own narrations of the significance of those specific places, often imbued in entangled controversies, allowing me to gather their views, anecdotes and memories.

The last decade and period of my research, from 1997 to 2007, has often been referred to as 'India Shining' by representatives of political life, media domains or personal contacts. The term was heavily criticised for various reasons, one of which was that economic growth had mainly taken place in urbanised India. The 'idea' in fact parachuted into various directions; some landings were soft and on fruitful ground, others, rather harsh and violent. However, the idea of 'India Shining' does shape the imagination of people, the urban development of a city such as New Delhi and its representations in new media technologies, predominantly for the new upper middle classes in India and overseas. It is the images and sites of a booming global city as New Delhi that offer a multifaceted panoramic window through which this study enables the readers to examine the highly ambivalent experience of change and transformation in neoliberal India. The stories told, images displayed and perspectives offered, are but a selection of a myriad others. The storyboard is my fieldwork, conducted through participatory observation, interviews and extensive multimedia analyses. By focusing on the ways in which members of the new affluent middle classes shape and appropriate the city as a stage, and how the media uses key concepts such as 'world-class' to cast the desire of visibility, I exclude those who have no, or very restricted access to this imaginary: the lower middle class, the rural and urban poor who, in many ways, are at the receiving end of globalisation and urbanisation. I propose, however, that it is by a better understanding of the fabric of the new middle classes that the processes of marginalisation of underpriviledge people through globalisation in India (e.g., the urban poor) become more transparent.

Many of my findings and contacts could not have been gathered without these years of my coming to Delhi in which I was able to establish well-oiled networks with people at various levels in different domains. Some of them are shop-owners, others are journalists, or scholars from a host of academic fields, some are students, and many are friends. Their helpfulness overwhelmed me at times and makes me wonder how I can return my gratitude. In particular, this is so since I am aware of the fact that a few informants will not share the arguments and interpretations revealed in the case-studies. The ethnographies in this book are my personal attempt to make sense of concepts that are possibly not on the informants' agenda, and even if so, valued and articulated in very different ways. The danger of misrepresentation is thus an underlying theme addressed in this study as it focuses specifically on concepts such as authenticity and representation, recognising them as highly subjective and context-based forms of discourse, concepts of which I am as much a part of as my informants.

Most of the names of informants have been changed and/or abbreviated, and only first names have been mentioned in order to safeguard their personal integrity. I am deeply indebted to several volunteer workers at Akshardham Cultural Complex in New Delhi whom I met at the site and engaged with in conversations over a period of almost three years. As an outsider to the Bochasanwasi Shri Akshar Purushottam Swaminarayan Sanstha (BAPS) faith, I am truly appreciative of those within the movement who shared their knowledge with me, invited me to their festivals and homes, guided me through the construction site before it was open to public and into the complex after its opening, sitting down and discussing specific issues, repeatedly and patiently dealing with my queries, even when on duty. I am aware of the fact that they might feel estranged and misrepresented by some of the observations I am sharing with the readers of this book.

My profound gratitude goes to all those informants involved in urban planning, be they architects, real-estate developers or lifestyle-specialists who gave me their precious time, often after working hours, in order to enrich my understanding of the aesthetics of residential housing, wedding event planning, spiritual healing, and creating infrastructure for overseas Indians. I was fortunate to be able to participate in two Pravasi Bharatiya Divas (PBD) events in Delhi, international gatherings of overseas Indians that are organised by the Indian government and the Federation of Indian Chambers of Commerce and Industry (FICCI). These events of 2003 and 2007 gave me an insight into the ways in which concepts such as 'India Shining' were circulated, challenged and even criticised. The visits underlined once again as to how important the returning overseas Indians are for all the sectors in which my case-studies are placed, both as 'hard facts' and fuel for imagination.

I am grateful to Lalit Batra, Miriya Chacko, Ravi and Sarita Chadha, Sunanda Ghosh, Sharad Goyal, R. S. Iyer, Sudheendra Kulkarni, Diya Mehra, Krishna Menon, Harini Narayanan, Jomy and Liz Thomas, Ramu, K. T. Ravindran, Frederick Riberio, Shiv Sagar, Reena Singh, Sangeeta Singh, Karanvir Singh and Harsh Srivastava. My colleagues, spread across various corners of this world, must be acknowledged for putting my thoughts in place or an alternative track, reading and critically commenting on parts of this work in various forms. These are Niels Gutschow, Sophie Hawkins, Ute Hüsken, Jyotindra Jain, Nic Leonhardt, Bao Do, Barbara Mittler, Christopher Pinney, Katharina Poggendorf-Kakar, Karin Polit, Sumathi Ramaswamy, William Sax, Shuddhabrata Sengupta, Kavita Singh and Patricia Uberoi. I have considerably benefited from discussions within and research enabled through the Collaborative Research Centre of Dynamics of Rituals of which I am a member since 2003. The project, to a large extent funded by the German Research Foundation (SFB 619), enabled me to collect data during fieldwork in Delhi as well as present my findings at various occasions at international workshops and conferences. With the generous support of the Cluster of Excellence 'Asia and Europe in a Global Context: Shifting Asymmetries in Cultural Flows' at Heidelberg University, this book could be published in colour, a rare luxury for the academic book market. I am also indebted to my students at the Department of Anthropology at the South Asia Institute and the Institute of Anthropology with whom I could share and discuss various aspects of the study, in and outside of courses that I taught over the last few years. Discussions with colleagues helped clarify various issues raised in this study.

The fabric and 'soul' of this book also owes much to my husband, Axel Michaels. Omita Goyal, Nilanjan Sarkar and Rimina Mohapatra from Routledge, New Delhi were most helpful and professional. I also wish to thank Sujata Patel, the editor of the Series 'Cities and the Urban Imperative' of which this volume is a part. I should add that the responsibility for arguments and errors made throughout the book is all mine.

Different parts of my research for this manuscript have been presented at conferences and workshops in Delhi, Berlin, Manchester and Vienna. Much shorter and revised sections of this study have been published elsewhere and appear as 'The Gated Romance of India Shining: Visualising Urban Lifestyle in Images of Residential Housing Development', in Moti Gokulsing and Wimal Dissanayake (eds), *Popular Culture in a Globalised India: A Reader* (London: Routledge, 2009, pp. 174–91) and 'The Enclaved Gaze: Exploring the Visual Culture of "World Class-Living" in Urban India', in Jyotindra Jain (ed.), *India's Popular Culture: Iconic Spaces and Fluid Images*, a MARG volume (2008, pp. 114–25).

I want to end this Preface with a remark on the cover of this book. The photograph was taken in 2006 on the inner Ring Road behind Lajpat Nagar in South Delhi, and shows the front side of CTC Plaza, a shopping mall for bridal wear. It employs words and images that appeal to the dreams and aspirations of beauty and wealth, of power, romance and 'whiteness' of skin as an indicator of the relevance of western concepts, remodelled in the context of economic liberalisation in India. The photograph also shows two massive pillars, like arches of a gateway to a palace, both with reliefs of guardian angels blowing a trumpet with one hand, and raising the other in a gesture of victory. The motif of triumphant angels has travelled from classical Rome to West Persia in the seventh-century AD and reached the Mughal Court in Lahore in the seventeenth century to which they had been introduced by Jesuit missionaries (thanks to Niels Gutschow for this information). A few weeks later, the two angels held up a hoarding that invited customers to 'Enter a magical world'. A few months later the whole building had disappeared, like a *fata morgana*, due to a governmental move to remove illegal commercial as well as residential structures in the city. The photograph thus captures the allegory of the city of Delhi as it nests between imagination, aspiration and politics of urban planning, the migration of concepts between Asia and 'the West', and the emergence and dynamics of new spaces of consumption and pleasure for a young and highly heterogeneous social group: the new Indian middle class.

ॐ

Every effort has been made to contact owners of copyright regarding the visual material reproduced in this book. Perceived omissions if brought to notice will be rectified in future printing. The publishers apologise if inadvertently any source remains unacknowledged. The following holders of copyright are owed thanks for their assistance, generosity and permission to reproduce material: BAPS, Delhi and Ahmedabad for images of the Akshardham Cultural Complex in New Delhi, especially Jyotindra (Janak) Dave, R.S. Iyer, Marcus Nuesser, Aumweddings, EICHER Maps, Eros City Developers, Assotech, DLF, Rosedale Developers and Omaxe.

Introduction to this edition

'Worlding Delhi': Updating middle-classness in urban India

Only a few years have passed since this book on the social spatialisation of economic liberalisation in Delhi with a focus on the emergence of a new middle class was completed and published in 2010. But there have been remarkable shifts and developments in terms of the ongoing urban growth in the city, the fabric of the middle classes within this dynamic field, and the scholarship on the theme since then. Research on urbanisation and the constitution of middle classes in the Global South, particularly South Asia, witnessed impressive growth and diversification, developing a more nuanced and multidisciplinary repository for a wide range of theoretical and methodological approaches.[1] It is neither possible nor intended to use this additional chapter to analyse and respond to all of them. Instead, this Introduction seeks to update and reflect upon the discussions in this book and the new research by outlining a selection of continuities and alterations.

This book explores the first decade of the new millennium along the axes of social spatialisation in Delhi with respect to the notion of belonging to, and becoming, a 'world-class' city, through the lens of middle-class aspirations and practices. It studies global imaginaries and cosmopolitan aspirations geared towards 'gated' lifestyles in real estate development; the alliance of recreation and spirituality in the spatial aesthetics and narratives of themed environments; and the emergence of a landscape of professionals and experts catering towards ritualised events and spaces of affluent middle classes with respect to the emerging wedding and beauty industries that cater to lifestyle declarations. In all three parts, leisure, consumption and prosperity are considered as strategic means of making the heterogeneous

---

[1] It is also interesting to note the differences of studies on India in comparison to China in the sense that qualitative research on India's neighbour, and 'cousin' in terms of GDP has breached out more into different areas of socio-cultural contexts and processes of globalisation and neoliberalism, as well as particular attention attributed to urban phenomena.

and highly dynamic middle classes visible, spatially graspable and available for analysis. Not only has Delhi's urban landscape and demographic data changed in those years, with the National Capital Region reaching a population of 22 million people, thus becoming the second most populated urban sprawl in the world.[2] The case studies and loci of this book too, have developed in their own particular ways since 2009.

A selection of the new approaches taken in research on urban Asia, and India in particular, are addressed in the following pages. Several kinds of studies have been selected for brief discussion here: there are those exemplary ones that discuss the urbanisation processes in the neoliberal Global South (e.g., Bharne 2013; Heiman et al. 2012, Mayaram 2009; Perera and Wing-Shing 2013; Roy and Ong 2011; Samara et al. 2013), placing the study of particular regional cases in the light of a critical repositioning of concepts such as globalisation and development, middle classes and global city. Since Ahmad and Reifeld's edited volume *Middle Class Values in India and Western Europe* (2007) further collaborative attention has nurtured research on the complex formation of middle classes in India (e.g., Baviskar and Ray 2011; Donner 2011). Increased scholarly attention has also zoomed in on particular case studies of mega-cities other than Delhi, headed by Mumbai and Bangalore, followed by Kolkata and Hyderabad (e.g., Nisbett 2009; Phadke et al. 2011; Radhakrishnan 2011; Shatkin 2014; Upadhyaya 2011). New research is also conducted on second-tier cities with 'world-class' aspirations that have fallen 'off the map' of rating agencies and global cities' scholars (Robinson 2002). These studies are crucial in many ways, one of which being the idea of how such emblems like 'world class' circulate and localise in 'regional hinterlands' and at 'peripheries'. Such cities are, for instance, Jaipur, Ahmedabad or Mangalore. But the research on the 'established megacities' has also changed, and thus Delhi has become a challenging field for geographers working on gender (Raju and Lahiri-Dutt 2010), mega-events (Baviskar 2011b; Sengupta 2010), or local middle class associations (Mehra 2009). Others have studied the ways in which 'world-class' aesthetics and imaginaries have been consumed and appropriated by groups outside the realm of the middle classes, such as 'slum dwellers' (Ghertner 2011) or how new technological urban networks shape a rhizomatic informal landscape of spatialisation (Sundaram 2010). Much attention has been geared towards the growing inequalities

---

[2] In September 2013, the 2013 World Population Data Sheet released by the US Population Reference Bureau listed the NCR with 22.7 million people (Rajadhyaksha 2013).

and power asymmetries between elites and non-privileged groups through economic liberalisation and urban planning. This critical approach in the humanities and social sciences sits equally 'queer' against often-raised enthusiasms for the late but impressive economic boom, the growth of consumerism, and the expansion of professional sectors and classes into knowledge production and the like. In this field, the new middle classes, which are the focus in this book, are largely held responsible for a growing social, environmental and economic insensitivity, and a widening gap of 'have's' and 'have-nots'. They are considered as vital players in the drawing of boundaries that allow or deny access for aspiring groups from 'below'. But, as this book also underlines, in all their heterogeneity and dynamics, they are equally affected by strategies of exclusion and inclusion, and by accompanying fears, experiences and risks of being 'pushed out' or 'falling behind' (see also Fernandes 2011: 76, 82).

Other 'World-Class' Cities

There are a number of attempts to challenge and bring more fine-tuning into the discussion of mega-cities and global cities. The growing interest in urbanisation comes in tandem with a mounting attention paid to economic liberalisation in the so-called Global South that speaks of shifts in power-relations of former centre-periphery hierarchies (the 'West' and the 'rest') towards a rather multi-centred, if not reverted power axis. Many of these new studies on cities are questioning what Loretta Lees (2012) has coined 'imitative urbanism', that is, the assumption that non-western cities must copy urban models from the 'West', and do so more or less insufficiently, risking lack and loss of traditions, dilution and inauthenticity of place and spatial practices, at the cost of rising exploitation and further growth and marginalisation of under-privileged sections. Global cities in Asia are seen as creative and productive in terms of developing their own 'language', 'logic' and 'biography' (Berking and Löw 2012; Hassenpflug 2010), self-evidently with inbuilt mistakes, and weakness, as any other city would too. In her co-edited volume *Worlding Cities* (Roy and Ong 2011), Aihwa Ong (2011a) suggests that 'Asian cities are fertile sites, not for following an established pathway or western blueprint, but for a plethora of situated experiments that reinvent what urban norms can count as "global"' (ibid.: 2). One could argue that the same can be applied as a lens of looking at the spatialisation of middle-classness, in terms of aspirations and globalised imaginaries as well as trans/local histories and trajectories. As a global space of capitalism and postcolonialism, Asian cities such as Delhi are part of a larger battleground in the sometimes cynical and absurd 'ranking race' for national and international investment and recognition. This has become manifest elsewhere, for instance in the advent of the Olympics in Beijing 2008 (Broudehoux 2009), or the FIFA World Cup in Rio de Janeiro (2014). The previously largely Northern conceptualisation of and view on global cities has been challenged with the concept of Global South urbanism, challenged in terms of concepts such as 'origin' and 'copy', access and participation, private and public. But it has also been challenged by an increasing attention paid to inner-Asian flows and translocal networks as crucial factors of understanding what Shail Mayaram (2009) coins 'other global cities', or what Jennifer Robinson (2002) terms as 'ordinary cities'. Moreover, the rising sensibility towards urban processes that go beyond a particular local focus and also beyond the 'West'–'East' dichotomy has produced studies on new connectivities and entanglements, allowed for a new, transcultural and transnational lens on social change and spatialisation in and through cities (Mayaram 2009). The first two parts of this book speak about what I coined as 'Dubaisation', and Aihwa Ong defined as 'hyperbuildings' (2011b). With this, she means a globally circulating urban aesthetic and architecture localised and spelt out in different ways and for various reasons, for instance, when it discusses citations from neo-Renaissance or Victorian architecture in real estate advertising, or when it considers the global currency of theme parks with particular focus on the notion of middle-class spirituality and public space (Srivastava 2011; see also Dupont 2005). Thus, this book also argues that a 'spiritual-cum-recreational-park' like Akshardham Cultural Complex, discussed in Part II, must not be seen as a 'simple' attempt to copy a successful Western model, but rather, to understand this in a way that Homi Bhabha termed as 'mimicry', a productive and reflexive practice of re-modelling, interreferencing and constructing of new solidarities and networks. Likewise, mega-cities in Asia should also be considered as the ground for the contestation of citizenship, civil society and cosmopolitanism. The city, as Ong (2011a) argues, should be seen as a 'field of intervention' and interaction, it should be understood as a locality and placed at a particular nexus of particular local, translocal and transcultural ideas of access to modernity and globality.

The idea of 'Worlding Cities' is a very productive one since it enables an outlook on booming cities that do not fall prey to the burden of 'global cities' to function as a financial 'pressure cookers'. It also helps establishing the urban — and in the case of this book, Delhi — as a new translocal contact zone, in which agents constantly negotiate and contest locality and globality, participation in space-making strategies, cultural entanglements and a 'cosmopolitan' lifestyle.

Ambivalent Fluidity of Middle-Classness

Two edited volumes have recently been published that outline several important fields of inquiry about why the attention to middle classes and cultural politics of urban space in India is both meaningful and challenging for discussions around economic liberalisation in the 'non-West'. One is *Elite and Everyman: The Cultural Politics of the Indian Middle Classes*, edited by sociologists Amita Baviskar and Raka Ray (2011). Another important edited volume that relates to the transnational mobility and imaginaries of the middle classes discussed here is *The Global Middle Classes: Theorizing Through Ethnography*, edited by Heiman, Freeman and Liechty (2012). The editors of the latter highlight a concern with contemporary forms of globalisation and the challenges to reposition culture, class and capitalism with mounting transnational mobility, with changing forms of consumption, reproduction and citizenship in contexts of liberalisation economies in non-Western regions. In their interpretation, class and space must be scrutinised ethnographically:

> We view cultural logics, spatial practices, and affective states not simply as superstructural reflections of economic conditions; we understand them to be dynamics that can and often do have material effects on economic futures — but cannot be reduced to it. That is, we see these material, affective, and symbolic dimensions of class to be dialectically intertwined in the production of class subjectivities and class relations (Heiman et al. 2012: 9).

They also point out the importance of studying middle-classness as a category of self-identification and aspiration (ibid.: 18–19), thus arguing for going beyond quantitative 'measurements' of who can be counted in and excluded from membership to 'the' middle class because of particular economic conditions (on this, see a very productive critique by Sridharan [2011]). Spatial practices and imaginaries would fall under such an explorative approach: the glamorous surface of a city like Delhi is often ruptured by zones of public neglect, if not decay and poverty. And yet, this surface works as an emblem for progress, forcing its way into the language of private media and glossy real estate brochures. Neither the malls nor the luxury condominiums are dominant in numbers, but they are hegemonic in quality. This could also be said of the representation of new middle classes in commercial media such as magazines, cinema and TV: the mediated and spatialised presence of middle-classness constitutes the same in the process, creating the impression of a dominant discourse and thus 'social fact'. Yet, 40 per cent of the Indian population still lives in poverty and not more than 26 per cent of households are said to belong to the middle classes (Baviskar and& Ray 2011: 2). The middle classes might not even make up the empirical majority but their emblematic power as 'mainstream' and economic powerhouse of a 'new India' is remarkable.[3] Seen in this light, they are considered as pioneers of a new enthusiasm and as key motor for the 'revamping' of cities as recreational spaces, business hubs and 'world class'. In *Appropriately Indian: Gender and Culture in a New Transnational Class* (2011), an ethnographic study on IT professionals in Bangalore, Smitha Radhakrishnan points out that this group makes up about 0.4 per cent of the workforce, even though their media presence when reporting about India's globalisation, seems to create another impression. The study also highlights that the myth of the middle class being open to all members of society alike is speculative and as studies of the IT 'class' show, members are predominantly urban and high-caste. Yet, they have come to be 'mainstreamed' to such an extent that they are commonly identified with economic liberalisation as a magic wand for social mobility too.[4] Even though Radhakrishnan does not address urban practices and spaces as key themes, it becomes clear that even the landscape of professional and leisure architecture, between private and public, such as office buildings, cafés and restaurants, or the potential intimacy of an enclosed space at home

---

[3] In a survey from 1998–99, the National Council of Applied Economic Research (NCAER) defines five income groups for middle-class quantification: low, lower-middle, middle, upper-middle and high — categories called arbitrary by Sridharan (2011: 36), who suggests three groups instead: elite middle class (more than INR 140,000 p.a. = €20,000), expanded middle class (from INR 105,000 p.a.), broadest middle class (from INR 35,000 p.a.) (ibid.: 37). The number of Mio people belonging to the middle class was estimated to be about 290 in 2000 (ibid.: 43).

[4] The 'old' middle class was made up almost completely of upper-caste Hindus (Sridharan 2011: 529), and even in 2000, 60 per cent of expenditure in cities was done by the same group (INR 2,000 p.m.). With the 1990s, an increasing number of non-traditional caste groups, lower caste farmers (from dominant castes) joined the middle classes (ibid.: 53). A Centre for the Study of Developing Societies (CSDS) survey has coined 20 per cent of all Indians as 'middle class' according to the following five categories for middle-class membership: self-definition as middle class; 10 years or more of schooling; residence in a brick-cum-cement house; white-collar occupation; ownership of at least a car/jeep/tractor/scooter/ TV (ibid.). Fernandes maintains that the middle class is not per se a winner of economic liberalisation but that instead, 'liberalization has had uneven effects on middle classes' (2011: 67).

constitute a relevant part in urban lives. With respect to the relevance of aesthetics in social spatialisation, particularly in the case of gendered spatial practices, mobility patterns and lived geographies of placement in the NCR, Tina Basi (2009) has written a fascinating ethnography of call centres, urbanity and women, while Nisbett (2009) explores the ways in which a city like Bangalore brands itself and allows for new social groups (here, middle-class youth) to shape and visually 'take place', for instance, in the context of friendship, educational training and courtship.

The various entanglements of consumption, space and middle-class constitution, the different 'speeds' at which, for instance, 'development' moves within space practices in India, have so far, and particularly with respect to South Asia, still been understudied. But, as Heiman, Liechty and Freeman state: 'Spaces are critical for subject making not simply in terms of marking the physical spatialization of class — which proximities are afforded and which curtailed — but it is in those very spaces that classed subjects are made' (2012: 26). This also includes the privatisation of public space. Of particular interest for this book is the emphasis on how, after having been 'deeply invested in creating spaces that [aim to] foster particular kinds of social relations, subjectivities, and practices' (ibid.: 18), states have begun to withdraw from various moments of urban spatialisation. This has left 'gaps', partly filled by new agents and networks such as private investment (real estate development), a growing landscape of experts managing private consumption (Part III), and the growth of a consumer-spirituality (Srivastava 2011) that enables parts of the new middle classes to further negotiate values, duties and access to 'privatised public space' (e.g., through *seva*, selfless work as devotion often reframed as charity, or through private-public undertakings). In *Elite and Everyman* (Baviskar and Ray 2011), emphasis is on the importance of acknowledging and studying variations in class compositions — not only within what is coined as 'middle class' but in the context of a social assemblage. This has not been done in *India's Middle Class* but the book is hoped to work as a trigger to further sharpen the different modes of social emplacement and competition in globalising cities. Research on resilience or resistance against 'Westernisation' or 'gentrification' is expanding, with a well-argued critique of ongoing, if not worsening inequalities by means of exclusion and inclusion, the granting or denial of rights of access and participation in belonging to a city. Yet, at the same time, more diverse and yet differentiated approaches towards the role various middle classes in urban spatialisation, and how they relate to strategic inclusion and exclusion will also need to be expanded (see Butcher and Velayutham 2009). The argument behind this is that there are most probably more entanglements and oscillation than possible to be thought of in a clearly binary and dichotomising layout of concepts (for instance, assuming allegedly clear boundaries between 'subaltern' and 'legal' city).

Spatialisation of Distinction: Naturalised the 'Deserving Few'

Most of the recently published research on neoliberal politics and their effects in India are geared towards the discussion of inequality, arguing that the new middle classes are a key factor of the hardening borders between the poor, and social and economic elites. Even though inequality is not so much the key topic of this book, instead, the concepts of distinction and conspicuous consumption feature centrally since middle-classness is seen as a form of habitus and a strategy of self-positioning in a (spatial) field of discourses.

There is, within the large pool of people associating themselves to (or being attributed with the label) 'middle class', a very vibrant life based on distinction and constant self-evaluation. One of the main criteria, and inherently celebrated in an 'Indian' context, argues sociologist Radhakrishnan, is merit. She quotes Zoya Hasan, who has highlighted the concept as a strategy of legitimising a 'chosen people' whose alleged uniqueness seems part of their 'DNA' (2011: 89). This way, personal worth and competence become imbued with inherited right to status. But in fact, once could also argue that the reference to 'deserving' a place in the upper echelons of new middle-class India refers to the ideology to have 'made it by oneself', quasi against all odds.[5] This fits in well with the first part of this book, in which I analyse a whole chain of advertisements using terms such as 'the deserved few', or 'belong to world class'. Several examples in *India's Middle Class* reflect a rhetoric that naturalises affluent middle-classness as belonging to 'the deserving few', alleging that the deeds, norms and values of such an exclusive group legitimises a certain moral code, and a special claim to place, visibility and recognition.

As Leela Fernandes (2011) points out in her work on the 'new' middle classes in India, an understanding of historical depth and contexts helps reveal that the constitution of 'new' middle classes carried forward

---

[5] How misleading this idea of individual mobility because of genuine ambition and competence is has been discussed by Craig Jeffrey (2011), as well as Patricia and Roger Jeffrey (Jeffrey et al. 2010) in their research on unemployment of youth as well as segregation through class- and caste-based access to education.

historical continuities (in terms of the importance of caste and religion) and other trajectories and discourses. These impact on today's spatialisation of inequality in today's booming cities (see Baviskar 2011b). Fernandes proposes a move away from a generalised conception of class towards an analysis of an 'intersecting forms of inequality' (2011: 61). For her, middle-classness, underlining identities in process rather than as 'things', is highly precarious, instable (2011: 60), and a field of discourse, with diverse groups trying to compete for their (improved) positions in a social field. This interrelationality is also underlined by Srivastava (2010: 364) as he highlights the significance of ongoing self-definition, reflection and contestation as middle class. People define their desire to belong to middle class (as a metaphor of having 'arrived' or being 'on the move up the ladder') in constant competition with other groups who might do so too, but allegedly not in a suitable way. Several studies have thus coined, and tried to declassify such a moment of distinction as less appropriate habitus of the 'new rich', thereby referring to the unsophisticated competence to cite from repositories of established, 'older' elites.[6] Within the ecology of groups contesting for middle-classness is an emerging hierarchy of more or less 'authentic' and 'productive' segments. Since 'productiveness' is not limited to economic capital, morality, that is one's contribution to and participation in the nation's wellbeing, plays a crucial role here. But the context of a nation's wellbeing, and who actually belongs to it, changed over time (see Mazzarella 2003). Time and again, the 'arrived' middle classes have been seen, and considering themselves as pioneering in constituting social reform movements (esp. in the late nineteenth to early twentieth centuries), national development or, more recently, protest movements staged in cities (see also Srivastava 2012: 57),[7] but also in terms of charity activities.[8] Such a self-definition as morally legitimised as 'elite' justifies spatial segregations in private places, for instance in the case of domestic

---

[6] With 'new rich', I do not mean a quantifiable number in terms of surplus money and income. Instead, I refer to 'new rich' (*neureich*) as a derogatory term used by members of the established and 'arrived' classes, referring to such people who have made 'fast money' without having the necessary social capital to appropriately prove their status. Their attempt to belong to an elite fails to convince their peers, which may likewise also indicate that they would not have been accepted anyway, and the criteria used for this are merely means of a rhetoric of exclusion.

[7] One such example of recent urban and middle-class based protest is the Anna Hazare movement (Sitapati 2011).

[8] This comes close to what Srivastava calls moral and surplus consumption (2011: 376).

servitude through which boundaries of public and domestic spheres are defined (Qayum and Ray 2011: 247).[9] Strategies like these, argue Qayum and Ray 'reproduce as normal an unequal society in which groups "naturally" divide along class lines and in which lower classes naturally serve the higher classes' (ibid.: 248).[10]

Media and Aesthetics of a (Provincialised?) Cosmopolitanism

This book's attention is to a large extent focused on visual and media imaginaries, on the creation of a middle-'class aesthetic in Delhi. Thereby local and global regimes merge and sometimes even replace each other. As Sharon Zukin has already argued in 1995, cities use aesthetics and certain urban sensoriums in order to underline socio-economic and cultural hierarchies and forms of spatialisation, to regulate and divert access to localities (see also Ghertner 2011). Especially the English-speaking media, but also privatised programmes, largely consumed by urbanised, educated audiences, have generated a fairly homogeneous environment of middle-class representation in terms of 'naturalising' the middle classes and of their particular foci on themes and discussions. Media and aesthetics form a constitutional facet of imagining and constituting affluent middle-classness in an often mega-urban setting.[11] Smitha Radhakrishnan's book *Appropriately Indian* (2011) is a relevant contribution to the ways in which access to a certain profession shapes a new social status — almost caste-like — within a changing society and highly urban environment, and how culture and globality spill into each other, constituting a locally embedded, if not provincialised cosmopolitan identity. Radhakrishnan's concept of 'cultural streamlining' as means of shaping '"Indian culture" into *appropriate difference* . . . to assert their (IT professionals, CB) symbolic position at the helm of a "new" India' (ibid.: 3–4) underlines the concept of new Indian middle classes as highly heterogeneous and aspirational (see also Sridharan 2011: 55–56) where difference matters — both for internal as well as external

---

[9] See Wanning (2009) for the Chinese equivalent.

[10] It is worthwhile to open up space for further research on equal developments in the Global South, e.g., to China, which undergoes enormous processes of urbanisation and economic liberalisation. On middle class morality and gated communities in Shanghai, see Pow (2007).

[11] Of course, as I elaborate later, media are not homogenous by any means and are differentiated in this book according to technology, genre, speed, and quality of circulation, to mention only a few aspects. See Sundaram (2010).

processes of distinction. The real estate development, triggering notions of 'world class' (Part I), the landscape of urban religiosity-cum-leisure (Part II), the new infrastructure of experts 'themeing' beauty and marriage (Part III), stem from transnational circulations of images, media and people.

What seems particularly interesting is how, in the light of economic liberalisation and social spatialisation, notions of public and private have (been) changed. Srivastava (2012) shows this in his study of lifestyle advertising and of a condominium in DLF City,[12] at the outskirts of Delhi. As one can find in this book (Part I), Srivastava also argues that the home and interior lifestyle items such as kitchens or children's rooms, are sites of 'consumerist cosmopolitanism' (ibid.: 70), and that the 'public' demonstration of living in such a place is part of creating middle-classness and globality. Likewise, he also takes notice of the ways in which a language of English aristocracy (if not colonialism) is tapped into, and how new expert cultures, for instance, of architects and interior designers to shape and convey a symbolic culture of material goods and expressive rhetoric, emerge (ibid.: 65). The advertising, event-based and themed spaces discussed in this book are stages and fields for such 'work in progress'.[13] In his exploration of newly emerging places and spatialisation practices, Srivastava looks at Akshardham Temple Complex as a trans-urban phenomenon of 'massive, socio-spatial transformation' (2011: 377). In his article 'Urban Spaces, Disney-Divinity and the Moral Middle Classes in Delhi' (ibid.), he studies Akshardham complex as a means of becoming middle class, as a form of moral consumption and phenomenon underlining processes of aestheticisation as social spatialisation: 'Its self-representation in terms of technological mastery, efficiency, punctuality, educational achievement . . . links it with the world of tollways, highways, Metro rail, shopping malls, city "beautification" and slum-clearance drives, and the creation of middle-class identity' (ibid.: 378). He thus supports the arguments raised in this book, by stating an interesting alliance between Indianness, consumer citizenship and (Hindu) religiosity as distinct urban processes (ibid.: 377). To him, what he calls 'surplus consumption', is a 'strategy of engaging with

---

[12] 'DLF' stands for Delhi Land and Finance Company, established in 1946, it is one of the earliest and by now largest real estate companies in India (see Srivastava 2012: 67–68).

[13] On the social aesthetics of gated communities in China, see Lo and Wang (2013); on the 'McMansionisation' of residential suburbs, see Heiman et al. (2012: 15).

the intensity of social and cultural changes introduced by [a number]) of global forces' (Srivastava 2007: 185), allowing for the demonstration of mastery over consumption by consumption (ibid.: 2011: 381).

Bubble in the Gated Middle

This book is not so much dealing with concrete everyday lifeworlds of urban citizens but with media projections and imaginaries that facilitate certain notions of a 'good' and 'happy' lifestyle that upholds a 'bubble' of the gated world (Part I), of gated zones of leisure and recreation (Part II) within what is often depicted as world of unordered, unhealthy and inconvenient 'nuisance' (see Bagaeen and Uduku 2010). The strategy of establishing exclusive gated condominiums or a 'public' site such as the religious Akshardham Complex discussed in Part II of this book allows for the mediatised and sensorial/aesthetic availing of the new middle classes as a homogenous and moral community that creates itself in this process (Srivastava 2012: 59).

There are risks associated to being 'in the middle'. Even members of the affluent middle classes have come to experience, or at least to take notice, of the precarious status of belonging, even to middle-classness (see pp. 16–21, this volume; and fn 5, this Introduction). With an economic growth of only 5 per cent in 2012 (compared to a staggering 8–9 per cent in the previous decade, with the exception of 2012, when it went down to 3 per cent, while India also has faced an import-decrease of 60 per cent for the second half of 2013), international and national markets, and whole professions have become alert and nervous, wondering how sustainable the economic growth, and thus also the middle classes are. The talk about the bubble of real estate development is accompanied by other debates on the risk of investment in a flexible lifestyle. Upward mobility, particularly through education, has had major hiccups, either through the much-debated reservation politics, through rural–urban asymmetries, or the fallacy of equal access to higher education and the private sector, for all alike. Social spatialisation reflects this in some ways, since increasingly, condominiums do not fill up anymore or malls stay abandoned and turn into ruins of a recent past, not even attributed with nostalgia but with anger and cynicism.

In studying urbanisation processes in India, the concept of 'worlding' cities seems an appropriate way to move away from teleological models of developmentalism and consumerism, allowing critique and also repositioning of the middle classes in a more creative field of encounters, be they social, cultural or political. This would open up the field for a discussion on the emergence of a localised cosmopolitanism as both provincialising and translocalising, on the relation between media imaginaries and spatial practices as social facts. It would also make accessible an arena that recognises both the interplay between the desire for 'homogeneous' imagined communities, staged in and through media and rhetoric of social spatialisation, and for ways of scrutinising everyday ruptures and differentiations, thus giving a more heterogeneous picture of India's constantly changing fabric of the urban middle classes. Hopefully this book further facilitates such conversations and engagement.

References

Ahmad, Imtiaz and Helmut Reifeld (eds). 2001. *Middle Class Values in India and Western Europe*. New Delhi: Social Science Press, DK Publishers, Adenauer Foundation.

Bagaeen, Samer and Ola Uduku (eds). 2010. *Gated Communities: Social Sustainability and Historical Gated Developments*. London: Earthscan.

Basi, J. K. Tina. 2009. *Women, Identity and India's Call Centre Industry*. Abingdon, New York: Routledge.

Baviskar, Amita. 2011a. Cows, Cars and Cycle-Rickshaws: Bourgeois Environmentalists and the Battle for Delhi's Streets, in Amita Baviskar and Raka Ray (eds), *Elite and Everyman: The Cultural Politics of the Indian Middle Classes*, 391–417. New Delhi: Routledge.

———. 2011b. Spectacular Events, City Spaces and Citizenship: The Commonwealth Games in Delhi, in Jonathan Shapiro Anjaria and Colin McFarlane (eds), *Urban Navigations. Politics, Space and the City in South Asia*, 138–164. New Delhi: Routledge.

Baviskar, Amita and Raka Ray (eds). 2011. *Elite and Everyman: The Cultural Politics of the Indian Middle Classes*. New Delhi: Routledge.

Berking, Helmut and Martina Löw (eds). 2008. *Die Eigenlogik der Städte: Neue Wege fur die Stadtforschung*. Frankfurt am Main, New York: Campus.

Bharne, Vinayak. 2013. *The Emerging Asian City: Concomitant Urbanities and Urbanisms*. Abingdon, New York: Routledge.

Broudehoux, Anne-Marie. 2009. Seeds of Dissent: The Politics of Resistance to Beijing's Olympic Redevelopment, in Melissa Butcher and Selvaraj Velayutham (eds), *Dissent and Cultural Resistance in Asia's Cities*, 14–32. Abingdon, New York: Routledge.

Butcher, Melissa and Selvaraj Velayutham (eds). 2009. *Dissent and Cultural Resistance in Asia's Cities*. Abingdon, New York: Routledge.

Donner, Henrike (ed.). 2011. *Being Middle-Class in India: A Way of Life*. London, New York: Routledge.

Hassenpflug, Dieter. 2010 (2009). *The Urban Code of China*. Basel, Boston, Berlin: Birkhäuser.

Fernandes, Leela. 2011. Hegemony and Inequality: Theoretical Reflections on India's 'New' Middle Class, in Amita Baviskar and Raka Ray (eds), *Elite and Everyman: The Cultural Politics of the Indian Middle Classes*, 58–82. New Delhi: Routledge.

Ghertner, D. Asher. 2011. Rule by Aesthetics: World-Class City Making in Delhi, in Ananya Roy and Aihwa Ong (eds), *Worlding Cities: Asian Experiments and the Art of Being Global*, 279–306, Oxford: Wiley Blackwell.Hassenpflug, Dieter. 2008. *Der urbane code chinas* [China's Urban Code]. Boston: Birkhäuser.

Heiman, Rachel, Carla Freeman and Mark Liechty (eds). 2012. *The Global Middle Classes: Theorizing Through Ethnography*. Santa Fe: School for Advanced Research Press.

Jeffrey, Craig. 2011. *Timepass: Youth, Class and the Politics of Waiting*. Stanford, CA: Stanford University Press.

Jeffrey, Craig, Patricia Jeffery and Roger Jeffery (eds). 2010. *Education, Masculinities and Unemployment in North India*. New Delhi: Social Science Press.

Lees, Loretta. 2012. The Geography of Gentrification: Thinking through Comparative Urbanism. *Progress in Human Geography* 36(2): 155–171.

Lo, Kevin and Mark Wang. 2013. The Development and Localisation of a Foreign Gated Community in Beijing. *Cities* 30: 186–92.

Mayaram, Shail (ed.). 2009. *The Other Global City*. New York: Routledge.

Mehra, Diya. 2009. Campaigning Against its Eviction: Local Trade in New 'World-Class' Delhi, in Melissa Butcher and Velayutham Selvaraj (eds), *Dissent and Cultural Resistance in Asia's Cities*, 148–67. Abingdon, New York: Routledge.

Nisbett, Nicholas. 2009. *Growing up in the Knowledge Society: Living the IT Dream in Bangalore*. New Delhi: Routledge.

Ong, Aihwa. 2011a. Worlding Cities, or The Art of Being Global, in Ananya Roy and Aihwa Ong (eds), *Worlding Cities: Asian Experiments and the Art of Being Global*, 1–28. Oxford: Wiley Blackwell.

———. 2011b. Hyperbuilding: Spectacle, Speculation, and the Hyperspace of Sovereignty, in Ananya Roy and Aihwa Ong (eds), *Worlding Cities: Asian Experiments and the Art of Being Global*, 205–25. Oxford: Wiley Blackwell.

Perera, Nihal and Wing-Shing Tang (eds). 2013. *Transforming Asian Cities: Intellectual Impasse, Asianizing Space and Emerging Translocalities*. Abingdon, New York: Routledge.

Phadke, Shilpa, S. Khan and S. Ranade. 2011. *Why Loiter? Women and Risk on Mumbai Streets*. New Delhi: Penguin.

Pow, Choon-Piew 2007. Securing the 'Civilised' Enclaves: Gated Communities and the Moral Geographies of Exclusion in (Post-)socialist Shanghai. *Urban Studies* 44(8): 1539–58.

Qayum, Seemin and Raka Ray. 2011. 'The Middle Classes at Home', in Amita Baviskar and Raka Ray (eds), *Elite and Everyman: The Cultural Politics of the Indian Middle Classes*, pp. 246–70. New Delhi: Routledge.

Radhakrishnan, Smitha. 2011. *Appropriately Indian: Gender and Culture in a New Transnational Class*. Durham, London: Duke University Press.

Rajadhyaksha, Madhavi. 2013. Delhi World's Second Most Populous Mega-City. *The Times of India*, 13 September, http://articles.timesofindia.indiatimes.com/2013-09-13/india/42039657_1_population-growth-mega-cities-mega-cities (accessed 23 September 2013).

Raju, S. and K. Lahiri-Dutt (eds) 2010. *Doing Gender. Doing Geography: Emerging Research in India*. New Delhi: Routledge.

Robinson, Jennifer. 2002. Global and World Cities: A View from Off the Map. *International Journal of Urban and Regional Research* 26 (3): 531–54.

Roy, Ananya and Aihwa Ong (eds). 2011. *Worlding Cities: Asian Experiments and the Art of Being Global*. Oxford: Wiley Blackwell.

Samara, Tony Roshan, Shenjing He and Guo Chen (eds). 2013. *Locating Right to the City in the Global South*. London: Routledge.

Sengupta, Mitu. 2010. The 2010 Commonwealth Games: Delhi's Worrying Transformation. The Monthly Review, 19 July, http://mrzine.monthlyreview.org/2010/sengupta190710.html (accessed 25 September 2013).

Shatkin, Gavin (ed.). 2014. *Contesting the Indian City: Global Visions and the Politics of the Local*. Chichester, West Sussex: Wiley.

Sitapati, Vinay. 2001. What Anna Hazare's Movement and India's New Middle Classes Say about Each Other. *Economic and Political Weekly* 46 (30): 39–44.

Sridharan, E. 2011. The Growth and Sectoral Composition of India's Middle Classes: Their Impact on the Politics of Economic Liberalization, in Amita Baviskar and Raka Ray (eds), *Elite and Everyman: The Cultural Politics of the Indian Middle Classes*, 27–57. New Delhi: Routledge.

Srivastava, Sanjay. 2007. *Passionate Modernity: Sexuality, Class, and Consumption in India*. New Delhi: Routledge.

———. 2011. Urban Spaces, Disney-Divinity and the Moral Middle Classes in Delhi, in Amita Baviskar and Raka Ray (eds), *Elite and Everyman: The Cultural Politics of the Indian Middle Classes*, 364–90. New Delhi: Routledge.

———. 2012. National Identity, Bedrooms, and Kitchens: Gated Communities and New Narratives of Space in India. in Rachel Heiman, Carla Freeman and Mark Liechty (eds), *The Global Middle Classes: Theorizing Through Ethnography*, 57–84. Santa Fe: School for Advanced Research Press.

Sundaram, Ravi. 2010. *Pirate Modernity: Delhi's Media Urbanism*. Abingdon: Routledge.

Upadhyaya, Carol. 2011. Software and the 'New' Middle Class in the 'New India', in Amita Baviskar and Raka Ray (eds), *Elite and Everyman: The Cultural Politics of the Indian Middle Classes*, 167–92. New Delhi: Routledge.

Wanning, Sun. 2009. *Maid in China: Media, Morality and the Cultural Politics of Boundaries*. London, New York: Routledge.

introduction: india shining

It's booming time in India. Touch the dust and it will turn into gold.
(Singh 2006: 9)

These lines from an article in the *Indian Observer*, a fortnightly journal published from Delhi predominantly addressing overseas Indians, read as if they had been cut and pasted from a report on a gold rush anywhere else in the world, or a line from a Hollywood western. In my conversations with members of the arrived urban middle classes between the years 2000–7, I found that this enthusiasm was replicated in various facets: by investors of all kinds, e.g., from real estate development; professionals from the growing service sectors and advertising world; overseas Indians, and lifestyle specialists. To many of them, 'India Shining' is another term associated with the desire and ability to enjoy and move forward into a new world, a world full of light, comfort and prosperity. The stunning career of this metaphor began with a massive media campaign launched under the same name by the Bharatiya Janata Party, then leading constituent of the Indian government, in the advent of general elections in 2004. In spring 2004, I accompanied L. K. Advani, the then Home Minister, on his *Bharat Uday Yatra* (India Shining Rally). This was a campaign that promoted India as the future global superpower of the twenty-first century, a country of unrestricted opportunities and achievement, with a citizenry proud of slogans such as 'Made in India' and 'there is no better time to be an Indian'.[1] Many of the occupations just mentioned, for instance, those of lifestyle experts (such as event managers), owe their existence to the notion that large segments of Indian society and economy

---

[1] The second slogan was one of several so-called 'points of achievement' published in Advani's Press Statement, Nagpur, 19 March 2004. To challenge its communalist image, the Bharatiya Janata Party (BJP) promoted itself as a party that considered citizens of all religions alike. For an analysis of the media campaign, see an interview with Ronald B. Inden (Sonwalkar 2004); see also Pinney (2005).

are rapidly moving forward, and upward. Such changes are based on the recognition that specific forms of lifestyle and flexibility are vital in order to increase economic growth — as opposed to falling behind — and that additional expertise is crucial for this. New professional groups, new leisure sites and practices are the most obvious markers of 'India Shining', as this study attempts to show. Several of the sites, spaces and events at which this 'Indian Dream' becomes visible and almost tangible, result from the process of economic liberalisation since the 1990s. Globalised capitalism, in particular since the new millennium, has produced a large and heterogeneous middle class that is distinctly different from the 'old' middle class. The dramatic speed at which India opened up to the world market and economic growth has also contributed to the production of new lifestyles that allow members of the new middle classes to both adapt to this change in terms of mobility and flexibility, and learn to perform and display the newly gained wealth and confidence. One of the most obvious 'testing grounds' and stages of new lifestyles are the city, media and religious practices (e.g., pilgrimage and marriage). They are the arenas where new identities are contested, where desires, pleasures and anxieties are given a face, narrative and direction, by a host of 'experts', media and events.

This study is not about the politics and ideology of a particular party such as the BJP and their *Bharat Uday* election campaign. It also does not claim to be a systematic and all-embracing investigation of 'the' middle classes; from an anthropological perspective, the complexity of the new middle classes requires many more and specific inquiries into this phenomenon. Instead, the case-studies in this book take particular images, media, sites and concepts to venture into the very powerful realm of 'India Shining' as an intangible coupled with a very concrete experience of globalisation, especially of transnationality and cosmopolitanism. This study is an investigation into the terrain of cultural globalisation that produces diverse strategies of flexible accumulation, new forms of identity construction and constitution of subjectivities. The new middle classes, despite their heterogeneity, are an ideal test case for the discussion here. To be sure, people who can actually afford to live these dreams projected by the concept of 'India Shining' are but few.[2] Access is limited, physically and financially.

---

[2] The annual growth rate of millionaires in India from 2000 to 2005 is among the highest in the world (accompanied by China, Argentina and Kazakhstan), averaging more than 15 per cent. By 2006, an estimated 83,000 millionaires lived in India; by 2008, India reached 141,000 (China: 373,000 and USA: 3,114,000;

However, I argue that the range of economic liberalisation, circulated and shaped by the media, by transnational groups and globalised concepts, make sure that notions such as 'world city' or 'world-class' reach more than 15 per cent of the Indian population who may fall into the category of 'middle class' in India.[3] Most of all, they shape, and even fire, the imagination of innumerable individuals who have access to those forms of media that circulate such images and concepts. It is in this way, following Appadurai (1997), that I stress imagination's role as a constitutive marker of modern subjectivity.

India Unbound and 'Feeling Good'

Many of the metaphors surfacing in the context of India's economic liberalisation are in one way or another related to visions of a country that has risen like a phoenix from the ashes, that engages in a 'gold rush' and other narratives of self-realisation appropriated from the 'American Dream', from which it is successively translated into an 'Indian Dream'. They highlight

---

source: wealth management advisors, Scorpio Partnership, 2008, www.scorpiopart nership.com-articles-recpressarticles.html, accessed 23 August 2009). More than 711,000 Indian consumers had more than US$100,000 in liquid wealth in 2006, according to the report *Inside the Affluent Space*, released in September by American Express, on the new wealthy Asian demography. By 2009, that number is expected to hit 1.1 million (Barker 2006). In 2004, the National Council for Applied Economic Research (NCAER) published a report entitled 'The Great Indian Middle Class' and estimated that in 2010 almost 4 million households will belong to the 'near rich' to 'super rich' category (with an annual income of INR 1 million to over 10 million, i.e., c. €18,000,00–180,000) (NCAER 2005: 43).

[3] The definition of 'middle class' varies greatly in terms of income. Categories defining the middle classes are (in ascending order): 'Aspirers', 'Seekers', 'Strivers', 'Near Rich', topped by 'Clear Rich', 'Sheer Rich' and 'Super Rich'. In their survey of urban consumers — 'Consumer Outlook 2005', 'India Retail Report 2005' by Images-KSA Technopak, Gurgaon, the global management consulting firm has differentiated the new middle classes into 32 million 'technologies babies' (8–19 years), 16 million 'impatient aspirers' (20–25 years), 41 million 'balance seekers' (25–50 years) and 9 million 'arrived veterans' (51–60 years). To grasp the heterogeneity of the Indian middle classes, I also relied on the works of Fernandes (2006: 76) and Varma (1998). Defining the new middle classes, Varma names 300 million 'aspirants', 300 million 'climbers', and 150 million 'consumers' (1998: 171). For detailed ethnography on the lower middle class in Kolkata, see Ganguly-Scrase and Scrase (2009).

enormous optimism and aspirations on the one hand, and on the other, give way to dramatic or subtle anxieties about being left behind, or left out. One informant from the arrived middle class would tell me that with economic liberalisation so many more things than before were possible, and that a comfortable lifestyle was in easier reach now: a weekend trip to Thailand or Singapore, regular dinners at five star hotels, and, with some more effort, access to one of the elite private schools in Rajasthan for children. But the same person might also alert me to the psychological pressures arising at the level of professional competition, social recognition, performance in family circles, and the tensions involved with respect to an increase in individual responsibilities and desire for independence.

The experience of manifold change due to economic liberalisation is often expressed in dichotomies of giant leaps from tradition to modernity, from old to new, as if, in principle, it was not possible for the one to accommodate the other; but India is one of the few exceptions where the impossible worked. Change is also placed on a teleological axis, narrating and associating India's development with self-empowerment and freedom. The ultimate source of freedom, for many, is that of individual choice, leisure and pleasure of consumption; the ultimate fear, simultaneously, that of a loss of heritage. In the year 2005, the Special Independence Day Issue of *India Today*, one of the largest Indian weekly magazines, promoted the slogan of 'India Unbound', defining India as a giant released and leaping forward into its predetermined future of economic liberalisation. The Editor-in-Chief, Aroon Purie, wrote the following:

> For many years, to India and Indians, independence meant political freedom but no more. Today as we look around us, we see a rapidly changing nation. India is on the brink of one of its most dramatic periods in its post-independence history and it has little to do with politics. It is almost as if India has been freed, again, from the shackles of its past … With all its traditions and heritage, India has become a forward-looking nation. When Indians now travel overseas they see more like them, doing business with the world, engaging with tomorrow … In an increasingly polarised world, India's position as an Asian giant with nuclear capabilities can be undermined no longer … Freed of the license raj, India Inc. has bloomed in a new economic climate, as it has always promised … Yet, through all this, India remains precariously balanced between two ages — the modern and the medieval (Purie 2005: 1).

The message generated here, however, is that a strong, confident and growing middle class is on its way to save the country and upgrade India's international reputation, shaking off the burden of the colonial past and the economic backwardness attached to 'Third World' countries. The case-studies in this book explore urbanisation, the transnational religio-spiritual market and the wellness and beauty industry as sites at which notions like tradition and modernity, change and continuity are related to each other in a field of tensions.

Certainly, not all citizens of India and critics of economic liberalisation politics would share Purie's vision. Whether the advent of the New Economy in India is liberating and enriching to all Indians alike is highly questionable, despite talk of the so-called 'trickle-down-effect'. The Indian government, for instance, has promised time and again to remove poverty by the year 2010. But while many surveys propose rapid increase of wealth from the aspiring middle classes to the 'super rich', the numbers of deprived households in India remain surprisingly stable.[4] It has been argued in fact that the BJP lost the general elections in 2004 owing to recent public incredulity against the extensive promotion of India as an economic powerhouse (see also Fernandes 2006).[5] Moreover, concerns have been raised as to whether the removal of poverty is not a slogan of neo-liberalisation, as part of 'India Shining' that admits no 'dark spots' on the glossy façade.

---

[4] Delhi has one of the highest per capita incomes in India, with c. INR 70,000 (c. €1,100) while the average per capita income in other cities is at INR 30,000 per year (Raman 2009). A household in India within the category of the 'deprived' earns less than INR 90,000 per year. In 1995, 80 per cent of Indian households belonged to this category! An NCAER survey in 2005 expected the numbers to fall below 50 per cent by the year 2000. But while in the years 1995–96, 131,176,000 households belonged to the 'deprived', projections for the years 2009–10 concerned 114,394,000 households (NCAER 2005: 43).

[5] In 2005, 27.5 per cent of the Indian population lived below the poverty line, with 25.7 per cent in urban and 28.3 per cent in rural areas. The per capita income per month defining the poverty line in Delhi was INR 613.00 (€10) (see 'Poverty Estimates for 2004–05', Press Information Bureau, Planning Commission, Government of India, March 2007). Reuters reports, 77 per cent of Indians, about 836 million people, 'live on less than half a dollar a day in one of the world's hottest economies', referring to the report of the state-run National Commission for Enterprises in the Unorganised Sector (NCEUS). The survey states that a majority of the people from the informal sector in fact lives on less than INR 20 (€0.30) per day ('Nearly 80 pct of India Lives on Half Dollar a Day', 10 August 2007, http://www.reuters.com/article/latestCrisis/idUSDEL218894, accessed 24 August 2009). See also n. 11 of this chapter.

Despite much of the reasonable criticism, what is relevant for this study and requires to be taken seriously is that a large spectrum of the English-speaking media, the English-educated urban middle classes as well as representatives and inhabitants of a growing occupational, housing, consumer and leisure infrastructure have responded to and recycled the notion of 'India Shining' as a viable concept of their own present and future. Leela Fernandes relates this growing visibility of the new middle classes, which is said to embrace approximately 300 million people, to the 'emergence of a wider national political culture, one that has shifted from older ideologies of a state-managed economy to a middle class-based culture of consumption' (Fernandes 2006: XV, see also n. 3, Part I of this work). She also highlights the shifts of taxation politics in the late 1980s through which middle class identities could become more visible and important (ibid.: 38).

A recurring mood shared by a majority of people I spoke to during my fieldwork was overwhelming enthusiasm about yet another BJP-slogan associated with 'India Shining': the 'feel good factor'. It is crucial to mention at this stage, that this mood was articulated by those profiting from economic liberalisation and that the interviews were taken before 2008. Clearly, the situation has changed completely with the global economic meltdown that has affected India quite drastically too, recording the slowest Gross Domestic Product (GDP) growth of the market value of goods and services in six years at 5.3 per cent in February 2009 (Mishra 2009). Until this dramatic shift in the perception of stability and progress had occurred, the notion of 'feel-good' suggested the theoretical possibility that citizens of all social strata could enjoy a good lifestyle and even 'make it big time'; that all doors were open and that, in terms of a promising career, there were no more restrictions by birth (that is, by caste or religion) and corruption. All that counted, in theory, was individual merit. Thus, many stories circulated in informal conversations about a person's unimaginable career and exuberant lifestyle. Most of these stories of the 'Indian Dream' are set in the booming IT and service sector, real estate development, the world of television, mobile technology or advertisement media, and the growing infrastructure for lifestyle experts, wellness, tourism or marriage industries. Salaries have indeed skyrocketed in 2006, and even trainees in the service sector (such as call centres or multinational corporations) bring home around INR 10, 000 per month (c. €180), with more qualified professionals working as business consultants or in the real estate sector earning around INR 100, 000 per month (c. €1.800), plus the facilities of a car and driver, coverage of rent, and so forth. 'Ordinary' salaries in the informal sector or government services are much below this.[6] However, various scholars have outlined that the disposable income does not necessarily define the ways in which members of the different middle classes identify themselves with and reproduce notions such as 'world-class', one of the key notions scrutinised in this book (see Fernandes 2006; Mazzarella 2005; Varma 1998). Instead I shall argue that it is the aspiration to become a member of both a cosmopolitan and nationalist class of Indians that characterises and fuels the imaginary of the 'global Indian', the 'global superpower' and even the 'global Indian takeover' (Gentleman 2006).

The newfound pride of identities 'Made in India' is to a large extent media- and economy-driven and is circulated as well as consumed in the domain of aspiring and affluent middle classes. For instance, weekly magazines such as India Today regularly come out with special issues in which 'Indians who made it to the top' are presented and ranked, be it in the steel industry (e.g., Lakshmi Mittal, industrialist), textiles, petrochemicals, telecommunication and finance (e.g., Mukesh and Anil Ambani from Reliance group), academia and economic analysis (e.g., Amartya Sen, economist), the culture industries (e.g., Neville Tuli, art auctioneer) or the global market of spirituality (e.g., Sri Sri Ravi Shankar, spiritual leader of 'Art of Living' or AOL). The 'market value' of such people, whose career is predominantly based on merit, not on birth into a particular caste or religion, has become the foundation for the shaping of a new moral universe and 'tool-kit' for those who aspire to belong to the most wanted citizens.

The last shot in the arm for the representatives of the global Indian takeover, and international recognition, was American Express's announcement of their introduction of the Platinum Club Card in November 2006. This move was made after the completion of a study entitled 'Inside the Affluent Space'. The survey revealed that India has more than one million people earning over US$ 1 million and that the growth rate had reached 25

---

[6] Until 2008, the salary of a professor in Delhi was INR 45,000 (c. €800), a senior journalist at one of the big daily newspapers earned about INR 15,000–20,000 (c. €300–400), a travel agent too would earn roughly around the same amount. Household servants in cities like Delhi receive salaries in the range of INR 4,000– 5,000 per month (c. €70–80), but because this kind of labour is informal it is difficult to establish concrete data. For further data on income, ownership and expenditure, see Fernandes (2006: 81–84). See also http://www.populstat.info/ Asia/indiag.htm (accessed 7 June 2007).

per cent.[7] Possessions and persona symbolise affluence: more wealth and more access are creating a lifestyle competition among India's affluent.[8] To be branded 'affluent' requires access to, as well as the competence to, perform the adequate dispositions and lifestyles. For many people who have quickly come to enjoy such amounts of money, this meant that they had to 'learn' how to become 'visible' and remain part of the 'I've made it'-club, as the American Express study terms this top segment of Indian society. Not without reason do lifestyle experts, lifestyle magazines or commercial media enjoy such demand.

Challenging the First World–Third World Divide

> Every time you go out shopping, remember you are a part of something big that is happening in India. Retail is the mantra of the moment. It's what that's driving investment. It's generating employment. Most significantly, it is making people like you think and feel a whole lot better about the way you can spend your money and improve your quality of life … Drive down a highway leading out of any of India's metros. Now look around you. What do you see? A landscape dotted with impressive high rises cased in aesthetically imposing steel and glass. Too much of steel and concrete maybe, but this changed landscape has a story to tell. It is the story of India's growth as a market. Inside those buildings plans are being drawn to bring a million new products and services to tens of millions of middle class Indians who have begun to expect more than the ordinary. Now shut your eyes for a moment. And think back fifteen years … What did this landscape look like then? Nice and empty for miles on end. What story did those barren arid stretches tell you? That we were a poor country that looked and felt poor. Maybe we are still a poor country. But surely we are less poor today than we were fifteen years back. Our metropolitan cities and their suburbs, however, do not look the type of a third world country … For better or for worse, Indians (especially middle class urban Indians) have become more nattily dressed, have learnt to exercise specific choices

---

[7] 'Inside the Affluent Space' was a survey conducted in Singapore, Hong Kong and other countries. It was commissioned by American Express Asia and the report was released in 2006. See *Rediff News*, 21 September 2006, http://www.rediff.com/money/2006/sep/21rich.htm (accessed 20 May 2009).

[8] According to tourism industry estimates, in 2005–6, 7.5 million Indians went abroad, 21 per cent more than a year before, spending US$5,100 per head — i.e., more than their European counterparts. In this, the Indian tourists lead among the Asian countries. Switzerland tourism statistics ranks Indians among the highest spenders (SFR 450 per day) — 320,000 Indians visited Switzerland in 2005. In 2005–6, Singapore received half-a-million Indian travellers per year (see Bobb 2007: 4).

over the brands, and developed enhanced skills in organising their lifestyles (Mookerjee 2007: 48–49).

This quote from *Celebrating Vivaha* (marriage), a leading Indian bridal magazine, paints a rather crude scenery of India 'before' and 'after' economic liberalisation. Most obvious, according to the editor's view, is the change in urban landscape and consumer choice. One can *see* the difference, one can *see* the changes taking place, and experience them too, and this is what seems to matter. The focus of comparison is predominantly the 'First World', but this is increasingly replaced by reference to other developments in Asian countries of the 'Global South': Singapore, Malaysia, and China. But the idea of a 'modernisation package' that is diffused from 'the West' to the rest of the world has slowly been discredited. Instead, we now see the emergence of 'entangled modernities' where the previous notion of centre (e.g., Empire) and periphery (e.g., colonies) has been rendered obsolete. Europe and (formerly) colonised countries are involved in a reciprocal relationship (see Conrad and Randeria 2002).

Certainly, the recognition of this breathtaking economic development is based on a reciprocal gaze of recognition of (and submission to) new realities. In the last few years, articles and books, both academic and journalistic, have focused their attention on 'India Shining' or 'India Rising', often in comparison with China's expanding market economy (see Basu 2004; Gill 2005; Jaffrelot and van der Veer 2008; Jha 2002). This focus has a somewhat peculiar entanglement with Orientalist discourses which underlines the seeming paradox that a nation so deeply entrenched in tradition and religion can come to the forefront by undergoing 'instant modernisation'. Such stereotypical notions can also be found in recent works dealing with India's economic growth, like *In Spite of the Gods: The Strange Rise of Modern India* by Edward Luce (2007) or *Mantras of Change* by Daniel Lak (2005), and German publications on the issue (Müller 2006; Ihlau 2006; both entitled *Weltmacht Indien*, or, 'Global Power India'. Many of these explorations by western authors are related to a bewilderment or even growing anxiety among members of western countries, that the new 'Asian tigers' — China included — will claim the status of an industrialised and 'First World' country soon, if not overtake western economies and hegemonies, triggering a kind of 'reverse colonisation'.[9] The 'old India' of Sanskrit scriptures, so desirably timeless for Indologists and Orientalists

---

[9] Harald Müller, Professor of International Relations, addresses a pecific western that ignores massive shifts at economic and political levels.

of all kinds, now leads the new scriptures, of information technology and business process outsourcing.

India's new image has also caught the highly ambivalent attention of Indian scholars, ranging from studies such as *The Great Indian Middle Class* by Pavan Varma (1998), *India Unbound* by Gurcharan Das (2002) or *Mistaken Modernity* by Dipankar Gupta (2000), to mention only a few.[10] In tandem with the glamour and fascination of this 'miracle' has come the critique that the fruits of economic growth were claimed by the affluent classes who allegedly could not care less that more than 50 per cent of households in India are 'deprived'.[11] While Varma criticises the new middle classes' reluctance to recognise their duty with regard to common welfare, particularly, the removal of poverty, and loyalty towards the nation state, Gupta states that the Indian middle classes and elites are caught 'between two worlds'; a 'shallow modernity' that only reproduces caste ideology on the one hand, and westernisation, which he associates with a public sphere à la Jürgen Habermas, in which universalistic norms and values are emphasised. With his concept of 'Westoxication', Gupta dismisses the aspiring middle classes and elites as alien, anti-national, immersed in 'superficial consumerist display of commodities and fads produced in the West' (ibid.: 21). Although Gupta admits that 'modernity' has its advantages over 'tradition', he stereotypes the first as a source of loneliness, competitiveness and seething dissatisfaction (ibid.: 9). Since extreme wealth and poverty are simultaneously present in India today, often next door to each other, his critical stance falls on fertile ground, despite the seemingly uncomplicated attribution of 'Westoxication' as being of lower value.

The narratives of a 'successful' process of modernisation by which Indians can embrace their cultural heritage and face the challenges of social or civil responsibilities must be seen in light of a growing reluctance of members

---

[10] The most elaborate sociological inquiries in this context are by Ahmad and Reifeld (2001); Deshpande (2003); Fernandes (2006); Jaffrelot and van der Veer (2008); Mazzarella (2003); Mishra (1961); Oza (2006) and Shah (1990).

[11] These numbers were released by the NCAER in 2002. See also Fernandes (2006: 82); Mazzarella (2005); Varma (1998) and Deshpande (2003: 135) (with a distinction between urban and rural India). The NCAER report on the middle classes of 2004 defines the 'deprived' (for the years 2001–2) as annually earning below INR 90,000, consisting of about 135 million households. While between 1996–98, around 80 per cent of the country's households were classified as deprived, the number is expected to fall to about 50 per cent by 2010, *The Billionaire Club*, November 2005: 43.

of the new middle classes to 'feel bad' about aspiring towards a capitalist lifestyle. After years of socialist economy, ranging from restrictions against the market of western goods to a moral universe that, in theory, promoted that less was better than more and that, first of all, the entire population of India had to be uplifted before economic liberalisation could be allowed into the country, capitalism was embraced and translated into a national virtue (Fernandes 2006). While capitalism was previousely identified with lack of patriotism, members of the new middle classes now consider themselves as motors of a new national revitalisation, both in terms of economy and moral values. And, as regards charity and social work, many feel that their involvement in new religious movements and organisations proves their caring for the welfare of society (see Béteille 2005b: 453–55). William Mazzarella has defined this as a shift of concepts from the duty of progress to progress through the pleasure of consumption (2003: 101). Pleasure as individual and collective progress, pleasure-driven consumption and display of wealth are thus relevant concepts for this study.[12]

New Citizens of the Globalised Nation

To identify the consumption-driven, largely Hindu, middle classes as citizens concerned with nationality seems paradoxical at first sight. Yet, authors like Mazzarella (2003) have explored the ways in which 'New Swadeshi' takes up a new realm of the Indian advertising industry, promoting that Indians uplift the Indian economy by supporting Indian production, while Arvind Rajagopal (2001a, 2001b) has argued that Hindu nationalism and economic liberalisation are closely connected. Several scholars have interpreted the shift from dutiful nation-citizen to consumer-citizen as creating another form of national identity. In their study of IT professionals in Chennai, Tamil Nadu's capital, Christopher J. Fuller and Haripriya Narasimhan maintain that members of this occupational group, 'are not Nehruvian nationalists, but, perhaps, paradoxically, the professionals who are crucially responsible for building a global economy based on information technology may be more committed to living their lives in India than many of their predecessors in India's aspirational middle class' (2007: 148). In her book about the new middle classes in India, Leela Fernandes makes a crucial point in arguing that despite the shifts

---

[12] As regards the moralising stigma associated with consumption, India is not alone: Heryanto (1999) maintains the same for Indonesia, and middle and upper classes in other Asian countries have similar experiences (see also Ngai 2003; Pinches 1999).

in loyalty towards the nation state, as it was idealised under Nehru, even today's 'urban middle classes are ... the central agents in this revisioning of the Indian nation' (Fernandes 2006: 66). Yet, she also highlights that the 'majority' of this nation seem to belong to the 'globalized middle class elite' (ibid.). Thus we find, in the economic liberalisation and urbanisation of India, a new and heterogeneous social group that negotiates concepts such as national identity and 'worldliness', tradition and modernity, in various ways that are based on new forms of cultural capital, power and aspirations of new social agents seeking to stabilise their position in a field of discourse (Bourdieu 1984).

The new enthusiasm about 'belonging to world-class' has various origins. Until the early 1990s, India seemed to be at the receiving end of 'modernity', positioned at the margins of the developed world, defined as a backward country and people. This image was promulgated both by the Indian political and economic elites as well as western countries and can be traced back to the expansionist and Eurocentric politics of imperialism and colonialism. Among the colonial elites in India, the notion gained dominance that western 'superiority', wealth and power resulted from new concepts of the nation state (e.g., capitalism) and its aligning institutions (e.g., bureaucracy, museums, school and higher education) and visual practices (e.g., surveys, photography). The imperial metropolis was conceived of as centre stage while the colonies were placed at its periphery (see Conrad and Randeria 2002; Delanty 2006). Flows of knowledge, power and goods were perceived as uni-directional, moving from a centre to its margins. Only if the margins became like the centre, so the argument went, could these nations become modern. This is also a view often shared by sociologists such as Louis Dumont or Max Weber in their discussion of the Indian caste system vis-à-vis European modernity, or the like (see Das 1993; Munshi 1988).

With anthropologist Ulf Hannerz we might follow the claim that these upwardly mobile and confident 'glocalised' Indians are 'elites of the periphery ... who tend to launch political campaigns of "authenticity"' against the alleged flow of modernity from an imaginary centre (West) (1996: 60) by challenging these centre–periphery relations. But this would be too simplistic an assumption. The question whether Indianness can be preserved only if westernisation is cleverly circumvented, is one that mistakenly assumes an either/or situation whereas, as we shall see here, in fact both are at work simultaneously (though not necessarily in harmony). The term 'glocalisation', first coined by Roland Robertson (1995), referring to the ways in which global flows are appropriated and transformed in various local contexts, would otherwise not make much sense. Instead, we must assume that modernity's flows and shifts are far more complicated, complex and entangled than scholars of anthropology have so far acknowledged.[13] The question is thus how we can trace and come to understand the management of meaning, the shaping of cultural capital, of glocal competence by drawing upon all kinds of 'archival' resources — be they material or imaginary. With their groundedness in participatory exploration and long-time qualitative research, ethnographies are particularly fit to face such a challenge. They can study how cultural repertoires are reshaped and adjusted to new needs and tastes. However, participatory observation is complicated by the fact that people, ideas, concepts and images do not stand still but move constantly, through various spheres and domains, and with different paces and meaning. To explore the local appropriation of a globalised concept such as 'cosmopolitan' and 'world-class', we must consider the impact of the non-resident Indians on the constitution of Indianness, of the different media technologies and specialists that are concerned with 'efficient' communication. Only by considering these different and yet intertwined levels can we 'fine tune' our understanding of globalisation and urbanisation in concrete settings. The entanglement of local and global facets of economic liberalisation becomes even more interesting and seemingly complex when we explore the issue through Mark Liechty's approach towards contemporary middle class desires in Nepal as 'being and acting worldly' within specific local contexts:

> The transformative work of cultural compromise that takes place as part of these global middle-class projects is less about 'westernization' than about the making of a local class culture (Liechty 2003: 252–53).

Therefore, the appropriation of global elements into a person's cultural capital, may serve individual aspirations not only to be part of a global society but also to be locally rooted and conscious.

Locating the 'Great Indian Middle Classes'

How do we picture the hydra-headed construct of the new middle classes by means of qualitative ethnography if other qualitative and quantitative studies already vary so drastically, struggling with definitions from income to

---

[13] See Clifford's work (1997) on diaspora and travelling cultures, Hannerz' work (1993, 1996) on transnational connections and megacities, and Appadurai's exploration (1997) of globalised modernity.

membership to terminology? In many of my conversations during fieldwork, with friends as well as informants, and most of all, in the booming landscape of lifestyle magazines, the notion of 'belonging to world-class' cropped up, as well as a strong desire to come to terms with the emerging middle class in India. These categories had obviously become crucial concepts of self-definition — not just scholarly applications. Yet, this desire for a homogeneous identity was paired with great confusion about what, or whom, it could *actually* mean and constitute, and how it should be attributed with meaning. One of the most obvious strategies was to draw borders of all kinds, in relation to upper class Indians, high caste Indians, low class and low caste Indians (though caste and class are certainly not considered identical), 'vulgar' new, and 'sophisticated' old classes. With respect to social change and segregation in Indian society, the question is what happens to the 'classical' markers of hierarchy and distinction, caste and purity; do they retain any further significance, and if so, when and for what reason?[14]

André Béteille has rightly argued that there is no single category that allows us to define middle class in India. One approach, he suggests, would be to look at occupation patterns, education and income. The new middle classes are highly heterogeneous, made up of 'professional, administrative, managerial, clerical and other white-collar occupations' (Béteille 2001: 77). In this study, I do not attempt to analyse the middle classes as an entity or 'essence'. Instead, I follow Fernandes, Liechty, and Bourdieu in tracing middle-class dynamic and complexity in and through its practices of distinction and regimes of pleasure. Fernandes proposes the very valuable concept of 'middle-classness' as a means of considering the experience and imagination connected with middle class. It seems to me that it is particularly the intangibility and 'fuzzyness' of 'the' middle classes as a category that leaves scope for multiple interpretations and underlines the importance of distinguishing the shaping of aesthetics and performance of 'taste' as a cultural resource among the newly emerging social groups. Furthermore, the group that has caught my attention is but a fragment of 'the middle classes'. Most of the addressees of the media, events and new sites of consumption I explore in this book are largely tailored and accessible for the upper middle classes and elites.

---

[14] For an excellent discussion of the Indian and Chinese new middle classes, see Jaffrelot and van der Veer (2008: 11–34). On the entangledness of concepts like caste and class, see also Béteille (2001: 82–83); Fuller and Narasimhan (2007); Fernandes (2006: 60–61); Liechty (2003: 14); Säävälä (2001).

Before addressing the importance of the notion of the 'world-class' as a desired status-related emblem and a strategy of distinction in a glocalised world, let me consider the concept of class in more general terms. What references to class are important to my explorations of the affluent and upwardly mobile new middle class in India? Class position and social status must be understood as dynamic, not as stable entities.[15] This section of the emerging middle class is an important concept of social fabrication and distinction, at once adding new meaning to, and challenging, notions of caste, ethnicity and kinship: 'those people carving out a new cultural space which they explicitly locate, in language and material practice, between their class "others" above and below' (Liechty 2003: 5). Leichty's observation points to the situation of being jammed between the ones below (who aspire to move upwards, and the ones above (trying to prevent others from moving up the ladder).

To ensure that the borders towards culturally and socially 'lower' groups can be drawn efficiently, and the position pointing towards upper classes strengthened, distinction is required. According to Pierre Bourdieu, distinction is an important element that shapes habitus, capital and cultural production. The properties of habitus are practice and dispositions. They render social practice and perceptions meaningful. The focus is on the particular kinds of activities by which a field of social positions and relations can be explored, for instance, as regards weddings.

Throughout this book, I have been guided by Bourdieu's concept of class and distinction as a means of symbolic contest. Class, according to Bourdieu, is a cluster of individuals who take up a similar position in social space that is determined by pedigree, symbolic and financial capital and class-consciousness. Social space must be understood as a field of cultural production in and through which social agents seek to position themselves by improving or stabilising their status, negotiating access to values and rules of the 'game' allegedly played. Class, then, can be seen as the struggle of different social factions over access to cultural space, the accumulation of prestige through the performative accumulation of various forms of capital by means of distinction and classification: economic (e.g., financial), social (e.g., relations and networks), symbolic (e.g., prestige, honour)

---

[15] According to Weber, class is a function of a person or group's position in the capitalist market. It can be understood in terms of a person's relations with production (bourgeoisie or working class), on the one hand. On the other, it connects to the consumption of goods and services in the market. A person's social status conveys lifestyle, education, training and socialisation. See Liechty (2003: 13).

and cultural capital (e.g., qualifications, competencies, skills). These are always spatialised, either by means of imagination, perception, experience or materialisation. The members of a class move in a space of lifestyles, not just a physical space — like a city — but a space in which symbolic capital is both a shaped and shaping force within the imagination. The city, for instance, is imagined as much as it is a social arena in which people compete for symbolic power, for an improvement or at least stabilisation of their individual positions and access to particular resources (see Hannerz 1980, 1993; Schiffauer 1997). Appadurai addresses a person or a group's 'capacity to aspire' as a cultural and vital competence in contemporary consumer societies, and in particular, in urban habitats (2004a: 59). It is tied to the desire for visibility-as-recognition, for having a voice (ibid.), and the competence to handle resources such as cultural capital. Class membership is thus also related to consumption as a constructive practice of distinction.

Consumption, distinction and class are closely connected: it is not so much a question of *what* is consumed but a question of *knowing how* to consume it that is at the heart of the matter when we explore images and strategies of the new middle classes in India (Uberoi 2008; Young 1999). At the top of the hierarchy of people who *know how* stands the specialist who manages taste (e.g., the designer or wedding planner). The connoisseur or expert in consumption matters follows suit. He knows how to celebrate consumption of, for instance, a French wine, knows how and when to serve alcohol to his guests, and how to behave at a five star buffet. While the colonial and postcolonial elites might have consumed alcohol on special occasions and thus see nothing special in continuing this habit, this applies largely to the cosmopolitan classes. For many members of the new urban and educated middle classes the consumption of alcohol in public has been socially stigmatised as a westernised and morally weak practice. Hence, to them, the introduction of drinks as a means of socialising is a challenge to some groups.

Moving Up and In: Caste Versus Class

In the age of neoliberalisation, class has become the key focus and platform of cultural production and consumption, and in particular, the affluent segment of the new middle classes, or what Pinches (1999) calls the 'new rich', underlining the fact that these groups share a consensus about their new roles, social positions and lifestyles, the 'common capacity for discretionary spending' and 'new forms of consumption and public display, derived largely from international middle-class fashion' (ibid.: xii; see also

Ganguly-Scrase and Scrase 2009). However, this heterogeneous, dynamic and predominantly metropolitan segment of Indian society is yet to come to terms with the idea of its own identity in the national and globalised economy and public culture. This process of negotiation evolves around etic and emic categories such as caste or tradition (*parampara*). It cannot be argued that traditional concepts like caste and kinship have been fully replaced. Instead, they still occupy centre stage in certain contexts, for instance, networking and marriage or funerary rituals. In other instances, it may be the rise of nationalist sentiments, often in view of colonial experiences, that generates ethno-nationalism and chauvinism based on communalist arguments and an alleged East–West dualism. Caste and class are a means of social stratification, two sides of the same coin, entangled and reinforcing each other in manifold ways. They are based on concepts of inequality and difference, both of which are always negotiated in particular contexts. One major difference between caste and class is that caste is a key characteristic of a closed system of stratification, and a person is member of a caste by birth. Caste confines a collective identity rather than an individual asset. Class, on the other hand, is considered to be an open system, encouraging and even demanding flexibility of individual social agents who come from all kinds of backgrounds and accumulate different kinds of capital to belong to a class (e.g., financial means, but also education). It is merit, not birth, that counts; performance in conspicuous consumption is valued more rather than mere ritual purity. Forms of mobility exists in both caste and class, though in the former, it is slowed down, if not discouraged on the basis of ritual, economic and social criteria. In contrast, in the ideal of the latter, namely, class, it is an accepted, if not crucial, property of capitalism.[16] It is this struggle and attempt of the middle classes to define both position and (aesthetic, performative, narrative) language in order to create distinction from other social segments 'below' and 'above' that is explored in this study. What makes up the cultural and symbolic capital of these new social groups who possibly have no other common denominator, no shared culture, history and memory but (solely) their desire to belong to 'world-class' and be recognised as a member of this group? How do they claim and 'defend' their status in this highly mobile and fluid transnational, 'mediatised' and urbanised society? When does 'merit' leave the stage in favour of 'birth's' entry on stage?

---

[16] Interestingly, Gupta points out that despite the acceptance of hierarchy within the so-called caste system, there is no consensus over how purity and pollution should be quantified on a gradational scale (2004: 130).

In today's South Asian societies, caste, as Liechty has argued, is still an important means of framing discourses around class status in particular, and social mobility in general. In her ethnography of the relationship between caste and class among urban middle classes in present-day Hyderabad, anthropologist Minna Säävälä maintains that Sanskritisation is not adequate enough to explain the aspirations or anxieties of economically well-situated lower castes. She highlights that 'the overarching objective of social action … is cultural re-interpretation of respectability' while rendering the low social honour assigned by caste irrelevant (Säävälä 2001: 294). There is, she argues, much competition and anxiety among lower and higher caste members within the middle classes to fall down the social and economic ladder, and to lose, as I suggest, their membership in the 'club-class'. To Säävälä, the fact of the popularity of high caste Hindu practices among low caste members of the middle class is not necessarily a sign of unchallenged Sanskritisation (ibid.: 298). She also questions the dichotomisation of secularisation and Sanskritisation after M. N. Srinivas and highlights that urban middle classes may use both in order to improve their prestige (ibid.: 300). Appropriation of high caste Hindu practices is part of the newcomers' strategy to accumulate cultural capital and present themselves as 'competent' custodians of high Hindu culture. In my case-studies, too, hierarchy and purity remain as important as classificatory dispositions as a high-caste, predominantly Brahmin concept of 'Hindu culture' and 'Hindu tradition'. There is, for instance, a recurring claim towards the common source and value-creating force of 'the Vedas' among members of the Hindu middle classes, in order to claim noble ancestry to a Golden (Hindu) Age, even by people from low caste lineage. By means of such a 'theming' strategy, members of the old and the new middle classes transform themselves into custodians of national values and cultural heritage as well as torchbearers of modernity.

Moving Down and Out: The Fear of Falling

In the period before the global economic meltdown, the notion of 'India Shining' not only shaped new forms of confidence but also new fears. Undoubtedly, the fears have multiplied since 2008, when the economic crisis also became a 'hard fact' in India. The fear of falling behind or losing ground and thus one's membership in the middle classes is ever-present and haunting for many members of the aspiring and arrived middle classes. It has bitter connotations for many. Many of my informants highlighted the speed at which globalisation had 'taken over' the Indian subcontinent and ways of life, and that some people's salaries had increased breathtakingly. It appears as though there has not been sufficient time to react adequately, with a cool head. Either one managed to jump on to the train or was left behind. This is how many informants described the experience of economic liberalisation. Several fears can be distinguished: first, of other upwardly mobile social groups claiming access to the same status domain; second, of not being able to compete; third, of failing in social and business relationships, and fourth, that one's competencies were recognised or treated 'fairly' in competition contexts.

For several years I followed the struggles of one particular middle class Sikh family whom I had befriended over the years of my coming to Delhi during my fieldwork. In fact, they are a mixture of 'old' rich and 'new' rich, insofar as the parents of my informant Neetu K. had once belonged to the old established classes of Delhi and Kolkata. In his conversations with me, Neetu would narrate a picture of childhood set in comfort, protected from falling. Nostalgic moments in conversations would reveal (and make me marvel at) memories revolving around the family's old mansion in Kolkata, and summer holidays in the Himalayan foothills near Shimla, imbued in a quasi-colonial lifestyle. But those days were suddenly over when, after the Delhi riots of 1984, the family lost its property and business, and had to start all over from scratch, elsewhere.[17] Neetu's parents sent him to one of the elite private schools in India, knowing that education was increasingly becoming important for upward mobility. It is interesting that his social networks from those days are still well oiled. With economic liberalisation, Neetu started his own business, first in information technology, thereafter in security systems for governments, business in general and residential housing. Partly out of personal aspirations and likings, partly to impress potential clients and business partners, Neetu and his wife Suneeta always sported posh cars, state-of-the-art stereo systems, and a Labrador dog. They went on holiday trips to Thailand or Singapore with the extended family, and sent their daughters to an elite boarding school in Rajasthan. By no

---

[17] The Delhi Riots refer to a period of civil and communal violence after Prime Minister Indira Gandhi was assassinated by her Sikh bodyguards in 1984. For months after this occurrence, Sikh inhabitants of Delhi became the victim of physical and economic violence (murder and looting) and social stigmatisation. The widespread violence marked the city as a dangerous space, and the state as a force that encouraged rather than protected against violence.

means did Neetu want to send them to a US-American high school, where, according to his view, they would only get associated with 'wrong' ideas and values. Neetu played golf with business friends at exclusive golf clubs in New Delhi and Noida, made it a habit to eat out in five star restaurants and presented gold coins to his best clients on Diwali, the beginning of the new financial year for Hindus. He did so even when his business was making severe losses. Yet, Neetu was highly ambivalent regarding what he called 'the whole middle class business', defining it as 'pretentious' (spending thousands of dollars for a designer item to give away on Diwali), 'unfair' (because others would be more successful despite the fact that he too offered top quality) and 'dishonest' (going to the temple or gurdwara in the morning, chanting prayers, and then cheating the whole day, yet pretending to be a devout son at home). Despite the financial loss, Neetu continued to spend money with credit cards, his debts increasing day by day.[18]

What is specifically 'glocal' about Neetu? Like many other entrepreneurs, he saw economic liberalisation as a great chance to improve his economic and symbolic capital, to remain bound to values and traditions through his family and open for cosmopolitan mobility and conspicuous wealth through his business and social networks. Neetu also represents a global trend in which more and more young upwardly mobile persons are drawn into the credit card market, and who fall victim to the temptation of taking loans in order to afford a nice car or an independent flat in a safe and high-rated area of the city, and so on. It underlines the belief that commodity consumption guarantees access to the desired upwardly middle-classness, to respectable social status and competence (Fernandes 2006: 72). And, it highlights the pleasures and risks emerging with the notion of life when viewed as a game of lottery.

Both Liechty and Säävälä have pointed out this fear of the aspiring and even the affluent middle classes in India who 'hang between high and low' (Liechty 2003: 61; Säävälä 2006: 392; see also Mazzarella 2005: 7). The option to choose among a wide variety of material goods, lifestyle designs, relationships, is not only promising but also threatening and in fact highly risky, with responsibilities taken and borne by individuals. The constant pressure to perform conspicuous consumption and be up-to-date with the latest lifestyle trends is also a way of securing onself from

---

[18] In 2007, more than 26 million credit cards were owned by Indians in India, compared to 220 million mobile phones (Bhupta 2007: 213–15). Introduced in the 1980s, they have moved from a reluctantly used item to a status symbol.

falling down and behind. In this context, the production and circulation of moral narratives of risk and rise is crucial in order to negotiate and legitimise what is socially acceptable and what is not. Liechty has most convincingly worked on this issue, arguing that different concepts of 'vulgarity' are produced and managed through which, for instance, the new rich can be distinguished as 'illiterate' newcomers by members of the 'old' or established middle class (Liechty 2003: 67–69; see also Abaza 2001: 116; Bourdieu 1984). Thus, the 'new rich' have to prove their credentials if they do not want to be discriminated against as 'pretenders' and 'fakes' (see Part III of this book). In several conversations, my interview partners would point out the difference between 'old' and 'new' middle classes in such a way. Often, they would indicate that it was, most of all, time and generations of 'good breeding' that placed the 'new' in the shadow of, and below, the 'old' rich.[19] Culturedness, taste and their adequate strategy of display, so it seemed, could prevent from falling. But it quickly dawned on many new members of the 'arrived' or 'aspiring' middle classes, that sophisticated taste and its display could not be possessed like money but had to be learnt, like a language. For these 'laymen', often stigmatised as *parvenus* by the established elites, lifestyle experts and media have become a safety net and educational platform to get the best and fastest access to the crucial 'knowhow'. But the access is restricted, and conditions and rules are constantly shifted by a host of different forces at work. According to Bourdieu, taste is a strategy of legitimising a particular practice as superior to others, by creating dichotomies of 'pure' and 'impure', 'cultivated' and 'vulgar' taste (Bourdieu 1993). Rather than a 'given', taste thus must be understood as an expression of class-consciousness, asymmetric production of knowledge and power. Members of the 'old' elites of New Delhi, for instance, would play out class distinctions by referring to themselves as leading the 'modest' but authentic Indian lifestyle of a 'cultured person' while 'newcomers' would be classified as embarrassingly overambitious, clumsy and vulgar.

Looking after One's Self

The 'feel good-factor', mentioned earlier, is a term used frequently by my interview partners to underline a particular sensuous experience related to economic liberalisation, city life and global lifestyles in general. While

---

[19] Fuller and Narasimhan (1997) define the 'old' middle class as a property-owning petite bourgeoisie, and the 'new' middle class consisting of educated and qualified professional and technical service sector employees.

older members of the middle class shared this view to a large extent, the importance attributed to the 'feel good' narrative seemed particularly relevant to younger people and professionals who constitute more than 60 per cent of the Indian population below the age of 30. This points towards the manifold ways in which one's self-perception has altered within the larger framework of transnational connections, images of urban lifestyles and the pleasure of consumption.

The importance of imagination, pleasure and agency of consumption and the shaping of alternative modernities in a wider frame of post-colonial history helps us to shift attention, away from modernity as disenchantment à la Max Weber, towards modernity as a new subjectivity, valuing the active cultivation and concerned care of the Self. Modernity as enchantment, even as healing, and the notion that one is almost obliged to enjoy life and look after oneself, is addressed by sociologist Gerhard Schulze in his study on the *Erlebnisgesellschaft* (The Society of Sensuous Experience). Here, he holds that people in consumerist societies are committed to the imperative 'Give your life a "good taste!"' (Schulze 1992: 34) and succeed in the 'project of a beautiful life' as part and parcel of capital production and risk prevention (ibid.: 40).

Where and how one lives and works is crucial for the outcome of the 'project of a beautiful life'. Prices for real estate in megacities like Mumbai or New Delhi have skyrocketed and made a cosmopolitan lifestyle almost as expensive as in cities like New York or Paris. Golf, tennis and wellness have come to be the most expensive and exclusive leisure-cum-business activities in India, and the national and international tourist industry is booming. Moreover, new religious movements have turned into multinational corporations, offering five star accommodation and services to those willing to pay for comfortable spirituality and best access to a spiritual leader. Being different by being exclusive and exorbitant is a major criterion for Indians belonging to 'world-class'. Miriya C., then manager of one of the first growing numbers of five star spa hotels in India, affirmed:

> Previously, you would go to a golf club or a wellness centre, or our hotel and either find top upper class Indians or foreigners. Nowadays, there are so many more Indians who go off on a shopping-trip to Singapore or a romantic weekend to Egypt, who care for a wellness treat at a resort and for a game of golf with business partners. You won't believe how much people are ready and able to spend! And look at the amounts of money people are eager to spend on housing and interior design!!! With such ease! It drives you crazy. They just don't care. I grew up with parents telling me to save money for the future. To

many of the 'Gen X' this does not count any longer (personal conversation, New Delhi, October 2005).

Conspicuous consumption is not only valued as investment in a better lifestyle but as a sign of one caring for oneself. Soul, mind and body must all be trimmed in good shape in a 'world-class' life. Above all, one's satisfaction and happiness must be visible for all. Watching people visit a shopping mall reminded me as much of a beauty contest as attending a mega-ritual staged by a new religious organisation such as the 'Art of Living'. Feng shui, *vaastu*-consultation, psychotherapy and visits to wellness centres are markers of the cultures of self-care and self-experience as much as they are sites of conspicuous consumption. One crucial condition of 'middle-classness' is its aesthetic and performative dimension, and some of the strategies of making itself visible and desirable are discussed in the case-studies to follow. The aesthetic dimension of the new middle classes has a strong 'corpothetic' impact, and is part of a careful choreography of seeing and being seen. For this to be efficient, the staging of visibility must be connected to and conveyed through an event, what Schulze calls *Erlebnis*, terming it as the foundation of modern society. The term 'Erlebnis' cannot be translated into English. At best, it could be identified as an eventful sensuous, deep and immediate experience.

Why is the concept so relevant? In fact, it seems to mark a shift from *Erfahrung* as a robust experience to Erlebnis as a flatter and more intangible form of immediacy. However, taken as a signifier of modernity and modern lifestyle, Erlebnis should not be mistaken as a less rich and thus 'cheap' form of mass-mediated experience. The key domains discussed in this book, in which the constitution of the new middle classes and their desire for the 'world-class' surface, are located on the level of transnational networks, media production and consumption and urban space. The public space is shaped by a new consumer logic where class can be playfully performed and affirmed as care of the self. At the same time, as we shall see later in this study, even though it sports the surface of playfulness and equality, class is also part and motor of a social panopticon of control, discipline and surveillance, of the 'enclave gaze'. Erlebnis links imagination and social facts, structure and practice. Arjun Appadurai has defined imagination as a key resource 'for experiments with self-making' (1997: 3) and refers to the idea of the 'imaginary' as a fluid 'constructed landscape of collective aspirations' (ibid.: 31):

The image, the imagined, the imaginary — these are all terms that direct us to something critical and new in global cultural processes: the *imagination as a social practice.* No longer mere fantasy, no longer simple escape, no longer elite pastime, and no longer mere contemplation, the imagination has become an organized field of social practices, a form of work, and a form of negotiation between sites of agency (individuals) and globally defined fields of possibility (Appadurai 1997: 31).

The discussion of middle-classness in the case-studies to follow is thus embedded in debates around the visual turn and the performative turn, which is why the concept of Erlebnis is so crucial for analysis. Imaginaries such as, 'world-class' are ways of managing meaning, 'means by which individuals understand their identities and their place in the world' (Gaonkar 2002: 4). Social groups such as the new middle classes in India depend on visibility, visuality and performativity, as well as on a culture of circulation and a competence (e.g., taste, 'being cultured') to manage and decode them.

Let us thus return to the concept of Erlebnis. Dictionaries would translate this as 'event' or immediate 'experience'. However, even this does not seem adequate.[20] Erlebnis is a particular sensory experience that takes place in the individual. Others may share it, and it can be collectively aspired to. But it is, simultaneously highly, subjective and self-reflexive, that is, a conscious response to something or someone. It marks a very special, intangible and unique occasion or event that remains memorable. It also designates an attitude towards life as joyful. The concept of the *Erlebnisgesellschaft*, that is, the experience- or event-society, as well as that of the lifestyle society (*Lebensstilgesellschaft*), proposes a society that places Erlebnis and lifestyle at the centre stage of their constitution of identity and practice (Richter 2005; Wöhler 2005). The reason being wanting to be able to say and show that one's life is intense, and thus meaningful.

Gerhard Schulze (1992) proposes that everyday life is turned into a 'project' (*Erlebnisprojekt*). He suggests that there is consensus among people about the 'task', even the duty, to live a life filled with Erlebnis. Only then can 'a good life' be lived and 'happiness' accessed. Consumption and leisure facilities and practices enable — but do not guarantee — Erlebnis. Nevertheless, three key factors responsible for the creation of *Erlebnisgesellschaft* can be outlined: first, the fact that more choice increases the desire for coordinated and 'guided' Erlebnis, possible with the help of all kinds of experts (e.g., feng shui or *vaastu*); second, the pluralisation of life-design calls for a more diverse landscape of lifestyle magazines, television programmes, even

---

[20] Gerhard Schulze approved this term in an e-mail conversation in 2007.

therapists; and third, crises derive from new forms of sociality that seem difficult to control but that also provide a very productive challenge and enrichment to modern selves. It appears that in the face of diverse options, relationships, friendships, love and spiritual bonding can be manufactured, managed, or monitored, as well as revitalised or revised individually (Schulze 1992: 77). Besides risk being a central factor constituting class distinctions, new forms of trust have to be negotiated top.

There is a high exhibitionist element to *Erlebniskultur*, on the one hand, manifest in the call to celebrate and display oneself, turning this into a constant choreography of self-becoming and self-making. On the other, there is an emphasis on the care for the self, a trend towards spiritual practices and communities in which too, to some extent, this desire for celebration of life and self are embedded. Yet, as we shall see in the course of this study, the effort is to also complement it with morality, to create a moral community of consumers. 'Culture' seems to be the most appropriate means for this, as it is translated into 'cultured behaviour' and 'repertoire'.

Cosmopolitan Lifestyles

How is the concept of the 'world-class' generated through media, events, places and people, such as experts, as they constantly move and negotiate between the global and the local? I propose that a particularly useful, though complex, tool for analysis is the concept of cosmopolitanism. However, the conventional definition of 'cosmopolitanism' is already slightly misleading because it means much more than one clearly definable practice and consciousness, for instance, connotating a certain open-mindedness and world citizenship. While there are several forms of understanding a quasi-elite cosmopolitanism that is highly intellectual, non-hierarchical and self-reflexive, I am more interested in the ways in which the term inflects a certain notion of class-consciousness and the constant evaluation and confirmation of hierarchical relations and difference on a vernacular level. Cosmopolitanism is a condition of several discourses based on civilisational superiority such as modernity, the modern nation state, capitalism and colonial enterprises (van der Veer 2002). What has been argued about the middle classes so far can also be applied to the concept of cosmopolitanism: cosmopolitanism is not a state but a discursive process through which the new middle classes in India (and overseas) seek to reach and stabilise their 'ideal' position in the social field. It shapes the ways in which people consume and experience pleasure, or anxiety. Unlike its 'elite' brother, 'popular' or 'vernacular' cosmopolitanism works along polarities (for instance, the East–West divide) and for people who do not necessarily belong to an intellectual class or established bourgeoisie. It tends to unite and appeal to particular persons as a moral community, often claiming moral superiority over others.

Gerard Delanty maintains that cosmopolitanism is about cultural translation. It is about the relation to others without overcoming the fact of difference. Cosmopolitanism, argues Delanty, 'entails the capacity to view oneself from the eyes of the other' (2006: 54). The cosmopolitan person is often looked at with ambiguity and scepticism: some define her/him as a desirable global player, member of the jet set elite, and at home in the world; others stigmatise her/him as being unfaithful to the nation state and moral community of national citizens. This latter image emerges in several of the chapters in this study, with the figure of the transnational capitalist class of overseas Indians. While consumerist attitudes and lifestyle define the cosmopolitan on the one hand, moral values matter as well. Steven Vertovec and Robin Cohen maintain that for those whose cosmopolitanism is understood as the accumulation of financial and cultural capital (taste), the question of developing an interest in the 'Other' does not really arise. This is the popular experience and taste elaborated by mobile groups as a skill to communicate with others alike. In the context of this study, cosmopolitanism is a practice of status-creation. It mediates between various levels of everyday world: the local, the regional, the national and the global.

How is the idea of cosmopolitanism embedded in the contemporary search of urban middle class professionals for an identity that caters to the allegedly dichotomous notions of modernisation and tradition in a global and highly transnational context? Who sells the idea, how and to whom? Who can afford to dream and, possibly, even practice 'cosmopolitanism'? In what way can we understand cosmopolitanism as a discourse through which modern selves shape in relation to others (Beck 2004)? What do we make of cosmopolitan Indianness as a world-view that claims openness but simultaneously generates exclusive enclaves and justifies social segregation of various kinds? How do the emerging middle classes attempt to both replicate and diverge from the global imaginary?

Cosmopolitanism today carries the fresh air of being an actual phenomenon that derives from unique conditions of globalisation, the vision of a new society and an ecumene of 'world citizens'. However, this is not entirely the case. The idea of the 'world citizen' is not identical with that of the 'world-class' referred to in this study. Many contemporary discourses are openly or subtly based on colonial rhetoric, on a colonial gaze, an effect of imperial encounters, and in particular, resulting from the

alleged dominance of the West over its colonies. Peter van der Veer calls
this 'cosmopolitanism with a moral mission' (2002: 17). The author is also
critical about the view that cosmopolitanism 'is often declared as liberating
alternative to ethnic and nationalist chauvinism' (ibid.: 15). The situation
today is remarkably similar. The postcolonial context still shows colonial
reminiscences, and even today's cosmopolitanism is 'cosmopolitanism
with a moral mission', for instance, along the lines of an alleged global
East–West divide, or the urban–rural divide. Cosmopolitans thus do
constitute a moral community.

In the context of economic liberalisation, the points of reference for
the practice of distinction today are much more varied than in colonial
India. This requires a high competence, or literacy, of the agents contesting
their positions in a particular field of discourse. Arjun Appadurai and Carol
Breckenridge underline these overwhelming opportunities and challenges
with respect to the creation of cultural capital:

> Today's cosmopolitan cultural forms contain a paradox. As forms, they are
> emerging everywhere, films, packaged tours, specialized restaurants, video
> cassettes and sports spectacles seem to be drawing the world into a disturbing
> commercial sameness. But as vehicles for cultural significance and the creation
> of group identities, every society appears to bring to these forms its own special
> history and traditions [social imaginaries], its own cultural stamp, its own quirks
> and idiosyncrasies (1988: 5).

Like under colonial rule, points of reference for the generation of distinction and lifestyle today are notions related to other dominant discourses —
in this context, westernisation and modernisation, on the one hand, and
tradition as cultural heritage, on the other. Patricia Uberoi argues that the
key arenas in which class is negotiated and staged (and thus important
instruments of class formation) are English-medium schooling, the growing
availability of consumer goods, new media technologies, and:

> Increasingly ... the transnational connections of the middle-class diaspora ...
> [T]his cosmopolitan, all-India middle and professional class is not conspicuously
> cosmopolitan in its kinship and marriage practices, and the same is true even of
> the very wealthy and of Indian diasporic communities (Uberoi 2006: 22).

In this book, I shall refer to different kinds of cosmopolitanism that each
point to different sets of dispositions (e.g., frame of mind, arrangement)
that generate the middle class habitus; a cosmopolitanism attributed with
globalised nationalism, auto-orientalist and occidentalist views, with
vernacular and elite discourses.

Cosmopolitanism relates people of a specific locality to larger global contexts, and, as sociologist Ulrich Beck maintains, points to a specific way of dealing with Otherness, and thus Selfhood (2004). A 'true' cosmopolitan, as previously argued, is at home in the world, a 'world citizen'. The concept of cosmopolitanism points towards the theoretical possibility that it provides open access to global markets for all. Moreover, it alleges to embrace cultural difference and expressions, the sharing of one political institution or the moral inclinations towards living a good life and to help other members of this moral community to live a good life too.

Now, in the light of 'India Shining', groups as heterogenous as the new middle classes make new claims to cosmopolitanism as a way of life. The claim is to belong to 'world-class' and still remain 'distinctly Indian'. In the Indian context, I shall argue, being cosmopolitan does not necessarily implicate identification with some world community or global citizenry. Instead, the term represents particular rights and interests and qualifies for access to a global 'first class' or 'five star' lifestyle. Furthermore, 'distinctly Indian' is a misleading concept too, for who can possibly claim the right to define this idea of an authentic, 'essential' cultural identity! The definition of Indianness reflected in the cosmopolitanism of the upper middle classes who want to belong to 'world-class' is more a reflection of orientalist facets of colonial India. For Ulf Hannerz (1996), cosmopolitans are also locals and this holds true of the neoliberal urban India too, since the notion of the cosmopolitan or the world-class can only be understood as the attempt to define Indianness. This refers to the fact that despite their aspiration to belong to a 'world-class' that knows how to make it everywhere in the world, cosmopolitans are structured by (and themselves structure) local dispositions. As a consequence, however, the celebration of a nationalist culture can be provincial in as much as transnationality can be provincialising. As Shail Mayaram argues in *The Other Global* City (2009), cosmopolitanism is essentially about the relationship of the self to an other, to a stranger, and cities are one such key place in which this highly complicated relationship is staged, in both intangible and spatially visible ways. In fact, cosmopolitanism can generate hegemonic cultural homogeneity and must be seen in the particular historical, national and political context that constitutes it (ibid.).

If we concur that cosmopolitanism creates new borders, inverted gazes and compartmentalised enclaves, and that the qualifying distinction 'cosmopolitan' is very often both a lifestyle label and a moral category, based on civilisational superiority, how do we venture into discussions around glocalisation and alternative modernities in order to understand the generation of cosmopolitan Indianness? Some dangers of misunderstanding cosmopolitanism as open discourse and consensus-finding among equal strangers have been outlined by John Urry and shall be further examined in the course of this book. Urry also highlights the 'so-called cosmopolitans' who seek to escape from the obligations towards the nation state and create their own protected enclaves, often at the expense of the locality and local (marginalised) people (Urry 2000: 7; see also Abbas 2000). In particular instances, the 'rural' or 'ethnic' Indian may be turned into an exoticised 'Other' quite like 'the West' is often occidentalised.

Cosmopolitanism, identified with 'world-class', seems to become an increasingly important asset for India because her governments, both national and regional, can employ it in order to appeal to overseas Indians and foreign corporations and businesses alike. The appeal raised through this rhetoric is for the NRIs to invest in India's economic growth, to help remove poverty and improve education. The label 'We are World-class Now' is very important to the overseas Indians, and besides opening up to investments in the real estate sector, for instance, the Indian government wants to present the country as stable and prepared to meet the western demand. There is thus a 'partial cosmopolitisation' or selective transnation-alisation at play in order to send out appealing signals to respective desired groups. Beck argues that 'deterritorialized ethnicity leads to a nationalism without frontiers' (2004: 446), offering multiple affiliations. This kind of nationalism rides on a wave of 'soft' or 'pop Hindu nationalism'. Quite distinct from what Habermas prognoses when he speaks of the middle class as pillar of a critical rationalist–secular mass that enabled public sphere to flourish, the middle classes in Asia have displayed a reluctance to imitate the European model of the bourgeois public sphere, producing instead an 'Indian' version of it:

> The new rich in Asia appear as likely to embrace authoritarian rule, xenophobic nationalism, religious fundamentalism and *dirigisme* as to support demo-cracy, internationalism, secularism and free markets (Robinson and Goodman 1996: 3).

Thus, we find a truly complicated form of glocalisation at work in and through the lens of this concept in the search for and claims made over the definition of a 'distinctly (Hindu) Indian' modernity as enclave cosmopolitanism.

I wish to conclude this section with the prototypical figure of cos-mopolitanism, the flâneur. The flâneur, a model from late-nineteenth century Europe, is a cultured person, a pleasure- and event-seeking expert of emerging capitalism and urbanism. For Walter Benjamin or Charles Baudelaire, the flâneur became an icon of cosmopolitan modernity. For her/him, viewing and buying came to be consumption as a stage play of pleasure; the performance of floating through urban arenas of capitalism is more important than the actual act of buying. Flânerie is an activity linked to the flâneur; it denotes glancing and strolling, and requires urban spaces as stage. Keith Tester underlines the importance of the recognition that the flâneur knows that (s)he is in the crowd, yet 'princely incognito' (1994: 4), dwelling in anonymity and observation. One of the key desires of the flâneur is to experience and enjoy 'purposeless' consumption, to be overwhelmed by the urban environs (e.g., arcades, theme parks) and at the same time to respond to it with certain degrees of snobbery and disinterest. The flâneur must know that (s)he is registered by members of the anonymous crowd in and through which (s)he moves, although not in person but by means of sheer appearance. One may argue that the flâneur is a cousin of the cosmopolitan in that (s)he enjoys the world as a shopping window. The flâneur must know where to go and how to perform in order to be seen, and must have the air of a cultured connoisseur. But (s)he is also a hedonist and ignorant of the Other — flirting with the surface rather than engaging with the backstage — and thus also un-cosmopolitan.

A city like New Delhi is being increasingly shaped according to the premises of the (Indian) flânerie: the spaces and themed worlds designed by real estate developers, the shopping malls and leisure parks, the consumption of tourist and ritual sites as part of becoming and displaying 'world-class' as discussed in this book, reflect this type of a person. One major difference, however, seems to mark the line between Europe of the nineteenth century and India today: the flâneur is never depicted as enjoying himself or herself alone, but always part of a group — mostly family members, or college and business friends.

Public Spheres

One of the key themes woven into the various chapters of this study is the notion of public spheres. I have already highlighted the flâneur as a new social type of modern lifestyle, flânerie as the responding activity, and commodity fetish as the source and aim of consumption. In the Indian context, we must not take the Habermasian or any Eurocentric concept of public sphere for granted. Instead, we must assume a different kind of flânerie, assuming that we deal with altered notions of personal identity, citizenship, publicity and common welfare (see Bhargava 2005; Kaviraj

1997).[21] All of these are phenomena that must take place in public in order for the new middle classes to constitute themselves, along with the notions of 'world-class'. Moreover, institutions such as governments, organisations like new religious movements and lifestyle experts seek to position themselves and regulate access to the public sphere, be it through urban planning and construction of leisure sites (Parts I and II of this book) or the creation of a wedding and wellness industry (Part III of this book). These social agents, collective or individual, are also concerned with concepts such as citizenship, public property and rights of access.

As in the case of the new middle classes, we are misled if we conceive of the public sphere as a static and neutral given. The public sphere is highly contested, varied and heterogeneous, and it is even argued that in the light of globalisation, the public sphere, as a domain of the commons, vanishes due to privatisation. Such arguments are often raised in connection to urban planning. Let me give one example. Paradoxically, a site like the Akshardham Cultural Complex (see Part II of this book), opened in 2005 next to New Delhi's colonial centre and the Commonwealth Games Village, is a result of both a new public domain enterprise and privatisation. Likewise, the new middle classes both open and close public discussions and spheres, thus contributing to the constitution of civility and its simultaneous censorship.

The particular state–society relationships in the 'West' involved a conceptual separation of the state and society in the shape of a vastly expanded state; a highly activated (but vague) society; and a set of concepts, institutions, and practices to ensure communication, negotiate interests and values, and allow for the largely non-violent resolution of conflicts between state and society as also among various segments of society. The space thus opened between state and society is usually referred to as the public sphere.

Instead of working with the concept of public sphere in the singular form, I prefer to use the plural: there are various public spheres at work, simultaneously, on a transcultural, national, regional and local level, as well

---

[21] About India's public sphere Bhargava maintains that it 'contains a distinct layer of alternative modernities … [N]otions of civil society and public sphere began to interact with similar elements in local cultural systems and eventually gave rise to a new kind of society and public sphere that replicates neither anything Western nor something local and indigenous. What we have instead is an altogether new phenomenon that escapes the interpretative grids of Western modernity and traditional cultural systems' (2005: 32–33).

as in the context of the mediascape that must also be considered as a public sphere. In fact, this notion follows Appadurai's concept of 'flows' (1997) and Hannerz's concept of particular networks (1992). Public spheres are not just located in one physical territory, or with one social group as Habermas (1989) would have it, when he terms the educated upper classes and bourgeoisie as being torchbearers of the public sphere in the European context. Habermas, for instance, conceives of the critical and self-reflexive bourgeoisie as a pillar of public opinion and participatory democracy, where social groups discuss and judge matters of public interest. Public spheres are part of social spatialisation; they can be closed down by some agents, and extended or opened up by others they can be semi or fully privatised, to cite only a few examples. Here, I am interested in the ways in which public spheres allow for the exchange of public views, for the constitution of publicity and for the staging of 'world-class' or other identities relevant to the understanding of glocalisation in India. Thus, the individual case-studies of this enquiry explore places, events, images and people that shape and are shaped by the various public spheres in and through which 'India Shining' (or 'India Falling'), is generated and circulated.

Sudipta Kaviraj, for instance, argues that a public sphere in India has never been open to all alike (and the question is whether this is not also the case in Europe). In fact, it has always been surveyed by certain powers and granted access to selected 'publics', whether they are defined via caste, education, religion, or else (1997). Though Indian elites and members of the new middle class (gentlefolk or *bhadralok* in Bengali) in colonial cities like Calcutta appropriated the western bourgeois concept of private and public, the upper castes altered this division according to their needs, rendering the public sphere impure and unworthy of feeling responsible for it. Public consciousness arose only in the course of the independence struggle, when the *maidan* (public park) was opened to groups of protesters against the colonial regime. The more important question is who aspired to use public spaces and transform them into a public sphere, i.e., a realm for creating public consensus and discourse. Partha Chatterjee (2003) maintains that the public spheres of Indian cities are becoming bourgeois now because they claim rights over moral citizenship but reserve them for a selected few, defining the others as 'populations'. Several scholars have worked on the public sphere in colonial India, and examined as to how it came to constitute a communal(ist) sphere in which notions of the nation state were shaped (Freitag 1989). Others explored postcolonial urban India in the context of mass performances such as the Ganpati festival in Bombay, whereby different discourses that take place within various groups are considered crucial for the multiple locations of the 'public field' (Kaur 2003). This is a connecting space of practice and its correlates, entwined with media spheres, and made up of the performance-oriented public sphere and activist (often subaltern or low class) public arenas. In this concept of the public field, the alleged oppositions of secular and religious domains can be constructively reconsidered.

Transnational networks generate their own public spheres by circulating images, goods and people along the lines of these transcultural, fluid borders. The figure of the 'world-class' cosmopolitan, or Ong's 'global nomad' (1999) emerges from the context of such flows, shaping transcultural and transnational publics. Mass-produced electronic media like the Internet form yet another domain of public sphere and discourse, with genuinely 'virtual' communities of 'netizens', for instance. The public sphere is not the sphere of the nation state, and yet, nation states impact on its constitution, for instance, in the case of censorship or minority rights. The ways in which the state binds its citizens to its national agenda (and vice versa), and, the ways in which citizens challenge the monopoly of the nation state, are crucial pillars of understanding the notion of public. Thus, it makes sense to argue for the existence of subaltern or other 'counter publics' (Bhandari 2006) as well as the old and the new middle classes as a variety of publics. On the global scale, transnational organisations, multinational corporations, and by and large, the power of capital, organise the constitution of the public spheres. The concepts of public welfare, citizenship, rights, and so forth, are negotiated differently according to each public sphere, even though they may partly overlap and enforce each other. Certainly, one of the key debates evolving around neoliberalism in India, and elsewhere, is as to what extent the public sphere of civil society is restricted and transformed into a host of private enclaves, interests and agents. Although this study does not claim to give a ready answer to this concern, it attempts to address it through the different case-studies presented here, as for instance, when the 'world-class' city is explored (Part I of this book), when a transnational religious–nationalist leisure complex is discussed (Part II), or the wedding and the beauty industry are examined (Part III).

This book explores various ways in which concepts of what 'public', 'publicity' and 'public sphere' are, or could become, are negotiated and manifested by different social agents driven with varying motivations. It examines thus quite remarkable consequences of how we shape notions of, and (de-)legitimise, 'the Other' (e.g., non-citizen) and ourselves. This study extends and develops Habermas' seminal work on the public sphere in three respects. First, the public sphere is not an intrinsically neutral

34   India's Middle Class

space between state and society, reserved for a critical public and elite.
Second, the role of the state as a historically factual and important player
in the shaping of public sphere above and beyond its regulatory powers is
challenged and transformed (for instance, with respect to market forces or
privatised cultural productions). Third, the public sphere is transnational in
character, not essentially coterminous with the national space and requires
new analysis of relationships towards 'home', 'roots' and 'routes' as well
as 'flexible relationships' (Ong 1999). Fourth, we must reconsider the role
of religion in secular societies such as India, for instance, when it comes to
the shaping of civic and urban religion (Srinivas 2008) and transnational
religio-spiritual movements, for it is particularly the new megacities of the
global South that seem to draw such new initiatives.

Research Context and Design

Until the early 1990s, class, urban spaces like megacities, leisure and
consumption practices as well as the phenomenon of imagination as a
social practice were often disregarded and considered as 'inauthentic', 'not
Indian enough' to be taken too seriously. With a view to my own inquiry,
this could be applied insofar as new professions, new spaces, urban slums,
residential colonies, shopping malls or leisure sites such as theme parks
have yet not gained much scholarly attention.[22]

Studies on the phenomenon of glocalisation in post-independence
India are so far relatively scattered. I only want to name Moti Gokulsing
and Wimal Dissanayake's *Popular Culture in a Globalised India* (2009) and Jackie
Assayag and Christopher J. Fuller's *Globalizing India* (2005). In particular,
they highlight the important role anthropology can play by exploring
globalisation 'from below', that is, the ways in which global phenomena
are appropriated, experienced, applied and modified, in a local context
and by different social agents. Another highly relevant inquiry into the
relationship between globalisation, Hindu nationalism and religion, caste
and class, is by Satish Deshpande. The economist and sociologist highlights
too that the concept of class has been marginalised despite its relevance in
Indian identity politics (Deshpande 2003).

In particular, multi-sited ethnography as a grounded method of cultural
anthropology, does justice to the complex and challenging conditions and

---

[22] For exceptions, see, for instance Appadurai (2006); Baviskar (2003); Deshpande
(2003); Fernandes (2006); Dickey (2002); Froystad (2005); Liechty (2003);
Mazzarella (2003); Osella (1998); Oza (2006); Poggendorf-Kakar (2001); Säävälä
(2001, 2003); Uberoi (2006).

contexts posed by newly emerging fields such as globalisation in urban and 'mediatised' domains. Such an ethnography explores the journeys of people, ideas, images and objects across borders of certain kinds and requests the researcher to move along, physically, diachronically and through a cross-disciplinary flexibility. To take New Delhi as a kind of switchboard for the various case-studies presented in this book makes sense: the capital city seeks to transform itself into a global city; it wants to draw capital and audiences of various kinds, while simultaneously seeking to firmly restrict access to the urban domain to a selection of groups. The Delhi government and the public want the city to become a financially lucrative and 'eventful' space for the affluent, and thus enable constructions such as the Akshardham Cultural Complex, a monumental religious leisure site along the banks of the Yamuna river. But to study the effects of globalisation in local contexts, with a particular focus on the new middle classes, also requires examination of the role of religion and of life-cycle rituals such as weddings. Last but not least, it is important to consider the way the markets open up for the search and 'care of the self', not only through religion but also beauty, wellness and tourism. In order to be able to do so in this work, long-time networks had to be activated, and new contacts sought and established.

An ethnography of 'India Shining' and urban lifestyle managers such as theme-event designers, wellness experts, feng shui teachers, public relations people and so on, responds to the new challenges posed to anthropologists of contemporary urban and global contexts. Modern life is fast and so is the lifestyle of those experts who feature centrally in this book. Research methods have to, therefore, adjust to the informants' mobility and lack of time. Ever so often I found myself hunting for interviews with professionals from all kinds of domains — they were either abroad, conducting a feng shui retreat in Korea or Japan, attending an international workshop on spa wellness in California, or just busy with business meetings in Delhi itself, in one of the South Delhi farmhouses or another exclusive enclave. Sometimes I would have to wait for weeks to get an interview; thus, multiple interviews with one person alone were a difficult thing to arrange since their days are usually fully planned from 9 a.m. to 9 p.m. Some of my interviews were thus conducted over the phone, through e-mail, in the car, as people travelled from the corporate office to the next meeting. Informants in the urban and professional fields are possibly as pragmatic as their counterparts in a mountain village. But they are also more aware of their public presence, the importance of how and by whom they are perceived and how this might potentially change their status. Quite a few experts denied an interview because they were aware of their much criticised role in neoliberal housing or labour politics (e.g., real estate development or BPO). Others did not care very much as soon as they learnt that their input would only end up in an academic book. By and large, however, I was received with curiosity and openness, generally backed up by comments such as 'Yes, this is really relevant, because it recognises that something important is happening in India!'

The complexity of people's movements in their everyday lives requires an equally flexible methodology. Nevertheless, the study's primary sources (see Bibliography at the end of this book) are based on semi-structured and open interviews (marked as 'personal conversation', including place, month and year of interview) with a host of people with whom I came to speak and whom I accompanied to various activities over a period of several years. The first names of most informants have been changed and surnames abbreviated. Getting access to some of the sites that I aimed at exploring in terms of their constitutive role for lifestyle experiences was often difficult. These were private or semi-public enclaves that require certain preconditions to be fulfilled: one must be member of a wellness studio, or a gulf club, or a fitness centre, in order to get in — yet, membership is not unconditional (prestige features highly) and is certainly not cheap. One must know people who live in a luxury condominium in order to be able to get access into one. One must not carry a camera, pen or pencil when entering the spiritual theme park for security reasons. In fact, repeated visits to the site of the BAPS sect involved strict examination from the side of the informants — whether or not I was trustworthy, really interested in (and even sympathising with) their agenda.

Beginning from the late-1990s, intangible and grey material was collected for this study: maps and plans of gated communities and leisure parks, advertisement brochures, posters, hoardings and news clippings as well as tourist souvenirs, DVDs, stickers, postcards and other paraphernalia related to the new lifestyle of the urbanised middle classes and the new sites of consumption and pleasure. A major source of information comprised hundreds of lifestyle magazines, ranging from bridal and spiritual magazines to ones concerned with home cooking, parenting, ageing, fitness, wellness, business, real estate and tourism, to mention only a few.[23] These intertwined forms of media are crucial when it comes to their capacity to educate 'uncultured' newcomers, creating immediacy and intimacy. Liechty writes

---

[23] Many of these media sources are currently digitised and annotated at the Heidelberg Research Architecture, part of the Cluster of Excellence 'Asia and Europe in a Global Context'. See http://www.asia-europe.uni-heidelberg.de/research/heidelberg-research-architecture (accessed 2 June 2009).

of the concept of the media assemblage as a methodological (as well as theoretical) concept: 'complex ways in which different mass media play off (and mutually promote) one another, as well as a host of other allied commodities ... forming an intricate web of linkages that promote and channel consumer desires in never-ending circuits' (2003: 260). This, he argues, creates a consumer ethic that affirms and 'naturalises' cultural values and habitus of the middle class and shapes, as I would propose, the new middle classes as a moral community.

A brief overview of the study's structure is appropriate here. Three main parts assemble multifaceted case-studies on urban planning, religious-leisure sites, and beauty and wellness industries. Part I explores the reshaping of urban landscapes through the global imaginary of 'world-class city' and lifestyle. It looks at the ways in which public space is remodelled through real estate developers and advertisement agencies in New Delhi, and how this relates to the aspirations of a new aspiring middle class that wants to belong to an imagined cosmopolitan elite. The section traces various lineages of these seemingly new concepts and argues that orientalism and colonialism are major sources of identity-formation. Much attention goes to the relationship of public and private space, the mimetic appropriation and alteration of foreign taste into 'distinctly Indian' properties.

The ways in which religious practice comes to figure as a motor for the creation of national heritage in the context of a rising leisure and consumption-oriented urban habitat like New Delhi is central to the case-study of Part II. The section examines the recently opened Akshardham Cultural Complex (ACC), built by a rather marginal yet transnationally well-connected and economically affluent sect, the BAPS from Gujarat. Key focuses are the fields of tension that arise in the context of a site that addresses at once 'classical' pilgrims and urbanised (often overseas) visitors and tourists, both Indian as well as non-Indian. Finally, it considers how particular forms of gaze and behaviour enforced at the site reflect larger concerns about a 'disciplinary society' and ritual efficacy.

Part III continues to examine the relevance of heritage and ritual with a shift of perspective on the wedding and the beauty industry. Lifestyle and event managers are the major group of investigation as they convey their opinions about pleasure, caste or physical and spiritual wellness. The ways in which codes of conduct are elaborated and performed compose additional material in the discussion of 'world-class' distinction.

PART I

ತ

Belonging to the World-Class City

꒐

The year 2007 marked a turning point in human development: for the first time ever, it emerged that the majority of the world's population will no longer live in the countryside but in cities. In this context, megacities (with more than 10 million people) assume a special importance, in particular because only one-fourth will be located in the so-called 'First World'. What are the cities of the future going to be like when, as UN demographers say, more than half of the world's population live in them, with more than a dozen 'hypercities' located in Asia alone?[1] How are the cities imagined, by and for whom? How is lifestyle in a megalopolis envisaged and who can afford these imaginaries?[2] In what way are public space and place contested, spurred by what symbolic means and socio-economic or political intentions?

This section explores the ways in which economic liberalisation in urban India has generated different desires and anxieties linked to the idea of belonging to 'world-class' — and thus being cosmopolitan — in the context of the new urban middle classes in India. The key focus of this section is the creation of an imaginary of the 'world-class city' in and through visual representations and texts of real estate advertising. Images and texts are considered here as narrative moments conveyed by real estate developers, architects, urban planners and housing activists in various conversations

---

[1] The UN Population Division 2004. In 2005, the urbanisation rate of South Asia was 30.3 per cent, as against 15.6 per cent in 1950 (Heitzman 2008: 175).

[2] On an average, 160,000 people move into cities around the world every day (China: c. 14 million p.a., India: c. 10 million). It is estimated that 400 million Chinese will migrate to urban landscapes in the next few years, compared to 300 million in India (Nilekani 2006). According to the 2001 Census of India, c. 29 per cent of the Indian population lives in urban areas, a figure expected to rise to over 40 per cent by 2021. With an urbanisation of 28 per cent, India is still behind China, where 40 per cent of the total population constitute the urban population (see Just et al. 2006: 9). In 2006, Delhi's population reached 15 million (compared to 410,000 in 1911 and one million in 1951); more than 50 per cent live in unauthorised or settlement colonies. The year 1992 marks a rapid decline in workmanship in the organised sector — a rise of unemployment, close-down of manufacturing sectors and industries and falling employment in the unorganised sector (Hazards Centre 2006a: 3). See also UN Habitat's World City Report 2006/07, http://www.unhabitat.org/content.asp?cid=3397&catid=7&typeid=46&subMenu Id=0 (accessed 22 August 2009).

and media technologies. They are considered as strategic means by which social space is structured in the context of neoliberal urbanisation. Even though it is clear that the projected real estate dreams can be lived only by a few (mainly members of the professional elite), the advertising material that is circulated reaches larger audiences who can at least aspire to such dreams, and partially translate them into 'reality'.

This kind of imaginary and geo-physical spatial structuring has very local and manifest consequences for the city's shape and its inhabitants. The material explored here points us to the aspired shifts and concrete plans towards the realisation of the world-class imaginary: India's transformation from being a Third World country to a First World country; Delhi's transformation from 'walled city' (the name referring to Shahjahanabad, the pre-colonial part of the city) to a world-class city; and last but not least, the creation of 'First Class' citizens and, consequently, 'Third Class' citizens. I suggest that in the ethnographic material analysed here, we find a keen desire of different sets of experts in the field (architects, journalists, therapeutists, urban planners, event managers, etc.) not only to 'teach' members of the aspiring middle classes about the 'good life' in a 'world-class' city but to turn them into a moral community of citizens united in their commitment to link pleasure and consumption in such a way that they strengthen economic growth and thus the welfare of India and her people. Seen in this light, consumption can be represented and justified as an activity that improves the lived-in-world for all. Consumption's phantasmagorias promote success and belonging as well as equal treatment on the basis of merit, granting access to a 'good life' to those who allegedly 'deserve' it. Simultaneously, and rather silently as regards the global imaginary of the world-class, social groups are defined who are denied access to this city of light. Hence the distinctions of citizens versus population, public versus private, rightful versus illegal, clean versus dirty, and safe versus dangerous, are important categories for the analysis of spatial discourses in this section.

This part investigates the notion of belonging to the world-class city Delhi in various ways. It explores several intertwined spatial topographies of the national capital, for instance, different categories of imagined and real inhabitants of the new spaces opened for 'world-class' living. Furthermore, it examines two domains in which changes due to globalisation and urbanisation become most obvious: the shaping of New Delhi into a landscape for shopping as a leisure activity and for residential housing. Key focus in the latter case is on the newly constructed gated habitats and the 'themed lifestyle' promoted through them. The chapters trace some of the types and themes historically. The last chapter of this part (Chapter 5) discusses how the desire for socio-spatial segregation is legitimised and idealised, and what kind of social community, particularly in view of class and citizenship, is constituted with the emerging urbanism of a megacity such as Delhi.

Central to this section are the ways in which a megacity like New Delhi is imagined with respect to economic liberalisation, especially for whom it is imagined, and what implications this might have for community-constitution and social spatialisation. In the course of the various sub-sections, I explore the creation of what I call the enclave gaze, a particular way of looking at the world and oneself from an encapsulated, insulated perspective. I relate this enclave gaze to the question as to what extent public sphere and discourse are altered in this context. I argue that the notion of belonging to the world-class is crucial to understand the 'efficacy' of the enclave gaze that is generated in the imaginary of the global city. The enclave gaze is part of a selective perception of reality that shapes the life-style aspirations and identification of the new middle classes, and presents them as a themed narrative. Furthermore, I maintain that the enclave gaze, and the associated lifestyle imaginaries, call upon and revitalise colonial narratives. In other words, new middle classes are responsive to neocolonial and auto-orientalist rhetoric through which they hope to improve their status and legitimise their claim to 'world-class'. The 'world-class' city is conceived as a visual if not multi-sensuous, spectacular delight; a full-fledged Erlebnis of what I call 'Dubaisation'. It is eventful, safe, clean and ordered to such an extent that it seems artificially 'out of this world', as if it was located on a strange and distant planet called 'India'. As with Dubai's armies of cheap construction workers, those who build and 'oil' the city of Delhi, thus rendering it functional, are marginalised, if not stigmatised, and equipped with the minimum of right to belong.

This section is based on a range of ethnographic case-studies, including extensive use of visuals as ethnographic sources. The body of data selected for the analyses in the following chapters has been collected over a period of almost three years (2004–7). It consists of around 450 advertisements from English language-lifestyle and real estate magazines, newspapers, predominantly collected between the years 2005 and 2007, and about 50 field trips through and beyond New Delhi, to malls, real estate offices and condominiums. Many of the 48 interviews with urban planners, architects, designers and lifestyle practitioners I have consulted for the purpose of this section were conducted in buildings that are the outcome of recent eco-nomic liberalisation: private apartments in Gurgaon with several bedrooms and large balconies, office outlets in Noida and Faridabad, headquarters of real estate developers in South Delhi, new commercial complexes around

Connaught Place (CP) or towards Gurgaon, and even a new theme park next to the National Highway towards Greater Noida. Other places were less glamorous: housing activists and some of the architects I visited repeatedly received me in densely populated, so-called 'unauthorised' colonies, for instance Kirti Village in South Delhi, and for a few days in 2003, I conducted participatory observation following the demolition of north India's largest 'slum', a cluster of unauthorised colonies along the Yamuna Pushta (embankment). Particularly, employees of real estate developers were very cautious and defensive to start with which is probably also caused by a very ambivalent response to the construction boom in Indian megacities, including rumours (and facts) of corruption and other illegal methods of urban planning and architecture. My fieldwork has been impacted much by the mobility of informants from the real estate sector, many of them changing their employer like nomads would change grazing grounds, embarking for more lucrative sectors ever so often, be they in Delhi, Dubai or elsewhere.

Three Ventures into Delhi

A megacity like Delhi is ideal for an investigation of various 'glocal' flows at work in India over the last two decades. Three anecdotal glimpses shall enable different ventures into the dynamics of urban change. The first example gives a perspective into the transformation of a typical middle class neighbourhood in West Delhi. The second one is a vignette of changes taking place in the general lifestyle infrastructure of the city, through the retrospective eyes of a person who grew up in South Delhi. The third venture serves as bridgehead to the discussion of the most recent real estate developments, at the time of this research.

Venture 1: Many of my friends and colleagues, as well as their parents and grandparents, have lived in Delhi for long. Though there are on-going complaints about the city, such as regards the traffic and pollution, most of them are very fond of the city, and have their families and other friends living nearby. In fact, several of these families may have already bought plots of land in South Delhi or West Delhi, possibly a bungalow each with a small garden and roof terrace. In the years after Independence, plots of land and houses in New Delhi were allotted in bulks, first to refugees from different regions, and later to different kinds of government employees. This way, people from a region or similar income and occupational group would often share a neighbourhood. Quite visibly, many of the localities have changed within the last decade or so: take, for instance, the condensed neighbourhood of Old Rajendra Nagar, close to the booming Punjabi shopping hub Karol Bagh, and within reach of CP (part of the colonial layout). Old Rajendra Nagar is populated by former refugees from the Punjab region who settled here after Partition in 1947, when South Asia underwent rapid urban growth, in part because of dramatic migration flows (see Navina Gupta 2006; Heitzman 2008). Old Rajendra Nagar lies right behind the ridge, or green belt, that surrounds central New Delhi. Whereas in the late 1990s, the small alley in which one of my friend's house is located, was populated by one or two-storeyed houses with relatively simple facades, today, most of these houses that were built after Partition, have been replaced or have undergone a complete facelift. Now almost every house sports four to five storeys and a facade decorated with rococo balconies and the like. Finding parking space in the alley is now close to impossible: each and every family has approximately two or three cars. Many invest in their private property. My friend's parents are lucky; they bought the property for relatively little money in the 1960s. With the modest salary of the parents, both of who were government employees, the family lived a correspondingly modest lifestyle — possibly visiting relatives in Kolkata for Diwali and Durga Puja, and going abroad every few years. Had they wanted to buy the property today, they probably could not have afforded it for real estate prices have more than tripled. Of course, my friend's parents find that the place has become narrow and congested and they no longer know most of the neighbours. But they would not move to a modern condominium despite the fact that they could probably sell off their property in Rajendra Nagar for a very good price. To them, the idea of living in a newly built township is not appealing.

However, there are people who prefer to move into an integrated township or condominium, as another befriended couple from the same area did, with their two small children. Even having rented a spacious flat in Rajendra Nagar, they aspired to have 'their own' place, in a residential area with easy access to all everyday facilities: 24 hours electricity and water supply (facilities which are hard to find in a place such as Rajendra Nagar). They finally moved to East Delhi, one of the booming and previously marginalised areas across the Yamuna river, where one construction site or high-rise building stands beside another, with only a few pockets of older colonies left now. Mary tells me that she feels more isolated now; friends don't come to visit them as often any longer and she and her husband return from work even later at night. With both their parents living in south India, they depend on a maid for looking after the children. The promised park nearby is a muddy garbage dump for now. But the Commonwealth Games of 2010, hopes Mary, will improve the quality of life soon, especially since the Commonwealth Village is so close.

Venture 2: This journey begins with a journey back in time. In an essay entitled 'Learning to Belong', New Delhi is remembered by Pavan Varma (1998), a former diplomat and author of various books on the Indian middle classes:

> I first came to Delhi as a one-year old child in 1954 when my father, who was in government, was posted to the new capital of India. My first memories are of growing up in Man Nagar, now called Rabindra Nagar, a residential area only inhabited by government servants. Man Nagar was then almost at the periphery of New Delhi. Outside its gates was the seductive wilderness of Lodhi Gardens. New Delhi was a small city. It was the city of Lutyens and Baker, largely homogeneous, a bureaucratic city symbolising power rather than money ... When the first traffic lights were erected, people were amused. Raj Path was then still remembered as Kingsway, Queen Mary's Avenue had not yet been christened Pandit Pant Marg ... Absorbed in its new-found importance, New Delhi was essentially more a hierarchy than a city, presided over by the privileged layer of senior bureaucrats, established politicians and old money (Varma 2001).

This anecdote enables us to draw parallels and indicate differences that are relevant for this section. We learn that Delhi was still predominantly structured by architecture and memory sites of the British era when it transformed into the capital of independent India. Varma writes about the homogeneity of the neighbourhoods, assorted according to the occupational hierarchy within the government service. In Varma's memories there was no other transfer of power and people, it seems. But there in fact was: hundreds of thousands of Sikh and Hindu refugees arrived in Delhi shortly after Partition, mostly from the western part of Punjab. They were equally allocated in special camps or resettlement colonies, or in neighbourhoods that had previously been occupied by Muslims who had left their homes out of fear (Navina Gupta 2006). Varma also tells us about the 'wilderness' of Lodhi Gardens outside his protected colony. Today, this park is one of the most 'orderly' public places, much appreciated by the upper middle classes of South Delhi, who go there walking their dogs, jogging or meeting friends. Finally, we hear that 'old money' and bureaucrats would mingle with politicians. As of now, many of them are still around. But their impact has been restricted by a new world of business(wo)men from the corporate world or service sectors, by traders and shop-owners from Punjab, or even Gujarat, who moved up the career ladder. New Delhi is a pulsating megacity, and as national capital still more bureaucratic — possibly more conservative than Mumbai. Perhaps, no other city demarcates the shifts between the 'old' and the 'new' middle classes today better than Delhi.

Venture 3: Having witnessed the transformation of parts of the metropolis over a period of 10 years, and incorporating the views of Delhiites as well as visitors returning to the city after many years of absence, the impression I have of many places is that in terms of architecture and aesthetics, public and private facilities and access to them, parts of New Delhi have changed beyond visual and physical recognition, particularly during past and upcoming mega-events such as the Asian Games (1982) and Commonwealth Games (2010) respectively. More flyovers, more malls, new business towers have come up here and there; in many places *jhuggi-jhopris* (squatter settlements, with partly proper structures) have been cleared. The city's streets and air have become cleaner due to the official policy of natural gas public transport; the city is more efficient now in terms of public and private transport; and the growth of an affluent middle class has led to a boom in the access to diverse sites of leisure and consumption: e.g., fitness centres, day spas, designer shops, lounge bars and cafés.

The on-going construction of the Delhi Metro since 2002 and the advent of the Commonwealth Games 2010 improve life and 'upgrade' the city in many people's eyes. Delhi's government firmly aims to turn New Delhi into a 'world-class city', for 'world-class people'. In a variety of contexts, one gets to engage in or overhear conversations about the new urban sensations available for consumption to the citizens of Delhi: the sprawling malls of Gurgaon or Noida located in the peripheries of the capital, the fairytale-style wedding theme events at luxurious farm houses in South Delhi, the latest culinary pleasures at the buffet in five star hotels or a new restaurant, the screening of an offbeat film at one of the multiplexes in West Delhi, or the opening of a massive theme park-like monument and pilgrimage-site across the polluted Yamuna (see Part II of this book). At the same time, one can also hear and read stories of massive demolitions of unauthorised *jhuggi*-clusters (shanty colonies) along the same river, the dislocation of hawkers and people dwelling in one of the many ancient sites that cover the city, and the drastic reduction of licenses for rickshaw-pullers in the old city of Delhi. The most recent demolitions of 2005–6 also affected unauthorised structures of the middle classes, especially, individual shops and shopping malls, residential houses or posh restaurants.[3] But in the light of the economic meltdown, the steady rise of its key sectors, real estate development and retail, has slowed down and revealed the ambivalence of economic growth. In May 2009, real estate company Emaar MGF, a joint

---

[3] In 2006, a demolition drive by the MCD in Delhi increased investors' insecurity. Unauthorised buildings of the middle classes and higher income groups were

venture of properties giants from Dubai and India, who announced the creation of 'new India' on hoardings throughout the city's rich south (see Plate 1.3) in constructing the prestigious Commonwealth Games village next to the ACC, had to accept a massive loan from the state government to meet the deadline of finalising construction by 2010 (Hussain 2009).

New Delhi, the capital of India, seems to have moved far beyond Varma's memories and has become a 'record-breaking' city that competes with Mumbai and Paris for the status of 'world-class city'.[4] 'World-class' has become a buzzword of the new economy in India, demarcating its upward mobility, or spatial gentrification, thus moving into the world-city pantheon.

The ways in which Delhi is being fashioned since the 1990s reveal the imagining of a new and utterly different city. By making itself available for particular forms of consumption and lifestyle, to particular and predominantly new groups of inhabitants, Delhi turns into a patchwork of new parts, rendering old ones invisible, or disturbing in the perception of the new inhabitants. These 'parts' happen to be located in the city of Delhi, or the bordering National Capital Region (NCR). One could argue that so far, at least, these new parts of the New Delhi are a network of places, or topography that is set apart from the city. It remains to be seen whether the 'old' and the 'new' topographies grow into each other, and if so, in what way.

'Whose Culture? Whose City?' is the title of an essay by urban sociologist Sharon Zukin (2005). This question certainly applies to the new visions unfolding for New Delhi. The images used for the projection of Delhi as a 'world-class' city both address and reflect the desire of members of a new, affluent transnational class for particular economic and lifestyle environments that are still in the shaping. These desires correspond with indigenous as well as (neo)colonial concepts of social purity. The people addressed by the metaphors (mentioned earlier) as well as the imaginary

---

demolished and shops in residential areas closed down (*Real Estate Watch. Building Greater India* 1(4), October 2006: 10, see also Sharma 2006b). On 15 September 2006, the Houses of Parliament passed the Delhi Laws Act (Special Provisions) 'to amend the Master Plan and ease the pressure exerted by the Supreme Court on commercial establishments' (Gupta 2006b).

[4] Certainly, Delhi's urbanisation cannot be isolated from that of other megacities in India: Bangalore, one of the top 10 new tech-cities and Asia's fastest growing city (known as the 'Silicon Valley' of India), Pune, ranking among the top five Indian cities for IT exports (with about 40,000 professionals), Kolkata, on the threshold of an IT/BPO revolution, and finally Chennai, the IT and BPO-hub of south India (see Heitzman 2004).

of real estate advertising (in the following discussion) are local upper
middle classes and local elites in addition to what Aihwa Ong (1999) has
called 'global nomads', i.e., people who settle down in a particular place
or many under the conditions of comfortable work and housing. In order
to be attractive for such professionals and their families, city governments
gear up through private organisations in private–public ventures and
offer political and economic stability, attractive credits and access to state
of the art infrastructure or real estate property. They reflect remarkable
confidence and enthusiasm in the idea of Delhi's transformation through
'India Shining' — as for example, the following advertisement by the Delhi
government in view of the Commonwealth Games of 2010 that would
take place in the capital:

> Delhi — At the Top of India: Delhi is a vibrant dynamic masterpiece, one of the
> greenest capital cities in the world running the world's largest environmentally
> friendly public transport system. Sitting at the top of India both in its physical
> location and overall development Delhi is a masterpiece waiting to be
> explored.[5]

A similar initiative, organised by one of the largest English-language newspapers in India, *The Times of India*, was *Chalo Dilli; From a Walled City to a World City*.
It advertised the Commonwealth Games, commercial centres, proposing
yet again a 'gold rush' mood:

> Today, we stand at the tipping point. Waiting to be rocketed into higher orbit.
> Alongside world-class cities like New York, London, Paris, and more … What
> do we have going for us, and what more will it take for Delhi to get there …
> And here's the best part: would you believe that Delhi is perhaps the best placed
> to emerge as 'The World City'? Most world-class cities are good at one thing or,
> at most, two. There is hardly a city in the world that represents the confluence
> of the most promising political, economic and cultural realms as perfectly as
> Delhi promises … It's time we got together and made Delhi the super city it is
> longing to be. *Chalo, Dilli!*[6]

The images and metaphors explored here are part of what Sharon Zukin has
called the 'symbolic economy of the city' (2005). They are all concerned

---

[5] See http://www.qbtpl.net/cwg/bid_history/html/WHY-DELHI-FOR-2010/
main.htm (accessed 12 April 2007).

[6] See http://chalodilli.indiatimes.com/articlelist/1393834.cms (accessed 28 April
2007). The text plays with freedom fighter Subhas Chandra Bose's battle-call 'Dilli
Chalo' (Go, Conquer Delhi), which is now replaced by the reference to 'Move, Delhi!'
(I thank William Sax for this remark.)

with the creation and address of a 'cultured' cosmopolitan citizen aspiring to belong to 'world-class', also by means of making a statement by living in a particular place.

The advertisements promoting Delhi as a 'world-class' city are a means of social distinction and reflect a particular view as regards who belongs to it and who does not, who can afford to aspire to this belonging and remain outside of the imaginary realm. To be sure, more people aspire to be part of the comfortable life projected in the images and narratives of a cosmopolitan lifestyle than can actually participate in. We will see, for instance, that the advertisements discussed here shape a desire for 'world-class' lifestyle by playing upon dichotomies such as safety and threat, cleanliness and dirt, purity and pollution. The envisaged world-class city of New Delhi will be a 'themed city', clean and slum-free by 2010, the time when the Commonwealth Games take place in Delhi, as Chief Minister Sheila Dikshit announced in January 2008.[7] The following pages explore this vision of the new 'city fantastic' that delivers unending pleasure of consumption to those inhabitants willing to join: 'Global Living for Global Indians' (Plate Ia).

Plate Ia: 'Global living for global Indians'. With this slogan, real estate developer Assotech addresses potential buyers at the upper end of the real estate market. Detail of an Assotech advertisement, Indirapuram, NCR (2006).

[7] See http://news.oneindia.in/2008/01/25/cm-unfurls-flag-unveils-vision-of-slum-free-delhi-1201265184.html (accessed 20 May 2009). However, this statement was revised a few months later when the government had to admit that these ambitions had to be postponed. See Rajeev Ranjan Roy, 'Delhi will not meet slum-free target by 2010', http://www.igovernment.in/site/delhi-will-not-meet-slum-free-target-by-2010/ (accessed 20 May 2009).

the city fantastic

Conspicuous consumption is one of the key markers of the new, affluent middle classes in neoliberal India in their desire to be visible. However, as highlighted in the Introduction, the knowledge of how to display wealth, as well as selecting particular events and stages for this display, is required for such performative and public self-affirmation. The city of Delhi has undergone major spatial restructuring in order to turn itself into a comfortable and spectacular space for consumption (see Srivastava 2009). Shopping as pleasure and leisure activity, as well as national progress, demands new sites (malls), efficient mobility (roads and parking), and the desire of individuals to belong to a group of people who want to see and be seen (flânerie).

The concept of the shopping mall was introduced to Delhi in the 1990s, along with the concept of the multiplex, an air-conditioned cinema hall for the upper market. Compared to traditional bazaars where shops are often found along a narrow but crowded, noisy alleyway in a mixed neighbourhood, the concept of the mall offers parking, seclusion, air-conditioning, retail shopping, background music, playgrounds, food courts and the feeling of floating in time. The mall is intended to turn shopping into an 'experience'; it is meant to be understood as part of the lifestyle of the cosmopolitan elite. Malls are usually made up of several galleries around a main plaza, escalators, elevators and security personnel. Most malls offer a wide variety of items and activities. There are themed malls too, for instance, wedding and jewellery malls, which cater to the most important life-cycle ritual in India: the wedding. Another recent development is to clad the mall within a themed architecture: for instance, of an Italian city, a market square or a palace from Greek or Roman antiquity (see Plate 1.1).

Like the world fairs, the arcades or the leisure parks of European metropolitan cities around 1990, the shopping malls of Delhi are a crucial element of choreography and stage of a new modernity with its sensoriums. They attract audiences of all kinds, ranging from 'time-pass' flâneurs, affluent local customers and tourists of various kinds. Shopping complexes such as Shipra Mall in Indirapuram (Plate 1.1) and Gurgaon's Mall Avenue, with almost 10 malls placed along a highway (Plate 1.2), have meanwhile

Plate 1.1: The themed architecture of Shipra Mall, one of the first of its kind in India, Indirapuram, NCR (2006).

Plate 1.2: The mall functions as an effective advertising screen and soundboard, with loudspeakers blaring out latest hits and shopping announcements. The Metropolitan Mall on Mall Avenue, Gurgaon (2005).

become tourist spots and leisure sites (see Narayanan 2006). Large real estate developers and builders like DLF, Eros City Developers, Omaxe or Assotech have come up in the last 10 years, or even earlier. One of the oldest realty business groups in New Delhi is Ansal, which built the first residential condominium in 1969, the first commercial skyscraper in 1968 and the first shopping mall (Ansal Plaza) in north India in 1999.[1] Malls and real estate hoardings are the most obvious and condensed emblem of India Shining and, based on the fact that New Delhi and the surrounding National Capital Region (NCR) have the highest per capita income in India, there seems to be no end to the construction boom.[2] In particular, on weekends, hundreds of families, married and unmarried couples and friends seek the enclosed and air-conditioned walls of these new worlds, less to shop, so it seems, but mostly to see and to be seen.

The mall visit is an entirely new activity in India. Such spaces for flânerie were previously not available in or even concerned heritage sites, memorials, museums or temples. But the fact that shopping is more than just buying flour and rice, or a pair of trousers, refers to a lifestyle concept in which 'public space' is required and it accounts for leisure activities of such people who have time and money to spend demonstratively, as part of self-affirmation. Since consumption as pleasure is a new activity and offers a new open space in an urban environment, the 'how' of consumption must be learnt. Accordingly, visiting a mall is a particular urban activity and marks urban competence. I have seen many so-called 'mall rats' (mall visitors), probably visiting a mall for the first time, who seemed unsure of how to behave, not daring to enter one of the many retail shops behind glass facades, or walking freely up and down the aisles and escalators. Behaviour is restricted and observed everywhere, starting with guards in uniforms at the entrance gates. There is video surveillance in order to keep unwanted elements out of the malls: security guards and controls make sure that people below a certain 'standard' must not enter a mall. 'This is a clean place', a security guard of a mall in Gurgaon tells me, 'we check that no beggars or rickshaw-drivers or hawkers enter this place'. The 'social control' effect creates different hierarchies and accessibility to a public space such as a mall in Gurgaon. For instance, there is a difference between the

[1] See Narayanan (2006). See also http://www.globosapiens.net/delhi-travel-tip/shipra-mall-3948.html (accessed 1 June 2007). For general information about shopping malls in Indian cities, see http://www.megamalls.in.
[2] See Roy (2005a). The average per capita investment in Delhi is INR 5,410 (c. €97), while the per capita income is as high as INR 51,664 per month (c. €920; see Kackar 2005: 16).

customers attracted by the malls in Gurgaon and the underground Palika Bazaar in New Delhi, one of the earliest shopping malls situated right in the centre of CP. If we go by Mona Abaza who proposes a typology of malls, Palika Bazaar is a 'popular' mall, as opposed to a so-called 'chic' mall of the elite (2001: 108–10). It is a relatively unrestricted underground market that has been the city's canse of pride in the 1980s. But in as much as CP's popularity declined in the 1980s, and other shopping opportunities emerged elsewhere, Palika Bazaar's image went down by the late 1990s, with filthy nooks, shops selling blue movies and semi-pornographic magazines illegally imported from overseas. With the opening of a huge Metro station at CP, and the revamping of parts of Delhi into a 'heritage city', since 2000 the site is changing once again. Globalised retail shops have displaced traditional individual shops, and restaurant chains and exclusive bars with live music now provide entertainment in a previously run-down and rejected area. CP has turned into a popular tourist and nightlife magnet for the affluent middle class.

Sites and goods of consumption are interrelated: due to economic restriction policies, until the 1990s, international brands had to be acquired abroad. There were no Indian lifestyle or interior design magazines and while foreign ones were available from hawkers, they were often already a few years old and expensive. I remember how puzzled I was when I noticed that IKEA catalogues, available for free in Germany, were sold for something like INR 300 on the pavement in the late 1980s. Export limitations had 'protected' the Indian urban market — and customers — until the early 1990s from being 'flooded' by foreign goods and images of global lifestyles through satellite television. Today, luxury brands are available in India, with their numbers rising daily, and chain stores opening in luxury malls and five star hotels in India. Moreover, the variety of imported and domestic lifestyle, fashion or travel magazines available in local markets is substantial, serving as handbooks or guides in lifestyle matters.

The variety of, and the speed at which, lifestyles can change, improve, and have to perform a certain flexibility is evident in the advertisements as well as the conversations with representatives of real estate developers. Potential buyers have no time to select furniture for their new habitat. Therefore, upmarket flats are already furnished. Alternatively, an interior designer is hired. Architect Fredrick R. explains:

> Private high-rise apartment blocks are a relatively new thing to Delhi. Previously, apartment buildings were government-built, subsidised, and were not more than four to five stories high. Increasingly, young people with high salaries want the most modern space available, move into projections of 'London Lofts' or 'Spanish Villas'. Who buys? Multinational corporations who have settled down

in Gurgaon in the last five years or so recruit young people, IT graduates and business students, offering them a good salary, accompanied by a 'packaged lifestyle' (personal conversation, New Delhi, April 2005).

Mostly, the consumers of the themed lifestyle visualities and visibilities are professionals from the service sectors of information technology or retail, possibly working for one of the mushrooming call centres or multinational companies in New Delhi or the surrounding region. They are members of a heterogeneous new flow of people: young, flexible, career-oriented professionals with a high degree of formal education who shape a new and yet very powerful trend of transnational and domestic migration within the emerging new economy. Their monthly salary might be as much as their parents earn per year. Clearly, we have new patterns of a consumer culture and subjectivity at work here. Working hours of professionals may well last 10–12 hours per day, and comfortable work and living environments are desired to reach utmost results and relaxation. At the same time, no long-term commitments can be made by these 'global nomads' (Ong 1999) in the flexible workflow prevalent these days. The motto of flexibility and mobility complicates long-term urban planning. Yet, the notion of belonging to class because one lives in a particularly stable and valuable habitat is two-fold. According to architect Fredrick R., Gurgaon will have to be rebuilt completely in a few years ahead from now, or will become a ghost city. It is already 'drowning' in chaos, mostly due to the fact that Gurgaon consists mainly of privatised land, acquired by private developers such as DLF, one of the largest real estate developers in India. Unlike Noida, says Fredrick, Gurgaon has not been planned for a sustainable future. Instead it was put together haphazardly in a patchwork way, without an overall vision in profit-oriented manner. Investors and developers consciously banked on profits over a very short time span, and promoted the vision of an exhaustive lifestyle for the elite.[3] Critics have even started to raise questions as to how much longer the real estate and mall boom might last.[4] In fact, the global meltdown has badly affected the real estate market in cities like Delhi, where prices fell by nearly 30 per cent in 2008.

Opinions on the alleged over-saturation of the real-estate market have varied over years. In fact, Sales Manager Sanjeev K. from Omaxe, one of

---

[3] In 2007, Gurgaon had almost 20 malls, Delhi and the National Capital Region listed almost 40. In 2008, some of the Gurgaon malls closed down for a day per week due to inadequate electricity expenditure and lack of visitors. See Ahuja (2005), Baruah (2005), Narayanan (2006).

[4] See Special Issue of India Today 30(5), 7 February 2005.

the largest real estate builders in India, with branches all over the country, about 700 employees, and with several themed malls in planning, told me, quite logically, that contrary to Fredrick's dark painting of the downfall of malls in Gurgaon, he was rather optimistic:

> Gurgaon is still the hub for call centres and MNCs in India, with a huge business infrastructure that requires facilities like malls and apartment blocks. So many people arrive, live and work in Gurgaon. Why should they have to drive to Delhi every time (personal conversation, New Delhi, April 2005)?

Likewise, he claimed that themed malls on interior design and lifestyle would be profitable undertakings, offering exported furniture and upmarket white goods, partly on lease. Such malls are needed wherever a lot of new people settle down, buy flats and look for adequate interior design, yet do not have enough time to look around. Sanjeev, further, said:

> Many people, especially mobile couples, and people from abroad (whether Indians or foreign corporates, so-called 'expats') are looking for interior design that suits their taste. In the future, people will buy more and more from malls; malls will be everywhere — they are the best solution, there will be no more conventional street markets in the traditional style anymore (personal conversation, New Delhi, May 2005).

Off the microphone he admitted that he himself shops in those very street markets because he knows the shop-owners, items can be tailored to his needs and prices are negotiable and reasonably lower.

The boom of retail and residential real estate development in Indian cities is not unique to the subcontinent. The success of malls can be seen in China, where malls have sprung up much earlier and in higher numbers. In 2005, the seventh biggest shopping mall of the world was opened in China. In neighbouring countries like Nepal, a shopping mall and huge advertisement buildings signal hopes in economic growth, even though the economy might still be eons away from India's average economic growth of 8 per cent per year. However, India still lags behind China, and the USA. The Delhi Development Authority reacts to infrastructural weaknesses, monitors the growing demands for retail as well as for hotel rooms and proposes to manage malls better.[5] At the same time, mall growth is still seen as an indicator of economic prosperity and stability in India. In 2004–5, the Delhi Development Authority sanctioned 24 malls, with a majority of 13 malls coming up in West Delhi.

---

[5] For the year 2007, 343 shopping malls were planned in India — compared to three malls in 2001. In 2005, almost 100 malls were operational in India. Further,

The shopping malls, leisure parks and multiplexes of the metropolitan city today are what the arcades of the second half of the nineteenth century were for Walter Benjamin: sites of consumption and utopian imagination. In some ways, Benjamin's observations, made more than 70 years ago, about the European metropolis Paris in the nineteenth century, parallel what India's megacities witness today in terms of new emerging economic classes, new spaces and activities linked to the *Erlebnis*, the experience of modernity, of which the key experience is the consumption of fetishes, and the cultured, hedonistic flâneur — the protagonist of emerging modernity and urbanity, of taste and distinction. The arcades, certainly, were sites for the consumption of luxury items, stages of conspicuous consumption, of conscious display of competences embodied in 'taste' that allowed the 'actor', the flâneur, to express distinction while belonging to a particular class, a knowledge of the world, or more specifically, of the fashionable goods circulating in the world, and the meaning seemingly tied to them. There was a theatrical and entertaining aspect to them, even educative: 'World exhibitions are places of pilgrimage to the commodity fetish', writes Benjamin (1999: 17); they 'glorify the exchange value of the commodity' (ibid.: 18) and, one could add, at least, partly *suggest* free access and even belonging to the various circles of distribution, circulation and sites of the cosmopolitan culture of consumption. However, even then we find strategies of classification and stratification among those who are granted full or restricted (or even no) access to this world of phantasmagorias. Being a result of a boom in the textile trade, of colonialism, the arcades were, according to Benjamin, 'a world in miniature' (ibid.: 15), connecting colonial sites of production with sites of consumption of the colonising powers through which goods, people and ideas would be circulated, encoded and decoded with meaning and value. Lastly, the arcades were not so much nodal points of transcultural entanglement but indexes of a 'functioning' and efficient society à la Fourier, utopian in character, harmonious and disciplined — the sites of conception of a new man/woman, of a new affluent class of people. Paradoxically though, here too, the promise of equality of access to cosmopolitan membership was a farce since class distinction through cultural capital remained a crucial element of marking difference.

---

93 malls were to be built across 14 major cities: 54 malls in New Delhi, 23 in Pune, 12 in Mumbai and four in Lucknow. 'The NCR comprising New Delhi, Gurgaon and Noida will witness the maximum activity with 18 retail malls … to be oper-ational in 2005. A popular mall can pull up to 60,000 visitors on a weekend' (Bhupta 2005a: 11–13). By 2010, the year of the Commonwealth Games, 22 new hotels are said to come up, ranging from exclusive to budget establishments (Das Gupta 2007).

Both cities and arcades are sites of production and representation of
new subjectivities. This is particularly crucial when we return to the notion
of the 'world-class city', as we seek to position the discussion on Delhi's
transformations and locations on the global map in the wider realms of
urban anthropology and identity politics. In an article about the world city,
Anthony King argues that the city is at once a fluid space and an imagined
habitat, both structure and practice, with constant movement between
the two (1995: 215). The city, according to him, 'is in fact many cities,
consisting of various representations', a cultural construct that shapes by
means of imagining, be it through symbols, metaphors, desires, where
meaning is ascribed to the experience of modernity in and through urbanity (ibid.: 216). King distinguishes two ways of exploring the imagination
of cities through representation. The first one is focusing on the 'built
environment, the physical and spatial form of the city' as a 'representation of economic, social, political, and cultural relations and practices, of
hierarchies and structures'. The second way is that of highlighting visual
representations, aesthetics, equally filled with symbolic meaning (ibid.:
218). 'In many more ways than one, the world(-class) city becomes a
place where the symbolic economy of new cultural meanings and representations takes place' (ibid.: 228). To me, this is an important remark that
connects well with Sharon Zukin's statement about the symbolic economy
of the city in which the understanding of what 'culture' is controlled by
means of tagging. In order for the visual representation to 'click', we must
understand that the city unfolds on various, sometimes overlapping, levels
(e.g., economic, symbolic, cultural, political), connecting different public
and private spheres along different hubs.

The aesthetic and spatial fabric of a city like New Delhi might also be
enforced by the embraided transnational relationships of cities, enabling
the flow of certain concepts and categories of people. In his exploration
of world cities, Ulf Hannerz maintains that the cultural role of world
cities challenges anthropologists to consider the fact that a sense of place,
and the identities emerging from it, must not be seen isolated any longer
but 'complemented by one of cultural flows in space' (1996: 127; see
also Schiffauer 1997). He differentiates the making and shaping of world
cities by, first, distinguishing four transnational categories of people who
develop particular relationships with the world city, such as businessmen
or migrants. Second, he defines the city as a stage for spectacle; third, as a
cultural marketplace; and fourth, as a site where different relationships of
centre and periphery are played out. But apart from this horizontal factor
of ideas flowing in and through these various levels, the imagined city is
also a local and regional phenomenon with vertical consistence. Thus, no

matter how global a city might be, we must investigate the local trajectories on which it shapes too. For this, let me turn to the discussion of the global city and how it is appropriated in the Indian context of the desired transformation from a 'backward' country to a 'global player'.

From Third World to World-Class City

Many members of the aspiring and arrived middle classes perceive the malls, business districts and multiplexes as signs of economic growth, confidence and potential membership to the 'world-class'. Real estate development is imbued with the aura of India's transformation from a 'Third World' country into a fully developed country, and likewise, Delhi's transformation from a 'Third World city' to 'global city' or 'world-class city', as in the *Dilli Chalo* campaign. If we take Appadurai's concept of imagination as a social practice, it has the potential to create 'social facts' and shape space. In this imaginary, such a global city and the lifestyles that are shaped with it seem to have more affinities with other world-class cities such as Dubai, Shanghai or Singapore than with the hinterland — appealing to people who aspire to be part of a 'jet set'-cosmopolitanism and global nomadism. Real estate advertising propagates this vision of creating a 'New India', populated by beautiful and happy people, heralding 'new lifestyles' (see Plates 1.3 and 1.4).

Along with the middle class, the metropolis and various sites of conspicuous consumption have become the nodal points and visible 'evidence' of this transformation to the 'world-class'. The idea of belonging

Plate 1.3: 'Creating a New India'. Real estate hoarding at Khan Market, New Delhi (2007).

Plate 1.4: 'Building the New India'. Real estate advertisement by DLF, Gurgaon (2006).

to and being world-class literally 'takes place' in and through a range of strategies of spatialisation (Lefèbvre 1991), and is built upon the idea of a transnational, yet traditionally rooted, cosmopolitan community and lifestyle. The different kinds of material analysed in this chapter clearly show that the imaginary of the world-class city and global lifestyles dominates the public sphere and media of popular culture (such as newspapers, magazines and hoardings) to such an extent that they come across as 'real', suggesting that the only route the city, and its inhabitants, can and must take is towards the globalised Indian city, no matter how disparate reality and the ideal might be.

What is the 'global city', or the 'world city'? In his book *Transnational Urbanism*, Michael Peter Smith argues for a contextualisation of the global city as a historical construct (2001: 49). In the case of Delhi, we can see that there is constant cross-referencing of cities aspiring to be 'global' along a diachronic and synchronic axis. This is reflected, for instance, in terms of European prototypes of the early twentieth century (Paris and London) or contemporary phenomena of urbanisation such as in Dubai or Shanghai. Smith maintains that global cities like London, Paris or Tokyo share 'highly mobile, transnational processes of capital investment, manufacturing, commodity circulation, labor migration, and cultural production' (ibid.). Saskia Sassen, who coined the term 'global city', understands the global city as a space in which a shift surfaces from manufacturing and production to finance and business services. She also considers the global city as part of a web of different modes of circulations — of money, people and goods, weaving global cities into a hierarchical geography of late-capitalism. Global cities, argues Sassen, are command and control centres (see 2001a, 2001b, 2002). To some extent, the 'global city' depends more on its relation to other global cities than on flows of exchange with its hinterland. This does not mean, however, that the direct environment is rendered irrelevant. The competition of 'global cities' over their 'world-class' status in the urban pantheon is fierce, and to some extent is generated by an insecurity about who belongs to the aspiring and affluent class that would bring in the desired capital. There has been a substantial amount of criticism that Sassen's model of the global city must be revised and expanded by including the rapid urbanisation of cities situated in non-western and 'backward' countries in scholarly explorations (see Mayaram 2009; Butcher and Velayutham 2009). The recent years show a growing tendency of global cities shaping in so-called developing or emerging countries, the 'global cities of the South'.[6] Members of the transnational management class, cultural experts such as urban planners and advertising agencies, spearhead New Delhi's imagined — and partly actual — transformation from 'Third World' or 'Third Class' city to what I call 'world-class' city.[7]

---

[6] In 2005, Mexico City led the hierarchy of world cities among developing countries in terms of population, followed by Mumbai (19 mio), Sao Paulo (18 mio), Delhi (18 mio) and Calcutta (14 mio) (see Shatkin 2007: 3).

[7] In fact, 'II-Tier' cities such as Pune or Surat move to the centre stage as they become attractive hubs for global investors owing to the partly miserable infrastructure of cities like Bangalore.

Ambivalent Imaginaries of Village and City

Although the concept of the global city requires understanding of urban connections across the globe, the relationship between the city and the countryside must be considered too, in particular, when we explore Indian cities. The projection of new 'Indianness' and world-class lifestyles has led to a change of status in large cities like Delhi or Chennai amid the rhetoric of national growth and pride. From the megacities, so it seems, wealth accumulated through globalised economic networks can be diffused into the rural areas. The image of the promising city — the city of dreams — has come a long way from Gandhi's idealisation of the village as the prototype of change and identity in India. This vision of rural India may be as much a utopian projection as the dichotomous notion of the city as a parasite living on the expense of the rural countryside and draining it out. The city is often looked upon with suspicion that is nurtured by the assumption that city life is linked to modernity, and modernity, in turn, to westernisation. A relatively rigid anti-urbanist perspective nourished the pro-rural agrarian perspective. This perception lasted until the early days of economic liberalisation, when cities such as Delhi or Mumbai turned into bridgeheads of globalisation, catalysts of an increased import and export of goods, ideas and people. To ensure that the perception of the village as an 'ideal-typical' miniature of India can be perceived as essentially modern, the village is idealised as a backward, timeless, but 'balanced', organism while urban habitats are associated with inhumanity and machine-dominated activities and identities, very much like the 'classical' nature–culture-divide (see Nandy 2001). As a result, people living in the city were seen as corrupted by capitalism and modernity's ideology of hedonist individualism, spoilt and detached from their roots, deterritorialised and homeless. The middle class, a specific phenomenon of modern civil capitalist societies, was perceived as the epitome of greed and selfishness, and had to succumb to the moral idea of selflessness and responsibility towards all. Thus, the figure of the steady farmer and romantic hero emerged against that of the 'hedonistic flâneur' or 'capitalist exploiter'.

Ashish Nandy is by no means alone in the assumption that the relationship between village and city is complicated and highly ambivalent. Scholars such as Sudipto Kaviraj, Arjun Appadurai, James Holston, Partha Chatterjee, Sunil Khilnani and Krishna Menon have highlighted the importance of the city in the modern Indian imagination in order to understand the currents underlining today's transformations of public spheres and citizenship. Despite the fact that state institutions of the early years after independence promoted the 'making of an ideal citizen' (such as the documentary films of Films Division of India; Roy 2007), nationhood was mostly tied to the transformation of rural India. Blockbusters like *Shree 420* (directed by Raj Kapoor, 1955) or *Awaara* (directed by Raj Kapoor, 1951) present the stories of the high aspirations of the innocent (educated but unemployed) villagers seeking their fortune in the promising metropolis. Yet, what they find is anonymity, unhappiness, greed, corruption and moral decay; in short, emotional poverty and moral decay. Against the strange city surfaces the trope of the village as a familiar and knowable site. In this imaginary, the 'essence' of India lies in the Gandhian village. The city is an untameable beast, deeply profane, seemingly inadequate for the religious-spirited Indian. Yet, as Sunil Khilnani writes in *The Idea of India*, though the backdrop of India's modernity may still be the picturesque village:

> their very exclusivity, and the spreading of rumours of their opulence [and progress], have made the cities universal objects of desire — all who dream of the ransom of modernity, who peer at its spectres on television and cinema screens, dream of some connection with the city (Khilnani 1997: 109).

Even though this desire existed before the 1990s, the 'mythification' of endless possibilities has intensified since then. This is, as we shall see shortly, carried forward by the presentation of the megacity, the world city of New Delhi, as the ultimate banner of the model of the American-turned-Indian dream.

Previously, disenchantment and resentment were likely modes of relating to the city, defining it as a place where traditional social relations such as the joint family, kinship networks and religious practices would be replaced by a 'homeless' place inhabited by strangers, following materialist lifestyles and extreme individualism, and imbued by strong economic competition (see Nandy 2001: 25). On the flip side, the city was also perceived as a space for unimaginable possibilities for individual upward mobility and self-realisation, where choice was available as a constant companion to one's life. Anthropologists have often privileged the exploration of village communities, caste and kinship issues over hybrid urbanisation and class issues. Such entities were understood as more 'authentic' as opposed to the heterogeneous and fluid fabric of modern lifestyles. For various reasons, the assumption was made that modernity or globalisation were not entangled with rural life, and that the one excluded the other. Yet, these dichotomies enforced each other too. Especially for the educated elites, as Ashis Nandy argues in his exploration of the Self in Indian imagination, where 'the village of the mind shapes the city of the mind, too' (ibid.: 19):

the village of the imagination has become a serene, pastoral paradise. It has become the depository of traditional wisdom and spirituality, and of the harmony of nature, intact community life and environmental sagacity — perhaps even a statement of Gandhian austerity, limits to want, and anti-consumerism … (I)t is a counterpoint to the city (ibid.: 13).

Like Appadurai's argument about the transfer processes between imagination and social facts, Nandy maintains that this image of the village as ideal future impacts on today's public awareness and life. Other scholars have promoted the village as the central category of national identity and nationalist movements (see Srinivas 1987). Mohandas K. Gandhi even proclaimed the city to be a 'helping hand' of the colonial rule and global market politics. In *Young India* (1921), he said: 'The city people are brokers and commission agents for the big houses of Europe, America and Japan. The cities have cooperated with the latter in the bleeding process that has gone on for the past two hundred years' (Gandhi 1966: 288–89 in Jodhka 2002: 3346). Elsewhere, 25 years later, Gandhi maintained that the city was predominantly a white enclave, a bubble of foreign presence:

When the British first established themselves firmly in India their idea was to build cities where all rich people would gravitate and help them in exploiting the countryside. These cities were made partially beautiful; services of all kinds were made available to their inhabitants while the millions of villagers were left rotting in hopeless ignorance and misery (Gandhi 1982: 232 in Jodhka 2002: 3346).

However, Gandhi also acknowledged that the city bred open-mindedness, that better education facilities were available and that untouchability did not play such a great role in work and social life as it did in the village (ibid.: 3347). However, while Gandhi promoted the idea of the village republic as the ideal model for Indian society, critics such as B. R. Ambedkar perceived the village as a site of ignorance where the ghettoisation of 'touchables' and 'untouchables' persisted (ibid.: 3351). Even today, many scholars, as well as middle class representatives perceive the city as decadent, ugly, dirty and criminal, its inhabitants as individualistic, uncultured and mundane. But economic liberalisation has altered this perception: now, the world-class city became the flagship of development — the lifeline that could gentrify India, including its poor populations, promising wealth, health and a good life to all. The idealised and domesticated village is still the object of desire of the urban elites, smiling nostalgically through the mask of heritage and the 'ethnic chic' (Tarlo 1996).

the enclaved gaze: living abroad in india

T he focus of this chapter is on how 'globalised' and 'Enclave India' are imagined, visualised and sanctioned in and through lifestyle aesthetics. Within the city, the shaping of such lifestyle aesthetics represents the desires of the upper and rising middle classes of 'India Shining' and a 'good life' (see Schulze 1992).

The iconography of the housing and lifestyle advertisements reflect a desire for seclusion — even 'social purity' (Fernandes 2006) — indicating clearly demarcated borders between an 'inside' world, allegedly filled with order and peace, and an external world, allegedly infused with dirt and disorder. The real estate advertisements reveal the gatedness of the worlds they seek to sell. One such image is the aerial view of brightly lit buildings, often set in the backdrop of the night sky. Indeed, the townships, often designed in a circular shape, look like spaceships that have just landed on earth, and tend to create the effect of 'Planet India', showcasing virtual satellite towns (Plate 2.1). Then there is the category of the view

Plate 2.1: 'Discover the Ideal Land'. A Gulmohur Greens advertisement, East Delhi (2006).

on the greenery and leisure activities possible around 40–50 storeyed high-rise apartment blocks, usually depicting a swimming pool, mothers playing with their children, small group of people attired in business suits engaged in conversation. Very often it seems as though the people have been superimposed onto the setting by means of a cheap computer program, using cut-outs and quotes from other advertisements, possibly western magazines (the models are usually white-skinned). In effect, such advertisements could be found anywhere in the world, addressing affluent buyers. With a few exceptions, such as 'Gulmohur', a reference to an Indian tree, Indian real estate vocabulary is primarily western, reminding one of the colonial era or US-American equivalents (see Dupont 2005).

The visual material drawn upon here could not have been found in the 1990s. It includes advertisements promoting life in gated townships, from lifestyle and real estate magazines and newspapers to builders' brochures and hoardings along major roads. There is a certain surreality that comes with the construction of a hoarding a mid barren land occupied by huts of construction workers or even a slum waiting to be removed in the course of further construction work (Plate 2.2).

To me, those visions of 'globalised India', or 'Planet India', emerge at the crossroads of cosmopolitan and folkloric distinctions that impact, what I call, the 'enclaved gaze'.[1] Inspired by John Urry's exploration (1990) of the

Plate 2.2: Construction site, with workers' *dhabas* (eateries) in front of a squatter's settlement, Indirapuram, NCR (2006).

---

[1] Urry coined the term 'tourist gaze', a practice involving all senses, through which identities and world-views are shaped discursively and performatively in the act of looking.

'tourist gaze', I consider his work for my analysis of the ways in which the new middle classes are encouraged to look at Delhi, from the point of view of a secure, set-back enclave. The enclaved gaze is an inverted gaze, circumambulating itself in a narcissistic way, pretending that it can do without the world outside. This gaze imbues a particular way of looking at the world and oneself, cast from an insulated perspective. I relate the enclave gaze to the extent to which public sphere and discourse are altered in this context, for instance, through the privatisation of public space (Glasze et al. 2006). I argue that the notion of belonging to the world-class is crucial in understanding the 'efficacy' of the enclaved gaze generated in the imaginary of the global city. The enclaved gaze is part of a selective perception of reality that shapes and legitimises the lifestyle aspirations and identification of the new middle classes. Furthermore, such a gaze and associated lifestyle imaginaries call upon and affirm colonial narratives to underline 'world-class' identities. Mazzarella (2003) has termed this 'auto-orientalism', that is, the use of India and Indianness as an exotic trope by Indians themselves. It becomes particularly visible in advertisements that orientalising self-stigmatisation is a means of distinction addressed against an (occidentalised) modernity, declared as western and foreign. The enclaved gaze is thus a discursive look that may see but exclude discomforting and irritating elements from its frame by heightening the pleasures allocated within the frame. It celebrates its beholder and the world upon which (s)he looks in a way that permits sidelining the world outside the enclave or 'Planet India'.

Earlier I mentioned the challenges faced by the new middle classes in generating adequate cultural capital and 'literacy' to be able to belong to the 'world-class', and to know how to suitably perform the new lifestyles of (upper) 'middleclass-ness'. The deregulation of the market economy in the 1990s increased the circulation and availability of such images and lifestyles that were linked to the idea of a 'good life' as an on-going choreography of the upwardly mobile middle classes, promulgating ideals of individual flexibility, affluence and cosmopolitanism, so crucial for the shaping of cultural globalisation, for the notion of 'global nomads' and 'flexible citizenship' (Ong 1999).

A key notion in this context is 'global', and it is mostly identified with the 'world-class'. Real estate builders such as Ansal or Assotech circulate their message with images such as in their advertisement 'Eleganté: Global Living for Global Indians' (Plate 2.3). The text of the real estate advertisement suggests that, 'a global concept deserves a global audience' and we see a young couple dressed in western clothes looking out of the grand window of a high-rise apartment building. Their enchanted gaze rests on a cityscape that could be located anywhere between Singapore and

Shanghai — or even a completely imaginary site. More important than the actuality of the trope is the fact that in its appearance it seems somehow delocalised and replaceable in its claim to be 'truly international' (Plate 2.3).

Plate 2.3: 'A Global Concept Deserves a Global Audience'. Assotech advertisement for a luxury condominium in Noida, NCR (2006).

In another advertising brochure published by Assotech for their Eleganté project, we learn that a German kitchen with white goods as well as a sky lounge for a unique cosmic experience come as part and parcel of the 'lifestyle facilities', and that launches of these apartment buildings have, simultaneously, been held in hubs along, what could be called, the 'diasporic lifestyle axis', i.e., in Dubai, USA and Canada. By now we can sense that the audience in this picture is made up of a new 'species' of the Indian. Its members represent the constantly moving 'career nomad' who touches ground according to the availability of lucrative jobs and work permits, in India or abroad, with increasingly fluctuating residential addresses and high expectations in lifestyle environments. Many of them might have turned into fairly wealthy employees at a great speed, and it is, in particular these 'newcomers' to wealth who seek guidance of the abounding lifestyle and 'taste' experts today. For instance, in order to follow the latest trend in interior design of a kitchen opening into the dining table and living room, the inhabitants of such a flat would not rely on the idea of seclusion and ritual purification of their kitchen, as necessary for a traditional Hindu household. The new concept of the open kitchen also points towards new ideas of family rituals in the context of 'world-class' lifestyles. Here, cooking becomes a part of leisure, familial and convivial activities. Another novelty for middle-class households is that parents and children have their independent bedrooms, with attached bathrooms. At the same time, certain ritual practices such as feng shui or *vaastu* are revived and they enjoy great popularity in new residential areas. The 'global Indian lifestyle' allows harmonious coexistence of apparent paradoxes such as tradition and modernity, the 'indigenous' and the 'foreign', to the extent that these categories are highly entangled. Several of the 'authentic' Indian concepts (like *vaastu* and *yoga*) have had to come a long way before they were termed suitable for modern Indians, and very often this was after they had been appropriated and remodelled in a western context.

To me, one slogan of a real estate advertisement represents particularly well the relationship of new urban planning to the already existing urban space: 'living abroad in India'.[2] This slogan seems paradoxical and yet appropriately fitting for what is actually happening: the new urban spaces are quasi-colonies, islands or planets of a different kind, only partially connected with their physical environment that lies between them. In many

---

[2] Opera Garden, a real estate developer, advertises their housing estates with the following slogan: 'Get ready to live abroad in India!', *Hindustan Times*, Property Supplement, August 2006.

conversations with real estate developers, architects and members of the middle classes living in New Delhi, I learnt that those spaces in-between were considered as unnecessary and unpleasant, and that they had to be avoided or eliminated, and infrastructure like streets had to be improved to safeguard a smooth transfer of inhabitants from one island to another. To be sure, at some locations in New Delhi or Gurgaon, the difference could not be more drastic. If one were to leave the secluded and air-conditioned apartment block of Beverly Park II in Gurgaon, for instance, as a pedestrian, one would have to look out for deep holes in the pavements, and for cars speeding down the avenue. Often, the land between malls, highways and condominiums that has not (yet) been 'developed' lies carelessly abandoned (used as car parking space or, simply, resting place for strolling buffaloes and cows), and even main streets are flooded after strong rainfall (Plate 2.4). In many cases, they would have been agricultural fields, before they were given up and/or sold to real estate developers by local farmers. In some cases, bordering farmland is still in use (Plate 2.5).

Comfortable open or enclosed public space for retreat is a rarity in New Delhi and NCR, and it is a logical consequence that particularly affluent inhabitants are willing to pay extra in order to surround themselves with greenery and functional infrastructure. The governments of Haryana and Delhi, too, seek to upgrade infrastructure and eco-zones, knowing that this

Plate 2.4: One of the main streets in Gurgaon after rainfall (2006).

Plate 2.5: Agricultural life at the rims of 'Enclave India', Gurgaon (2006).
Source: Photograph by R.S. Iyer.

is not only a necessity for the citizens but also a 'pull-factor' for investors and business in general.

Making Delhi a 'Happy' Place for Modern Maharajas

All great cities have a great skyline. Delhi too. From being a completely horizontal city, it is now reaching for the skies with luxury condominiums and penthouses with swimming pools. There are plans to build the world's tallest building in Noida which will be taller even than the Taipei 101, the currently tallest on the planet. If countries like Korea, Indonesia, Thailand and Taiwan can fashion themselves into super cities, there is no reason why Delhi can't do the same. Together, let's make it happen.[3]

This appeal of the media group Times of India was part of the campaign (Plate 2.6) in 2005 to urge the citizens of Delhi to 'help Delhi make a leap to a World City' (see Introduction of this book).

In my view, this slogan symbolises a change of public sphere and civility, a change in the ways inhabitants of the city could experience and relate to the city, and the ways in which some groups were addressed and asked to help to change the city, while others were not. It allows us to highlight the

---

[3] See http://chalodilli.indiatimes.com/articlelist/1393834.cms (accessed 21 April 2007).

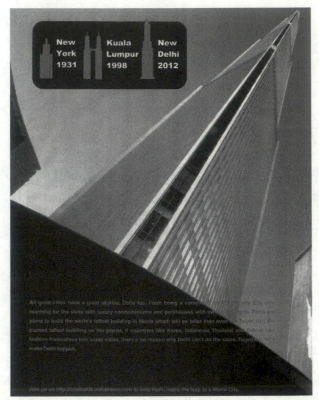

Plate 2.6: 'All Great Cities Have a Great Skyline'. Advertisement from the *Chalo Dilli* Campaign, *Times of India* (2005).

hierarchical distinction made between 'citizens' as rightful inhabitants and the moral community of the city and 'populations' as social groups viewed as possibly necessary, but unpleasant (see Chatterjee 2003).

For the Privileged Few: Deserving 'World-Class' Living

The first time I came to Gurgaon, one of the satellite boom-towns of privatised economy at the outskirts of South Delhi, I was perplexed, besides all the visual stimulations and spatial experiences offered by shopping malls, modern office blocks, condominiums and construction sites, by a hoarding of a township called Sahara Grace. The hoarding was placed beside one of the boom-town's malls and entitled 'For the Modern Maharajas' (Plate 2.7). Despite all the other hoardings near by and the buzzing visual and spatial dynamics of a trendy location like M.G. Road (the main road connecting

Plate 2.7: 'For the Modern Maharajas'. Sahara advertisement on Gurgaon's 'Mall Avenue' (2006).

Mehrauli, in South Delhi, with Gurgaon, quite different from Mahatma Gandhi Road which is also known by the same name), this particular banner stood out for various reasons. Partly, I was struck by the inherent contradiction of the hoarding: I associated maharajas with a nostalgic grandeur of large palaces set in pre-colonial and colonial history rather than state-of-the-art and high-rise apartment blocks made of concrete, one of the many sites among commercial condominiums and other privately guarded communities. Likewise, my attention was caught by a rather overtly elitist rhetoric addressing a growing audience of people who bought into the seemingly contradictory rhetoric of modernity paired with the nostalgic vision of royal grandeur and patriotism.

Yet, by browsing through newspapers or real estate journals and observing the booming satellite cities of megacities like Kolkata, Delhi or Bangalore, and smaller cities like Lucknow, Jaipur or Amritsar, one comes across many similar depictions of the 'good life' that are staged for the pleasure of consumption and the shaping of distinction for the new affluent élites. The viewer is offered visions and views of a 'five-star life' with the promise of 24 hours security, water and electricity, a clubhouse, swimming pool and fitness centre, maybe even a hospital and a school. The items and places on display, catalysing imaginations and desires, are just one part of a whole range of new pleasures and spaces that have emerged since the 1990s and intensified since the beginning of this millennium. Some of the most eye-catching examples available in print media, packed in special folders and printed on glossy paper, are the advertisements of luxury villas like Gurgaon's Ansal's Florence Marvel, Omaxe Luxor Apartments and Penthouses, and Assotech's Windsor Park. The advertisements present festively lit individual villas with huge windows, balconies, and terracotta tiles. The new consumer-citizen does not look up to India's dams as symbols of development, as (s)he might have done with pride under Nehru's socialist economy rule. Rather, it is now to the new residential colonies with lakes and golf courses, and glass-bodied skyscrapers reflecting business (wo)men in western suits, equipped with laptops and BlackBerry phones that shape the globalised imaginary of 'New India'.

The advertisements, most of them published in 2006, show blocks of high-rise buildings assembled around parks with English lawns, flowerbeds, lakes or swimming pools, and shady trees. As points of identification, people feature too: meditating businessmen, women sipping coffee in the morning while reading their e-mails. Further catchy lifestyle definitions are added, such as 'Life is all about how you live', with the backdrop of a city-skyline at night.[4] Other popular slogans are 'Luxurious cottages for the privileged few' (Shri Housing), 'World Class Lifestyle with Punjabi Spirit'[5], 'Reflections of Class ... Hurry, don't be left out!' and 'Experience Class Luxury — World class indulgence' (both by Parsvnath). Prestige Estate Projects in Bangalore promote: 'Prestige Shantiniketan. A Lifestyle Property that India has never seen before ... The result? You don't even have to step out for anything. Except to see how the rest of the world lives'. Real estate giant Omaxe even presents itself with utopian designs: 'Dreaming bigger dreams. And making this world a better place to live'.[6] A deluxe brochure for Assotech Éléganté announces that 'Éléganté gives a flight to your ego and lets your pride soar high.' Villas and apartments are laid out according to ancient *vaastu* principles and an environment-friendly habitat, with a hotel in proximity, facilities for old people's care, parking space, jogging track and yoga hall. In fact, religion and rituals are markers of class in the real estate business. Supply and demand constitute each other in complicated ways: taste structures, and is structured by, global as well as local dispositions of persons and qualities of habitats. Despite the fact that the real estate market carries all signs of globalisation or 'world-class standard', it shows an

---

[4] AIPL Cityscapes Delhi, 2006, see www.aiplcityscapes.com (accessed 20 April 2007).

[5] Vrindavan Gardens, Amritsar, Elite County Developers Pvt. Ltd., 2006.

[6] Likewise, Parsvnath, another pan-Indian real estate developer, sports the slogan of being 'Committed to Build a Better World'.

appropriation of glocal elements too. I use the term 'glocal' here because what seems to be 'aboriginal' has been exported to the West in the course of the twentieth century, transformed, and re-imported as an exotic lifestyle item in the late-twentieth century. In facts, no matter how international the buyers, architecture, design or lifestyle quality offered in any of these places are: religion and tradition continue to matter even in these modern environments and convivial communities. In many niches of lifestyle design, and consequently in residential housing too, 'capitalist spiritualism' emerges as a means of conspicuous consumption and distinction (see Carrette and King 2005). Eros employee Rohit B. highlights the fact that 'spirituality' plays an important role in their impression management for marketing policies: 'We even offer *vaastu* consultation for future tenants, with the only condition that the façade of the house must not be changed; changes can only be made internally. One could even call all this a "*vaastu* craze"' (personal conversation, New Delhi, March 2005). Assotech markets itself as *vaastu*-conscious, knowing the upper new middle classes desire for custodianship over cultural heritage:

> *Vaastu shastra* is of the belief that your home should be designed in such a manner that the positive forces override negative forces, leading to a positive cosmic field that infuses residents with contentment and prosperity … At Assotech we make all possible efforts to create vaastu compliant complexes to bestow on the dwellers all the energies and bring harmonious balance between an individual and nature.[7]

For the first time a real estate developer also catered to the Hindu clientele that is keen to worship outside of the private shrine at home but yet within the compound of the condominium. Advertising a 'rejuvenation of the mind in modern times', real estate developer Parsvnath constructed a temple called Sarveshvar Dham Mandir at Parsvnath Estate in Greater Noida with a ceremonial consecration of deities for the enclaved public in January 2005, located just opposite a golf course (Plate 2.8). The advertisement promises visitors spiritual relief from the stressful challenges of the world outside the enclave. Real estate developer Parsvnath presents itself as caring for the needs of its customers' health, happiness and spiritual balance.

Beyond the culturalist perspective on the buyer's alleged desires, the *bhoomi puja* (worship of the earth, considered to be auspicious for the building) is part of every newly completed construction site. It is believed that

---

[7] See http://www.assotechworld.com/index.php?option=com_content&task=view&id=6&Itemid=14 (accessed 4 August 2008).

Plate 2.8: Spiritual privacy in the enclave. Newspaper advertisement for the opening ceremony of real estate developer Parsvnath's Sarveshvar Dham Mandir, NCR (2005).

it also gives better returns to the investors of residential or commercial buildings. If the bhoomi puja happens, it is a clear sign that the construction work is bound to take place. In the light of a booming real estate market, with many projects being announced but not necessarily taking off the ground, this is an important trust-generating aspect for investors.

The notion of 'class' as status-marker for those belonging to, and claiming power over, New India, surfaces everywhere: especially reflecting in names such as 'The Nile', 'South Avenue', 'Mayfield Gardens', or 'Royal Residency', may they be in Gurgaon, Faridabad or Noida, Ludhiana or Pune, the new residential sites have 'everything that spells class': 'the interiors are tastefully designed in neo-modern style with an enchanting view of the picturesque surroundings' (Parsvnath advertisement, 2006). Whatever 'neo-modern' might be, the slogan does not require further explanation: it refers to a global visual imaginary that immediately associates 'quality' and modernity.

These visual quotations often come to life only after they merge in the viewer's mind and exhibited along a plethora of slogans. The advertisement for Ansal's Florence Marvel at the construction site in Gurgaon's Sushant Lok reads: 'Unveiling the Art of Timeless Living. Ansal's Florence Marvel. Luxurious Villas with personal swimming pool, golf putting greens & open air bar on the terrace' (Plate 2.9).

A newspaper version of the advertisement carries the additional line, 'Inviting those who belong to class. See it, to believe it!' Underlining these associations is the projection of a competent consumer with 'classic', 'eternal' and good taste and way of life. References are made to golf (a sport imbued with a high degree of symbolic capital) inviting relaxation and business conversations, as well as to people who would regularly host garden or roof terrace parties equipped with open-air bars, indicating the growing acceptance of alcohol as a [western] signifier of class and sophistication. Like the trend of the kitchen opening into the living room, the consumption of alcohol is a new phenomenon of life-styling that has been integrated into residential housing. Alcohol has been previously associated with unsuitable behaviour and low 'westernised' morals, and it is only since the 1990s that its consumption has been 'domesticated' and attributed with 'class' among members of the affluent classes. In conclusion, the addressee is assumed to have financial and symbolic capital and confidence, or at least the desire, to *belong to class*. 'Belonging to class' means 'to be special' or 'to have made it', to be part and parcel of a trendsetting transnational elite immersed in impression and lifestyle management, and 'class'.

Plate 2.9: Ansal's Florence Marvel. Hoarding at the construction site, Gurgaon (2006).

What we find in the advertisements for a city like New Delhi is a form of social spatialisation through images and narratives of an exclusive lifestyle, which underlines the widening gap between the 'deserving' and 'selected' few and their counterparts. To a great extent, the images I discuss here show the profusion of open green space and living space. However, it requires mentioning that most Indians still live in small flats and houses, i.e., one to two rooms per family unit, and that cultivated nature is a luxury item.[8] They will never afford to buy one of these properties. But they will be able to include these glimpses and notions of a 'good life' in their aspirations and imagination, which then, in turn, shape the cultural logic of globalisation.

The members of the groups addressed by the advertisements such as the ones mentioned are relatively clearly defined. They are 'transnational elites', 'the dominant class in the world city, and the city is arranged to cater to their life styles and occupational necessities' (Friedman and Wolf 1982: 322 in Hannerz 1996: 131). Negotiations of the world-class drift between having to express taste by the knowledge of trends and yet performing exclusiveness. In his book on images and lifestyle, Stuart Ewen argues that to members of the aspiring and affluent middle classes, the notion of 'being special' is crucial and the desired development of lifestyle is enforced through advertisement images. These images, in fact, convey a 'feeling' of being exclusive (1988: 58). This requires a distinguishable set of 'images, attitudes, acquisitions, and style' (ibid.: 62), and even if 'the 'lifestyle' ... is not realizable in life, it is nevertheless the most constantly available lexicon from which many of us draw the visual grammar of our lives' (ibid.: 20). In this context, images of status and style become the social currency or the symbolic and cultural capital used for the distinction of the on-going project of 'living a good life', one that is exercised in an increasingly mobile, fluid, commercialised and globalised world (see Ewen 1988). As a seemingly distinct style, it also suggests the existence of certain visible indicators and ways of placing them strategically, creating the imaginary notion of a clear-cut border between those who belong and those who don't, the 'haves' and the 'have not's' in social space.

The visibility of the 'have's' and the invisibility of the 'have not's' is reflected in Ronald Inden's work on Bombay cinema. The new middle class imagined in this and the following advertisements, and its 'visual lexicon'

---

[8] Deutsche Bank reports that 70 per cent of Indian households do not possess more than two rooms. Prognoses underline the fact that the numbers of members in a household will sharply decline while the demand for space continues to rise (see Just et al. 2006: 20).

of identification converges with what Inden calls a 'new transnational cosmopolitan class of Indians' (1999: 48). Their Arcadian visions of lifestyle, as Inden argued in his analysis of the Hindi blockbuster *Hum Aapke Hain Kaun...?!* (Who Am I to You?! directed by Sooraj R. Barjatya, 1994), are set in worlds where 'the masses have virtually disappeared. Only the elite are present' (ibid.: 59). Whether it is filmi heroes and heroines or modern maharajas on the hunt for luxurious residential apartments, they all float playfully in a 'suburban utopia' (ibid.). Thus, the visual popular language of Bollywood and Gurgaon shares the same imaginary, developing a similar 'enclaved gaze' that draws borders and excludes those Indians who do not (or must not) have any access to the 'world-class'. The visibility of the Self produces the invisibility of the Other or, as we shall see in the following discussion, makes the latter open to exotic consumption and further 'stereotypisation'. The question as to whether the new middle classes have no concern with struggles of the outside world corresponds with Pavan Varma's critique of a declining moral, social and ethical responsibility of the new middle classes against the masses of poor and uneducated people of India in his book *The Great Indian Middle Class* (1998). Yet, as Fernandes (2006) argues (see Introduction to this book), also in concurrence with Ong (1999), the new middle classes have developed a different kind of national identity and responsibility. They consider themselves as promoting economic growth by spending money and see themselves as custodians of Indian culture, tradition and moral values, for instance, by contributing to charity activities in religio-spiritual organisations. Moreover, real estate developers, like private entrepreneurs, engage increasingly in philanthropic activities. One such example is real estate developer Omaxe who launched a girl child care initiative in September 2006.[9] Many of the upper middle classes belong to the cultural category of 'global nomads'. With a high degree of physical mobility and career flexibility, with social and economic networks defined along the lines of class rather than caste, the city to those people will predominantly be a 'service' institution. What matters to them, thus, is the smooth access to international lifestyles and infrastructure, sites designated for high quality experiences (malls, theme parks, hospitals) and a supportive and efficient structure that caters to their desire of hygiene, security and mobility.

---

[9] The project is called *Kauwahakni* and addresses 'issues related to the plight of women with a focus on persistent problem of illiteracy of girls among the rural masses of India', as the Omaxe Foundation homepage states. See http://www.omaxefoundation.co.in/events_kauwahakni.php (accessed 8 June 2007).

Five Star(+) Homes: The NRI-Factor

Who is qualified to belong to world-class living in India? What are the markers for this distinction? Who buys the places on offer in real estate development and who lives in them? A large part, sometimes as much as 50 per cent of the buyers investing in real estate, are members of the transnational, imagined cosmopolitan community and belong to the group of over 25 million non-residential Indians. Quantitative details could not be obtained at the time of completing this book, and it is particularly difficult to even estimate it due to the fact that some return to India permanently, some only temporarily, some for the sake of holiday or old age security, others only for investment. Rohit B., then Deputy General Manager (Sales and Marketing) for Eros City Developers, one of India's largest players on the real estate market, says:

> Since a few years, NRIs invest more heavily in real estate, some do it for investment only — mostly people in their 30s onwards, double income families who have an annual income of around 30–50 lakh rupees. Others do so because they envisage to return to India after their retirement, and are even in their 50s (personal conversation, New Delhi, April 2006).

Besides sentimental reasons and the general attraction of the growing market for investors, there is, in Rohit's opinion, another reason why overseas Indians living in the USA are investing in India: insecurity has increased since the attacks on the World Trade Centre on 11 September 2001, and following a backlash against Asians, the feeling that India has now become a safe and even comfortable haven is being cultivated among NRIs (personal conversation with Rohit B., New Delhi, October 2005).

Eros City Developers produce lifestyle habitats for members of such transnational groups. They develop luxury apartments and villas, malls and complete townships, and cater towards the desires of the affluent middle classes with the appropriate narrative contexts, that is, conscious theming.[10]

---

[10] Eros luxury apartments cost around INR 1.5 crore plus (c. €30,000), independent houses cost, at the minimum, INR 2.25 crore (c. €40,000). Some built villas have a private pool and the plot size is between 800 and 1,000 m². In the upcoming and well-planned township of Noida, residential condominium projects range from INR 30–85 lakh per unit (1,200–3,000 sq. ft, c. €55,000–€1.5 mio) in so-called Grade-A residential buildings (Verma 2006). In comparison, while apartments in Manhattan are available at an average of INR 40 lakh per sq. ft (c. €71,500), house buyers in particular neighbourhoods in a city like Mumbai have to cough up INR 70 lakh per sq. ft (c. €125,000). *India Today Buyer's Guide*, 2006, 1(1): 17).

The NRI has become a key consumer of the real estate imaginary and politics of the 'world-class' city. While Eros taps into the residential and the overseas market, developers like Rosedale from Kolkata focus specifically on the NRI market. They appeal to potential customers by way of nostalgia:

> There's no denying it. Only an NRI can truly understand the yearning an NRI feels for his home. Or even what he looks for when he does come home … [E]very little thing is just the way an NRI would want it. After all, you can't just call any place home (Rosedale developers' brochure, Kolkata, 2007).

This text advertising the real estate project Rosedale in Kolkata, offering a 'fully-loaded residents' club' plus 'senior citizens' apartments', predominantly addresses those overseas Indians who, as it seems, belong to the stream of 'reverse migrants' (Plate 2.10). This new category differs from the so-called 'twice migrants', another term from south Asian migration history that refers to people who have moved from India to another country to yet another country, for instance, to Uganda and then the United Kingdom. Reverse migrants are people who come to settle in the country of their parents or ancestors, in this case, to India, largely in response to

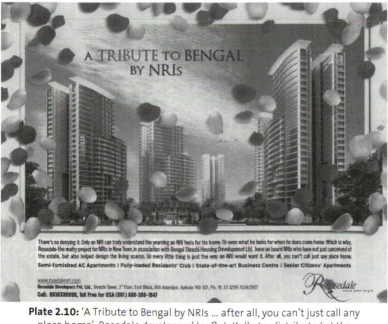

Plate 2.10: 'A Tribute to Bengal by NRIs … after all, you can't just call any place home'. Rosedale developers' leaflet, Kolkata, distributed at the *Pravasi Bharatiya Divas*, Delhi (2007).

the economic growth. Reverse migration also points at the complex and flexible strategies of attachment to a place, underpinning the agency of rather privileged diasporas to make a conscious choice in moving across, to and fro, and in between.

The development of the real estate market in 'world-class' cities like Delhi needs further contextualisation. Both the free market and the nation state are catering to the NRI, trying to tap into this social segment's interest to invest in and even return to India. The Indian government has done so by institutionalising a substantial annual gathering of NRIs and PIOs (People of Indian Origin, not holding an Indian citizenship) — the *Pravasi Bharatiya Divas* (Day of Overseas Indians) in one of the megacities of India each year, with the expansion of the Ministry of Overseas Indian Affairs and with regional ministries of overseas matters.[11] The assumption underlining these attempts to appeal to the NRIs through the rhetoric of 'homecoming' is that the overseas Indians are essentially 'homeless cosmopolitans' with no moral obligation to any locality but India (see Schiffauer 2004: 94–95).[12] Against this, Schiffauer holds that locality is a 'means of identification with a landscape' that does not require rooting in descent, nationality or religion (ibid.: 98). Instead, it has strong sensuous connotations that emerge by means of 'sharing a place rather than values or ancestors, … smells, sounds, tastes, and rhythms' (ibid.). Identification of cosmopolitans with a locality can happen when an aesthetic relation is formed, when favourite sites are defined, when a longing to belong surfaces. The next example illustrates this quite lucidly by tying locality to memories of 'home'. Images provide essential stimulation for such an aesthetic identification in that they shape and create a new, imagined landscape associated with 'home'. Interestingly, there is a meaningful wordgame that indicates a shift of the meaning of 'NRIs in the 1990s: while before that, they were often, in jest, referred to as 'non-reliable Indians', the wave of returning wealthy and investment-friendly migrants turned them into the 'national resource of India'. Many real estate developers bank on a certain nostalgia of NRIs to return to India, and to invest in their home country.

The Rosedale advertisement (Plate 2.10) appeals to the alleged desire of NRIs to return to their 'roots', remembering their childhood days,

---

[11] On the PBD, see http://www.pbd2007.org/; also Ministry of Overseas Affairs homepage, http://moia.gov.in/ (accessed 27 August 2007).

[12] The discussion on the alleged 'faithlessness' of NRIs is continued in Part III of this book.

knowing that the idea of home is enforced by memories and the nostalgia
of returning to where one grew up, where one originated from:

> No matter where you are, if you have lived in Kolkata, its memories will always
> remain a part of you. The afternoon cricket matches in the alley, eating *bhog* at
> the *para pujo pandal*. Think! Why do these memories keep coming back? Because
> Kolkata is in your DNA. Now you can relive these memories again. By living
> in Rosedale Gardens. And what's interesting, is that the experiences you'll be
> gathering here will be packaged better than yesteryears. Because, the changing
> times have added a fresh perspective to the old ones. The coffee house 'addas' are
> in the Baristas, the matinee show at Priya cinema has been replaced by movies in
> the multiplex INOX. In spite of the topsy-turvy times before, the globalisation
> takeover, Kolkata retains its infectious never say die attitudes. So, it's time to
> rewind those memories and unwind in Kolkata (Rosedale brochure, 2007)!

The advertisement maintains an essential identity — of belonging to
Kolkata — one that is imbued in the genes, that only has to be rediscovered
and affirmed by 'paying tribute'. It suggests a kind of happiness linked to
stereotypical notions such as playing cricket in the alley, talking for hours
in a traditional café (*adda*) — of having endless time to enjoy life. The
advertisement further suggests a lifestyle transformation which has taken
place in cities because of economic liberalisation and globalisation, with
Barista (the Indian answer to Starbucks) and multiplex cinema halls for
the upper middle classes. Nostalgia without memory (Appadurai 1997) is
what the real estate brochures convey, only that this nostalgia is wrapped
in serviced apartments and an old-people's home.

With prices of flats ranging from INR 50 to 100 million, with parking space per car for the price of INR 250,000, Rosedale moves along
the high end of residential apartment housing.[13] It can actually afford
to approach only wealthy NRIs who consider themselves jet-setters.[14] In
fact, the condominiums seem to be functioning and conceptualised like
a multinational corporation. I collected information material about

---

[13] See http://www.rosedalenri.com/apt-payment-price.html (accessed 25 March
2007).

[14] 'Since a lot of Keralites are working abroad and have substantial disposable
income, real estate is a best bet for them to invest in their own state … Till two years
back, as much as 70 per cent of our clientèle comprised NRIs. But now, as more and
more locals are opting for better lifestyle and modern living, their share has gone
up. Nevertheless, NRIs constitute 50 per cent of our total clientele', says K. Lava,
managing director of Foundations and Structures Private Ltd. Kochi (Kulkarni
2006c: 38).

Rosedale and talked to the junior management staff of this organisation at the *Pravasi Bharatiya Divas* (PBD) in New Delhi in January 2007 where quite a few real estate developers had set up information stalls. Here, I learnt about the massive overseas expansion of the real estate market. Amit, a public relations manager of a 'seven star'-condominium in Gurgaon, told me that he had just returned from a real estate fair in Dubai, where his firm approached rich Arabs as well as Indians living in the Arab Emirates as potential investors and buyers. In fact, real estate developers from Dubai are investing heavily in overseas property. It might be neither anecdotal nor incidental that at the PBD 2007, one real estate developer asked me whether I would like to work for him, promoting their projects in Germany, for he had heard that there were many affluent Indians who might be interested in such investments.

An employee of Assotech, one of the major players of luxury residential housing and entire townscapes, told me that 70–80 per cent of the flats were already sold out before the construction had finished, mainly to NRIs, retired couples, and young professionals in a nuclear family set-up with a salary starting from INR 100,000 per month.[15]

But does Rosedale's slogan 'Touch Your Origin' really work? Do all overseas Indians crave to return to their home town, where possibly some of their family members are still living? Iqbal Naroo, from Naroo Constructions in Goa, has his doubts:

> Demand from NRIs is mainly from Gujarati buyers settled in places like London. They are basically people who hail from small Indian towns like Porbandar, Rajkot and Jamnagar, and immigrants from Uganda who later shifted to the UK. They are currently buying property here because they have a strong bond with their country but are not interested in investing in their home towns for various reasons. After leading an upmarket lifestyle abroad they do not want to retire to their village in India. They are more keen on buying a home here and make flying visits to their home towns whenever they find time (Kulkarni 2006b: 44).

---

[15] India is the youngest nation in the world with 70 per cent of its total population younger than 36 years, making up a large workforce and eager consumers, also named LUCKIES: the Labelled, Urban, Chilled, Kicked-with-Life Indians. In fact, 660 multinationals have brought overall business of more than US$1 million annually to India, employing over 3.5 million Indians, with India controlling 44 per cent of the global offshore outsourcing market for software and back-office services (such as call-centres whose total revenues in 2004–5 was about US$17.2 billion; see David and Unnithan 2005: 18).

This is an interesting statement because it shows how conscious and very diverse choices are made as regards what and where 'home' is. Possibly a young family decides to buy property in India now because they want to invest, spend a holiday away from the overseas home, but decide against the 'conventional' way of staying with relatives. For many, this could mean an involuntary reduction of their independence. What becomes clear is that manifold strategies are developed to tap into the NRI market, some by referring to the nostalgic rediscovery of a personal past, others through that of regional or national heritage, still others by finding that life in India can be like life anywhere in the 'developed' world. Some buyers never come to permanently occupy the property; instead, if they are NRIs, they might stay on a temporary basis for a holiday or a business trip. Alternatively, they rent the place out to corporate professionals, or offer it as a holiday site to other NRIs or family members who live abroad as well. Rosedale, for instance, even provides services to survey empty flats while their owners are abroad. Whether or not these new communities grow together as solidary neighbourhoods, and whether an identity beyond class, develops in such residential housing colonies remains to be studied further. Owing to the global economic crisis, however, NRIs have become more cautious in investing in the real estate market as well as playing with the thought of returning to India to find a better lifestyle for less money.

Since 1993 it has become much easier and lucrative to invest in India, and both the government as well as real estate developers do their best to convince investors of the economy's stability. As regards the domestic market, many members of the aspiring and affluent middle class addressed by real estate advertisements are single people or young professional couples. They may also be nuclear families with rising disposable income, which contributes to the growth of home loans and tax incentives provided by the government. Demand for land, especially in the metropolitan regions, is high and extremely competitive. One consequence of this is that land prices have risen by as much as 100–150 per cent in 2006 and regulators such as the Reserve Bank of India or the National Housing Bank have started worrying about a bubble forming whose collapse is only a question of time.

There is a rush to get into what the recent study by American Express has called 'Inside the Affluent Space'.[16] India has been benchmarked as a 'hot destination' for foreign developers and investors, even called the 'land of abounding opportunities'. From American Express' report *Inside the*

---

[16] The report in 2006 explored economic growth and investment options in several Asian countries. See n. 7, Introduction to this book.

Affluent Space to Deutsche Bank investment funds to banks and investors in the Gulf countries, people and institutions everywhere are reacting to the prospect that owing to rapid population growth, rising incomes, decreasing household sizes and a housing shortage of about 20 million units in urban India, extensive residential construction is required. However, it is not specified as to for whom these residential units must be built (Just et al. 2006). The global real estate consulting group Knight Frank has ranked India fifth on the list of emerging retail markets, and in fact booming sectors range from the growth of IT and BPO (Business Process Outsourcing) industry, retail, hospitality, health, tourism and education. Estimates go as far as calculating 10 million new housing units per year by the year 2030 (Mohamed 2006). Developers already experienced in luxury, master-planned townships in the United Arab Emirates have offered joint ventures both with the private and the public sector, for instance, in the context of the Commonwealth Games Village next to the ACC (see Part II of this book).[17]

'Dubaisation': Experiencing the Themed Enclave City

Many references in advertisements and conversations have been made to the booming city of Dubai. As if it was a miracle from *Arabian Nights*, or a futuristic dream of urban planning, Dubai triggers a host of desires and aspirations (see Plate 2.11). Undoubtedly, we can witness a process that I call 'Dubaisation', a redefinition of public venues and urban spaces along the lines of a dense chain of spectacular — and semi- or fully-privatised — sites and events (see Zukin 2005). I derive the term 'Dubaisation' from

---

[17] Investment opportunities for non-Indian citizens in the Indian real estate market are not as attractive as they are in Dubai. While Dubai is witnessing a real estate explosion attracting international investments and allowing foreign ownership of property, providing resident visas upon purchase, India encourages foreign investment on a restricted access basis only. A foreigner is not permitted to buy property unless (s)he is granted permission by the Reserve Bank of India and spends more than 182 days at a stretch in India or opens a tourism-related company in India (see Kulkarni 2006a; Simpson 2006). Affluent professional Indians have several connections with the United Arabian Emirates and the market shows strong signs of expanding towards those countries, too. The India Real Estate Expo 2006 was in fact held in conjunction with the Worldwide Property Show at the Grand Hyatt in Dubai, with the UAE expressing a significant interest in exploring high investment opportunities in India. *Realty Plus*, 2006, 3(1): 129.

Plate 2.11: 'Dubaisation'. Part of the 'Creating a New India' Promotion by Emaar and MGF. Hoarding at Khan Market, New Delhi (2007).

Alan Bryman's concept of the 'Disneyization of society' (2004; see also Part II of this study). With this notion he proposes that the concept of theme parks, an eventful enclosed space, spreads through society and that urbanisation and personal subjectivities are impacted on in this process.[18] I consider the theming of cities as the making available of space as a narrative of lifestyle and consumption as pleasure. 'Dubaisation' denotes a recent development of urban planning located in the previous periphery of modernity, in places that earlier did not seem to matter much in terms of global/urban networking. As opposed to Disney World, Dubai has an origin outside the realm of fantasy and themed environments. It is the world's greatest shopping mall and dream oasis. It seems to be the perfect simulacra of the 'Global South' that inspires other cities that were formerly at the periphery.

Enjoyment and pleasure are centre stage of urban experience and marketing, and cities become 'event-zones' with 'topographies of taste and spectacle' (Legnaro and Birenheide 2005: 13; see also Mbembe

---

[18] Bryman argues that 'social institutions and practices increasingly resemble theme parks', that cities are turned into theme and entertainment spaces, and that culture and history are 'sanitized' (2004: 5–6). On the city as spectacle, see also Stevenson (2003).

2004). Hassenpflug (2008) has termed this phenomenon of the performative city 'citytainment'. The city transforms into a living museum
or theme park, as Michael Sorkin has already suggested in the context of
urbanisation in America (1992a: xv). The transformation takes place in
patchwork patterns, not completely — some are privatised, others publicly
accessible. The concept of the 'themed' environment refers to the design
of a public or private space or site according to a particular theme that
invokes pleasure and aspirations. For instance, a restored part of an old
city can be a 'themed' environment, as in the case of Old Delhi, or colonial
Delhi, as much as an ethnic village within the city that presents traditional
folklore, ethnic consumer goods and lifestyles to tourists and other visitors
(see Tarlo 1996).

'Dubaisation' in this context refers to the city that ambitiously and confidently realises the birth of a utopian dream of luxury, efficiency, safety and
leisure, supporting Achille Mbembe's concept of 'superfluity' (2004). Dubai
is a good example of an imaginary becoming a social fact. The city by the
Arabian Gulf has shaped itself as the ultimate utopian and record-breaking
experience (*Erlebnis*), embedded in what Mike Davis has defined as 'Sinister
Paradise' (2005). It is a place transformed into a roller-coaster of sensations
and a patchwork of what every aspiring world city desires: the latest state-
of-the-art in terms of architecture and leisure, of 'cultural heritage', and a
mosaic of global styles. It is a perfect alliance of private and public sphere,
with no shortage of investors and consumers. Indeed, in these notions of
a city, images of Beirut's famous Hanging Gardens, and other paradisaical
and spectacular urban associations come to merge. Today, Dubai has
become a place of leisure pilgrimage, quite like the world exhibitions and
fairs of Walter Benjamin's Arcades Project (1999). In the nineteenth century, the world fairs of London or Paris were spectacles of consumption,
assembling 'the world' in a location that served the desire of a society, or
'civilisation' — the British Empire, the French colonial power or the United
States of America, for instance — to both invent and present themselves as
world power (see, for instance, Benedict 1983; Brown 2001).

Dubai invents itself into a living emblem of the penultimate, exciting,
Arcadian world-class city, or a spatialised telenovella of *Arabian Nights*. As
an exposition of various themes ready for consumption: world history,
world art, Arabian tradition and folklore, futuristic residential and leisure
sites, and gigantic architectural adventures, all are presented in such a
way that they seem virtually 'touchable'. The presentation and promise of
almost unimaginable affluence and activity in Dubai (and, increasingly, in
neighbouring countries of the Gulf region), has affected discourses about

globalisation and modernisation in India, especially when it comes to the rhetoric of 'world-class cities' such as New Delhi, Mumbai, Chennai or Kolkata.[19] As a consequence of the notion that — quite like the 'gold rush' metaphor used in the context of returning overseas Indians — there is an unbelievable surplus of floating capital only waiting to be tapped, many slogans projecting India's megacities as global boom-towns in fact recycle the terms and vocabulary of megacities from the Global South (such as Dubai, Singapore, Shanghai or Kuala Lumpur). In this new chain of associations of power, the global cities of the Global North (New York, Berlin or Paris, for instance) are pushed into the second row where they are rendered as nostalgic models of another modernity.

The growth of a city such as Delhi and its surroundings, as it becomes available to the upwardly mobile sector of the middle classes, is partially shaping such lifestyle visions by following a politics of theming. Through this, certain sites of the city are turned into a complex of events and sensations. This is, to some extent, also a marketing strategy of a city that facilitates initiatives that seemingly add to its desired reputation as being 'world-class'. Such initiatives lead to the gentrification of particular localities that might have been previously unattractive and inaccessible. One striking illustration is the Metro network in Delhi where construction is still underway. The Metro, in itself a spectacle of modernity, suddenly made it possible that Old Delhi could be reached easily and comfortably, reinforcing its transformation into a heritage, leisure and consumption site for the new middle classes. This is also true of the Akshardham Cultural Complex, a mega-site of themed religious architecture and experiences that draws upon the growing popularity of leisure-religion and New Age capitalism (Part II of this book).

Despite their use of local elements of tradition (e.g., the *vaastu* model of construction), most of the enclaves of 'world-class' cities like Delhi are remarkably non-local. Many malls have turned into replicas of each other,

---

[19] According to Trammell Crow Meghraj Property Consultants Private Limited, one of the leading international property consultants in India, the 'hottest growth areas' and 'A-grade' cities are: the NCR (Delhi, Ghaziabad, Gurgaon, Noida), Mumbai, Kolkata, Chennai, Bangalore, Hyderabad, Nashik, Pune. See *Realty Plus*, 2006, 2(5): 32.

The boom in the UAE has also started a debate about new forms of slavery by means of using cheap migrant workers from South Asia to build palaces of consumption. The 2007 PBD addressed exploitation of those workers, asking the governments of the respective countries to ensure safety and a decent quality of life for the workers.

even though some have started to appear unique and themed in terms of their architecture (see Plates 1.1, 1.2 and 3.1). Once inside, one easily forgets which mall one has entered. The same counts for the residential housing complexes or condominiums. The next chapter thus takes a closer look at the idea of the enclave, traces its local and global history and explores, among other aspects, the tension-loaded relationship between diversification and standardisation.

'insulate!' the celebration of new gated habitats

These days in a place like New Delhi, when leaving for Gurgaon, for instance, it is possible to drive on a road along a residential area for a long stretch without being able to either leave the road or divert by turning right or left, like in US-American suburbs: there are high gates, walls, watchmen, even surveillance cameras that prevent one from doing so. Likewise, in the opposite direction, when driving towards Greater Noida, one is struck by plots of land on which completely new master-planned communities are mushrooming, often still just announced by glamorous hoardings promoting new shopping paradises (Plate 3.1), lush green townships, world cities, exotic islands as future habitats in a place like New Delhi and the NCR.

Get a
brand showcase
that draws
all eyes, like
never before.

Plate 3.1: Eros promotion of 'Marketplace', a new themed shopping mall, NCR (2005).

Source: *Hindustan Times*, Delhi, 25 July.

These enclaves within the city do not seem to take any notice of their environment, and it appears as if, according to architect and critic Michael Sorkin (1992a: xiii), 'what is missing ... [is] the spaces in between, the connections that make sense of forms', and these enclaves tend to act as if the space between integrated townships was just a means of transport from A to B, if at all acknowledged as such.

One of the key arguments of urban anthropologist Ulf Hannerz is that a city is a network of networks, and that a world city is characterised by both access to diversity and diversity of access. By these means, a culture of communication unfolds that is inherently 'urban' and 'open', ideal-typically 'cosmopolitan'. In the case of the real estate rhetoric of the 'world-class' city, there is certainly an associated pantheon of images granting access to diversity for affluent consumers — relating to different lifestyles, parts of the world, its history, and so forth. But this alleged openness to each other is also imbued by the tendency of social groups to compartmentalise their lives within enclaves, in terms of residential, outdoor leisure or work domains. Hannerz puts this phenomenon in illustrative words:

> The reaction to diversity on the part of these inhabitants of the world city may be to shield themselves from it as much as they can, by living in their very own neighbourhoods, or if affluent enough, in a house with a doorman ... These are the people of the centre wanting the periphery to go away from their doorstep, or at least to show up there only discreetly, to perform essential services. 'You've got to insulate, insulate, insulate,' as someone says in Tom Wolfe's New York novel, *The Bonfire of the Vanities* (1996: 134).

To cope with alleged insecurities of various kinds thus becomes very much part and parcel of the urban way of life: 'The basic rule of the urban way of life is: Keep your distance' (Siebel and Wehrheim 2006: 32). In this kind of spatial hierarchisation, the space surrounding these enclaves becomes an allegorical no-go-zone.

Splendid Isolation, Perfect Solitude

To have all the trendy and seemingly necessary facilities to live a good life, in a centrally located and well-connected place, among others alike and yet remain still independent, surrounded by privacy, even by solitude, seems to be an ideal lifestyle in a busy city. This vision is also reflected in the following advertisement that appeals to the affluent and mobile consumers' desire to live 'the way the world lives', in Assotech's township Windsor Park in Indirapuram, NCR. A man in a western business suit is shown to meditate on the lawns, assumingly of his apartment block (Plate 3.2).

Plate 3.2: 'The Way the World Lives'. Assotech advertisement of Windsor Park, Indirapuram, NCR (2005).

Source: *Hindustan Times*, Delhi, March.

The images of lifestyle in urban India paint a utopian vision of safety and peaceful seclusion. In other advertisements too, no crowds populate the advertisements, only couples, or maybe business friends, and the words 'peaceful' or 'quiet' are repeatedly mentioned. This idealisation of solitude as indicative of wellness is new and worthwhile to explore. To some extent, the desire for solitude may derive from Hindu asceticism, especially, when a householder is expected to withdraw from his family and worldly life in order to seek *moksha* (liberation or release from the cycle of rebirth). Generally put however, the desire for solitude is not common among traditional Indians. Quite to the contrary, wanting to be alone is an attitude stigmatised as being anti-social. More critically, I would argue, the ideal of solitude is a crucial part of the bourgeois public sphere, underlining a different notion of personhood, where the individual requires 'rest' from socialising in order to be 'fit for work and leisure'. Further, it represents a longing for withdrawal from what is perceived as aggressive, distracting and even criminal (see Caldeira 2005). This is evident in the Parsvnath advertisement that promotes an enclave temple for stressed-out urban souls.

There is certainly nothing wrong in wanting solitude, in particular in a city like Delhi and in the context of ubiquitous social control enforced upon individuals. However, these kinds of advertisements enforce a class discourse rather than a critical reflection of urban planning and social change: being away from the crowds is a statement about luxury and status. Thus, what we can see here is that with those new residential areas a new desire for a modern identity is promoted, one that appreciates silence and solitude as qualities of a 'better' lifestyle. The desire to distance oneself from the city, to be at ease, away from the chaos of the streets, markets and shops, is one that is recreated in the advertisements and by the media in general. Thus, reads the Victoria Gardens advertisement (Plate 3.3): 'In a city full of concrete, a living garden resort to live and breathe. In Delhi … One step into this living garden resort and you'll forget the blues of concrete city life.'

The image of the meditating businessman or the mother walking her child along a lakeside certainly reflects the lack of such spaces in urban India and the precious privilege to have access to them. Artificial worlds seem to be the only place where hassle-free movement is possible. This urban experience of quasi-claustrophobia is also mirrored in the remarks of an informant from the aspiring middle class working in the service sector who maintains that private space is a problem in the city of Delhi and that 'the general attitude of the city is one of intrusion' (October 2006). Public parks in Delhi are never quite hassle-free, full of flâneurs and voyeurs of

Plate 3.3: Solitude away from the chaotic city. Advertisement for Victoria Gardens, Negolice India: 'All your five senses will be enamoured and you will experience a lifestyle that is beyond belief, in the heart of Delhi' (2006).

Source: Hindustan Times, Delhi.

all kinds. Public places such as Café Coffee Day or Barista are there, but to sit and chat there is an expensive undertaking for people belonging to the aspiring middle classes. Many families I know could only go to places like *Dilli Haat* — an open-air market in South Delhi with stalls offering regional cuisines on hot and humid summer evenings; others would go to religio-spiritual sites that have increasingly started to incorporate large open spaces, such as the ACC across the Yamuna. There is hardly any other open-air place that is available in the evenings where children can run around freely and adults can sit down with drinks and snacks without having to pay a fortune. Thus, it is not so much the fact that lower middle class and poor people do not enjoy investing in their home, or like to go out for an evening stroll, or even seek peace, away from the crowds. It is the lack of such free spaces.

Club Class

Such a 'privatopia' (McKenzie 2006: 9), secluded from the everyday garb of the public, is also promised to the potential buyers of a gated township called Vatika City in Gurgaon:

> For some a Home is more than just an address. It's a statement … Live the way the world's jet-set prefers … [apartments] nestled amidst contemporary townscape architecture and located within the lush settings of Vatika City. Artistically designed for the discerning few, the limited edition apartments speak of opulence and extravagance … Fully air-conditioned. Hermetically sealed, sound proof environs [sic!] … State-of-the-art security.[1]

It is a strange combination of desires of the 'world's jet-set' and the 'discerning few', showing how closely tied totalitarian security and individual freedom, spatial exclusion and inclusion, the longing for prestige and respectability and social anxieties can be. The outside world is 'switched off', life only happens behind well-guarded walls and under video-surveillance.

The idea that new worlds can be built from scratch is hollow if not filled with 'life'. In fact along with solitude we see new forms of socialising emerge, in particular, 'clubbing', emphasising the growing importance attributed to peer groups and friendship. The residential housing townships and their clubs are promoted as if they were an extended family. Indeed, this is a form of conviviality through which kinship, caste and region are rendered marginal. Instead, new networks move centre stage. My informant Neetu K., for instance, spends a lot of leisure time with business colleagues, some of who were formerly his schoolmates; others came to be his friends during work, or the golf club. Indeed, it remains to be seen whether new forms of socialising are generated under the new conditions of urbanisation and globalisation. One of the largest real estate developers in north India, DLF, presents itself as:

> Building the New India. Homes for India where neighbors become friends. Offices for India where work becomes a pleasure. Recreational places for India to keep minds and bodies healthy. Shopping malls for India to indulge in its favorite brands, food and entertainment (see Plate 1.4).[2]

---

[1] See http://www.vatikagroup.com/Residential/VatikaCityGurgaon/home.html (accessed 15 September 2008).

[2] DLF Advertisement, First City, October 2006: 37.

The world and all that one desires in a nutshell — this is what the housing developer promises, and this is, possibly, what the new middle classes with their ambitious work ethic and world-class taste aspire to: a village without a 'real' village's social control, hierarchy, and alleged boredom and provincialism.

In her ethnography of gated communities in the USA, anthropologist Setha Low argues that these new residential 'ways of life' mirror a 'new version of the middle-class American dream precisely because it temporarily suppresses and masks, even denies and fuses, the inherent anxieties and conflicting social values of modern urban and suburban life', as if other societal alternatives were not available (2004: 11). She also proposes that globalisation and economic liberalisation have led to a breakdown of both social family and kinship structures, as well as to a decline of credibility of the state and governance. Low considers this 'breakdown in local control' as a source of threat to many people who prefer to live in a gated community because it seems emotionally warm and physically safe. Yet she argues that '[t]he creation of gated communities … is an integral part of the building of the fortress city, a social control technique based on the so-called militarization of the city', a 'new form of social ordering that conceals, displaces, and regulates people or activities' (ibid.: 17).[3]

I disagree with Low as regards her claim that social structures are 'breaking down'. In the case of urban India, studies have shown that social structures and networks are only transformed, adapted to new work conditions and lifestyle aspirations. Thus, as Patricia Uberoi argues, it may look as if the joint family falls apart in the context of modernisation. Instead, it distributes its various generational and marital branches into smaller households (see Uberoi 2004).

Fortress Delhi

Low's observation about the creation of gated communities as a new social control technique, based on fears of disorder and security threats, can be applied to the agenda of new gated communities only to some extent in a city like New Delhi. The language of real estate advertising is very much in tune with the polarisation of the inside and outside, the safe and unsafe, the orderly and disorderly. In fact, there is a growing concern among upper

---

[3] On the militarisation of urban space, see also Davis (1992a). Oldenburg's study (1984) of colonial Lucknow explores urban planning and surveillance in the light of morally imbued 'conditions' that shape colonial expectations and argues that the colonial city had to be safe, orderly, clean, loyal and pay to get support.

middle class families as to whether they can still trust their maids and other household servants. Moral panic evolves (and is often fired by English-language media) for instance, around the kidnapping of a baby from a middle-class family by the maid from Bihar (one of the poorest states in India), or cases of murder of a citizen by his or her servant because the door of the bedroom was left unlocked (see Dickey 2000). There is also growing fear as to how unsafe Delhi's streets are, particularly at night, especially since members of the middle classes have fallen victim to burglary, kidnapping and even gang rape. However, compared to cities in Latin America, for instance, streets in Indian cities are still far from being the stage for criminal outbursts. In my view, both residential as well as commercial townships do not only encourage the creation of an enclaved gaze but also generate a gaze of surveillance. By this I mean a spatial structure that reflects the desire for control, surveillance and transparency in order to be able to spot 'outsiders' or 'intruders'. But there is also a panoptic gaze enforced on the inhabitants of gated communities. In what way? It is by establishing rules according to which the residential community has to live (e.g., no games on the lawns, silence during noons and evenings, no potted plants in the balconies), and the presence of watchmen, cameras, security control, etc. a gaze of self-control is only forced upon and internalised by the tenants.

Recently, 'smart' homes have come to be promoted by companies in India, and Closed Circuit Television (CCTV) surveillance is being increasingly employed in private and semi-private spaces such as condominiums or religious leisure sites such as the Akshardham Cultural Complex. Luxury townships highlight their elaborate security systems. Why is the issue of safety and security so central when it comes to promoting new residential townships and initiatives? Siebel and Wehrheim underline that the felt presence of security systems is part of a rhetoric and aesthetic of self-legitimisation, and increases the distinction between 'haves' and 'have-nots', between the 'deserving few' and the 'undeserving many',

> to the extent that security as a public good becomes a privately acquirable (and desirable) commodity, security becomes another element of social equity. Cities appear to be fragmenting more and more into places for social groups that have access to security and places for social groups who cannot afford this commodity and who are defined as a risk for others.[4]

---

[4] '"Security" is one of the biggest growth markets in the world. In addition, mixed forms are emerging in the form of public private partnerships in which cooperation between formal and informal controls are organised in a wide variety of security partnerships (neighbourhood watch)' (Siebel and Wehrheim 2006: 29).

From this, they conclude that 'this calls into question another fundamental precondition of public space: its general accessibility' to everyone (Siebel and Wehrheim 2006: 35). As a consequence of the felt insecurity (often deriving from news reports on television and weekly magazines), the desire for enclosed communities which can afford and legitimise restricted access grows. Since the late 1980s, in Delhi and other megacities there has been a growing trend of installing gates in residential neighbourhoods of the wealthy, and the numbers are still rising. At night, the numbers of gates within a neighbourhood are populated by security guards who write down the number plate of each and every car or vehicle that enters and leaves the colony (see Falzon 2005). Even the number of personal security guards recruited for individual houses has risen drastically. However, Siebel and Wehrheim hold that the 'thesis of the decline of publicness is one of a series of decline myths about the big city' (2006: 36). In the case of Delhi, one could argue that one reason behind creating gated neighbourhoods, such as Defence Colony or Greater Kailash II, is simply based on the desire to restrict traffic flow. The other reason is linked to status: if one belongs to a certain class, a watchman is necessary. In fact, a lot of middle-class anxiety revolves around the vulnerability of the safety of the daughters as they move in and through public space.

With the example of the 'smart home' as well as in many instances of visiting condominiums or malls, I am reminded of Michel Foucault's interpretation of Bentham's panopticon, the model of a prison-tower that allows the watchman to put each and every prisoner under surveillance, and brings the prisoner to internalise the watchman's gaze by means of self-control. Foucault (1977) understands the panopticon as an allegory of modernity reinforced through total discipline and complete surveillance, fostering the emergence of the disciplinary society. Based on the concept of panopticism as a means of creating power and control, the panoptic gaze also leads to an internalisation of specific 'codes' assumed to be given and relevant in order to live in a 'functioning' society. The panoptic gaze is, thus, one of internalised self-control and self-discipline on the basis of the external eye of social and moral control. The panoptic gaze and the enclave gaze overlap to the extent that both relate to the fact that there are safe havens from which the outside world can be rendered visible on the one hand and distanced behind walls on the other. In my view, the modern gated community, with its rules of self-regulation and techniques of surveillance, is such a panopticon.

According to Mike Davis, the panopticon design is particularly suitable to create and segregate what gated communities define as *pariah* groups (1992b: 226; see also Narayanan 2006). To anthropologist Teresa Caldeira, writing on different notions of crime that unfold in Sao Paulo's gated communities of middle and upper classes, these 'artificial' communities display a longing for independence and freedom 'both from the city and its mixture of classes' (2005: 328–29). Arguing that the patterns of distribution of social groups, activities and goods in the city are still distributed along the lines of segregation, she further writes that since the 1990s, 'a new aesthetic of security shapes all types of constructions and imposes its new logic of surveillance and distance as a means for displaying status, and it is changing the character of public life and public interactions' that largely prevailed in the 1970s (Caldeira 2000: 231). For Caldeira, condominiums are not just private worlds for the elite but 'fortified enclaves' that turn inwards and reject any form of interaction with the outside world that lies behind the high walls and entrances with security guards. Several advertisements explored for this study highlight the fact that stepping out of these islands of splendid isolation is not required, for 'life' is within the fenced boundaries. Thus, the enclaved gaze underlining the images discussed so far is also imbued with a longing based on anxiety, or fear, of being disturbed, threatened, if not swallowed up, by a disorderly, uncontrollable public. Through the lens of the enclaved gaze of the 'global nomad', integration into the global community seems of more relevance and is perceived as more familiar and 'natural' than the local worlds of the bazaar or the *gali* (narrow alleyway through a neighbourhood) outside. I would even argue that the desire to spatially separate from the alleged chaos and dirt outside is also related to the fact that neither Indian upper middle classes nor returning Indians overseas want to acknowledge that India is not 100 per cent 'world-class', and that there are 'dirty' spots that prevent the country from joining the 'First World'. If they do recognise the poverty, the reaction is often that it is not 'their fault' and not 'their responsibility' to challenge this condition.

Gated Cities, Glocal Cities

Why are gated communities successful models of housing?[5] How do they differ, what history do they have — global and local? To whom

---

[5] For a further analysis of the types of Indian gated communities, it may be helpful to draw upon Blakely and Snyder's categorisation of gated communities in the USA: (1) lifestyle community — security and separation for leisure activities and amenities for retirement (2) prestige community — the fastest growing residential form in the USA, creating and protecting one's place on the social ladder, and (3) security zone community — protecting tenants from alleged criminality (1997: 39, 42).

do they appeal, and why? Across the world, and in growing numbers, condominiums or enclosed townships are privately managed. They mirror the privatisation of public space and the desire of emerging middle and upper classes to develop and live distinct lifestyles in secure seclusion. As Glasze, Webster and Frantz propose, they 'result from and cater to an internationally mobile global elite labor force' (2006: 3), a social group that responds to an 'increase in social, ethnic, income and lifestyle heterogeneity within cities with an attendant rise in fear of "others"' (ibid.: 4). Gated communities are not a product of economic liberalisation but have a much longer history. Traditional gated communities in India may have been shaped for various reasons: memberships in caste, region, or religion were probably the most prominent ones. These ties were often upheld despite industrialisation and increasing flow of work-migration into large cities, when many traditional ties and loyalties were loosened in favour of new ones. Yet, studies on urban growth and spatialisation in northern India have found that by no means does this point towards an affirmation of the common cliché of the city reduced to crude forms of anonymity and interest groups. Neighbourhood groups, often with well-maintained and controlled links to the village or rural regions, shape the face of a modern city. Gated communities like 'Rosedale' in Kolkata or 'Windsor Park' in Indirapuram, may be global in nature, because they address a 'global audience' of the 'deserved few'. But they are simultaneously firmly rooted in local contexts. Even though the recent growth and popularity of gated communities is a worldwide phenomenon that surfaces, in particular, in the rising urban centres of the global south, gated communities have very cultural-specific histories and spatial segregation is an on-going practice. Some enclaves have their roots in relatively homogeneous neighbourhoods that recruit their members along the lines of ethnic, ritual and religious relations, for instance, the mohalla, a north Indian form of housing where clusters of houses, often with spatial segregations, were enforced along the lines of specific caste-like or caste-based groups. Masselos argues that mohallas were to maintain occupational, social and religious cohesion, and thus regulated access to and identity of the mohalla even in industrialised cities like Bombay (2007: 18–22). Like the mohallas of Bombay or Kanpur, the pols of Ahmedabad are neighbourhoods tying the individual to the city through regimes of social control and regulation. Industrial growth has not disrupted this fairly traditional form of living, whether organised by caste or religious group. The pols maintain stability by organising social activities, availing occupational security and regulating participation in ritual affairs and tax matters. Membership to a pol contributes much to a person's social status and identity, and exemption from a *pol* community might have drastic consequences in terms of isolation (Doshi 1974). Depending almost exclusively on the free market, however, I wonder how the new gated communities of the global city establish their regulating mechanisms, if not by means of class and financial capital. Once tenants move into a condominium, residents' welfare associations seek to ensure the constitution of social cohesion (see n. 5 of this chapter).

Furthermore, Indian cities have gone through spatial segregation in the context of colonial town planning, where 'white town' and 'black town' would also be signifiers of colonial power politics based on concepts of race (see Kosambi 1993; Masselos 2007; Oldenburg 1984; Patel and Deb 2006). Housing colonies for state administrators were built right after the birth of independent India, as Pavan Varma remembers in his description of childhood days in Delhi at the beginning of this chapter. An administrative city like Delhi is also one of such gated communities that emerged after Independence through employment positions of its members within the governmental sector. Particular neighbourhoods were thus often populated by high-ranking officials or bureaucrats of lower rank.

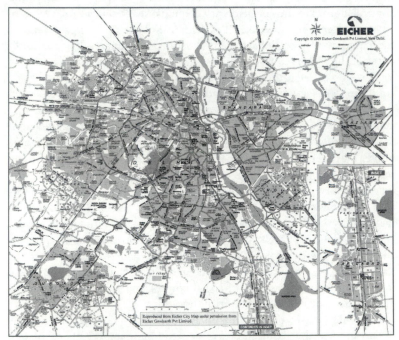

Plate 3.4: Map of Delhi and suburbs (2009).

Source: © EICHER. Used with permission.

Most of South Delhi was structured that way after Independence. But the new gated communities that emerge with economic liberalisation since the turn of the last millennium show that it is predominantly class and money that matter first and foremost. It remains to be seen and studied as to what lifespan and dynamics these completely new structures have, who moves in, when, why, is for how long, and in what way — if at all — identification with, social cohesion, and 'belonging' to the site and its other inhabitants, is shaped.

Partly because of lack of space in a city like New Delhi, most new town-scapes emerge at the fringes, often in clusters of townships, and across the border spilling into neighbouring states such as Haryana and Uttar Pradesh (Plate 3.4). These neighbouring states seek to attract investors with special tax benefits and highlight their infrastructural visions and competence.

As we search more recent sources of today's gated communities, we are first of all led to the powerful diffusion of the American enclave model (Glasze et al. 2006: 2) and to late-nineteenth-century European concepts of town planning, including 'suburbia' and 'Garden City'. In these models, 'zoning and city planning were designed, in part, to preserve the position of the privileged' and to 'privatize community space ... civic responsibilities' (Blakely and Snyder 1997: 8). Garden cities, maintains Sorkin, are also re-flections of a desire for complete surveillance and Cartesian order (1992a: 213). Gated communities and their cousins — integrated townships — are conceptualised as holistic and self-contained lifestyle communities where work, home and play can be fused.

Gated communities render visions of ideal security and community visible. In the 1970s, such communities in the USA were built for retirement, country clubs and resorts, for instance, Leisure World in California (see Low 2004); the 1980s saw gated communities built around golf courses (Blakely and Snyder 1997: 4). In the early 1980s, they became a key residential element in the USA:

> Millions of Americans have chosen to live in walled and fenced communal residential space that was previously integrated with the larger shared civic space ... Many feel vulnerable, unsure of their place and stability of their neigh-bourhoods in the face of rapid change (ibid.: 1).

Gates are a common item of upper middle class and higher-end segments of the American society today. 'The new fortress developments ... are also a search for socio-spatial community — the ideal community ... [in which] all resources ... would be open and shared by all the citizens of a locality' (ibid.: 2, see also Low 2004). The idea of a gated community as a moral cosmopolitan community is confirmed in real estate advertisements and conversations with tenants in condominiums in India. The new middle classes' idea of a moral community does not necessarily include a feeling of responsibility for those who have no 'membership':

> Gated communities manifest a number of tensions: between exclusionary aspirations rooted in fear and protection of privilege and the values of civic responsibility; between the trend toward privatization of public services and the ideals of the public good and general welfare; and between the need for personal and community control of the environment and the dangers of making outsiders of fellow citizens (Blakely and Snyder 1997: 3).

So, it all depends on constantly evaluating advantages and disadvantages of private versus public interest, it seems. But not all socio-spatial segregation went along the same track as the gated communities in the USA. Socialist models in the Soviet Union, where living was strictly regulated and controlled, sought to create societies with no claim to individuality and particular status. Geographers Lentz and Lindner observe that the previously controlled space of a city like Moscow became available to the urban public only for a short time after the fall of the Soviet Empire, falling victim to the new regulations and rules of the privatised real estate market shortly thereafter (2003: 50). Until the fall of the Soviet regime, the formation of a public was — seemingly paradoxically — only possible in the domain of the (semi-)private. It could be neither state-based nor bourgeois. This is what Lentz and Lindner termed 'private publicity' (versus 'official-publicity') (ibid.: 51–52). Yet, the state reached even into the intimate domain of the private space; everyday life of the 'citizens' became the property of the state. Like Hardt, Lentz and Lindner pinpoint a spatial and social withdrawal of both the state and the civil society, concretely, from the public sphere in the Putin era, and strengthen the call for a 'stronger hand' of state authority and the image of a legally dominated public.

Let me conclude this chapter with an ethnographic example that sums up some of the points discussed earlier. I have mentioned that the city has often been associated with the strange and the unfamiliar against which the village community emerged as the familiar and known (see Keith 2005: 15–16). The popularity of condominiums, club culture and residents' welfare associations has to be seen in this light. They are parts of a strategy that responds to the desire for warmth and the protection in a somewhat alienated world and surrounding. In many interviews with tenants at new condominiums in Delhi's suburbs, I was told stories of an otherwise rare, or lost, communal warmth and security that painted the private enclave in the context of a safety zone or a protective family. In a personal conversation, reiki master Aneeta C., for instance, described how informal and warm, life in the enclave of Beverly Park at Gurgaon was, despite the fact that out of the 160 apartments, only 50 per cent were permanently occupied; the other half was temporarily rented or used by the owners themselves. The primary criterion for selection into the gated community is, first of all, money. However, in conversation, real estate agents claim that they look at customers with great care and choose only those who 'fit in' according to class membership, sometimes even birthplace. Caste and religion, however, do not seem to be openly declared categories according to which the real estate market functions.

Aneeta and her husband Atul travel abroad and within India for at least a third of the year, conducting feng shui and reiki workshops or visiting one of their siblings who is married and lives in London. Likewise, Aneeta explains that many other tenants at the site predominantly still lived abroad and visited India in the pleasant winter months, most of them wanting to return after retirement. To be sure, this is one of the key reasons for the existence of gated communities in the USA. However, in India this phenomenon also points towards the growing tendency among older family members to live alone. Their children either live abroad or have a fluctuating lifestyle or prefer to live on their own, yet possibly close to the parents.

Each and every tenant of Beverly Park, Aneeta insists, is 'one of their kind', maybe not so much in terms of place of birth and caste or religion, but in terms of their belonging to the same class of 'educated' and 'cultured' people. There are monthly meetings with the gardening group, another group has formed around the theme of spirituality, of which she is an organising member. Each month, she told me, they invite outsiders for lectures, for instance, from the transnational spiritual organisation Art of Living (AOL).[6] Holi and Diwali are jointly celebrated in the condominium's court.

Aneeta emphasises, time and again, how comfortable life in Beverly Park and proudly shows me around the pool and fitness centre, the beauty

---

[6] The AOL was founded in 1981 and is headed by spiritual leader Sri Sri Ravi Shankar. It calls itself a non-religious organisation, catering towards the needs of individual development and happiness, by means of relief work, research (e.g., Ayurveda) and meditation techniques. AOL is transnationally organised and has Indian and non-Indian followers. See www.artofliving.org (accessed 9 December 2009).

parlour and hairdresser, a desperate chèf waiting for customers, the bio-waste site, the clubhouse and the lecture hall. Like all condominiums, this one too claims to provide 24-hours water supply, electricity backup and two-tier security control (guards, video cameras, reception). Both water and electricity are considered to be luxurious resources elsewhere in Delhi, a city where even some posh South Delhi neighbourhoods receive water for only a few hours per day. Everything one desires in an anonymous megacity like Delhi seems to be right here: privacy, solidarity, exchange and neighbourly concern. When I met Aneeta at her flat in 2005, she had just returned from visiting a neighbour who had been released from hospital. She had given him healing (through reiki). In our conversation, she observes how wonderful it is that one could be there for each other. 'It's a great community here!' she declares enthusiastically, 'they [at Beverly Park] make you feel at home, even with simple things like all-round electricity and water!'[7] Before coming here, the couple lived in a farm house at Sainik Farm, for almost 10 years, and before that in Greater Kailash I, a wealthy neighbourhood in South Delhi. But she desperately wanted a garden. Now she has to give up her dream because the Residents' Welfare Association, of which her garden group is a part, advises against having potted plants in the balcony for safety reasons. This is so because potted plants on balconies in high-storeyed apartments could fall and injure someone. Aneeta explains that after having moved to Sainik Farm, they found that her husband's business was declining. For that reason, they bought the flat in Gurgaon, now worth at least double of what they had paid then, and feng shui-'approved'. Like members of other gated communities, they participate in the monthly gatherings of the Residents' Welfare Association, visit the clubhouse for social events and talk in a way about the community of tenants as if it was an intimate relationship of deep trust and concern that connects them all.

Several aspects of contemporary gated communities are reflected in Aneeta's comments. The Arcadian community is constantly evoked in the rhetoric of real estate development. Low argues in her study of US-American gated communities: 'gated community residents infuse their desire to recapture physical elements of their childhood landscapes ... but this desire is entangled with an unconscious longing for security they identify with living behind gates and walls' (2004: 77). Advertisements promote

---

[7] The topic of the luxury condominium as a functioning and caring, family-like community finds reflection in the film *Delhi Heights* (directed by Anand Kumar, 2007).

child-friendly zones and playgrounds, something that is certainly difficult to find in the 'city outside'. However, in several conversations with tenants of condominiums as well as real estate developers it became evident that these zones were often much smaller than suggested and strictly controlled by laws of order and noise prevention: 'We have two hours per day, between 1 p.m. and 3 p.m., where no cars must drive into the driveway and children must not play ball. Thus, there is such blissful silence and peace!', maintains Aneeta. Quite possibly, this desire for silence is shared by many of the retired inhabitants of the gated community at Beverly Park of which quite a few are retired officers and admirals, and their wives.

This brings us back to my previous definition of the 'first class' citizens in which the notion of an affluent moral community of citizens is juxtaposed with that of the 'population'. Residents' Welfare Associations (RWA) are such moral communities that shape new forms of neighbourhood locality, inclusion of members of their class and exclusion of 'non-citizens'. They work on the 'beautification' and care for the safety of their neighbourhood. Partha Chatterjee holds that:

> [i]n metro after Indian metro, organized civic groups have come forward to demand from the administration and the judiciary that laws and regulations for the proper use of land, public spaces, and thoroughfares be formulated and strictly adhered to, in order to improve the quality of life of citizens. Everywhere the dominant cry seems to be to rid the city of encroachers and polluters and, as it were, to give the city back to its proper citizens (2003: 178).

Batra and Mehra (2006a) have observed a similar radicalisation of bourgeois organisations that aspire to create enclave-like fortresses and conceive of slum-dwellers as encroachers and polluters of land who block the beautification and gentrification of a neighbourhood and even the whole city. They also argue that in the context of neo-liberalisation, the new middle classes have become increasingly reluctant to object to violent slum demolitions by bulldozers and police forces (see Batra and Mehra 2006b). 'Populations' only have a right to claim such participation if they behave like citizens, an almost paradoxical request.

taming the public city and other colonial hangovers

iscussing the relevance of notions like the 'public' and 'private' in India, Partha Chatterjee (1993) has convincingly argued that the private–public dichotomy was shaped during the colonial era by reproducing gendered notions of private and public space ('private' as female, preserving and stabilising culture and tradition, 'backstage'; 'public' as the political domain in which men could actively position themselves, 'frontstage' — the public as a domain theoretically open to all), with a bourgeoisie that cherished ideas of the intimacy of home, the family, and even the idea of the nation as an extended family. Yet, the transfer of the European type of the public and the private (which was in itself remarkably heterogeneous) to the Indian context did not take place directly, but was in fact constantly contested and altered. The colonial city, as several studies have shown, was based, quite like its European cousins, on spatial segregation. It worked along the axis of attributing or withholding rights from particular groups. As opposed to the working class versus the elite tension, the Indian case was complicated through skin colour, religion and caste. Particular narratives implying social anxieties (for example, moral and civic decline) and desires (such as the rise of an underdeveloped city to the status of a world or global city) are tied to the imaginary of the city itself and undergo change over time. In fact, the central question is: how rise and decline, gains and losses are defined and legitimised, and by whom. To a great extent, the discourse evolves around notions of threat and security, order and hygiene, the public and the private.

The global city is not so different from the colonial city in terms of its complex network with other global cities, shaping and contesting each other's progress as 'command centres' (Sassen 2001b). The old imperial maps still influence the circuits of globalised culture and capital, impacting what Dawson and Edwards term 'new imperialism of economic global-ization' (2005: 3). Some aspects of urban planning in India today can be traced back to the colonial origins of modern town planning, and several reasons for the 'neocolonial hangover' will be addressed in the following discussions, underlining Sassen's thesis of the need to explore the localisation of global cities.

India's urban visions parallel others worldwide. At the same time they are imbued with the experience of colonialism, socialist government planning, bureaucracy as well as American town planning (Menon 1997: 2932). 'Handbooks' of colonial town planning still enforce today's urban planning. Architect and urban planner Krishna Menon argues that the colonial past still continues to linger in the ways in which the modern Indian city is imagined despite the fact that the awareness of the inadequacy of western models in another cultural-specific context is on the rise too. The ways in which Indian cities are imagined by town planners today, argues Menon, is against the indigenous needs and habits of urban living, and 'derived from British town planning experience in the belief that they are universal and modern', progressive and rational (ibid.). The models of the Garden City and the City Beautiful served as a backdrop to country-house architect Edwin Lutyens' plan of the imperial city of New Delhi. The Garden City, developed around 1900 in England, the heart of the British Empire, emerged at a time when the grim urban plight and the understanding that the urban poor were a moral and health threat in industrialised and booming cities of the kingdom led to the development of the idea of an 'oasis' as a refuge and a safe haven. It was understood to be a holistic entity, a counter-strategy against the uncontrolled, dirty city centre. Polarised in such a way, beautification in capitalist Europe went hand-in-hand with slum eviction, where the squatter settlements were forced to make space for the gentrification of a sanitised bourgeois public sphere, quite like the slum evictions in Delhi in the new millennium.[1] However, one of the most drastic examples of the implementation of foreign concepts of urban planning in Delhi is the Master Plan, established with the help of the US-American Ford Foundation in 1962, through which a model city is envisaged that both creates and controls its subject citizens, mapping them onto strictly drawn zones.[2] In fact, the Master Plan ignored

---

[1] In the year 2005, for instance, 385,000 people were rendered homeless in two months as 83,000 slums were demolished (Koppikar 2005). In this process, approximately 150 acres of land were 'set free' for real estate development, with one acre selling at about INR 10.5 crore (Bhupta 2005b). The ironical facet of slum demolition, however, is that slum-dwellers, who constitute 60 per cent of Mumbai's population, occupy only 6 per cent of the city's land (Sharma 2005: 16).

[2] In the 1960s, the state became concerned about the control over urban growth. Helped by Ford Foundation experts, it developed the concept of a Master Plan

the dynamics of urban living, and the proposed growth of the city sidelined the practicalities of mixed land use (residential, commercial, manufacturing, etc.). In other words, it did not work as a 'tool to serve the needs of a diverse and dynamic society' (Menon 2006). Post-independence Delhi emerged on the foundations of medieval Old Delhi and the colonial city. Particularly, in the first two decades after Partition, with massive migration flows and the attempt to establish the capital of a young country, tensions between the planned and the unplanned city surfaced.[3]

The fractured vision of the planned and the unplanned city haunt the idea and realities of New Delhi today. Sudipta Kaviraj elucidates how the colonial regime imagined the city as civilised, clean and orderly, and how this vision generated the perception of the public sphere as a space of representation through which the public could be constituted and disciplined (see also Khilnani 1997: 124). 'Public space' in the colonial era did not invite all people alike. Instead, access was restricted and granted only at special occasions such as parades and royal visits or to Indian employees of the British Raj.

The performative stages of today's elites might well constitute a similar element of representation, restricting access to allegedly 'public sites' of conspicuous consumption in places such as malls and theme parks. As today, the colonial city too was filled with ambiguities that move between desire and disgust. Partly this is based on a paradigm of tradition versus modernity, projected upon the alleged rural–urban divide. The history of ambivalence in relation to urbanisation is not new and surfaces as part of social spatialisation on a global scale.[4] For Benjamin, writing on Paris in the nineteenth century, the urban 'temples of the bourgeoisie' were indicators of megalomaniac phantasmagorias 'rendered in stone' (1999: 24) and

---

(see Mann 2006; Singh 2007). DDA became the implementing agency: 'On the pattern of modern European cities', writes Lalit Batra, 'separate areas were allocated to be used for housing (43 per cent), movement (22 per cent), industry (5 per cent) and green belt area (22 per cent) (2005: 24). Each plan is meant to provide solutions for 20 years.

[3] Baviskar notes that 'the building of planned Delhi was mirrored in the simultaneous mushrooming of unplanned Delhi' (2003: 91). This dialectic rendered some space for negotiating legal and illegal initiatives — 'jurisdictional twilight zones' (ibid.: 93, see also Batra and Mehra 2006a, 2006b).

[4] Walter Benjamin writes about Paris in the second half of the nineteenth century that it was based on an imperialist form of investment capital, when 'speculation was at its height', with Georges-Eugène Baron Haussmann during Napoleon's reign. Haussmann's aim was urbanisation according to a master plan that affected the

yet, he proposes that 'the world dominated by its phantasmagorias ... is "modernity"' (Benjamin 1999: 26). Almost at the same time as the demo-litions of neighbourhoods in Paris took place, settlements in old parts of Delhi, the so-called 'Black Town' were erased. Much of this followed the dramatic challenge of British rule by Indians in the 1857 'Mutiny'. The main axis of spatial segregation divided the new colonial city from the old part of Delhi: 'the colonial state demolished large parts of Shahjahanabad, laying down railway tracks that tore through its heart' (Baviskar 2003: 90). For Sunil Khilnani, the colonial city functioned like Paris, a stage on which the spectacles of power could be played out through a display of British sovereignty and rule, where the colonial subjects could be disciplined (1997: 118).[5]

Both in India and Europe we can witness the desire of colonial and other elites to be in control by disciplining public and private space and everyday life conducts. They engaged in what Kaviraj describes as a civilising process of relentless surveillance, policing, restricting and imposing (1997: 85). The idea that the public is in fact accessible to all alike is primarily a European notion, highly idealised and conflicting in colonies and other non-western domains. Though there were rules and obligations in traditional Indian society, they were predominantly based on particular sects, caste rules or religious laws. Even institutions like the panchayat were local and did not consider developing an imagined community of citizens that would share a consensus about public welfare, or rendering the question of birth marginal. A lot of social and educational charity unravelled in the religious sphere; again, not a homogenous but a complex patchwork of heterogeneous 'publics', with particular rituals and regulations (ibid.: 89):

> What is precisely missing in these traditional Indian contexts is the notion of a universality of access, the idea that an activity is open to all, irrespective of their social attributes (ibid.: 90).

---

whole city: 'Haussmann's expropriations g[a]ve rise to speculation that border[ed] on fraud' in which a 'hatred of the rootless urban population' surfaced (Benjamin 1999: 23). Even though securing the city against the barricades of the proletariat was crucial, the aesthetic appeal of the perspectival gaze was equally central: 'This ideal corresponds to the tendency ... to ennoble technological necessities through spurious artistic ends. The temples of the bourgeoisie's spiritual and secular power were to find their apotheosis within the framework of these long streets' (ibid.: 24).

[5] On the city as theatre, see Hannerz (1980: Chapter 6).

Instead, Indian society is 'governed by the logic of segregation' (Kaviraj 1997). I hold this to be a crucial observation as regards urban development and the enclave gaze in India today, enabling the smooth transformation to the 'caste' system of condominiums and club culture. Parks are possibly the only public space in postcolonial India, as they are open to cricket matches, demonstrations, lovers on their romantic walks and family picnics. In fact, the idea that middle classes would leave their house for a leisure trip is relatively new. This is interesting especially because members of the new middle classes, in particular, Brahmins, consider the space outside their house as (ritually) insignificant, one for which they do not have any responsibility. As opposed to domestic privacy and purity, civic space as well as natural space did not really matter, until, as I argue, leisure as a form of conspicuous lifestyle came to be highly valued and linked to public spaces as arenas of the display and experience of this lifestyle. Now, the public space became a domain contested by many, and in particular for members of the affluent middle classes as a mark of lifestyle-space and stage.[6]

Staging Themed Histories and Traditions

In this section I explore the ways in which the idea of theming lifestyle and space in real estate advertising plays a leading role in terms of creating notions of 'world-class' by means of referring to history as cultural heritage. History and heritage are appropriated to celebrate the confidence of the 'new maharajas' and help them stage their alleged cosmopolitan knowledge. Cultural heritage and history, in fact, give a new face to global cultural capitalism.

In *Whose Culture? Whose City*, Sharon Zukin argues that culture is a 'means of controlling cities. As a source of images and memories, it symbolizes "who belongs" in specific places' (2005: 286). In my opinion, cosmopolitanism emerges as one of the key themes of identification. Local heritage and its preservation as well as historical knowledge as part of the desired symbolic capital, is another. The city's symbolic economy occupies centre stage — in particular 'its visible ability to produce both symbols and space' (ibid.). The enclave world must offer 'the basics' of a world-class lifestyle: a beauty parlour, supermarket, fitness centre, club house, even a hospital. It is a world *en miniature* (Benjamin 1999: 17), a place in which the pleasure of conspicuous consumption is both heightened as a spectacle and naturalised as

---

[6] This also applies to the new leisure activities of trekking, wild-water rafting or biking — all of which are new to the middle classes, who were previously not too attuned to the idea that nature could be viewed as a space of value and leisure.

4

a 'right' of the middle classes. But beyond offering these, the enclave world must also arouse desires, attract attention and entertain the audience by means of a theme or a mega-narrative. Overlooking, as opposed to reliving, India's stigma as a 'developing country', many of the enclave narratives are intertwined with a nostalgic projection of a 'Golden Age' of 'Indianness' and the longing to revitalise this glory through national pride, festive pomp and religious traditions. The display of wealth and self-esteem requires care and competence. 'History' and 'heritage' add depth to national pride and cosmopolitanism. Moreover, knowing one's own and the world's history certifies a person as 'cultured', prestigious and 'with taste'.

It is by no means just Indian history to which references are made. In the historical parade of real estate theming, the new maharajas transform into new pharaohs, new Caesars, and so forth. Omaxe, one of the big real estate developers in India, appropriates and reinterprets ancient Egypt for one of its latest apartment townships, 'Luxor' in Gurgaon (building 400 apartments in nine towers). The advertisement heralds it as follows:

> World's greatest civilization now comes alive in Gurgaon. Luxor Apartments and Penthouses … The place where Egyptian grandeur mingles with ultra-modern lifestyle … Do call us to know more. We promise it will take you into a different world altogether (see Plate 4.1).

In the nine towers that accommodate 400 apartments, one can find Egyptian architecture, hieroglyphs on walls, coloured sand-stone, Egyptian paintings on the wall, and Luxor-inspired domes (Karir 2005). Indeed, Dubai does not seem to be too distant from this spatial choreography. Could it be that these condominiums are the new pyramids of the modern world? Another Omaxe residential project at Gurgaon represents 'The Nile':

> Nile provides the perfect combination of modern amenities and a serene setting far away from the maddening crowds of the city, making a perfect landscape for a place you'd like to call home. Nile's namesake has been called the world's greatest ancient civilization. Every nook and corner of Nile tells stories of ancient Egypt's glorious history. The mighty river Nile cradles historical cities like Cairo and Luxor. A sprinkle of Egyptian architecture amidst lots of open space and sunlight futuristic planning makes it a modern day landmark. Its palaces, monuments, temples and tombs speak accolades of Egypt's grandeur and glory, leaving its visitors awe struck. Just like what Omaxe's Nile seeks to do … you have a home even the pharaohs of Nile would be proud of![7]

---

[7] See http://www.omaxe.com/main.php (accessed 4 March 2007).

Plate 4.1: Egypt in Gurgaon. Newspaper advertisement of 'Luxor' by real estate developer Omaxe (2005).

Source: Indian Express, 7 May.

Judging from online illustrations (the building had not been completed at the time of writing this book), we find high-rise buildings like any other condominium, with the slight difference that small onion-shaped peaks top the towers of the apartment blocks. The promises sound rather like a narrative from *Arabian Nights*. Yet, real estate advertising and the booming tourist industry are not far apart here, and hinge on popular commercial Hindi films of the 1960s, where newly wed couples would go on a grand tour around the world for their honeymoon.[8] The global imaginary generated is based on the desire of the new affluent middle class to explore the world and travel abroad, to more exotic sites than Paris or London. While one's own apartment seems to invite and reflect the world, and theming of lifestyle turns the world into a theme park, it might be possible that soon the pyramids of Egypt will be sidelined in favour of travelling to one of the spectacular cities in UAE.

History as Neocolonialism

History — Indian or world history — is the recurring motif through which real estate advertising is 'theming' space and lifestyle. Historical knowledge is part and parcel of a person with cultured behaviour. Moreover, the real estate rhetoric even promotes the conspicuous consumption of history. Text and image reflect the production of transcultural connections, of a 'world-class' history, where 'Indian culture' and the 'Hindu Golden Age' emerge as an intertwined topography with that of Greek antiquity, the Roman Empire, the Egyptian pharaohs and Romanticist notions of the Grande Tour. The Grande Tour undertaken by upper-class Europeans between the seventeenth and the nineteenth century can be understood as an educational exposure both to the cultural heritage of classical antiquity and the Renaissance, as also to the ideas of aristocratic and fashionable European society. Real estate advertising and architectural styles invites the imagination of buyers to undertake such a journey of the world-class. Significantly, luxury travel packages to Egypt and other tourist destinations are very popular among Indian tourists, reflecting the curiosity and confidence of the rising middle classes to travel around the world, and incorporate the world at home. On a global scale, in fact, colonial lifestyles are back in fashion, and in many

---

[8] Some of the films featuring Indians as globetrotters and diverse exotic sites as the stage on which this habitus could be displayed are: *An Evening in Paris* (directed by S. Samanta, 1967), *Dilwale Dulhania Le Jaenge* (directed by Aditya Chopra, 1995) and others.

ways, Dubai spearheads this trend in terms of catering to a form of colonial nostalgia and auto-orientalism (see Davis 2005). While the Orient was constructed by the Occident in the context of European imperialism and colonialism, today those formerly 'orientalised' use the same stereotypes in fashion and lifestyle, something that Emma Tarlo (1996) has termed the 'ethnic chic'.

What applies to Dubai comes as a challenge to every world city trying to attract investors and tourists, although, in a less extreme form. The display of a collected world history is also manifest in the following illustration, taken from a brochure from Eros City Developers for Rosewood City, Grand Mansions II, Gurgaon.

Many advertisements call upon a repository of 'history' as if it was possible to see it unfolding in front of one's eyes like a catchy film. The slogan on the front-page of the Eros brochure suggests the potential buyer to internalise the following: to 'seek out a kingdom worthy of thyself' quoting a command that Alexander the Great had apparently received from his father (Plate 4.2). This request has been superimposed upon a baroque entrance of a huge house, which, of course, is not quite in tune with the architecture of Alexander's period. In many ways, Europe serves as an index for historical depth and for the visualised distinction of those 'who made it', be it antiquity, medieval baroque or romantic landscape gardens and late-nineteenth century-suburban garden cities. 'Europe' still counts as an honourable label with export quality. To an extent this might be true, since Europe has been associated for so many centuries with cultural superiority, success and a powerful imperial and colonial expansion as well as international recognition (see Dupont 2005).[9]

Why might Alexander the Great from Greece be so appealing to India's 'modern maharajas'? As the brochure suggests, he was an 'all conquering and free spirit', the 'most prolific conquerors of all times', and he even came to north India! Such a place (India) is for those 'forever seeking more out of life'. Alexander can also be more easily quoted since, unlike Mughal invader Babar more than 2,000 years later, he left India after a relatively short period, and returned to where he belonged. Thus, viewed in today's light, Alexander

---

[9] India's visual and architectural mimicry is similar to other countries which have witnessed economic liberalisation, for example, China's Shanghai or Russia's Moscow (Glasze et al. 2006). However, for a further exploration of this apparent similarity, the different political and historical contexts and flows of transcultural exchange should be considered.

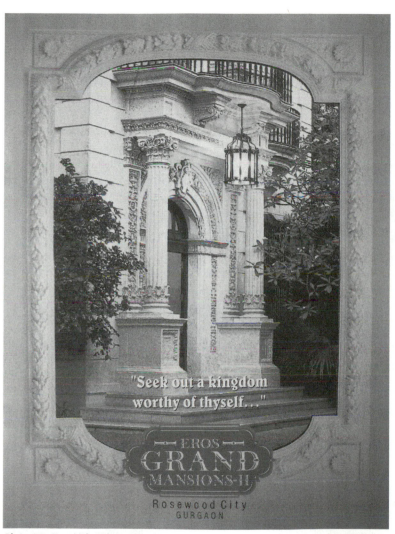

"Seek out a kingdom worthy of thyself..."

EROS
GRAND
MANSIONS-II
Rosewood City
GURGAON

Plate 4.2: Royal lifestyle — the European way. Eros brochure for Grand Mansions II, Gurgaon (2005).

does not carry the burden of forced conversion or demolition of religious sites, objects and beliefs. Maybe because of this, the notion of conquering can be used to capture imagination, without the controversial baggage of alleged sixteenth-century introductions by Islam. The architecture in the

Eros brochure represents 'stately elegance and generous spaces ... classical perfection and grand proportions ... conquering the modern world of lifestyle yet once again ... against constraints of space'. These promised quality standards are often lacking in a megacity like Delhi. In another Eros brochure, we are reminded of Inden's statement on Bombay cinema's enclavic gaze on an 1990s Arcadia where he argues that India seems to be freed from poverty, and luxurious lifestyle has come to occupy centre stage. The brochure advertises luxury villas that promise to unveil a 'saga of unparalleled lifestyle' for the 'deserving few', the conquering and the power-hungry: '[F]inally, couches can be placed far apart ... you can give that big and exquisite Persian carpet its due place'. Likewise, a guide to 'good living' is wrapped up in the following promises from the Grand Mansions project, where each villa offers five bedrooms and furnished with imported bathroom fittings:

> Parthenon-like balconies, stately corridors, magnanimous reception areas with water bodies mingle easily with Jacuzzi, en suite bathrooms, modular kitchen ... An ancient architecture conquers the modern age constraints of space and economy to broaden your world, while modern lifestyle and privileges make life amidst this glorious architecture a phenomenal experience (Eros City Developers' brochure, Grand Mansions, 2005).

Clearly, the notion of unlimited space is a scarce luxury good like the notion of solitude. To 'have space' is also associated with having enough lifestyle, 'cultured taste' and material goods to fill this space with. What the brochure meant by 'Parthenon-like' can be guessed easily given that the origin of the term appears in the temple architecture of Greek antiquity. The eclecticism imbued in this quote mirrors the excellent portrayal of popular architectural styles and middle-class attitudes in north India by architect Gautam Bhatia who coined the term 'Punjabi Baroque'. The quote from the brochure highlights how the appropriation of different international styles indicates a desire to belong to the world-class. It further indicates the playful adaptation and appropriation of status symbols, transforming them into something one owns, the indigenous perspective of self (Denslagen and Gutschow 2005). For the Indian architect, this style is a representation of a creative attempt to establish taste and distinction by including elements from a vast range of other styles:

> Chandni Chowk Chippendale, Tamil Tiffany, Maratha Chauvinism, Bengali Asceticism, Akali Folly, Marwari Pragmatism, Punjabi Baroque, Bania Gothic, Bhaiyya Eclectic, Brahmin Medievalism, Parsi Propriety and Anglo-Indian Rococo, among others, are all part of the permanent collection of the streets,

the new urban galleries, the architectural canvas on public display (Bhatia 1994: 32).

These visualised and spatialised fused styles of specific and honourable cultural achievements in space and time are an effort of the new middle classes to prevent being classified as 'provincial' and 'uneducated', to display cultural competence, taste and style in 'world-class' knowledge about architecture and lifestyles.[10] By knowing one's own and world history, or at least pretending to know, one qualifies as belonging to the educated and 'chosen' elite. What we find visualised in the advertisement of Victoria Gardens in Delhi is a neocolonial elite that seems to care for specific references to localities of symbolic prestige but ignores its surreal de-location. The text of the advertisement reads thus: 'History is blooming once again. Inspired by the Victoria Gardens of Kolkata and the royal lifestyle from the imperial era, comes Victoria Gardens in Delhi' (see Plate 3.3).

Similar phenomena of theming the city through historicising and aestheticising it can be found in cities like Shanghai. Urban sociologist Hassenpflug has coined notions like urban parody, urban aestheticisation and citytainment (2008: 122) to underline the appropriation of 'European' power and history as the exotic Other in neoliberal China. Is all this eclectic and ignorant arrogance of a parvenu class a reflection of the aspiration to become a dominant elite? Or, can we see a playful engagement with entangled histories and styles in this patchwork of imaginaries? Is this cosmopolitan engagement with the other, or is it lifestyle cosmopolitanism that pretends to be open but is enclaved and xenophobic? In his exploration of Shanghai and Hongkong, Abbas remarks that in China too, there was a particular creativity and reciprocity involved in 'imitating' foreign styles of architecture that came along with the shaping of new public and social spaces. In his view, these were spaces of a kind 'that could be appropriated by the Chinese themselves and used to construct a Chinese version of modern cosmopolitan culture' (Abbas 2000: 775). Thus, what we find in globalising India today, is not just a simple replica of an original from elsewhere but its authentic appropriation and alteration. It is based on

---

[10] The export of European architecture to other global sites is discussed by Abbas (2000). Exploring Shanghai in the 1920s and 1930s, he heralds a 'shallow' kind of cosmopolitanism by quoting different styles of international architecture, be it Tudor, German, Spanish or Russian: 'styles imported from elsewhere — a shallow kind of cosmopolitanism, a dream image of Europe more glamorous even than Europe itself at the time' (Abbas 2000: 774).

delicate transcultural asymmetries and flows that challenge us to revise the very concepts of modernity.

Heritage City

Before the Metro connected Old Delhi with New Delhi in 2005, upper and middle-class people from New Delhi were generally reluctant to visit the overcrowded bazaars, *mohallas* (neighbourhoods) and (*galis*) lanes of Chandni Chowk, Kinari Bazaar or Parantha Gali. Even though the area is known for its food specialities and extravagant wedding sarees and accessories, firecrackers and other consumer goods, access to the region (e.g., parking, bus services, etc.) was difficult and time-consuming. Once there, many visitors of the densely populated web of the old city, with its narrow lanes and congestion, dreaded its dirt, pickpockets, and so on. In order to appeal to the upper middle class consumers' taste for the exotic and their desire to move without hassle, several attempts were made to turn Old Delhi into a controlled consumption and leisure zone of its own kind. This must be understood in the light of global trends such as 'new urbanism' and 'heritagisation' that have come to impact the city too, especially its medieval and Mughal monuments and colonial architecture.[11]

Along with senior politician Jagmohan, Vijay Goel from BJP (MP from Chandni Chowk and former Union Minister) was a key figure in this context. Sensing the market-value of Old Delhi with its 'charming' architectural past attracting heritage-seekers, more so in the light of its 'polarisation vis-à-vis a rapidly modernising New Delhi, he published a book entitled *Delhi: The Emperor's City: Rediscovering Chandni Chowk and its Environs* (Goel 2003). The book was launched at the five-star Ashok Hotel and hosted prominent guests such as the former Home Minister L. K. Advani and Prime Minister A. B. Vajpayee. The launch was designed as a themed spectacle in which Goel appeared as a modern maharaja, a proud and cultured 'Dilliwalla' (man from Delhi). The launch intended to give the press and visitors like me a glimpse into the world of Chandni Chowk, while it was conveyed at the same time that they were participating in 'something useful' by supporting the idea of transforming Chandni Chowk into a 'Heritage City' and help preserve deteriorating buildings. Further, the event built on the so-called 'bourgeois environmentalism' (Baviskar 2003), suggesting that anyone

---

[11] New urbanism is a movement towards emphasis on traditional neighbourhood design. The critique of it is that aesthetics is elevated over practicality and that public spaces are turned into semi-restricted spaces of pure and dense leisure activities.

opposing the transformation of the 'filthy' and chaotic Chandni Chowk in fact opposed legalisation, and supported non-conforming industries as well as the street hawkers and rickshaw-pullers who congest the streets of Old Delhi. This approach reflects strategies of 'urban spatialisation' of 'upper-class concerns around aesthetics, leisure, safety, and health' (ibid.). The predominant force that pervades such an approach to city planning seems to be the seductive charm of a city of *Arabian Nights*, holding for the new world-class citizens an exciting flavour of lust and danger.

Moreover, the previously shared imaginary of Old Delhi as an uncon-trollable place of decline and dirt is replaced by a new vision that projects a sanitised and safe space. The new vision depicts Old Delhi as an open-air heritage museum, a walk-through picture book, an imaginary that found large support among the middle class Delhiites. On the one hand, marketing Old Delhi's heritage was sensed as a powerful potential for investments as also for the tourist economy. On the other hand, architectural traces, as a reminder of a golden past, appealed to their 'nostalgic hearts'. Old Delhi was suddenly visualised in its magnitude; it became the other side of the coin — the part that would complete and complement Delhi as the world-class metropolis.

Other incidents of such urban 'heritagisation' include the Red Fort, the planned development of Yamuna's embankment, virtually competing with the river banks in Paris or London, and the opening of the Akshardham Cultural Complex, a site that was built despite heavy criticism and even a (failed) court case because of the disputed land it was built on (see Part II of this study). Jagmohan, also known as 'Demolition Man' (or the Indian answer to Baron Haussmann in Paris), responsible for the removal of 'illegal' squatter dwellings in Old Delhi during the Emergency, became Union Minister, of Urban Development and Poverty Alleviation, Tourism and Culture in 1999. One of his central visions was to transform the Yamuna embankment along the Red Fort into the kind one finds in Paris. Commenting on the removal of slums along the Yamuna in this context, he argues that urbanisation needs a recognition that this approach cannot please all:

> Paris was a slimy area before 1870 and all the slums were resettled or removed by a person called Baron Hoffman.[12] He was very much accused of sending the people away and so on, but he organized Paris, created huge boulevards, parks, beautiful places and created an organized way of life, and now Paris has

---

[12] He refers to Baron Haussman; see n. 4.

become a hub of tourists who come from all over the world … as a tourist spot, Paris alone is earning much more than all our cities combined. Why? It is called vision and problems of poverty are solved like this (Jagmohan quoted in Bharucha 2006: 167).

The arrogance with which Jagmohan displaces the 'vision' of slum-dwellers with his own is remarkable and might in fact be very similar to that of Haussmann more than 100 years ago, who felt that not only would dirt and chaos be removed but also political instability — this was a time of unrest. Further, Jagmohan mentions Hauz Khas, a former urban village that has undergone dramatic changes and is today a quasi-'walk-in' heritage museum (see Tarlo 1996).

Delhi is not the only city witnessing the combination of heritage and modernity in residential and commercial lifestyle-projections. Though the trend is not monopolised systematically by megacities as of yet, it does surface at places with a condensed flow of financial capital and international exposure (e.g., Shanghai). Causes for these kinds of flows are the booming wellness industry, tourist industry and the wedding industry (see Part III of this study). One example is Cochin in Kerala. Another is the city of Udaipur, a centre of domestic and international tourism, of Indian destination weddings and honeymoons, known as the 'city of lakes and palaces' or the 'Venice of the East', attracting 1.2 million foreign tourists per year. Currently, a 'world-class' shopping and retail complex is being planned by the name of 'Celebration Mall'. The conceptual Palace Mall is designed like a Rajasthani palace with domes, equipped with water bodies on all storeys of the mall, recreating the ambience of the royal grandeur of a bygone era. Different themes are drawn from local history and architecture of Mewar.[13]

Furthermore, it hosts a health club, a Thai spa and other wellness facilities. Advanced India Projects Limited plans similar conceptual malls in Amritsar, Gurgaon, Dehradun and other sites.[14]

The economic boom produces a pantheon of structured experiences and controlled spaces (*Erlebniswelten*), where visitors are turned into consumer-flâneurs. By February 2006, 23 malls had been built in Delhi's National Capital Region. However, compared to the US, France or Singapore, India's

---

[13] See http://www.eproperty4u.com/fprlist.php?pid=33 (accessed 20 June 2009).

[14] See http://www.advanceindia.co.in/retailudaipur2.asp?id=Udaipur (accessed 2 March 2007).

total retail space is still modest, with only a 2 per cent share of super-markets and speciality stores (Tiwari 2005). The small kingdom of Dubai has successfully combined the experience of shopping and tourism, with two of the largest shopping centres in the world (Dubai Mall and Mall of Arabia). Considering the huge potential of the tourist economy, urban administration, real estate developers and private entrepreneurs are now getting enthusiastic about preserving traditional architecture and urban structures such as Hauz Khas, Old Delhi or CP.[15]

To illustrate the importance of this expanding trend, it should be noted that the real estate developer Omaxe has decided to build a second 'Connaught Place' in Greater Noida in Uttar Pradesh. In New Delhi, the site has been the commercial hub, since the days of the British Raj, and regarded as the architectural marvel and symbol of the metro's centre of business power. It has lost its unique importance only within the past 10 years with the emergence of other shopping malls and market centres. The layout and construction plan of the proposed new CP will be different — for example, it will be square in shape, not circular, with all four sides open. Yet, some of its original features (recently revamped and 'upgraded') like corridors and pillars will be copied.[16] It is worthwhile mentioning that the preservation of the original CP was neglected until the start of the new millennium, when the government of Delhi decided to upgrade the whole area as a business district, to facilitate access by building a Metro station and encourage other visitors by creating a small heritage-park with water fountains at its centre. Slowly, the landscape of CP is changing: the old shop-owners cannot afford the escalating rents any longer, and as a result, more and more retail chains are moving in.

'Green Delhi': Themed and Tamed Nature

In the preceding discussions, I mentioned that parks in Delhi are about the only places in which 'nature' can be publicly enjoyed. The city government as well as environmentalists are becoming increasingly aware of the fact that trees are the lungs of the city and must be preserved, and that nature is not only beautiful but also important. In the last few years, more and more urban migrant villages have been cleared in order to 'protect

---

[15] On Hauz Khas, see Tarlo (1996). Chandni Chowk and Connaught Place are now directly connected by means of the Metro rail, facilitating access and avoiding traffic congestion.

[16] The design is by the well-known architect Hafeez Contractor, with partners Larsen and Toubro. See http://www.hafeezcontractor.com/ (accessed 4 March 2007).

nature' and prevent encroachment.[17] Simultaneously, free space is getting increasingly scarce and many trees are felled to create parking space, for instance. Delhi's ridge is protected natural area and yet also known to be a place where people come and dump their domestic garbage. As public space is reduced to the few parks and historical sites of the city that are not restricted yet, middle class people of Delhi find it increasingly difficult to spend their leisure time in the open. At the same time, advertisements create the aspiration that nature equals luxury, health and happiness. For those affluent professionals who do not want to restrict their movement to indoor fitness studios, shopping malls or leisure parks, the idea of the enclave park becomes a cherished alternative.

Different urban planning models have come to stand for the social spatialisation of cities over time. In the case of New Delhi today, these are the 'Garden City' and the 'City Beautiful' (see Menon 1997). While the 'Garden City' has been appropriated from the expansion of English cities and the change of labour culture around the year 1900, the 'City Beautiful' is a concept that has been shaped in the US about the same time, mainly in response to a perceived threat of inner-city poverty. There is a certain amount of cross-fertilisation with the British aesthetic concept of the Garden City in the ways in which the 'beautification' of cities purportedly improves the citizens' morals, health and civic participation. These concepts have been criticised as another form of social control (of the bourgeois elite) over an allegedly unruly population. 'Natural' environments were, thus, thought to uplift moral value and create civic virtue.

Some parts of New Delhi seem to burst with promises of the 'City Beautiful' and the 'Garden City' while others promise to do so (Plate 4.3). Advertisements for a 'Green City' or the 'world-class' are building deliberately on the notion of 'exclusiveness', stressing a certain lifestyle of 'global players' and the nostalgia of a grand past, as we have seen earlier. The gated or enclaved gaze, however, is also shaped by reference to nature and 'naturalness' — both visions of a desired paradise on earth. In the advertisements, the culture–nature divide is blurred for a split second, when sights of Arcadian landscape gardens are included, visually and metaphorically, suggesting the utopia of meadows covered with morning dew, of silent locations of meditation, of drifting into endless gazing into a scenery of exotic domestic flora and fauna where the evenings are filled with peacock screams and laughter from the pool nearby instead of car and truck noises,

---

[17] One example is the eviction of the allegedly unauthorised colonies in Bhatti Mines, located at the fringes of the capital, bordering Haryana, in 2006.

Plate 4.3: Hoarding of 'Green City', Noida, NCR (2006).

lack of water and electricity, or the unpleasant sound of a landing aeroplane. This utopia, in contrast to urban traffic and stressful day-to-day life feeds into a growing desire among the urban middle classes for artificially created areas that allow easy access with maximum possibilities for light entertainment: the birth of the themed zones, be it a gated community, a fun park, a mall or a golf course (see Morris 2001).

The pleasure of enjoying nature and silence are frequently mentioned attributes of the new private enclaves, and of the new cosmopolitan classes intending to inhabit them. The joy of nature as a luxury and leisure item reflects a genuinely modern and capitalist characteristic, defining status and 'cultured behaviour'. Consider, for example, the advertisement by Windsor Jaipuria's Sunrise Greens: 'fresh mornings, quite [sic!] evenings', which highlights the contrast between two images. The first image shows a man sitting on a picnic bench, contemplating with an unlimited view into the greenery (only his back and laptop bag can be seen). The second image depicts a fortress-like cluster of apartment blocks surrounding a rather caged and tamed garden. A similar description comes from Amrapali Village, Indirapuram 'set amidst the fresh winds of an unpolluted atmosphere and landscaped gardens'. The more anarchical, ugly, dirty and noisy the open city seems to be, the better sells the promise of a packaged and gated Eden.

'Real' nature, however, lies outside the fortress of the gated community, and indeed, different images of nature prevail and shape the everyday lives of the people living there, where meditation on a park bench or on a lawn is probably unheard of. Partly farmland, partly deserted land waiting to be fenced and turned into another colony, the contrast between themed and unrecognised nature could not be more drastic (see Plates 2.4 and 2.5).

Many real estate developers propose to protect nature and biodiversity. The claims on nature and its consumption through protection and its enjoyment as status symbol mirrored in these projections, has been referred to as 'bourgeois environmentalism' by scholars such as Amita Baviskar (2003) (see also Bharucha 2006). Here, the concept is used to define the reorganisation of urban space according to the desires of the elite to possess and control nature. Architect Menon, too, has referred to this desire as a reminiscence of colonial ways of imagining the Garden City (1997). The desire to control nature completely draws one's attention to the fear of misfortune that might strike suddenly at any given time (McCarthy 1994: 157; see also Schulze 1992). Agricultural land and jungle have to make place for artificial sceneries of paradisaical appearance. Often, real estate developers emphasise that parks and gardens in their integrated townships or condominiums contribute to the region's ecological prosperity. The stamp 'ecofriendly environment' is repeatedly used. But to what extent it camouflages exorbitant use of water and electricity remains to be tested. Some condominiums market themselves by announcing that they protect nature, nurture roses, palm trees, exotic birds and butterflies. This is often done in reference to a powerful trend within the rising middle classes, where successful world-class lifestyle is associated with health food, exercise, a relaxed mind, and a conscience with respect to nature and environmental issues. These properties are restricted and thus part and parcel of the concept of the artificial enclave.

To conclude this section, it could be argued that the iconography of the 'enclaved gaze' reflects the taste and desire of a new affluent and confident Indian middle class. The visual regime of this popular cosmopolitan imagination flaunts the notion that it is possible to distinguish oneself from others by putting on display (and thus shaping) a cosmopolitan lifestyle environment, or at least the idea of what it could be like. The pictures discussed are imbued with the desire to 'belong to class', to be 'world-class' and for a control over the allegedly disorderly, uncontrollable public. This public includes both urban space and people who move and live in it, trying to control, clean and seal off the 'wanted' from the 'unwanted' elements. Nature surfaces centrally in this attempt to control the environment. It can only be enjoyed for leisure and relaxation if it is surrendered and turned into another enclave.

ordering the city and its citizens

In the previous chapter, we saw that a city such as New Delhi is entangled with various globalised forms of social spatialisation and architectural aesthetics, most of which derive from colonial urban planning. A major trend in this context is the theming of certain zones as heritage spaces on the one hand, and of green zones that refer to regeneration and health, on the other. The enclave gaze prevails in that access to the city as a public space, and a public stage, is still restricted and opened only to what Chatterjee (2003) refers to as 'citizens' (versus populations). In the race for the title 'world-class', cities such as Bangalore, Mumbai or New Delhi assign particular status and rights to particular social groups. Amita Baviskar and others underline the paradoxical fact that in this attempt, groups of low social and economic status are not acknowledged insofar as their involvement in constructing the 'underbelly' of the city, and informal services such as collecting garbage, is concerned (Baviskar 2003; Bharucha 2006). Partha Chatterjee has talked about the 'proliferation of segregated and protected spaces for elite consumption, elite lifestyle and elite culture' (2003: 144). There are, I suggest, different spheres and kinds of 'visibility' that help us differentiate the politics of granting rights of access to the public sphere. There is the visibility of the aspiring and affluent classes, played out in public and semi-public physical spaces like five-star hotels, malls, multiplexes, residential townships and restaurants. At the same time, there is the visibility of those segments of society that are rather unwanted, aesthetically unappealing (to the bourgeois eye), and associated with dirt (Kaviraj 1997) and crime. To me, this construction of a dichotomy seeks to legitimise the drawing of borders along the lines of citizenship and personhood: 'first-class' or 'world-class' citizens versus the 'second-' or even 'third-class' population (not citizens). To some, even the status of citizen is denied, as we shall see subsequently. The issue of glocalisation moves into this segregation because, put broadly, the idea of the global city is part of a global discourse while that of citizens is specifically local.

But who belongs to the category of the 'first-class' citizens of the 'world-class' city? Are all these factors linked with a withering of public space, as Hardt (1995) or Sorkin (1992a) have suggested in their multifaceted explorations of urbanisation and civil society? Do we, as some have suggested, witness the decline of civil society along with the emergence of private cities, gated communities, and special economic zones — all this under video surveillance? Along with Sharon Zukin (2005), we may ask 'Whose city is it?' Who are the legitimate citizens catered to by the state government in all these discussions about private–public alliances and civic agency? Who is made into an illegitimate citizen in the course of these negotiations (Masselos 1991)? What we can certainly observe is a discussion about authorised and unauthorised housing settlements (and their tenants) and a strong legal debate about who owns what, who protects whose land and interests, and the selling-off of public interests and rights to private entrepreneurs and investors. What kind of functions of the city are changing in this context and is this all based, as some housing activists suggest, on the greed of elites wanting to establish New Delhi as a 'world-class city', a playground for their own interests? What are the markers in terms of architecture and urban development that indicate the changes taking place in a city trying to keep up with the development of other megacities in India and across the world?

Socio-political and economic aspects of urbanisation involve an on-going process of negotiating the conditions to open the city for social groups that are relevant to the city's prestige and thus considered as citizens, and, conversely, to close the city for those who are considered 'useless' and 'threatening'. Historians have well documented the social segregation and definition of citizenship in the context of urban planning in colonial India (for instance, Kosambi 1993; Masselos 1991). In his article 'Are Indian Cities Becoming Bourgeois at Last?', Partha Chatterjee (2003) explores contemporary processes and proposes a distinction between 'citizen' and 'population'. While citizens have the moral duty and right to share the sovereignty of the state, populations have no right to make moral claims. As a consequence, he argues, those 'with' rights, deserving the status of a citizen, try to rid the city of its encroachers (ibid.).

The imagery discussed hereafter reveals a strong desire of real estate developers and advertisement agencies to appeal to, and simultaneously create, a cosmopolitan class of citizens. Subsumed under this fuzzy notion are groups who have fluid capital that can be invested, flexible lifestyles, and who aspire to 'state-of-the-art living standards'. Consequently, the people at the periphery or seemingly outside the discourse revolving around the 'world-class' and the 'Global City' do not feature in the Indian advertisements: there is no mention of the cheap labour of the armies of migrant labourers actually involved in constructing what is projected in those advertisements. Such groups remain 'backstage' and rendered invisible.

Instead, in the new world-class city, finance and service sectors are given space to expand and to be visible to investors on the basis of their function as 'command points' and tools of expansion of capitalist globalisation (Sassen 2001a: 3). In Delhi, for example, central business districts are constantly upgraded and made more efficient especially in terms of telecommunication and transport connectivity; integrated townships offer special economic zones, and more. Likewise, and connected with this change in professional urban space, public space too transforms according to the priorities set for the creation of a world-class city. State governments, private investors and consulting firms like McKinsey have a crucial say in this respect. Both the improvement of infrastructure and cleanliness are of great relevance in this context and lead to a different engagement with underprivileged groups. Partha Chatterjee maintains:

> The result has been, on the one hand, greater assertion by organizations of middle-class citizens of their right to unhindered access to public spaces and thoroughfares and to a clean and healthy urban environment. On the other hand, government policy has rapidly turned away from the idea of helping the poor to subsist within the city and is instead paying the greatest attention to improving infrastructure in order to create conditions for the import of high technology and the new service industries ... [T]he new metropolis will belong to the managerial and technocratic elite and a new class of very highly paid workers (2003: 144; see also Batra and Mehra 2006a).

The megacity is always under pressure to be attractive to potential investors and business at large. In the past few years, India's cities have become symbols of national and international progress, development and confidence. This shows a shift of emphasis in the Indian national economy and self-understanding because large cities were more of a burden and blind spot of development than a resource. The shift also reflects in the 'nick-names' associated with some of the 'great' cities: Hyderabad is known as 'Cyberabad', Bangalore as 'India's Silicon Valley' and Mumbai as 'Shanghai'.

As mentioned before, notions of risk and threat of decay are as much associated with the 'global city' as the notion of 'India Shining'.[1] In the Indian urban context, a report of McKinsey & Company triggered that fear,

---

[1] The fear of falling behind is part of Mike Davis' argument about the architectural boom in Dubai in that the planners of such cities — as they enter partnership with private developers — generate certain fears in order to streamline or even cage the critical potential of a citizenry (Davis 2005; see also Oldenburg 1984; Zukin 2005).

not only in Mumbai, but elsewhere too. It released a report entitled *Vision Mumbai: Transforming Mumbai into a World-class City* (McKinsey & Company 2003), in which 'recommendations' were presented to private investors and government institutions to 'improve' the quality of lifestyle in the commercial capital of India by the year 2013. In order to make Mumbai a 'centre of choice' all over Asia, the report demands an economic growth of 8–10 per cent per year (e.g., through development in health care, IT and media), an improvement of mass and private transportation, an increase of housing availability and affordability, and effective governance and strengthening of public–private relationships and resources.[2] Ignoring the fact that Mumbai has been a vibrant international metropolis for over 100 years, McKinsey offers a deficient view of the city's condition. They present idealised models of the successful transformation of cities from urban decay to urban glamour by pointing at Shanghai and Bangalore. The McKinsey report evoked the fear that Mumbai could not compete with other megacities who allegedly perform better, and deliver more.[3]

Moral Citizenship

In this section, I will explore the notion of what I have termed as 'first-', 'second-' or 'third-class' citizenship and relate them to a larger moral discourse on citizenship. According to Appadurai and Holston, cities have always been a site of contested identities related to the public sphere, be it identities related to race, gender, class, caste or religion (1996: 188). Citizenship is closely linked to nationhood. Yet, in the context of cosmopolitan identities and transnational networks, it must also be seen as a more complex practice of negotiating solidarity, value and meaning, quite like what Ong's term 'flexible citizens' suggests (1999). By this, she refers to citizenship as a 'felt' or 'experienced' notion of transnationally active social agents ('global nomads') who consider themselves as being able to choose between and practise different kinds of citizenship. Rather than thinking of citizenship as a 'natural given', it is actually a notion embedded in discourses aligned to privilege and power, and emerging in particular spatial, political and ideological contexts that must be carefully

---

[2] This includes 'upgradation' (gentrification) of slums and resettlement and the creation of 'islands of excellence': museums, parks, urban plazas and hospitals (McKinsey & Company 2003: 30–32).

[3] The McKinsey Report alleges: 'Mumbai fell from 26th place in 1996 to 33rd in 2000 in *Asia Week*'s rankings of the top 40 cities in Asia' (ibid.: 3).

analysed. Appadurai and Holston also refer to the allegations that on the one hand, 'cities may be re-emerging as more salient sites for citizenship' and on the other:

> citizens are producing new notions of membership and solidarity. As a whole ... in many postcolonial societies, a new generation has arisen to create urban cultures severed from the colonial memories and nationalist fiction on which independence and subsequent rule were founded (1996: 189).

However, with respect to India and the material that is explored in this chapter, I argue that a new colonial rhetoric is emerging as well as a new form of nationalism which is not bound any longer to principles of market regulation and Nehruvian responsibilities of uplifting the entire nation. The upper middle class and elites celebrate a language that recollects the grand days of maharajas and palatial self-representation. The paradigm of nation-building has shifted from the rural 'as the fundamental expression of the indigenous and authentic' (Appadurai and Holston 1996) to the city as the symbol of economic growth.

The cities projected on the real estate advertisements discussed here reflect a deviation from, and potentially replacing, 'nations as the important space of citizenship' (ibid.) and move towards a rather new virtual space of the transnation. This kind of transnational citizenship seems to underline a loyalty towards the transnational imaginary of the world-class rather than a national passport. It also addresses the attribution of citizenship according to the 'productivity' of persons with respect to 'national welfare'. There is an exclusive notion of citizenship at work here. It defines the category of 'non-citizens' as opposed to 'deserving' citizens who make the city 'world-class' and have committed themselves morally to this societal vision: 'Their objective is to privatize or dismantle public spaces and services and to implant zoning regulations which in effect keep the undesired out' (ibid.: 191).[4]

A new category of 'first-class citizens' has moved to the centre stage recently: the non-resident Indian (NRI). This group of people, part of a huge trend of reverse migration, has so far hardly been considered in earlier studies. The overseas Indians are often perceived by planners and developers as the *kamadhenu* (the wishful cow in Hindu mythology which

---

[4] In his exploration of new urbanism and Disney theme parks Cunningham maintains that both share the search for a 'modification of behaviour and feeling through design' and see 'cleanliness as a neighbourhood virtue' (2005: 119).

grants wealth and wishes), ready to return and to invest and/or live in their 'motherland' and make it rise and shine. This is tied with the desire to rediscover cultural heritage and traditional values. They are appealed to as 'first-class' citizens by real estate developers and the government alike, with attractive offers and a host of privileges.[5] Moreover, they also feel like first-class citizens. Says Vijay A., an IT businessman who lives in a luxury apartment in Gurgaon:

> I came to India after having lived a very comfortable life in California. I wanted to help run the country. I expect that it works for me too, and offers me a good lifestyle. My apartment is my island. I can't help feeling relieved when I return from work and stressed when I leave the gates behind. If I can, I avoid leaving the condi [condominium] at weekends. Why should I expose myself to India (Vijay A., Gurgaon, September 2006)?!

This statement displays a certain reluctance of Indian employees in the service sector who come from overseas to acknowledge the difference between an enclave life of 'India Shining' and the realities outside the imaginary and physical gates. Instead, living in India, and 'running it', often sounds like a pragmatic and rather detached business deal or development project and is at times imbued with a patronising top-down perspective. The question 'Why should I expose myself to India' emphasises an enclave gaze that considers 'backward' India with embarrassment, a provocation to those who attempt to make the country a better place to live. Such perceptions also legitimise the demarcation of the 'ugly', 'unhealthy' and 'dangerous' zones as well as their removal.

Cleaning up for Pleasant Spaces

Looking beyond the projection of the imagined 'world-class' city that has been predominantly discussed so far, we now move to the other side of urban planning in 'India Shining'. This section considers different voices — of real estate developers, architects, town planners and housing activists in order to explore the tensions and conflicts related to the transformation of Delhi into an imagined 'world-class' city. Many critics of real estate development in India have shown great concern with respect to social housing. In particular, they protest against the aggressive slum demolitions in megacities such as Kolkata, Chennai, New Delhi and Mumbai. For instance, 400,000 slum-dwellers were evicted in Mumbai in 2003–4, and

---

[5] I am grateful to Katharina Poggendorf-Kakar for our conversations on 'first-class' citizens in Delhi.

authorities of the Delhi government evicted over 300,000 people in the area of Yamuna Pushta, the city's biggest slum cluster, in 2004. Some voices maintain that the recent strategy of large-scale slum 'clearance' is based on the need for more real estate development land, be it for commercial or housing purposes. On the one hand, squatters' colonies may occupy prime space in the city. On the other hand, they are a thorn in the eye of urban planners, whether from the private or the public sector. They allege that the visible poverty and dirt puts off investors, business people and tourists and thus harms the reputation of the city. This is visible in Mumbai, where run-down textile mills are sold and converted into malls and luxury hotels, and where slums along major streets have been removed. In the case of New Delhi, major slum demolitions took place along the embankment of the Yamuna river, for instance, in favour of a central business district and an entertainment district with a quasi-spiritual theme park (see Part II), high-rise buildings, parks, clubs, golf courses, and so on.[6] Many housing activists have argued that the middle classes witnessed the removal of slum-dwellers without raising much protest. Batra and Mehra (2006a, 2006b) and Butcher and Velayutham (2009) for instance, consider this as a sign of a decrease in public responsibility, and a radicalisation of middle-class values in terms of defining what they consider as 'their space' and 'their rights'. Surveys undertaken by housing activists have found the percentage of pollution caused by slum-dwellers is not as high as often officially stated (Roy 2005b: 8).

Several voices, ranging from the architect and urban planning theoretician Krishna Menon to activist Lalit Batra and scholars such as Diya Mehra, as also the Hazards Centre (a support group and resource centre based in Delhi, surveying and protesting against slum demolition and improper resettlement), share Partha Chatterjee's view that economic liberalisation has encouraged a shift in the middle classes' relationship with the large groups of squatters which encroach upon unauthorised land.[7] It has also

---

[6] In fact, only 6 per cent of Mumbai's land is encroached upon by 'illegal' housing colonies, a challenge to the cliché of slum ubiquity (Sharma 2005). About 573 acres of prime land were to be released for the opening of mill land towards real estate development. According to Hafeez Contractor, a giant real estate and architectural bureau, 372 high-rise buildings could be erected at these newly 'vacated' sites, accommodating more than 100,000 people (Bhupta 2005b: 25).

[7] Hazards Centre in New Delhi conducts and offers research, documentation, training and consultation. They facilitate alternative frameworks on urban policy, planning and practice on issues such as land and housing, transport, water, environment, governance and livelihoods. See http://hazardscentre.com (accessed 22 August 2009).

altered their attitude towards the legal boundaries that define private and public spaces, the notion of encroachment and access (see also Siebel and Wehrheim 2006). While in the 1970s, these colonies were often tolerated, if not perceived, as a part of civil society that had to be carried along and uplifted, the emerging neoliberal rhetoric of the 1990s and the first years of the new millennium display a different stance. Members of the middle classes seemed to have the 'given' right to actively participate in the making of public opinion. But while the population outside the frame of legal housing technically had the right to receive developmental help or social welfare, it had no right of moral claim to the sovereignty of the state.

Hazards Centre attempts to challenge Delhi's alleged transformation into an exclusive, world-class and 'clean' space of middle-class environmentalism. It argues that since the 1990s,

> the landscape of urban India has morphed out of recognition. From mixed neighbourhoods to exclusive elite conclaves, from hundreds of informal markets to a score of glitzy shopping malls ... the change has been rapid and palpable. While a few privileged welcome the changing face of the city, for the majority of the poor and working people ... these changes are quite inhospitable ... The toiling majority of urban India is being made to bear the burden of giving a minority of 'citizens' a taste of what it is like to live in a 'global' city (Hazards Centre 2006b: 3).

However, the central government has also taken steps to remove urban poverty, reform urban governance and improve urban living beyond those available to social and economic elites. In 2005, the Jawaharlal Nehru National Urban Renewal Mission (a branch of the Ministry of Housing and Urban Poverty Alleviation) was launched, seeking to transform the allegedly 'inefficient' public sector into a space that attracts investor-friendly firms in Indian cities comprising larger than one million people. Nevertheless, critics claim that even this initiative is predominantly market-driven, encouraging the real estate development and builder lobbies to acquire big plots of land and drive out the poor, and not recognising the lack of local self-governance (Mukhopadhyay 2006: 879). Thus, the main point of criticism is that despite the announcement that urban reforms are implemented, the profit finally goes to investors and real estate developers.

Celebrating Religion, Real Estate and the Megacity

According to Sharon Zukin, culture is the driving force of economic growth for cities, the symbolic capital to which a whole range of social agents claim and seek access. City governments and real estate developers — in order to attract new residential tenants, tourists and investors — instrumentalise 'culture'. Religion and ritual practices, too, can be translated into cultural capital, as we shall see in Part II of this book. Religious pilgrimage has never been one of Delhi's 'unique selling points', though it has one of the most important Sufi shrines which draws many Muslim pilgrims to the Nizamuddin neighbourhood. Delhi's role on the sacred map of Hindu pilgrimage is only marginal. In the recent years, religion has come to serve as a marker of class and nationhood in the city, generating new flows of social groups — the middle classes — and their desire for conspicuous consumption. This is set against a picturesque backdrop for exotic narratives and imaginaries as well as a growing entanglement with spirituality and patchwork religion. The growth in numbers and visual presence of sites of Hindu leisure religion in New Delhi and the NCR can also be seen as a sign of 'soft' *hindutva*, i.e., the emphasis on ancient Hindu culture and religion as the greatest common denominator for 'Indianness', and the 'Indian way of life'.

There are several instances where real estate development projects, in particular for commercial and leisure purposes, have been legitimised by marking the first step of construction activity with a religious or spiritual theme of architecture. Such projects also justified the developer's 'right' to remove 'illegal structures' (Dasgupta 2006). Parks or religious places often spearhead spatial transformations, and it is not unlikely that they are encouraged and followed by entrepreneurial real estate development projects. This strategy banks on the assumption that there is less protest against such significant restructuring of space because of the respect for the religious sentiments of people (an idea itself highly disputed since the demolition of the Babri Mosque in 1992). This applies to 'Vedic Village' in Kolkata as much as Nehru Place, where a '*basti* of 5000 families was evicted in 2001 ... to make way for a "spiritual park"' (Batra and Mehra 2006b: n.p.). Spread over 125 acres of sprawling fertile farmland, Vedic Village is a bungalow estate set in a gated complex within an international spa resort. It is located in one of the most developing areas of Kolkata, opposite the upcoming Knowledge City where key IT players are setting up business. Since the new millennium, Kolkata has turned into a boomtown that challenges its negative (highly colonial) stereotype as the 'city of slums'.[8]

As regards Delhi, the most recent, and certainly spectacular, piece of spiritual-cum-real estate development is the Akshardham Cultural Complex,

---

[8] Sovan Tarafder examined urbanisation in Kolkata, in particular a theme mall called 'Swabhumi — The Heritage Plaza'. See http://www.swabhumi.com/home. html (accessed 24 August 2007).

a large site run by one of the fastest growing new spiritual movements in the subcontinent. It hosts theme halls, water fountains, several gardens and a monument. The site was opened to the public in November 2005, located close to India Gate and Connaught Place, the colonial heart of New Delhi (see Plate IIa), and is the case-study of the next part of this book.

Another aspect in which culture is instrumentalised to control the city can be seen in sites such as the Vedic Village: the theming and 'festival-isation' of urban space as a symbolic struggle over the definition of a new national culture in the light of 'India Shining'. Different parts of a city like Delhi are turned into 'event zones' — such as the shopping malls, leisure parks, heritage sites and central business districts, to mention only a few. The city itself becomes a theme park (see Gottdiener 2001; Hassenpflug 2008).

Space must be made, if necessary cleared, to turn the city into a stage for spectacles, for people to identify with and participate in the 'world-class' city project. Mega-projects like shopping malls and condominiums, as also a site such as the Akshardham Culture Complex (ACC) — a mixture of pilgrimage site and theme park — serve various kinds of agents with economic, social and political interests as national heritage and tourist items, as anchors for the envisaged business hub or motors for gentrification. There are several reasons why a monumental site like Akshardham could be constructed along the protected Yamuna river bed. It attracts religious tourists and can be projected as a monument of national heritage and pride without sporting an offensive Hindu nationalist rhetoric.[9]

There is another wave of urban planning that is particularly clear in the context of the ACC: the Commonwealth Games slated to take place in Delhi in 2010.[10] Quite like the Olympics in Beijing, the Commonwealth Games too cut deep into the urban fabric, raising real estate prices by more than 250 per cent. Whether it is a coincidence or not, the Commonwealth Village, built to cater to almost 8,000 participants and officials, is envis-aged to be located right opposite the ACC (Plate 5.1). The location is not

---

[9] The relationship between BAPS and Hindu nationalist ideology and politics is, however, kept backstage, despite its strength. The main connecting figures are L. K. Advani — then Home Minister, and recently prime ministerial candidate and leader of opposition (BJP), whose election constituency is in Gujarat (the stronghold of the movement) — and Narendra Modi, Chief Minister of Gujarat — a staunch Hindutva leader as well as promoter of Gujarat's transformation into an economic powerhouse of India.

[10] It is interesting to compare this to urban planning during the preparations for the Asian Games in Delhi in 1982, when South Delhi got a face-lift (see Batra and Mehra 2006a, 2006b; Tankha 2006).

Plate 5.1: Map of Akshardham Cultural Complex and the Commonwealth Games Village displayed on a signboard, East Delhi (2008).

unimportant: until the BAPS claimed the land, it was a protected 'jungle', like most land along the Yamuna river. Opposite the 'jungle' was the so-called 'Yamuna Pushta', one of the largest *bastis*, or unauthorised colony, in north India. Approximately 300,000–400,000 people lived there until demolition moves were executed between 2001 and 2006 (see Batra and Mehra 2006a, 2006b).[11] A similar protected area was the embankment on which the ACC was built and opened in 2005. Writer Rana Dasgupta argues in a blog:

> [Hundred] acres of shanty housing and small-scale industrial and agricultural land were progressively taken over by the temple developers over the last decade.

---

[11] The Annual Administration Report of the Delhi Development Authority announced that between 2003 and 2004, 354 'demolition operations' were carried out, almost 300,000 acres of land 'made free of encroachments', more than 13,000 'structures of kucha, pucca and semi pucca nature were removed' (pucca refers to solid housing structures, while kucha refers to fragile hutments). To authors Batra and Mehra this equalled the 'transfer of Rs 4,000 crore from slum dwellers to the DDA in just three years!' (2006b: n.p.).

The pristine complex that now stands there is much better propaganda for the new India … The temple is a symbol of the new city: hygienic and emptied of the organic past, monumentally modern, bristling with surveillance cameras and security, and inspired by a steely, expansionary, highly distilled ideal of Indian culture that can provide the logic and momentum for India's imagined global supremacy (Dasgupta 2006).

Whether or not, temples have an 'organic past', as Dasgupta nostalgically evokes, the quote informs us of the massive rhizome restructuring the city's fabric by choosing a religious motto as the allegory of a new cultural nationalism in the era of late capitalism. The symbolic value of ACC is closely linked to the hope that it will lead to the infrastructure development of not only East Delhi, previously an area with little prestige, but highlight the city of New Delhi as a whole the world over and attract millions of Indian and international tourists. While some talk of the demolition of residential and natural space, others applaus the so-called beautification and transformation of the city into commercially lucrative land. Large residential projects are said to have already sold out before construction is complete, and property prices have soared. Ideal-typical models of the beautification and 'recreation' of European metropolitan cities are cited, where the embankments right in the heart of cities like Paris and London have become major tourist attractions. In January 2007, the then Minister for Delhi for Urban Development, A. K. Walia, announced that the Delhi Development Authority's plan to revive the Yamuna river bed had been considered, making available 7,300 hectares of land. Only 3 per cent of this new land, according to the statement, was said to be used for residential housing and commercial development. As much as 85 per cent was to be dedicated to so-called 'recreational activities': creation of green spaces, water sports, a racecourse, tourist cottages, camping sites and pleasure parks. Whether or not, however, such a definition of 'recreational' is non-commercial can be questioned.

In the case of the ACC, privatised real estate investment, town planning and new spirituality seem to have joined hands. Architect and urban planning theorist Krishna Menon emphasised in a personal conversation in March 2006 that in the attempt to transform the Yamuna embankment in the heart of New Delhi into an Indian Paris, simultaneously promoting global sites and events such as the ACC, the Commonwealth Games of 2010 and the Metro, some major global players are involved. One such player is Fairwood Consultants. Fairwood, according to Menon, is not just a large organisation: 'They have also come to represent the 'new India', create desires and pretend to deliver fulfilment instantly' (personal conversation, New Delhi, March 2006). Fairwood used to be involved in projects in China, where the 'turbo'-city was developed even earlier and in full gear, with entire townships being planned (like Lingang outside Shanghai) and megacities like Shanghai or Beijing being revamped in order to turn them into global economic hubs. While in China the state still controls such activities, India's economic liberalisation in the 1990s has led to a boom in the privatised sector, with a huge demand for new residential and commercial areas. This is most probably the reason why Fairwood 'returned' to India in the late 1990s. The company is part of large investment projects, a global capitalist player. For some time, but not any longer, Fairwood had teamed up with representatives of the Delhi administration to transform Delhi's riverbanks into a world-class environment. To enforce that plan, ten thousands of millions of rupees are needed, money that real estate or banks and hedge funds could invest. Akshardham set a trend for others, argues Menon, and the state functions as intermediary in all these contexts. In partnership with Fairwood consultants, a real estate company with offices in India and China, the Housing and Urban Development Corporation (HUDCO) published a proposal to develop the Yamuna river bank in New Delhi, a project estimated to cost INR 80,000 crore,[12] and allegedly funded by commercially exploiting 10 per cent of the reclaimed land. The ambitious project aimed at building large commercial areas, ten thousands of residential flats, water reservoirs, stadia for Commonwealth, Asian and Olympic games, promenades, fitness centres, leisure clubs and golf courses (see also Shukla 2007). The idea was never realised but reveals Delhi's ambitions, also articulated in the Master Plan of 2001, to envisage the city along other river cities like London and Paris.

---

[12] 10 million = 1 crore.

conclusion

To sum up, Part I of this book explores how social control over the imagination, representation and actual planning of urban space has been stimulated and enforced by real estate advertisements. The primary objective in this process is to unravel the complex symbolic and spatial strategies appropriated and executed by a variety of social agents in order to shape manifold references to the idea of the 'world-class' city. The 'world-class' city is more than a geographical location. It is what Soja defines as 'simcity': 'the composite product of the restructured urban imaginary' (2000: 339), a 'patchwork quilt of specialized residential communities' (ibid.: 341) based on social segregation, with an extended family of simulated cousins at the so-called Gold Coast in Spain, the outskirts of Moscow or Sao Paulo. It connotes particular cosmopolitan lifestyles, desires and fears of those who aspire to belong to it. The global city is under high pressure to perform in order not to fall behind in the race for the 'world-class'. Since it must provide aesthetic appeal and professional infrastructure for people and institutions with an interest in the highly mobile service sectors and transnational capital flows or commodity circulation, the city is increasingly following the patterns of a multinational corporation (rather than a state government). In this process, the concept of the colonial city (as well as lifestyle) continues to remain relevant, and the 'world-class' city is imagined once again in terms of dichotomies such as 'order' and 'disorder', 'civilised' and 'uncivilised'. Moreover, it legitimises the categorisation of its population into 'first-class' citizens vis-à-vis a 'mass' of people who are not considered part of this moral community that contributes to the city's growth and success. This is of course a highly cynical hierarchisation since the 'masses' contribute crucially to the functioning of the city (e.g., construction work, domestic work, transport and waste removal). Discussed in particular are the attempts of the new middle classes to become a dominant group and influence power relations, and consequently social spatialisation. The visual rhetoric examined here highlights the desire to attract investment and potential buyers by promising access to 'belong to the world-class'. It also points to various tensions contested in the discursive field of social spatialisation, for instance, between the 'clean' and 'dirty', 'safe' and 'threatening', 'belonging' and 'place-less', first-class and third-class citizens.

One key argument is that an 'enclaved gaze' is generated in and through real estate advertisements. Such a gaze legitimises the rights of particular groups to have access to a privatised space, lifestyle and world-view or 'privatopia' that is restricted to others. This gaze aims at surveying, controlling, disciplining, sanitising and, if necessary, visually and physically excluding certain sections of the population from the 'club of the world-class'. Another argument proposes that architectural as well as symbolic mimicry are on-going processes of appropriating and transforming elements and sites in a way that enables the creation of the imaginary of neoliberal cosmopolitanism. However, it is also seen that this cosmopolitanism is both transnational and nationalist, generally supporting the constitution of a privatised and bourgeois public sphere based on colonial prototypes of identity construction and spatialisation. Finally, it is argued that history, cultural heritage and religion are key elements through which control over the city are sought to be executed, through which the city is marketed by private investors and state representatives ('private–public partnership') and that several examples suggest that religion is used to spearhead further real estate development in a particular and contested area such as the ACC. The primary aim for developers is to transform a locality into a chain of artificial and entertaining sites that appeal to outsiders and possible investors as themed events and festive heritage that constitute the spectacle city.

Another strategy is to spatially divide and exclude 'ordinary' India from 'New India' by establishing gated zones of residential living, consumption and work as if it were a different planet. As a result, India becomes distant and strange, while the new sites are rendered as world-class and 'authentic'. But the flip side to this urban segregation is that the idea of 'real time' capital excess and lifestyle surplus has recently been challenged. Buyers had to realise that the promises given to them about keeping the city's 'other', unwanted reality, outside the gates of the condominium and providing them with 'world-class' standards were not kept. New tenants of luxury gated communities found that the pools were not filled with water, tennis courts and children's playgrounds were never built, the 'promised land' filled with chirping birds and bubbling water fountains did not materialise (see Gentleman 2007). As a result, the number of Residents Welfare Associations and tenants' protests increase, and pressure is put on real estate developers as well as ministries such as that of urban development.

Let us briefly return to the question raised at the beginning of the book: How are the cities imagined, and by whom? How is lifestyle in a megalopolis envisaged and who can afford these imaginaries? In what way are space and place contested, by whom and with what symbolic means? We see that the 'world-class' city suggests an affiliation with transnational circuits of capital flow rather than its hinterland. However, the productive forces feeding the city in terms of basic amenities are visually and physically marginalised, if not excluded. One reason is that late-capitalism privileges not the celebration of production but the production of celebration and consumption. What counts is the shaping of a themed surface and performance-oriented conspicuous lifestyle. Aspiring members of the new middle classes must know how to belong by knowing how to 'speak' and 'read' the language of cosmopolitan taste. To be sure, this rhetoric is not fixed but constantly negotiated and shaped anew. It must provide both orientation towards the world and the locality. It is from within this field of tensions between the global and the local that we understand the making and shaping of today's megacities.

In short, the enclaved gaze is the other side of the coin of cosmopolitanism. It might be open to the world of the spectacle of glamour, celebrating multicultural lifestyles in the manner of the world fairs. But it tends to ignore and marginalise the world outside the gated community, rendering it as an exotic spectacle that can be distanced because of its otherness or appropriated and commodified.

PART II

ॐ

A Spiritual Mega-Experience:
The Akshardham Cultural Complex

T his case-study explores the shaping of modern selves as moral selves through particular aesthetic means, spatiality and ritualisation in the context of a relatively new religious movement. The organisation, Bochasanwasi Shri Akshar Purushottam Swaminarayan Sanstha (hereafter BAPS) is a spiritual–religious community (*sampradaya*) and a charity organisation structured like a multinational corporation. From being a rather enclavic and highly localised organisation from Gujarat in west India, it has entered the centre stage of national and transnational support and attention. Much of its global presence is due to the construction of monumental temples and cultural complexes in urban centres in India and overseas since the 1990s, as well as an extensive and sophisticated use of a wide range of media. Through their strong urban presence, their use of media and mega-events, members of this organisation — and newcomers or outsiders — gain knowledge of the transnational network and activities as if they were members of a close-knit neighbourhood where distance and time did not matter. Temples and media technologies help Swaminarayan think-tanks to create a shared cultural identity and stage the organisation as the custodian of Indian cultural heritage and morals in a way that makes it look 'naturally' legitimate. It communicates the feeling of 'partaking' in something of great global and historical importance. Cities like Atlanta, London, Nairobi or New Delhi are the physical nodes that make the global presence and growing importance of BAPS 'real'. The organisation is particularly interesting because it is regionally rooted and transnationally connected — conservative and innovative, exclusive and inclusive. In the light of economic liberalisation in India, BAPS has moved from its position as a relatively marginal set-up to one of the fastest growing new religious movements with incredible material wealth, confidence and transnational visibility. Urban hubs speak of the transnational dissemination and networks of BAPS members that have shaped along the lines of the history of the Indian diaspora since the nineteenth century. New Delhi as the locus of the most recent construction of a mega-site, speaks of the organisation's transnational importance and flexibility, for the flows of global nomadism are channelled back to the 'homeland' — not to Gujarat, but the nation's booming capital! Where businesses invest in real estate, religious players too, have come to invest in the city as a source of capital.

This case-study is not so much an analysis of BAPS. Rather, it is an exploration into the ways in which this ambitious religio-economic initiative could fall on fertile grounds in the context of urban planning of a 'world-class city' like New Delhi. Smriti Srinivas (2008) has termed this new presence of religion in secular and urban spaces 'urban religion'.

Furthermore, this part of the book investigates the desire for a flexible, prestigious, easy-to-apply-spirituality and a national identity based on specific notions of (mainstream Hindu) cultural heritage, generated for a growing urban middle class and an increasingly transnational consumption culture.[1] Somewhat complementary to Ong's notion of 'flexible citizenship' (1999), Sudhir Kakar's term 'flexible Hindu' points to the habitus and eclectic lifestyle of a predominantly urban, educated middle-class person who can be, at once, traditionalist, nationalist and 'globalist' (2006: 38). More than religion, spirituality and cultural heritage seem to have become key terms of identification for these new cosmopolitans. Finally, this venture also considers different regimes of authenticity played out at the geophysical site in Delhi and through various media technologies, such as Internet websites, DVDs, audio-cassettes, multimedia dioramas, and more, emphasising the importance of exploring a complex composition of representation.

What I look at are the ways in which these 'modern selves' are designed, and regulated, by BAPS to offer different audiences a wide range of identification and participation, providing members and sympathisers with means of guidance and instruction. The BAPS ideology proposes that a moral community can be constructed and spiritual happiness found only with the help of a guru (spiritual guide), life conduct (not lifestyle) and with a particular emphasis on rituals. It also offers to potential members an ideal transnational and national society en miniature and serves as a custodian of Indian cultural heritage.[2]

This part of the book focuses on the Akshardham Cultural Complex (ACC) in New Delhi, a large structure that opened its gates to the public on 7 November 2005, and has since stirred discussions about the legitimacy and authenticity of the place.[3] The ACC is an expression of the

---

[1] For a definition of 'spirituality', I follow Possamai who argues that 'with secularization, the cultural presence of traditional religious institutions has diminished, but the search for a more personal connection to a religion, that is, for spirituality, has increased' (2005: 37; see also Heelas and Woodhead 2005).

[2] Lord Swaminarayan (1781–1830) was born in Uttar Pradesh and settled in Gujarat after travelling through India, preaching, building temples and becoming head of the religious sect of Swaminarayan Sampradaya (see Williams 2001).

[3] 'Akshardham' is the term used to define the heavenly abode of the Supreme, in this instance, Lord Swaminarayan. ACC is also called Swaminarayan Akshardham, Akshardham temple (mandir) or monument.

process of blurring the boundaries between religious belief and profane consumption and leisure activities through the promotion of a set of codes of 'aestheticisation', 'monumentalisation', commodification and 'museumisation', based on the new middle classes' crucial desire for visibility, morality and a 'good life'. For the successful self-legitimisation of the site, followers as well as ordinary visitors are required to internalise certain new codes of convention. In this context, the borders between the concepts of pilgrimage centre, monument, shopping mall, flag-store of a multinational corporation, merchandising giant, luxury condominium, museum, shrine and temple are blurred beyond recognition. This is to such an extent that in December 2007 the committee of the Guinness Book of World Records declared ACC as the largest Hindu temple structure in the world. The labelling of the site as 'sacred' is to some extent surprising insofar as the authentic BAPS temple (*mandir*) is not even part of the gated structure which includes the Monument, the exhibition halls, the pond, and the IMAX hall. The temple used by the majority of Swaminarayan followers, in fact, lies outside the high walls of the leisure complex. This is also a way of keeping large crowds away from what is intended to be a rather intimate site of gathering and religious practice for locals and BAPS *satsangis*.[4] The same holds for the large satsang hall, where followers get together on occasions such as the visit of the spiritual leader Pramukh Swami Maharaj (see Plate IIa).[5] As of late, however, the Monument too is referred to as 'temple' by BAPS members.

Places and institutions like ACC do not emerge just like this, and everywhere. In fact, ACC provides us with a perspective of the relationship between imagination, social life and the production of urban space in late-modern capitalist societies. Being neither solely a leisure space nor a religious site, it is a function of urban real estate development and the shaping of new social and economic elites and lifestyles. I argue that much like a theme park, ACC is structured by, and creates, a culture of civility, security and safety that idealises urban space and thus creates a new ideal of urban religion as part of the public sphere consisting of consumer-citizens.

---

[4] *Satsangi* is the term for a 'companion of the truth', for followers of a religious path or a member of a religious fellowship or *satsang* (Williams 2001: 241). When mentioning satsangis, I refer to full-time volunteers working at the ACC. Part of the satsangi's duty is to contribute around 10–20 per cent of their annual income to the organisation.

[5] See http://www.guinnessworldrecords.com/adjudications/071220_largest_hindu_temple.aspx (accessed 24 August 2008).

The case-study presented in this section investigates the ACC, a monumental site that opened its doors to the public after just five years of construction — another record-breaking fact that is often promoted. Built with the help of 4,000 BAPS volunteers, 7,000 artisans from the famous *sompura* caste from western India and supervised by dozens of *sadhus*, the ACC quickly turned into a magnificent cultural symbol of 'India Shining'.[6] It seemed to be the cure to the experience of disenchantment in the secularised and commercialised lifestyles of 'the West', allowing religion in to shape the 'world-class'. From now on, Delhi as a global city would sport not only the state-of-the-art Metro system or the Commonwealth Games of 2010, but also a national heritage site based on Hindu religious principles and practices. Probably for the first time since the violent demolition of the Babri Masjid in Ayodhya in 1992, Hindu–Muslim riots and the ensuing debates on the role of religion in the secular nation state of India, Hindu religion could be put on display again without apologies. In fact, it could even be associated with the rise of new national confidence and global cultural citizenship.

The opening ceremony of ACC was a mega-ritual, visual and multimedia spectacle of international standard: 20,000 participants were present at the site, millions of people witnessed the ritual via television broadcast.[7] The Prime Minister of India, Manmohan Singh, was present, as well as the then President Abdul Kalam and the leader of the opposition at the time, L. K. Advani (from the Hindu nationalist Bharatiya Janata Party). President Kalam's speech referred to the fact that with such voluntary enthusiasm as shown by the BAPS members, an ideal for all Indians alike, BAPS Akshardham should be understood as 'India's civilizational heritage in dynamic form'. The speech concluded with the appeal for a post-1992 nationalism:

> Akshardham has happened at the dawn of 21st century with the commitment and dedication of one million volunteers. What has happened today at Akshardham inspires me and gives me the confidence that we can do it! The realization of developed India is certainly possible before 2020 with the millions of ignited minds like you (Kalam 2005).

---

[6] A *sadhu* in this context is a renouncer of the world, a Hindu ascetic who has received initiation and taken the vows of Swaminarayan asceticism (Williams 2001: 240). BAPS sadhus are clad in saffron robes and call themselves *brahmacharins* (renouncers), follow radical vegetarianism, strict gender separation in daily matters and movement and live in celibacy.

[7] See the DVD *Swaminarayan Akshardham New Delhi, Dedication Ceremony* (2006). Clips of the opening can be found on http://www.akshardham.com/souvenir/dedicationceremonydvd.htm (accessed 28 June 2008).

This clearly ties BAPS' concepts of voluntary service to selfless nationhood, and re-established (Hindu) Indian identity, or ecumenical Hinduism (Vertovec 2000) as the motor of economic progress and international confidence. But it also shows an inclination to resolve the relationship of individual and larger societal units by emphasising individual responsibility for one's own life and simultaneously a strengthening of community as the ultimate source of values and meaning. The tying together of spiritual awakening and economic development for nation-building (ibid.) is interesting because instead of religion as the basis of cultural heritage, it is spirituality that is mentioned (and thus the accusation of being communalist can be sidelined). Kalam's remarks are also interesting insofar as the citizen's duty to work selflessly for the national good is reintroduced by tying it directly to economic development.

After the monumental opening that was broadcast live on various private, religious as well as national television channels, all kinds of labels gained currency. In personal conversations, BAPS volunteers referred to it as the 'Vatican of India', associating global religious attention and importance to it. Others called ACC a 'Hindu Disney World' (a distinction which is already quite an orientalist way of tourist guidebooks dealing with the colourful richness of south Indian temple architecture), and some critical voices referred to it as inauthentic, pompous capitalism and nationalism. No matter what stance we may take, here we face a new phenomenon of enclaved and yet transnational lifestyle designs that do not shy away from celebrating religious/leisure time and experience as part of cultural globalisation, appropriating structures from theme parks for the purpose of being both entertained and enlightened, and aspiring to become markers of a newly emerging class of globalised and yet 'culturally rooted' citizens. It must be emphasised that within the BAPS *sampradaya*, this terminology is bound to fail and mislead because other categories are valorised, other contexts matter. Thus, different emic perspectives have to be considered and respected. Because I am interested in the ACC as a phenomenon placed within larger discourses on urbanisation, media and transnational migration, much of my analysis will probably not reflect the views of BAPS members.

This case-study sets out with a description of the ACC's topography, its layout and architecture, followed by an exploration of different social agents who work at or visit the site. Thereafter, the question of the ACC's 'efficacy' is raised as to what fills it with meaning and authenticity, and in what way. The key focus is on ritual performances and ritualisation at various points and in different contexts. I propose that a ritual hierarchy is shaped at the ACC through which power, control and distinction are created and circulated. In discussing a range of ritual performances, the highly ambivalent modes of switching codes (e.g., between religion and secularism), appealing to multiple senses and competences, moralising gaze and habitus are explored. A major part of this case-study investigates the creation and fixation of stereotypes as well as strategies of inclusion and exclusion at local, regional, national or transnational and virtual levels.

This section is the result of three years of investigation into the spatial and media productions of BAPS, with a focus on ACC in New Delhi and some research at ACC in Gandhinagar as well as the BAPS temple in London. Besides participatory observation before and after the opening of the Complex to public, interviews with BAPS satsangis, ordinary visitors as well as critics, a vast range of intangible material from various BAPS home-pages and paraphernalia from BAPS shops (e.g., DVDs, books, pictures, postcards and calendars) have been collected, annotated and evaluated. Satellite photography and a plan of the monument's architecture have been used too.

Framing the Site

At first sight, the immense cultural and symbolic power attributed to this place is surprising. Why? First, one would imagine that national leaders of a secular nation state typically privilege secular sites over sacred sites. Second, the ACC is a thoroughly new place with no sacred predecessor and history. Its location is unusual given New Delhi's previous irrelevance in the 'sacred geography' of Hindu pilgrimage sites in India. Yet, it is significant that ACC was not built in any of the sacred cities like Haridwar, Dwarka, Puri or Varanasi but in the national capital whose location is of much more importance. From within the BAPS, ACC has been attributed with a purpose: it is said to assure India's spiritual and economic progress and to possess sacred status in its materialisation of the vision of Yogi Maharaj, the spiritual leader of BAPS and Pramukh Swami Maharaj's predecessor:

> A Mandir on the Banks of River Yamuna … A Wish Fulfilled … In the heart of India's capital, New Delhi, and on the banks of the holy river Yamuna, the mandir emerges like a glistening pearl … a monument to Hindu spirituality and ancient architecture … Delhi is the capital of India and there the sovereign *Purushottam Narayan* is to preside.[8]

---

[8] *Purushottam* stands for the supreme person and highest divine reality. See www.swaminarayan.org/news/2003/02/NewDelhi/index.htm (accessed 30 September 2006).

Index

1 Monument	7 Ghats
2 Sound and Light Show/Musical Fountain	8 Temple
3 Theme Hall 1 (*Sahajanand Darshan*: Hall of Values)	9 Food Court
4 IMAX Hall (*Mystic India*)	10 Souvenir Hall
5 Theme Hall 3 (*Sanskruti Vihar*: Abode of Culture)	11 Parking
6 Abhishek Mandap	12 Garden

Plate IIa: Detail of a satellite picture of Akshardham Cultural Complex. The red colour demarcates green vegetation as per GIS photography (2008).

Source: Marcus Nuesser, GIS-remote sensing laboratory, Department of Geography, South Asia Institute with support from Cluster of Excellence 'Asia and Europe in a Global Context', Heidelberg University.

The quote reflects the attempt to create both a pilgrimage site with a myth-ical origin (vision and destination) and a cultural and national heritage centre. This way, ownership can be claimed over culture (i.e., 'high' Hindu traditions). This rhetoric, part nation-building, part spiritual awakening, is echoed by a prominent BAPS swami who argues that ACC is an 'integrated complex of ancient Indian civilizational heritage' (Sadhu Swayamprakashdas 2005: 18). National pride, self-sacrifice and spiritual enlightenment are presented as intertwined preconditions of a 'New India' rising to become a global moral leader.

I visited the ACC several times before the public inauguration in November 2005, speaking to several satsangis (at devotional congregations) and participating in various *aratis* at the temple next to the ACC or *satsangs* in the assembly hall.[9] It was truly impressive to see the speed at which the site grew, and to listen to the enthusiasm articulated by those people involved in the construction work in one or another way. Two weeks before the public opening, ACC opened its doors to BAPS satsangis, the press and VIPs, following a very strict list of daily entries. More than 8,000 volunteers from the *sampradaya* were involved in the opening procedures, for instance, in preparing food for the inpouring thronging visitors, becoming public relations officers or guides, looking after security, transport, accommodation and decoration.[10] Volunteers had come from BAPS centres all over the world to participate in *seva* (voluntary work). The place was like a beehive, filled with activity and good spirit. Most of the people I spoke to underlined how happy they were that they could play a role in such a historical moment of national importance. During my research on ACC, I grew particularly close to a joint family in which every member was a BAPS satsangi with experience of overseas migration and had a prominent status within the movement's hierarchy. At the time of the opening, almost every family member was at the site and had arrived from Nairobi, Atlanta, Beirut and London. Some had moved to Delhi in order to be at the service of BAPS, current spiritual leader Pramukh Swami Maharaj and the construction of

[9] *Satsang* is a regular congregation of the community of devotees (satsangis) who gather to listen to discourses by the swamis and chant devotional hymns. BAPS members are expected to visit the temple daily, attend the weekly *satsangs* and *sabhas* (mostly gender-separated meetings). There are weekly children and youth group meetings, again, divided according to gender.

[10] Out of 8,233 volunteers listed, 6,753 were male. Most of the women worked in the kitchen (see Sadhu Swayamprakashdas 2005: 84). After the opening, many female volunteers worked as guides.

ACC; others had come to stay only for a few months to help during the intense preparation times and the opening. At the time of construction work as well as after the site was opened, most family members were full-timers and had been delegated their *seva* at the ACC, to look after the public relations work, the VIP guests or the 'ordinary' visitors.

ACC is situated at the riverbanks of the Yamuna, a stone's throw from the colonial and posh centre of the capital (Plate IIb). Even around 2000, East Delhi had a very low status compared to the city on the western side of the Yamuna. Now, due to an aggressive and expansionist real estate market, with new integrated townships like Greater Noida coming up, East Delhi and bordering parts of the NCR are in the process of being gentrified. As a USP, ACC has contributed much to this upward mobility.

Even before the public opening of ACC, Nizamuddin bridge came to be referred to as the 'Akshardham flyover'. In fact, even the Metro station (under construction then) was to be named 'Akshardham Station'. As of

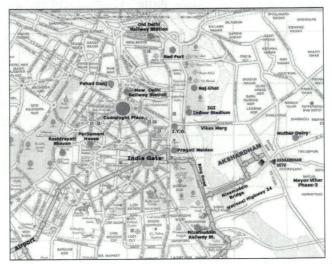

Plate IIb: Location of the Akshardham Cultural Complex, with other popular tourist spots in New Delhi nearby, especially since the British Raj (India Gate, Connaught Place, etc.) to the left.[11]

Source: © BAPS, http://www.akshardham.com/visitorinfo/index.htm (accessed 15 November 2009). Used with permission.

---

[11] © BAPS. Used with permission. See http://www.akshardham.com/visitorinfo/index.htm (accessed 30 September 2006).

November 2009, this station has become operational in view of the Commonwealth Games, 2010. On approaching East Delhi from this road, ACC emerges like a phantasmagoric oasis in a desert (Plate IIc). It certainly is a site that intends to impress, seduce and appeal to business people, visiting tourists, Delhi's affluent citizens, BAPS followers and religious pilgrims alike. Interestingly, it does so by means of offering itself to the 'masses' as a quasi-temple, a monument, a museum, a place where miracles happen, an event, a knowledge institution, and more. To its curious visitors, the Akshardham Complex promises it all: the 'authentic' taste of the ancient (Vedic/Hindu) past, the experience of going on a pilgrimage through India, of executing rituals for personal wellbeing and salvation (*moksha*), the encounter with great spiritual and national figures and knowledge systems, and a multi-sensuous spectacle. In order to legitimise itself as a spiritual authority beyond the borders of its own *sampradaya*, BAPS refers to and appropriates broader familiar aspects of history, religion and mythology that are very often part and parcel of the national school curriculum or diaspora cultural production. ACC is the youngest among the other religio-spiritual complexes and features prominently on the list of Delhi's tourist attractions. The city and the organisation are united in the desire to compete for national leadership and 'world-class' status.

Plate IIc: Approaching the ACC from the 'Akshardham flyover' (2009).

The Pilgrimage

'Swaminarayan Akshardham is a gigantic success story', reads the introductory text of the special issue of *Swaminarayan Bliss*, the bimonthly magazine of BAPS brought out at the inauguration of the site. Now, what makes this a ritual topography? I shall describe only a few points of attraction of this 'success story', adding more details in the course of the chapters to follow. Hundreds of stones carved in Rajasthan were brought to Delhi to be assembled at the site and used for the construction of the Monument and the colonnade.[12] In several brochures, the colonnades are named *parikrama*, referring to the circumambulation of a sacred site during pilgrimage. ACC contains over 60 acres of land, buildings, courtyards and themed landscape gardens (see Plate IIa). Even entering the site has a certain ritual character because one must let go of all worldly items (with the only exception that one may carry a wallet and bottled water). After passing through a thorough and even more rigid security control, visitors are channelled through ornate archways and shrines, to a huge reception hall where information can be sought from one of the many volunteers (more than a dozen at any given time) who work as spot-guides, or from information panels that carry both visuals and text (in Hindi, Gujarati and English), explaining the background of the ACC and the BAPS. A replica of Swaminarayan's feet in a pond awaits the visitor and here, many people start donating money by throwing coins into the water and making a wish. The vista then opens up to the Monument built with pink sandstone, 141 ft high, 316 ft wide and 356 ft long — the view is overwhelming (Plate IIc).

It is said that the Monument is created in consonance with principles of ancient Hindu temple architecture across India, after consulting one of the most famous Indian temple architects in the western region, involved in previous BAPS temple initiatives. The Trivedis are known for their elaborate work on Jain temples, and embrace the lineage of grandfather, son and grandson — members of the craftsmen of the *sompura* caste.[13]

---

[12] The term 'Monument' refers specifically to the heart of the ACC — the particular building in which the images of the founding figure and his disciples can be found (Plate IIa).

[13] The Akshardham Monument at Gandhinagar, completed in 1992, was built by Chandrakand Sompura from Gujarat's capital, a master architect for Jain temples in Gujarat who created the monument in the Haveli tradition, following the ancient architectural doctrine of the *stapati shastra*. The Trivedis were also involved in the construction of BAPS temples overseas in the USA. I am grateful to Niels Gutschow for this information.

Inside the Monument are *murtis* — divine statues of Swaminarayan and his Guru Parampara, i.e., the four spiritual leaders of the BAPS and Swaminarayan's best devotees as well as other deities from the Hindu pantheon. The Monument is built without steel and consists of 234 carved pillars and nine domes; its outside walls (*peeth*) called *parikrama* (sacred circumambulation), and the domes inside are covered with figurines of sadhus, deities and animals depicting stories from different mythologies and the life of Swaminarayan. The claim is repeatedly made that all the elements incorporated in the overall structure of the Akshardham Cultural Complex have been derived from the ancient *shilpashastra* (code of architecture) and thereby directly connect with the Hindu 'golden age' of pre-Islamic India.[14] Before or after visiting the Monument, one can purchase a ticket for the three theme halls for INR 125 (c. €2.20).[15] Visitors to the musical fountain (that starts at sunset) need to pay, in addition, INR 20 (c. €0.30). Entrance to the site itself is free. A visit of the theme halls does not only cost a considerable amount of money; it also requires extra time period of approximately two hours.

The three halls are rhetorically linked to Hindu ritual practices, pilgrimage and *darshan* (broadly defined as seeing and being seen by the divine by paying obeisance to and looking at a murti — a sacred idol or image). Raymond B. Williams, who studied the Swaminarayan Movement for over ten years writes: 'Sadhus say that Akshardham [at Gandhinagar, the first complex, finalised in 1992] extended the concept of *darshan* by adding *pradarshan*, which refers not to seeing the images of the god but to observing an exhibition' (2001: 178). Elsewhere he reports that 'one sadhu explained the development of these large exhibits in this way: "People come to the temple for *darshan* to develop their spirituality; they come to the exhibitions for *pradarshan* in order to gain understanding"' (Williams 2001: 180). Thus, education, cultural competence, spiritual experience and devotion come to converge in the ACC.

The first theme hall is entitled the 'Hall of Values' in English and 'Sahajanand Darshan' in Hindi, referring to the sacred experience of seeing,

---

[14] The ACC homepage exhibits the key important sites at the ACC with photograph galleries (www.akshardham.com/whattosee/). It is claimed that the over 7,000 artisans working voluntarily on the sculptures in and around the Monument were spiritually and morally uplifted. A detailed description of the different architectural elements and their meaning is given in the special inaugural issue of *Swaminarayan Bliss*, (October–November 2005: 36–44, 49–63).

[15] There are concessions for large groups and children who are charged INR 50 per head (c. €0.45).

i.e., experiencing Swaminarayan's childhood and youth (he was called Sahajanand in his youth) while visiting the 60-minute audio-animatronics show with films and dioramas. The scenes are said to communicate the importance of vegetarianism, non-violence (*ahimsa*), family harmony, morality and prayer. While the dioramas take the visitors back into the eighteenth century, into Swaminarayan's life, the semi-documentary films portray BAPS and their spiritual leader Pramukh Swami Maharaj in the context of an Arcadian presence. There are scenes of children playing happily at the stairs of a BAPS temple, close-ups of young men listening carefully to their teacher in the building, the spiritual leader walking through beautiful gardens, accompanied by some swamis. The overall message is that one is responsible for one's life and spiritual wellbeing and that one must have 'professional' guidance for this task, from a guru such as Pramukh Swami Maharaj.

The second hall houses the IMAX cinema, and is called 'Neelkanth Darshan', where one can experience the divine sight of the young Lord Swaminarayan, at this stage of his life known by the name 'Neelkanth', on his way to sainthood. A 40-minute feature film takes the viewer on a pilgrimage through the whole of India, journeying the most sacred sites and tracing the map of sacred India: rivers and mountains, temples and *ashrams*, from north to south, east to west. The film (shown on a mega-screen of 85 × 65 ft.) aims at familiarising the visitor with eighteenth century-India, narrating that Neelkanth's actions and values were all aimed at a betterment of society's morale and religious belief and practice that were in a process of decline, destruction and disbelief. 'Neelkanth Yatra' (pilgrimage) was shot at 108 locations (108 being a sacred number in Hindu philosophy), with a cast of 45,000 people, again ending with a view on today's relevance of having a guru in order to attain salvation and happiness.[16] In a slightly edited form, the film is shown as *Mystic India: An Incredible Journey of Inspiration* to a global audience interested in Indian wisdom, culture and religion.[17]

The third and last theme hall is called Sanskruti Vihar (literally, abode of culture, translated as 'India's Glorious Heritage' in an ACC leaflet), that consists of a 12-minute long boat ride through the 'world's oldest village life and bazaar in Vedic India', allegedly world's first university at Taxila,

[16] The 70mm-film was produced by a team of BAPS sadhus, director Keith Melton, script writers Kamlesh Pandey and Mose Richards, based on two years of 'authentic research' on eighteenth-century India and Neelkanth's life, books and drawings published by the British government or travellers and explorers visiting India at that time (Sadhu Swayamprakashdas 2005: 50).

[17] See www.mysticindia.com (accessed 22 August 2009).

scientific laboratories of rishi (holy men). Here, the visitor learns that plastic surgery as well as gravitational law and flight studies were developed and discovered in the Vedic age. Visitors float by dioramas depicting classical arts and performances and leave the hall with Swaminarayan's message of world peace and harmony. Altogether, there are five audio-animatronics shows, 81 dioramas and 800 fibreglass figures in the theme hall complex (Sadhu Swayamprakashdas 2005: 32).[18] The computerised shows are in Hindi and, upon request, in English.

The three halls can only be accessed through a ticket control booth. Upon entering and leaving, one passes by the so-called Vedic *Yagna Kund*, the fire pit (translated as 'step-well' in several brochures on ACC, Plate IId) of Vedic sacrifice — also the site of the musical fountain in the evenings. The musical choreography is claimed to represent important life-cycle rituals (birth, marriage, death) and Vedic traditions of sacrifice, as we learn from a description on ACC's website:

> The fascinating web of life on earth is intricate, precise and beautiful. Its fragile network shows an uncompromising interdependency between man, nature and God. Therefore what we receive for sustenance by way of earth, water, fire, air and space, we need to repay and sacrifice with body, mind and heart. To fulfil this function in life, India's great sages and rishis established the yagna tradition. They chanted mantras, offered grains and ghee in a sacrificial fire (*yagna kund*) to appease the deities of earth, water, fire, air, etc. *Yagna* means to sacrifice or generously give in appreciation to others.[19]

Water is a key symbol and narrative motif at the ACC. Not only does it provide an over-abundance of greenery in a city known for its notorious

---

[18] According to a key coordinator of the theme halls, the boats weigh 2.5 tons; the water is 1.5 meters deep; and the technology, as with the other dioramas, is bought from Germany and the USA. It is important to maintain the water so that it does not become smelly, the boat-ride is smooth and silent (the boats are not pulled), and the colours do not fade too quickly because of humidity. In the halls, 600 human figures are exhibited, including the smallest (dark-skinned) robot in the world (Jayesh V., personal conversation, March 2006).

[19] Allegedly, it is the world's largest step-well: 'In its center lies an 8-petaled lotus shaped *yagna kund* designed according to the Jayaakhya Samhita of the *Panchratra* scripture. Its perfect geometric forms testify to ancient India's advanced knowledge in mathematics and geometry. At night the center comes to life with a colorful musical water fountain that echoes the Vedic sentiments of India'. See http://www.akshardham.com/whattosee/musicalfountains/index.htm (accessed 4 May 2007).

Plate IId: The step-well of the musical fountain, with the IMAX cinema hall and the large statue of Neelkanth in the background, New Delhi (2006).

Source: © BAPS, http://www.akshardham.com/photogallery/musical fountains/index.htm (accessed 6 December 2009). Used with permission.

lack of water, it has mythological and religious symbolic meaning and serves major ritual functions of purification. The ritual functions of water and their association with ancient Vedic traditions are repeatedly woven into the visit, turning it into a chain of 'ritual citations' and experiences that draw upon familiar, yet larger, ritual complexes. Between the IMAX hall and the step-well stands a 27 ft. high bronze murti of Neelkanth (Plate IId), which is also available for sale as a small figurine from the souvenir shop at the exit. Several female satsangis told me that they have a similar small statue at home and worship it daily (see also Plate 8.1). When I visited the site a year before the official opening, in early 2005, I was told by a full-timer that the musical fountains are like a constant ritual pouring of sacred water over the divine statue (*abhishek*), thus creating a new mega-ritual in modern times. While circumventing the Monument clockwise, the visitor passes by another lake, called Narayan Sarovar. It surrounds the Monument almost completely. This is another reference to the centrality of water in pilgrimage, combining the worship of ancestors and water deities through steps (*ghats*) and coming in physical contact with the sacred substance as well as the idea that particularly sacred ponds carry the water of other sacred rivers lakes, and the sea. Narayan Sarovar contains 'holy waters from 151 rivers and lakes sanctified by Bhagwan Swaminarayan' and water pours through 108 fountains in the shape of cow heads (*gaumukh*) made of metal (Sadhu Swayamprakashdas 2005: 27, 40).[20] This follows the principle of 'replicating' the entire sacred territory of India in one 'vessel' and thus allowing the devotee to go on an imaginary, yet 'real' pilgrimage. The ACC homepage on its website quotes from the ancient script Rig Veda to underline the sanctity of the site: 'Where there is pure water, there lies a pilgrim place and therein the gods sport (Rig Ved 4.9.3, Bhavishya Puran: 1.130.15)'.[21]

Another ritual site is Neelkanth Abhishek Mandap, a small pavilion made of carved marble, and situated at the lake that surrounds the Monument. Here, visitors can offer abhishek to the statue of Neelkanth by pouring water from the lake through a bronze vessel (*kalash*). There are various versions to the ritual that is always supervised by two aspiring sadhus, and usually a nominal amount of money is donated, ranging from INR 11 (c. €0.15) to 51 (c. €0.90) or even more. The *grihasthas* (householders serving the murtis) also perform abhishek for absent devotees who have donated a lump sum for a particular period. It is said that 'prayers for spiritual upliftment and fulfilment of wishes' (Sadhu Swayamprakashdas 2005: 40) can be made here and in fact, I met several people (all women) who had repeatedly returned to the site because of the alleged efficacy of these prayers.

The choreographed visit of the ACC ends with a walk through a lotus-shaped garden with panels that carry aphorisms by prominent people (Indian and western thinkers) and a possible visit to the restaurant (which simulates the famous paintings of the caves at Ellora and Ajanta) and finally the huge souvenirshop emulating the themed architecture of a temple, where all kinds of religious paraphernalia, ritual items, postcards, framed pictures, printed T-shirts, books and DVDs as well as a BAPS brand of ayurvedic medicine can be bought. In front of these two buildings is a courtyard. In fact, this is the only place in the open where people can sit and rest in groups without being told by guards or loudspeakers to move on. Those visitors who donate money in one of the boxes at the Monument and receive a receipt from one of the desks at the ritual sites, can later

---

[20] *Gaumukh* is also the name for the glacial source of the Ganga river.
[21] See http://www.akshardham.com/whattosee/mandir/narayansarovar.htm (accessed 28 June 2008).

pick up a small pink plastic box, with the photograph of the ACC on top, consisting of *prasad* (blessed sweets). To exit, one must walk along the high security walls of the site.

Including the theme halls and the musical fountain, a standard visit to the ACC lasts approximately four to five hours. On leaving the theme halls aside, a standard visit takes around two hours, depending on whether one partakes in the *arati* at the Monument or the abhishek at the pavilion, both rituals lasting about 10–15 minutes.

who is who at the ACC?

This case-study explores the variety of social agents present at the ACC, and the various functions taken up by them, both in terms of the ritual and organisational infrastructure provided by BAPS and the visitors, who may come as pilgrims or tourists, or both. One of the most interesting experiences for me was that none of the categories with which I tried to classify the groups worked for too long: for instance, the ritual specialists were also event managers and technology experts, the volunteers were both guides and devotees, and the visitors were devotees-cum-leisure tourists.

The concept of the ACC was developed by spiritual leader Pramukh Swami Maharaj (PSM, also referred to as 'the Inspirer'), and a team of about 20 senior swamis who headed different project units. While PSM is said to have provided the groups with inspiration and guidance, and made final decisions, other swamis were in charge of the acquisition of land and government-related work, design of the master plan, research for exhibitions, films, sacred objects, or historical scripts, the music programme (including the choreography of the musical fountain), coordination of local services, placement of the sculpted stones, supervision of the production of animatronics, the restaurant, the souvenir shop and so forth.

On the following pages, I will focus on the BAPS full-timers, the range of visitors, and the BAPS set-up. I am keeping BAPS satsangis outside the category of full-timers because their category is even more complex, and I did not collect sufficient empirical material on them in the course of my fieldwork.

Full-Timers

Full-time volunteers were asked to come to Delhi to undertake sub-organisational tasks such as engineering and construction consultancy. Vipul G. and his family, for instance, had been called by PSM from Nairobi where they owned a profitable industry and were strongly involved in

BAPS community work in the temple. Vipul was put in charge of a host of public relations activities. He and his wife and their relatives have since permanently settled down in New Delhi and serve as full-timers in the information and public relations section. Sangeeta J., in her mid-20s, had arrived from Atlanta where she lives with her husband, a senior BAPS satsangi. Sangeeta works in the BAPS' children's education and training section. She came to Delhi for a few months to support BAPS during the opening period of ACC. Like hundreds of other male and female volunteers at that time, she worked as a spot-guide, photographer and in the kitchen. Arpit D. worked in the media cell of ACC, having arrived from the USA in the summer of 2006. He told me that he had been very excited about having been called by PSM. A national scholarship winner with a background in Economics, his plan for the following summer was to go backpacking through India, with a BAPS swami, partly following the route of Neelkanth's *yatra* (pilgrimage). He was born (and grew up) in the USA and this was his first time in decades that he had visited his 'motherland'. Both Sangeeta and Arpit represent the growing group of overseas Indians who consider it a duty to invest in their home-country and simultaneously, their *sampradaya*.

There were many others who joined the army of volunteers at ACC since 2005, and most of them were not from Delhi. The majority was from BAPS' communities in the 'home-region' of BAPS — Gujarat in western India. Many volunteers (no precise numbers are available) had arrived from overseas where they and their families lived. The global network of BAPS is remarkable and has gained an almost mythical reputation in terms of the wealth the small community from Gujarat have accumulated in the last few decades and in terms of their conspicuous religiosity when it comes to opulent festivals and temple architecture.[1]

All full-timers I spoke to underlined the fact that they were very proud to be allowed to volunteer at ACC. In their view, they were part of a significant movement of mass awakening and national historical event. They emphasised time and again that selfless service (*seva*) was a pillar of their life conduct: 'When you are called by Him, you give up your previous occupation and put all your energy into volunteer work' (Vipul G., personal conversation, New Delhi, March 2006). But not all are chosen. In several conversations with volunteers I learnt that PSM also rejected people who

---

[1] See http://www.swaminarayan.org/globalnetwork/index.htm (accessed 18 July 2008). The site displays all major BAPS centres in Africa, Australia, New Zealand, North America, Europe and India.

had approached him with the request to dedicate themselves to full-time seva at the ACC or to even become a sadhu. He would instead ask them to complete a particular training that could then be of use for seva. This was the case with Jayesh V. who was in charge of the theme hall technologies and who had worked as a computer engineer for the Indian Space Research Organisation until he joined BAPS as a full-timer. His aim now was to become a sadhu. Once or twice a day, the volunteers at the ACC would go to the temple outside the Monument's compound for *puja*. Some would also participate at the *arati* performed in the Monument in the mornings and evenings. Thus, to say that the ACC is not more than a site of consumption is misleading. For many, it is a site of production of various kinds.

Visitors

Apart from the misconception that ACC is just a site of consumption, it would certainly also be misleading to say that it is only a site for the middle classes. Despite the fact that ACC is the centre stage of Delhi tourism and part of the global trend of creating museums and theme parks for a growing number of leisure and culture consumers, it is not just visited by members of the new middle classes. People from all class backgrounds, from different generational and religious backgrounds visit the ACC. Increasingly, foreign tourists are finding their way to the site although the large majority of visitors still consists of Indians. On a normal weekday, approximately 2,000 people visit the ACC. On a day of the weekend, this number can go up to about 5,000 or even more.[2] Less than 50 per cent of the visitors buy tickets for the theme halls; others do not want to pay this amount. For many lower middle class families, an entrance fee of more than €2 per person is a rather significant amount of money. Some others skip the theme halls because they come in tourist groups and would not spend more than two hours at the site so as to be able to see the other sites on the tour programme; another category of people give the theme halls a miss because they have been there before and/or just come for a leisure stroll around the arcades and gardens on a holiday or in the evening to enjoy the relatively cheap and good south Indian, Gujarati or western meals at the Food Court. There is a VIP hall where diplomats, prominent people from political or media world, as well as some foreign tourists are seated in air-conditioned lounges on white sofas, looking at large posters of the

---

[2] One of the full-timers claimed that it was 10,000–40,000 visitors per day. No official statistics could be accessed.

ACC or PSM. One of the senior swamis or a representative of the media cell may even meet selected male representatives. This separate building is guarded in order to prevent ordinary visitors from entering. Most Indian visitors come to the ACC in groups such as families or villagers; there are young couples seeking a romantic stroll, older married couples with their children and grandchildren, groups of dressed-up young men and girls sweeping across the marble (more as though they were strolling through a shopping mall), boys stopping by the sacred lake to playfully throw water on the girls (not without being immediately brought to order by the cautious guards). Many middle class families come in the evening, after work, for a walk along the lawns, on the marble, for pure leisure, especially because there are so few public spaces in Delhi for such occasions. Some may use the chance to visit the temple or participate in the evening *arati* at the Monument. On weekdays, school classes are guided through the site, and made to assemble for short lectures on BAPS and Swaminarayan, followed by collective prayers in front of paintings of Swaminarayan and PSM in the visitors' hall.[3] Visitors seem to come from different class and regional backgrounds, and even different religions, predominantly Christian and Sikh. Probably over 70 per cent of the visitors are followers of Hindu or BAPS belief.[4]

In terms of geographical regions, a senior PR representative of ACC told me, people come from all over India. A good number of visitors are overseas Indians visiting their relatives in India for a holiday, people who had heard of this 'wonder of the world' from friends or information through media. This is an important factor. It shows, on the one hand, that we have to acknowledge the growing interest of overseas Indians in national heritage and sightseeing, in tandem with the rise of domestic tourism and a dramatically improved tourist and pilgrimage infrastructure.[5] On the other hand, this must simultaneously point our interest to the fact that ACC must be seen in the context of the presence and influence of temples in the diaspora. It is relatively certain that celebratory discourses about ACC

---

[3] In February 2006, approximately 20,000 school children visited the ACC, according to an on-site school guide. BAPS also offers training for teachers, and in fact, the ACC has come to be a very popular spot for school visits. For groups over 20 people, the tickets for the theme halls are reduced to INR 50 per head (c. €0.90).

[4] However, so far no survey of caste denominations has been made.

[5] Many devotees from International Society for Krishna Consciousness (ISKCON), for instance, now embark on India-wide pilgrimages to see famous Krishna temples. (I thank Sophie Hawkins for this information.)

circulate through such global temple and *gurdwara* networks. The diaspora temples definitely serve a legitimising function, both at the global scale insofar as they reinforce religion as well as at a personal level through which they bind, root or connect people to home and locality. In this way, the ACC can even be defined as a 'diaspora temple'.

Some people come to worship at one of the ritual sites; others want to learn about Swaminarayan, or witness the musical fountain at sunset when the whole complex is festively lit. Most probably, the majority comes for various reasons at once, as it is relatively easy to find stimulation on multiple levels at the cultural complex. I could see, during my visits, several crowds puzzled by the change machines that returned coins in exchange for large denominations, lawn-watering machines and lawn-mowers, possibly seeing those devices of modern technology for the first time in their lives. They reminded me of those visitors from small towns or villages who come to Delhi in order to escalators in the Metro. Even foreign tourists (a minority) are viewed with similar curiosity by some of their Indian fellow visitors.

Thus, there is a whole spectrum of people who arrive at the site, equipped with different symbolic and financial capital, different regional and ethnic backgrounds, different desires and interests. Sadhna G., one of the full-time guides awaiting visitors in the large reception hall of the ACC, tells me that because of the different sets of visitors she prefers the weekdays to the weekends:

> On a weekday, you have school kids, very interested, and you have the educated crowds, mostly from the cities or from south India. On a weekend it can be so tough! Then you have busloads of villagers, uneducated and noisy people who make fun of Bhagwan Swaminarayan and us, who want to sit down on the lawns and have a picnic (personal conversation, New Delhi, October 2006)!

Having predominantly lived in small close-knit communities of fellow satsangis, many of the satsangis are exposed to the 'rest of the world' for the first time. This changes their self-perception as they find themselves confronted with people who have a different opinion and knowledge of BAPS and Swaminarayan. Furthermore, from an orthodox viewpoint, mundane citizens are of relatively low moral standard and possibly, ritually speaking, even polluting. The just cited quote also reflects that my informant tries to make sense of the visitors' behaviour by classifying them. She maintains that different kinds of behaviour are associated with different categories of people: there are the cultivated and the educated lot looking for more understanding and deeper experiences (middle classes), and there is the leisure-seeking superficial 'mob' that conceives of the ACC virtually as a fair-ground (lower classes, 'new rich'). There are the ones who go on a *parikrama* (circumambulation) and those who just want to go for a walk (*ghumna*).

One aspect I want to highlight, however, is that the middle classes too show the tendency to differentiate themselves as being more 'genteel' than the lower classes by stigmatising them as 'masses', as noisy and playful crowd that privileges picnic over pilgrimage. They do so by responding to the idea of a cultural repertoire of 'high religion' and historical knowledge of 'cultured people'. I shall subsequently explore the distinction of groups, taste and attributed behaviours as one of patronising, disciplining and infantilising allegedly 'lower class' members (see also Cross 2006). I will also explore the underlining motivation to transform visitors into consumers despite the rejection of flânerie. The heterogeneity of visitors turns the ACC into a truly complicated field of discourse that shall be elaborated in more detail after we have turned to the key agents behind the construction of ACC.

Purity and Spirituality: BAPS

A few words about the spiritual organisation behind the ACC. Founded in 1907 as a splinter group of the Swaminarayan Movement, BAPS is a relatively young religious organisation. In the course of the second half of the twentieth century, and mainly through transnational activities of its wealth-generating followers, it has become tremendously affluent in terms of its global presence, connectivity and following. BAPS is considered as a very prestigious socio-religious institution to which members of the aspiring middle classes, in particular, both in India and abroad, tie desires of upward social mobility. To many, belonging to BAPS means that they can draw upon well-oiled social and professional networks. In the context of this particular growth, the display of confidence of the organisation and its satsangis has been both fed by and resulted in a professional use of new media and event management as well as the creation of a global network of connectivity, or what Hannerz terms 'global ecumene' through the worldwide construction of temples, 'cultural centres' and the organisation of festivals as well as charitable work. The temple's identity as a spiritual and humanitarian centre, promulgating moral reform through ritual practice and voluntary religio-social service (seva) is central to this movement. Temple and ritual constitute the social and cultural fabric, or the 'cultural heart' (Falzon 2005) through which the community develops and promotes a shared consciousness and the notion of cosmopolitan Indianness. Within this rather impoverished notion of society and culture, ritual is considered as part of healing of modern selves, and seva is turned into spiritual upliftment through selflessness.[6] I argue that BAPS practises what Max Weber called 'protestant ethic' in the context of capitalist spirit, where individuals could accumulate or display wealth without becoming morally illegitimate for worldly success could be associated with salvation. What Weber observed in the early-twentieth century was clearly focused on Europe; in his analysis of the Indian caste system he would probably not have imagined that caste and class would complement each other, as in the case of the BAPS. According to his view, ritual and the alleged inalterability of world order suppressed flexibility, mobility and thus the development of capitalism. This, however, needs to be revised in the light of new religious or spiritual movements in India today where rational life conduct according to inner-worldly asceticism is a constitutive element of capitalism and modern culture, and that self discipline and control determine the new interest in (and relevance of) religion in modernity.

Clearly, BAPS has not emerged in a social or historical vacuum. Its rise was at a time when Max Weber wrote *Protestant Ethic and the Spirit of Capitalism* (1904–5). David Hardiman has argued that the Swaminarayan sect is 'an ideological voice of an emerging class of commercial farmers and capitalist entrepreneurs' that manages to appeal to people from lower classes and castes aspiring to gain upward class mobility (Hardiman 1988: 1907) — a case of Sanskritisation. He further reveals that recruitment of followers into the sect was primarly from among Rajput peasants, Patidars, Kolis, Kathis and artisan castes, very few from the old Gujarati elites or from dalit and *adivasi* groups (ibid.). It is also worth mentioning that a large section of the followers of Lord Swaminarayan are — like the organisation itself — educated, often professionals taking up leading positions in administration, the free market, and so on.

BAPS is a branch of the Hindu Swaminarayan sect (established in the early eighteenth century) with more than one million followers worldwide and spread across the world in 45 countries, active in more than 3,300 centres

---

[6] BAPS is based on gender separation during ritual performances, and promotes rather conservative gender roles (see Hardiman 1998; Williams 2001). They refer to Vaishnavism and have incorporated many elements of Hindu reformist movements of the nineteenth century, such as the centrality of congregational worship, the importance of the vernacular as sacred language, and so forth (see Dwyer 2004: 181–82).

and 700 temples. BAPS' Global Network has a greater presence outside South Asia than any other Hindu group (Williams 2001) — I counted 56 centres in North America, three centres in Australia and New Zealand, eight centres in East and South Africa and six centres in the UK. There are, of course, many more subbranches in each of the regions mentioned.

Officially, satsangis describe themselves as being part of 'a socio-spiritual organisation with its roots in the Vedas'. The BAPS' online mission statement claims the following:

> Founded on the pillars of practical spirituality, [BAPS] reaches out far and wide to clear the confusions and questions in our moral, social and material world of today. It teaches a way to lead a peaceful life. Its strength lies in the purity of its nature and purpose. The Sanstha strives to better the world by consolidating character in societies, families and individuals. This is done not just by mottos and slogans but by mass motivation and individual attention, through elevating projects for all, irrespective of class, creed, color and country. The Sanstha's universal work has received many national welfare awards and the affiliation to the United Nations. Its international network has flourished into 9,090 youth, children and women centers, over 770 sadhus, 55,000 volunteers, several hundred temples in India and abroad and the dedication of over one million followers.[7]

According to Raymond Williams, followers of Swaminarayan's philosophy argue:

> [that] at a critical time of social change and the breakdown of the old world-view, Swaminarayan took the best of the religious tradition in India and constructed a new and more adequate sacred world. Thus, they say, in the past two centuries in the face of increasing secularization and the weakening of religious devotion, the Swaminarayan religion has provided a revitalization of the experience of sacred person, sacred space, and sacred time (2001: 100–101).

In his analysis of the global religious Radhasoami movement, Mark Juergensmeyer has elaborated a convincing approach towards the sect's popularity among urban and transnational middle class circles, applicable to BAPS as well. He writes that the movement is characterised by:

> an appropriation of a truth greater than science, a therapeutic approach to the self, and the reestablishment of personal authority in the social realm — (and) appeal(s) to those who for various reasons have (become) tired of the modern

---

[7] See www.swaminarayan.org (accessed 5 May 2007).

world, but are unsatisfied with what the more traditional forms of faith offer as alternatives. They constitute a form of faith that is modern in a distinctly Indian way, for it is hard to imagine another culture that would have as easy access to notions of the truth as an active agent, the self as fluid, malleable entity, and authority as an element of intimate relationships (Juergensmeyer 1992: 296).

What we find here is a phenomenon that has already been 'diagnosed' in the context of global spirituality: devotion is simultaneously privatised and commercialised. In Heelas and Woodhead's words: spirituality's global popularity is the result of a synthesis of secularisation and sacralisation, caused by a 'massive subjective turn' of modern culture towards an individualistic and holistic lifestyle (Heelas and Woodhead 2005:10).[8]

While the 'subjective turn' might be a useful concept to analyse the relevance of new religious movements to individuals outside a *sampradaya*, this view would be misleading when exploring the fabric of the organisation. Neither do we find indications of an engagement with 'Self' nor is there any mention of 'lifestyle'. Instead, the emphasis is on self-realisation through non-individualistic seva and life-conduct. The ideals of mobility and flexibility or 'world-class' do not seem to matter.

Like several other neo-Hindu movements of the late-twentieth century and early millennium (for instance, Art of Living Foundation), BAPS claims to be a holistic, charismatic and social mass movement based on the selfless dedication and the equality of its members (seva, satsangis). However, they do not seem to consider abolishing religious and caste hierarchy. In many ways, this organisation promotes and carries forward several key notions of the reformist religious movements of the late-nineteenth and early-twentieth century in India by demanding a new rationalisation and prominence of certain broad 'great tradition'-beliefs, rites and values. Yet, by analysing the rites and rituals, ritual space and ritual agents at ACC, one thing becomes obvious: membership, hierarchy and purity remain important means of distinction and 'othering', through which new points of reference for dichotomisation, as well as new means of communication are generated. As regards the role of caste, BAPS is conservative. Even though caste distinctions among ascetics were abolished in 1981 (the Indian Constitution did so in 1948), Dalit ('untouchables' or outcastes) cannot be initiated into the order. In his portrait of the Swaminarayan order, Fuller argues that BAPS' devotionalism, 'is a powerful and partially modernized

---

[8] This statement addresses the turn towards one's own subjective experiences instead of the dogma of a 'higher truth'. See also Warrier (2005).

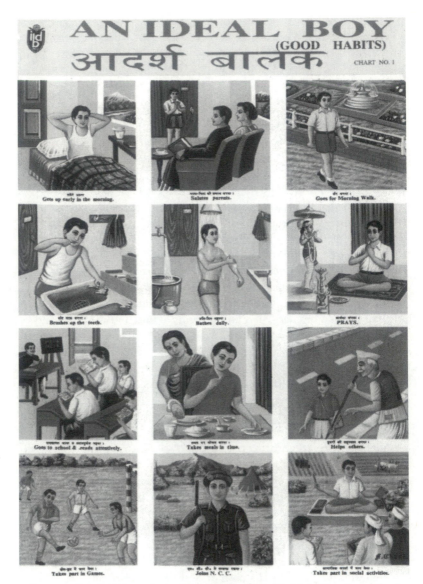

Plate 6.1: Pictorial life conduct of 'An Ideal Boy' (Good Habits). Educational chart, Indian Book Depot, Delhi (ca. 1950–60).

organizational expression of [hierarchical values]. The order demonstrates
very clearly how *bhakti* can be accommodated to institutionalized inequality in Hinduism and Indian society' (1992: 174). I argue later that
as a consequence, there are relatively stricter boundaries drawn between
'insiders' (satsangis) and 'outsiders' (the rest of society), 'educated' and
'uneducated', 'civilised' and 'uncivilised', 'safe' and 'threatening' characteristics defining categories of people. BAPS' organisational structure
reflects a moralising and theistic view of the dogma of moral guidance, self-
sacrifice for the spiritual leader, congregation of satsangis, and the quasi-
biblical authority of Swaminarayan's writings. The following comment
from the BAPS homepage on its website reminds us of educational charts
such as 'Good Habits' or 'Bad Habits' (Plate 6.1):

> The hallmark of the Swaminarayan devotee is that he or she devoutly begins the
> day with puja and meditation, works or studies honestly and donates regular
> hours in serving others. He/she observes the five principal vows: No Stealing,
> No Adultery, No Alcohol, No Meat, No Impurity of body and mind. Such moral
> purity and spiritual surety [sic!] add a deeper brilliance to all the hundreds of
> social services performed for a better life and salvation.[9]

To be sure, these are rules and regulations laid out for satsangis. Within
the community, there are weekly devotional gatherings (satsang) and
age-specific and gender-specific groups receive sacred texts from the
BAPS headquarters to study them. Like other spiritual movements, BAPS
promotes its important role in fields such as voluntary moral and cultural
care, social and educational activities, environmental and relief work.[10] Time
and again, this kind of voluntary service (seva) is emphasised to be one of
the basic pillars of BAPS. Such an emphasis comes handy in times when
there is talk about a general loss of social values and national identity. This
issue is picked up in President Kalam's inaugural address where he turns
the BAPS satsangi into the exemplar ideal national citizen: 'How can you
mix spirituality and social service? How can you separate the two? Those
who wish to sincerely serve society must be spiritually pure and only those
who are spiritually pure can sincerely serve society' (Kalam 2005). The
appeal here is that the BAPS' emphasis on seva aligns itself with a secularly
acceptable (e.g., modern) definition of religion as morality, or religion as

---

[9] See http://www.swaminarayan.org (accessed 22 August 2009).

[10] For more details, see http://www.swaminarayan.org/activities/index.htm
(accessed 2 July 2007).

the ethical code for modern citizens. This is a conscious shift and derives from the debates in nineteenth-century reform movements in India.[11] It also points towards a trend in contemporary politics to align citizens to the idea of the nation as a family, and, in turn, to national devotion as an extension of familial loyalty (*deshbhakti*). Representatives of different political parties used such rhetoric, be it Prime Minister Indira Gandhi (as 'Mother India') or members of the Bharatiya Janata Party.

With respect to the just discussed continuation of 'soft Hindutva', the ACC, despite its sectarian orientations, is truly a remarkable site insofar as it is one of the few 'religio-nationalist pilgrimage sites' or secular temples that were built or rebuilt in postcolonial India, such as the Bharat Mata temple in Varanasi or the Vivekananda Memorial in Kanyakumari. Such sites were meant to communicate concerns as regards the role of religion in a secular nation state and the notion of a both scientific and humanist spirituality appealing to the dutiful citizen. They are, further, a reaction to reformist Hindu movements seeking to create pan-Indian 'Hinduness', or Indian nationalists fuelling patriotic fervour by bridging specificities of caste, sect and even religious identities through the promotion of common denominators such as science, rationality and ambivalence over idolatry (see Ramaswamy 2006: 179). Finally, such sacred monuments could be linked with the celebration of a Nehruvian vision of secular India through which national identity and citizenship could be forged (see Brosius 2005).

Cosmopolitan nationalism is not so much related to individual parties any longer but to the desire to qualify for access to the 'world-class' by belonging to a particular nation — in this case, to India. The ACC must be seen as a vehicle of national resurgence in this light. Yet, simultaneously, it is a means to Indianise the project of modernity and to compete with the West without being sold out, possibly even creating a new form of cosmopolitanism as cultural superiority.

In my opinion, BAPS finds such widespread acceptance not necessarily because of its puritan moral agenda and dogma but also because of its emphasis on the lightness of ritual and emphasis on spirituality, of its competence to stage rituals as mega-events, of its promotion of a beautiful utopian society (i.e., the community of satsangis and swamis) and finally, of its celebration of India as a great ancient civilisation and global player. All these elements are particularly attractive to the aspiring urban middle

---

[11] However, even those were often apologetic of 'Hindu primitivism', and delivered in response to the 'Christian morality' of the colonisers (I thank Sophie Hawkins for this suggestion).

classes. At the ACC, BAPS engages heavily with conspicuous consumption and does not hesitate to use modern means of technology as a concession to urban and globalised lifestyles (as long as they follow BAPS' rules). Thus, despite the wide variety of people visiting ACC, the site exactly taps the new middle class desire to combine leisure, pleasure and ritual, while belonging to a community without committing everything, of voluntary work as worship (seva) and an imagined participation in (and revitalisation of) something of great historical and cultural value and importance for India and the world, spirituality acting throughout as foundation of cultural and national heritage.[12]

Finally, and this underlines the arguments just proposed, ACC and BAPS are well in tune with the pantheon of new forms of specialists that now provide their expertise for different domains of 'lifestyle' — wedding planners, interior designers, feng shui masters (see Part III of this study). The sadhus and swamis as ritual specialists too shift their emphasis and become event managers, public relation experts, or global players who belong to the jet-set community of 'rooted cosmopolitans'. Their agenda now is to 'sell' the message for a larger than ever audience, by means of aestheticisation, monumentalisation and historicisation.[13] Likewise, the desired mood of the 'customers' or 'clients' is one of 'feel-good', of celebration, beauty and pride. Even for ritual purposes, the religious specialist is taken away; there is direct contact between the devotee and the divine, the devotee becoming his or her own 'specialist', a consumer-devotee. The ritual technicians are substituted by the spiritual leader (guru) who bestows meaning and direction in life.[14]

---

[12] Dwyer reports that wealthy mercantile, urban communities are likely to join and patronise BAPS because 'its puritanical ideals offer an excellent foundation for business success' (2004: 190; see also Cross 2006: 642–43).

[13] This is with reference to contemporary spiritual organisations in India, such as the AOL or ISKCON, none of which claims national identity to be a central issue in their agenda.

[14] However, this does not question the authority of the Brahmin priest.

a question of authenticity

From what does the Erlebnis, the multifaceted and intimate, spectacular, and for many visitors, the overwhelming experience of visiting the site of the ACC derive? I propose that it is related to a seemingly paradoxical interest to be everything for everybody: to be at once a tourist site, a pilgrimage site, a site for spiritual enlightenment and national awakening, for entertainment and consumption, adventure and education about cultural heritage. It is a modern site of spectacle and conspicuous consumption, aspiring for the 'world-class' and cultural supremacy.

ACC wants to be a site that creates the desire in the visitors to belong to something greater than anything outside the walls (within which the Monument is confined) can communicate, to witness something of international attention, if not envy. 'Today, the West looks to the East for help for the "Indian Way"' was an often-heard statement even among people I spoke to at the ACC. The awareness that India's economic growth has puzzled the world to such an extent that it even threatens the alleged stability of previous hegemonies is emphasised repeatedly. But on the spiritual level too, India was spearheading, so goes the argument. This is in fact an old cry, going back to religious reformers and philosophers such as Swami Vivekananda (1863–1902) or patriotic writers like Bankim Chandra Chattopadhyay (1838–94) who made the point, around year 1900, that the disenchanted West must look up to the East for help in matters of the spiritual domain.

Many of my interlocutors argued that India was acknowledged for what it was, and still is: a Great Living Tradition, overcoming temporal weaknesses (such as economic underdevelopment) and creating synergies and energies of great help for humankind. The ACC is presented as one such prototype of confidence and self-reflection. While satsangis see in this an affirmation of their belief and life-conduct, members of the middle class in India and the transnational class of Indians overseas, may especially pay attention to this phenomenon in terms of its symbolic role as *Wirtschaftswunder* and beautiful habitat. In this context, the ACC functions as a theme park in which the idea of the 'production of celebration' or of spectacle has moved to the centre stage, and where both the sale of goods and of experiences are closely tied to the notion of a 'good life'. Crucial to this is the concept of leisure, where pleasure is generated by commercially produced recreational activities to fill time freed from work. Leisure should be understood as consumption of products that generate at once emotions and experiences (Clavé 2007: 158). Theme parks (and the ACC falls under this category), structure experiences by means of multisensory experiences and appropriation of historical heritage and traditional popular culture. They structure experiences and distinctions between people.

New media technologies, e.g., the musical fountain and the IMAX film 'Neelkanth Darshan', are employed at the Akshardham Complex to heighten the senses and attention of the audiences.[1] There is a well-orchestrated multitude of 'edutaining' activities and encounters for visitors of various kinds. Many of the sites and special items offered are also a source of remarkable financial inflow. Put simply, the ACC seduces and appeals to the visitors to participate in something special and transcendental. It is this interactive relationship, made up of spatial, aesthetic, familiar and innovative elements, that turns an ACC visit into a personal experience allowing visitors to imagine and articulate desires. Jayesh V., a full-timer specialising in the animatronics and theme halls, maintains:

> The theme halls as well as the IMAX film invoke an immersing experience for the visitors … The theme halls are to give pride, about India's glorious past. Once that is internalised, then you start to feel and take responsibilities; you feel morally responsible for the present and the future (personal conversation, New Delhi, March 2006).

To him, the criticism that the theme halls and the IMAX film are part of an ideological brainwashing or an emotional blackmailing initiative is irrelevant, if not absurd, because 'you have to generate the pride on your own'. The responsibility seems to be in the court of the audience. Nevertheless, this remark points towards the moralising environment of the ACC.

---

[1] The international version of the film is *Mystic India*. See http://www.akshardham.com/whattosee/giantscreenfilm/index.htm (accessed 3 July 2007).

Fake or Real? It is (Not) What it is!

There are many links between the aspirations of a 'world-class' city like New Delhi and the ACC. In accordance with Anton Clavé's study on the global theme park industry, I propose that the ACC, too, is a forerunner of future cities, a place where 'tensions are visually articulated between what is public and what is private, what is global and what is local ... [of] cities built solely for consumption' (Clavé 2007: 208). Let me name four common grounds shared by the ACC and a city such as Delhi. First, the ACC may partly be understood as a family member of the enclave, as much as condominiums such as Beverly Park, DLF Regency Park or Windsor Park in Gurgaon. Second, the terms 'global' and 'world-class' centrally feature in order to qualify and upgrade the value of a particular site, practice, and group of people or experience. Third, in its hermetically sealed character, the ACC instructs its visitors to behave in a certain way, explicitly different from the 'outside' world. Fourth, by means of re-building what could be experienced as a sacred world by followers, and by creating a desire to 'belong to' and to 'participate in' the projected 'class', a notion of 'the spiritual world-class' is shaped. It proposes paradisaical states on earth, a global brotherhood, a beautiful community that offers everything one might possibly ever have dreamt of in terms of spiritual, religious and national 'care' to its members. Along with being world-class, visitors/pilgrims are expected to reaffirm mainstream Hinduism as the 'Indian way of life'. This indicates a 'sameness-with-difference' and will later enable me to draw a connection with an argument about the centrality of 'cultural citizenship' and 'global Indian'.[2] Moreover, this is relevant for the further discussion of cosmopolitan Indianness.

The ACC employs 'cultural citizenship' (Punathambekar 2005) as a resource for national identity, a motivating force both tailored to the needs and desires of 'glocal Indians'. Here, religion becomes a tool in and through which a modern self can be projected, a self that shapes India's entry into the global economy and yet retains supposedly essential values, thus remaining 'genuinely Indian'. In fact, in writings and other mass media promulgated by BAPS, we find a strong rhetoric of claiming 'spiritual world leadership' and being a 'morally superior civilisation'.

There is the highly contested notion that in the domain of authenticity and consumption, ritual and religious practices can only be diluted to

---

[2] I am grateful to Sumathi Ramaswamy for her suggestions in this context.

become inauthentic and commodified. Indeed, many 'outsiders' I spoke to during fieldwork raised this question too.[3] As India increasingly opens up to the global economy, media technologies, leisure and tourism cultures, and as all of these domains become more and more aestheticised and commodified, can we diagnose the same for religious sites and experiences? Or is it instead that the various registers can be played out simultaneously, without putting 'authenticity' at risk? In short, how salient is the question: Is the ACC a heritage theme park of Hindu-Indianness that commodifies and stages 'authentic experiences' of spirituality or is it a 'real' pilgrimage site? I do not attempt to take either side but rather treat the field as a stage on which both seemingly paradoxical elements are 'naturally' intertwined. In this odd space, the fabric of modern selves is modelled and remodelled, and different forces constituting this field (for instance economic liberalisation and transnational connectivity) come together in a process of blending culture and capital (as well as capital interest), locality and globality. In his discussion of Chinese theme parks, Tim Oakes employs the concept of the 'authentic replica' as a means of circumventing the question whether something is 'real' or 'fake' (and judging the quality of experiences accordingly). He argues that even a replication can be regarded as authentic. Moreover, the quality-marker can not be the presence, or absence, of an original, because this is a Eurocentric apprehension of value (Oakes 2006: 170–71): 'Authenticity — as a regime of power — may also be claimed by groups seeking legitimacy within the broader frameworks of nationalism, civilization, or modernity' (ibid.: 172; see also Balme 1998). Instead, Oaks suggests the use of 'mimesis' as a concept with more scope to highlight agency. In that case, then, the case of ACC is not a simple 'copy' of a western concept. Rather, we have, here, a creative blend of different expectations and cultural resources for identity construction. ACC is the expression of a 'modern longing for the real … recast from an implicitly nostalgic urban and cosmopolitan look' (ibid.). The satsangis are not just puppets of a 'fake' world but actively locate themselves within a modern discourse on urban and transnational religiosity.

---

[3] Fieldwork was also undertaken at BAPS centres in Gandhinagar (Gujarat), Mumbai (Dadar branch) and Neasden (London) between March 2005 and January 2006. I could not speak to any of the swamis involved in the planning and execution of the Akshardham sites since the swamis follow a strict rule of neither talking to women, nor touching or even looking at them. In fact, this kind of treatment by the swamis is often legitimised by satsangis as a form of paying respect to women.

The ACC is part of an active shaping of a new public sphere that requires exploration because it promises — and delivers — different kinds of experiences — most of all, Erlebnis. A visitor to the site becomes, at once, the disinterested flâneur and the devotional pilgrim. Accordingly to the categories they meet, different competencies are required, and these, at times, come into conflict. There are different kinds of pleasure, yet sometimes they subtly overlap. The mundane flâneur seeks it in the production of desire and competence to consume, experiences the sensation of making the world available at his or her feet, and to stage himself or herself. The pilgrim on a sacred journey seeks pleasure in the unification with the divine, in the liminal state of being at a sacred site, and the search for transcendence.

There are different conditions and sites available to experience spiritual and worldly pleasure. The pleasure of being a flâneur at this heterotopic site is generated if the visitor is familiar with the concept of Culture (with a capital C!), the importance of national heritage, and the behaviour expected in museums and national memorials. The pleasure may be of another kind if the visitor recognises and appreciates ritual codes. Tim Edensor, in his study *Tourists at the Taj*, phrases this as 'culturally located ways of framing sites and arranging narratives' (1998: 13).

From an emic perspective, shared by most BAPS satsangis I spoke to, ACC, and their own activities within, are undoubtedly 'authentic'. First, there is the presence of swamis and full-timers who consider their work at the site sacred and a form of devotion (seva). One full-timer, keeping a diary in which she records observations about visitors' behaviour and questions, told me how much it insults her when she meets people who do not believe that she does not only work as a tour-guide for free but considers her work as blessed: 'People just don't get it that we are not a service provider; that this is like puja for us' (Anuj G., personal conversation, New Delhi, October 2006)! Second, the murtis of Swaminarayan and his disciples in the Monument are treated like deities; they are fed, puja is performed, and during the hot summer, they are 'cooled' with fans in the hot season: 'If even we use fans, why should they feel hot?' responded a volunteer when I asked him why ventilators had been placed in front of the statues (personal conversation, ACC, September 2006).

BAPS clearly has an ambivalent relationship towards structures such as theme parks, for on the one hand it seeks to entertain and appeal to visitors as consumers, while on the other, it considers capitalist leisure culture a force that dilutes those moral values that BAPS claims to revitalise. A question asked repeatedly by outsiders with a critical stance is whether the emphasis on ritual spaces and the practices tied to them only hide the fact that the complex is inauthentic, or even 'fake'. Devotees of different sects, however, do not always seem to share this view. To them, ACC is just another, enlarged and perfected version of already existing pilgrimage sites and religious festivals (see Sax 1995).[4]

Maybe, as a consequence, this means that we have to distinguish between the different kinds of visitors — the flâneur and the pilgrim — as well as varying ritual 'intensities'. Are the different forms of worship 'just for fun', commodified parts of a mega-experience for allegedly passive masses? Is the ACC a simple commodification of religion as a lifestyle item? How can we explain that people visit the place and firmly believe that it is 'real' in terms of the rituals they witness and participate in? Is this a pilgrimage site or a 'world-class' tourist site? Is this site a manifestation of 'soft Hindutva', i.e., the spread of national-chauvinist and xenophobic rhetoric in popular culture, as Leitkultur (volonté générale or welfare of the mainstream culture)? Or, does ACC represent a form of alternative secularism and modernity as part of a heritage that serves to underline national identity and spirituality that transcends religious borders?

The answer is certainly not simple, and I have tried to indicate one possible direction by highlighting Oakes' notions of authentic replica and mimesis. In my view, different perspectives on (and appropriations of) rituals must be contextualised, as well as different audiences, and motivations that dwell, subtly or overtly, behind them. I propose that it is through media and aesthetics that we can better understand the dynamics of the rituals put on stage here, with different overlapping and competing domains, be they of local, global, national, transnational, mainstream, popular, 'flat' or 'deep' nature. The danger in this chain of rhetorical questions lies in the presumption that a site can be either a pilgrimage place or a leisure site, but not both, and that by classifying a place and the production of meaning imbued in it we quickly turn to infantilising, patronising and colonising 'the other'. In fact, several recent studies show how pilgrimage and tourism today are closely intertwined and do not necessarily subvert or exclude each other.[5] Further, these studies highlights that the borders

---

[4] The concept of the leela ('God's play') in South Asia can be conceived of as both a religious event and a mundane spectacle, with the players embodying the deities (or demons) they perform as (Sax 1995).

[5] See Crouch (1999); Coleman and Eade (2004b), in particular chapters by Coleman and Schramm. The spread of religion has, to a great extent, followed trade routes, and vice versa. Thus, the entanglement has a strong historical quality and requires more research with respect to the Indian subcontinent.

between pilgrimage and tourism are not clearly distinguishable any longer (Badone and Roseman 2004; Coleman and Eade 2004b), and that a religious pilgrimage site can become a source of political tension and a secular site can become a quasi-religious place for collective memory. The alleged dichotomy of the secular and the sacred, of the orginal and the fake, does not necessarily arise in our case-study. For instance, *mela* (fair), travel/tourism and pilgrimage have a firm place in India's popular public culture as an ensemble. I am myself deeply ambivalent about the character of the site and its alleged 'efficacy'. But the search for 'authenticity' of the ACC is as problematic as diagnosing as naïve, people who bathe in the holy Ganga. The provision of ritual experience and practice in a carefully choreographed and glamorous place projects the ACC as an eventful — and for many people, an authentic site — even though it is also highly commodified. Authenticity surfaces by means of spectacle as well as citation from tradition, including other pilgrimage sites and rituals. Its power is based on modern selves' longing for Erlebnis.

Hindu pilgrims are, for instance, familiar with the elements of entertainment and of the replica temple. They would not consider it as a mundane 'copy' and thus inauthentic. 'Sacred spaces act as a means of reference, their association with nostalgia, heritage, community or the natural, allow us to find roots in a rootless world', proposes Richard Tresidder in an article about tourism and sacred landscape (1999: 144). Whether we appreciate this 'Disneyisation' of India's private as well as public sphere or reject it does not really matter — we cannot escape it because we are immersed in the conditions that produce these symbolic economies. The themed experiences increasingly come to dominate people's everyday lives (Bryman 2004) as Clavé argues in his study about global theme parks:

> [D]espite being productive places, they tend to mask the production processes so as not to condition the consumptive use their visitors make of them; and ... due to the necessary existence of commercial establishments and premises inside them, they seem to have the attributes of a public place. The imaginary character of parks is their main means of hiding the productive nature and private ownership of the space (2007: 193).

One could view the ACC in similar terms, with its dozens of donation boxes, refreshment shops, themed exhibitions, IMAX film theatre, and, of course, the souvenir mall and food court. The dominant narratives of a pilgrimage site and temple visit cover this 'Disneyisation' up to a large extent. However, such structures can be found even in pilgrimage and religious sites elsewhere in the world. What is more relevant, and will be discussed in more detail in the following discussion, is the fact that the site presents itself as a public and open space, but imposes rules and regulations, withholding the right of access for BAPS as private owners. More than the question whether this is an 'authentic' site or not, it is the production of a certain kind of habitus (dressed as 'cultured behaviour') and the surveillance and disciplining of visitors that, in my view, generates the more critical side of an institution like the ACC.

Meeting and Making Expectations

One indicator of how visitors might have responded to the ACC and what they highlight as positive is the online visitors' book. BAPS carefully takes stock of audience reactions, certainly in a selective manner. Towards the end of this chapter, I explore the observations from a full-time volunteer's diary of visitors' comments and behaviours that open up a different category of comment. The fact that BAPS responds to audience behaviour is clear in the ways details at the ACC have been subtly modified since its public opening. In the year I came to visit the site after its opening to conduct interviews with senior administrators, full-time volunteers and visitors, I could see several changes that obviously represent attempts to improve a particular appeal, in light of particular points of critique raised by visitors. Let me name only two very pragmatic examples: a refreshment stall selling popcorn and Pepsi was built next to the Research Centre, the Abhishek Mandap and the Monument. This was done in order to cater to the desires of visitors who did not want to walk the rather long distance to the restaurant located next to the exit. Before the opening, however, I was told by a senior satsangi that such elements of 'time-pass' would not feature at the Monument. Moreover, with BAPS being very concerned about the westernisation of Indian traditions, I was surprised, but possibly too conservative, to find Pepsi, pizza and popcorn instead of *samosas* and Limca or *nimbu pani* (lemonade). Furthermore, a digital photostudio had been built in order to allow visitors to have souvenir photographs taken in front of the Monument.[6] Obviously, many people had complained about not being allowed to carry personal cameras to the Complex or to use the service of *photowallahs* (professional on-site photographers).

In the 'VIP' area opposite the reception hall, visitors are given forms on which they have to state their impressions of the visit. These are then typed into the computer. The ACC homepage on its website too, has a visitor's book. Let us look at some of the visitors' statements that were

---

[6] One A2-size colour digital photograph costs INR 90 (c. €1.60). In 2007, the photographer told me that approximately 250 pictures were taken each day.

selected for publication. Most of them paint a picture of overwhelmed fascination and of being deeply touched. Suneet A., a doctor, writes in the online visitor's book: 'What started as a tourist experience turned into an overwhelming devout experience'.[7] We shall later see that testimonies and confessions are a major element in the self-legitimising narrative of BAPS. At the same site, a senior manager described his visit as follows; 'It is the perfect combination of spirituality and modern technology. I find in your institution a silver lining that there is still a chance to convert mother earth into a spiritual temple'.[8] This notion of magical transformation into an Arcadian state, fused with technology and spectacle, is underlined in a comment by a school principal. He emphasises professional efficiency, international standards of cleanliness and order at the ACC (see Plates 7.1 and 7.2):

> Within [a] short span after its inauguration, the whole team of Akshardham Complex is so much professional that it seems they are *managing* this complex since many years. This monument is like *Infosys of Spirituality*.[9] Lots of vibrations in each and every corner of this *Mandir* [temple]. Dedicated staff and *cleanliness* of Mandir add more vibrations … Every thing is well-maintained, all the facilities are *world-class*.[10]

The language and visual standards of global capital shape the metaphorical bridge between a spiritual place and a multinational corporation (MNC). This is certainly not coincidental. We find predecessors and parallels in mega-complexes of a similar kind, run by other new religious movements such as Sathya Sai Baba's hermitage Prasanthi Nilayam at Puttaparthi, Karnataka, or the main seat of Art of Living (AOL) in Bangalore, or ISKCON Cultural Centre in New Delhi (opened in 1998) and Bangalore (opened in 1997) — the latter is an architectural construction at the Indian IT-centre, fusing modern glass architecture with south Indian temple style.[11]

---

[7] See www.akshardham.com/opinions/others.htm (accessed 13 December 2006).

[8] Ibid.

[9] Infosys is the flagship of India's IT-success and its rising confidence as global player — a software company in Bangalore, India's Silicon Valley, which started off with an investment of US$1,000 in 1981, cashing annual revenues of US$1 billion in 2004 (see Fuller and Narasimhan 2007: 123).

[10] See www.akshardham.com/opinions/others.htm (accessed 13 December 2006); emphasis added.

[11] See www.golokanagchampa.com/temple.htm. For AOL in Bangalore, see http://www.artofliving. org/AboutUs/BangaloreCentre/tabid/233/Default.aspx (accessed 28 June 2007).

The ACC must be seen in a lineage of these and other sites and institutions that appeal to religious devotion and spirituality as a spectacle, for traditional pilgrims and middle-class devotees (often a conflated category). The fact that all these organisations are also charities and manage remarkable tourist flows must not be underestimated. This also makes them attractive to the city and state governments who can improve their national and international image by marketing these sites.

The emphasis on intense spiritual experience and transformation, business management and the ambiguity produced by referring to the ACC as a 'temple' and a 'monument' appear to culminate in the following remark by joint registrar from the Delhi High Court who almost poetically reflects on the elaborate and superior observation of 'Indian Culture' at the site:

It's a divine experience. The visit has taken us beyond the limits of time and space. The whole complex is a great mixture of architecture, science, faith, history and the human spirit to achieve perfection and excellence. We are glad to

Plate 7.1: The Monument at the ACC, New Delhi (2006).
Source: © BAPS, Delhi and Ahmedabad. Used with permission.

go through this overwhelming divine experience. I deeply feel from the core of my heart that this temple is the showcase of Indian Culture.[12]

This establishes the ACC as a 'museum'-like prototype and storehouse of 'authentic' Indian heritage. Rituals are a crucial link to this heritage-production, a means of communicating and experiencing a Golden Vedic Age. In sum, all voices seem to underline the 'efficacy' and authenticity of the site as an intense spiritual experience and education as opposed to the intensity of entertainment- and leisure-consumption. Yet we may also ask whether we should not acknowledge the element of ritual consumption that can be found at many traditional temples today, where possibly, with more ease as we might assume, devotees and leisure consumers fuse. In fact, the next step toward belonging to such a global 'ecumene' and 'home' is a small one.

The online visitor's book also highlights the educative power and use of this heritage site. A senior employee at Reliance, one of India's largest private sector enterprises, maintains that ACC is a 'must for any Indian — it reinforces our culture, is so peaceful'. To me, these comments underline the fact that at the ACC, BAPS tries to create in the visitors feelings of

Plate 7.2: The Monument lit at night, New Delhi (2006).

Source: © BAPS, Delhi, Ahmedabad. Used with permission.

---

[12] See www.akshardham.com/opinions/others.htm (accessed 13 December 2006).

participating in something larger than life, in a historic event, contributing to and witnessing the creation of 'paradise on earth'. Furthermore, the desire to belong to the 'in-group' is shaped. BAPS shapes itself as a custodian and maker of India's heritage and future, thus also responding to the middle classes' desire to care for the self, to accumulate and display wealth without 'feeling bad'.[13] Also, it enhances a portable spiritual cosmopolitanism in order to cater to the need of being both rooted and mobile in a transnational era. On one of my visits in October 2006, forms were handed over by the PR manager with the comment that BAPS wanted to collect quotes for the *Lonely Planet* travel guidebooks for Delhi and India. Indeed, one might argue that the conscious tapping of such communication media is done not only for foreign tourists. In fact, it is based on the realisation that a new generation of both young domestic and transnational Indians — be they heritage tourists, pilgrims, or both — increasingly falls back on such resources for their explorations of India as a 'foreign land'!

The structuring of control over particular experiences by drawing specific connections and associations is very efficient in the case of ACC and underlines the need for a thematised space to provide a perfectly organised atmosphere and coherence. Visitors get the feeling that they have entered an ideal public space, a quasi-'promised land of perfection' where the marriage between technology and spirituality would solve all of civilisation's problems, where a system of social order is presented to them, and invites them to be part of it, one that is clean, safe and regulated (see Clavé 2007: 31). The perfect private enclave!

---

[13] One example is the worldwide and online Satsang examinations and FAQs for school children. Even a webpage set up for 'Swaminarayan kids' underlines BAPS' agenda to legitimise itself as an authority on Indianness, cultural identity and values, particularly for Indians overseas.

a hierarchy of ritual performances

Senior satsangis at the ACC do not wish to generate the impression that it is a monumental commercial undertaking. Instead of being just a 'fun' place for leisure-seekers and flâneurs, offering 'artificial' experiences, the ACC is promoted as a place of national and religious devotion, a place for 'cultured' persons with a deep understanding of traditions and values. For this purpose, a variety of rituals and ritual sites have been 'institutionalised' and shape the main narrative of the spiritual journey. Rituals feature centrally at the physical site of ACC and BAPS homepages on their websites. They are not arbitrarily chosen but consciously and carefully choreographed to appeal to different audiences.

Humble devotion (*bhakti*) and proud nationalism (*deshbhakti*) are the core experiences that the themed environment of the ACC conveys to its visitors. The rituals that are availed of (for participation and consumption) differ in terms of where, for and by whom they are performed and with what intention. The question of framing the rituals is relevant here, as well as Erving Goffman's distinction of 'backstage' and 'frontstage' performances in terms of ritual intentionality and segregation. Furthermore, much emphasis is placed on the documentation and aesthetics of ritual performance, particularly in their media reproduction. This way, a sense of belonging to a beautiful utopian society is generated among devotees and observers. It is the sum of all the different kinds of rituals, sites and media technologies as well as the different groups that relate to them in different ways that turn ACC into a 'thick' and meaningful site, a site imbued with multiple meanings and demands for visitors with respect to their decoding and behaviour competences. Finally, the hierarchisation of rituals as well as ritualisation of visitors' behaviour defines qualities of participation, belonging and access to cultural competence and differentiation.

In order to establish itself as a full-fledged pilgrimage site, a storehouse of cultural heritage and a source of social and moral welfare, the ACC offers a chain of public and semi-public rituals, citations and sites of ritual performance along the guided routes that visitors are expected to follow and online worlds. Linked to the rituals and their particular contexts of encoding and decoding are different qualities and registers of 'purity' or 'authenticity' as well as rules of participation and the respective habitus of participants. Tensions may arise with respect to the blurring and moving of borders, be they geographical, aesthetic, experiential or ritual borders. To me, various frames underlining the ritual performances can be highlighted as follows: (i) Vedic rituals performed by the spiritual leader and other priests and selected guests; (ii) rituals performed by householders and visitors at the Monument and the Abhishek Mandap (see Plate IIa); (iii) citations from ritual performances or architecture as part of the overall rhetoric of ACC, and (iv) daily rituals performed by priests at the temple next to the ACC, clearly set apart from the daily bustle of the huge complex, attended by satsangis.

(i) The Vedic ceremonies are at the pinnacle of this cluster of rituals. From a high-caste perspective, they are — and make — 'pure' in every sense of the word. They are rituals performed only in the presence of swamis and male satsangis, with female satsangis separated from the 'happening', if they must be present at all. Non-satsangis are generally excluded from sacred occasions. A chain of such rituals was executed, for instance, during the foundation stone-laying ceremony in 2000[1] as well as the ritual inauguration and sanctification of the ACC between July and October 2005, a precondition for the public opening on 6 November 2005.[2] Despite the seclusion in which the Vedic rituals were performed, they were carefully documented and made available in the electronic media. Several such photogalleries can be found online on the homepage Akshardham at Delhi. On the one hand, they allow satsangis to retrospectively witness an important, possibly even uplifting, and purifying event. On the other hand, to satsangis and outsiders, they are evidences that ACC is *not* a theme park but a truly sacred site, authenticated by the presence of the divine and ritual specialists. The most elaborate sequences of Vedic rituals performed ahead of the opening were related to the Monument. Since all these sites received (almost) the same attention as a 'real' temple, the rites

---

[1] *Shilanyas vidhi* in the year 2000. See http://www.swaminarayan.org/news/2000/11/delhi/index.htm and http://www.swaminarayan.org/news/2001/07/delhi/photo01.htm (accessed 6 May 2007).

[2] See, for instance, the various *kalash pujas* conducted in July 2005, http://www.swaminarayan.org/vicharan/2005/07/01/delhi1.htm (accessed 6 May 2007) and Sadhu Swayamprakashdas (2005: 69–75).

performed, according to a BAPS swami, 'invoked the presence of God' (Sadhu Swayamprakashdas 2005: 69). This, then, gives the place a particular efficacy. After having sanctified the sites and the statues (*murti pratishtha*), Pramukh Swami Maharaj claimed:

> [w]hoever has *darshan* here will receive the fruits of all places of pilgrimage. Those who have *darshan* of Akshardham will have *darshan* of all avatars, deities and *paramhansas* … the *murti* of Neelkanth Varni has been consecrated. Offer abhishek. Maharaj will fulfil everyone's wishes. Maharaj will grant happiness and peace to all who come (ibid.: 71).

Plate 8.1: Worshipping the Neelkanth murti at the Abhishek Mandap, New Delhi (2006).

Source: © BAPS, Delhi, Ahmedabad. Used with permission.

Likewise, much attention is focused on the presentation of beauty of rituals and ritual performances at the site. This, for instance, is communicated through the photogalleries. The fact that the photographs of ACC were taken in terms of a particular aesthetic character underlines the conscious effort to monumentalise the site and the event. Both distance and nearness are created in the process, the former through an emphasis on the grandeur of the architecture, the latter through shots emphasising intimacy and immediacy. A picture-book aesthetics, i.e., an iconography based on symmetry and simple themes, can monumentalise what is otherwise sidelined as ordinary religious practice. This way, a certain 'authenticity' can be attached to the phenomenon, creating a desire in the beholder of the pictures to participate in this beautiful event, and movement.

The BAPS has demonstrated a two-fold strategy of self-presentation: for one, they use media documentation to intensify the perception of satsangis to be part of one large transnational family, to 'witness' the rituals a posteriori. Furthermore, new audiences can be addressed and appealed to through evidence of both the beauty and legitimacy of the organisation as 'authentic'.

(ii) The more 'classical' rituals are those performed on a daily basis. At the ACC, these are *puja* (offering), *arati* (waving the light in front of the deity), *darshan* (devine sight) and *abhishek* (pouring of holy water over the statue of the deity), and belong to the most widespread public ritual performances in a Hindu's devotional life. At Akshardham, they can be performed and witnessed in the temple outside the compound of the ACC, at the Monument and in the Abhishek Mandap (pavilion) situated opposite and separated from the Monument only through the Narayan Sarovar, a sacred pond that closes in the 'sanctum' (or *garbhagraha*, literally, womb), as it is often referred to (Plate 8.1).

(iii) Next, there are ritual performances that are represented as significant in (and through) the exhibits at the theme halls (film or diorama) and the choreography of the musical fountain. These are highly 'didactic' in terms of the message they deliver and the larger discourse in which they are embedded through the border narrative as well as the specific audio-commentary that accompanies the multimedia exhibits. For instance, time and again, the PSM is shown to be surrounded by his (male) followers, in an Arcadian setting of a temple, gardens, flowers and sunshine, as they sing, or engage in discourse or prayer. In the IMAX film *Neelkanth Yatra* or *Mystic India*, several mass-prayers are staged, such as at the *ghats* of a virtual Haridwar or in the courtyard of Akshardham (Plates 8.2, 8.3) — both scenes show a fascination with the monumentalised spectacle of hundreds of lit candles in the dark. These examples highlight the relevance of the rhetoric of the 'ecumene' and its guru, as well as the rhetoric of bringing light into darkness.

(iv) The last category consists of daily rituals performed at the temple next to ACC but almost hidden behind the high walls along the main ACC site (Plate 8.4). Access to the temple is possible only from another gate and clearly demarcates two different 'zones' and agents of worship. This *shikharbaddha mandir* has a *chal murti* that is served by swamis behind closed doors: it is fed, washed, and put to sleep. Five times a day, arati is performed by the priests, then the doors are thrown open to the devotees who pray

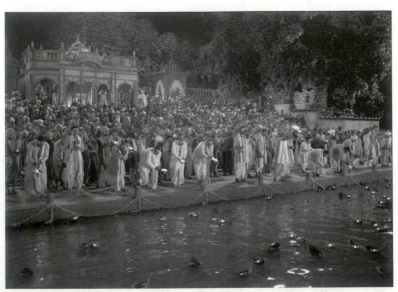

Plate 8.2: *Arati* at Haridwar. Still from the film *Mystic India* (2004).

Source: © BAPS, Delhi, Ahmedabad. Used with permission.

Plate 8.3: Inauguration ceremony, ACC, New Delhi (2005).

Source: © BAPS, Delhi, Ahmedabad. Used with permission.

Plate 8.4: The temple with the *chal murti* of Swaminarayan, situated behind the walls of the ACC, on the day of the Annakut festival, a day after Diwali, New Delhi (2006).

and sing in front of it, and during this one can avail of the *darshan*. This ritual is attended by dozens of saffron-clad swamis (*brahmacharin*) and satsangis separately seated according to gender. Very often, these devotees are the ones who reside in Delhi or the NCR. Only a few non-satsangis come for the rituals on a regular basis; most of them attend the annual festivals.

Intimacy for All

The BAPS shows great effort to stage ritual events that help transform the ACC into a major (Hindu) pilgrimage site, a site for intense personal devotion. As just discussed, BAPS is very busy organising, conducting and documenting (through a variety of media) a range of 'pure' rituals, and ritual sites that invoke this impression and turn it into a 'fact'.

The ACC encloses the 'Neelkanth Mandap', a pavilion for the performance of the abhishek, a ritual in which the divine object is consecrated by sprinkling water over it (ablution). A signboard in front of the entrance reads as follows, both in Hindi and English:

Abhishek. Ancient Vedic ritual of pouring holy water upon the head of God or his *murti* to honour him and to attain his blessings for inner peace and prosperity ... May this ritual fill our human life with his divine virtues of faith, fearlessness, huminity [sic], self-control, love and peace and also fulfil our innermost prayers and wishes.

On weekdays, the Abhishek Mandap is not very crowded, but on weekends there are queues of people waiting to be the first to make a donation (INR 11 per person) receive a *kalash* filled with sacred water from the lake facing the pavilion, and then pour it over the beautifully decorated statue of Neelkanth. Before doing so, visitors-turned-devotees may receive a small colour picture of Akshardham, Neelkanth and 'the Inspirer', a *janeo* (sacred thread), and a *tika* (mark of sandalwood or vermillion on the forehead indicating the divine) from one of the two householders who serve in the pavilion and feed the murtis in the Monument. Interestingly, however, every time I visited the pavilion, the ritual was conducted in a different way, with or without a souvenir (a picture card or a thread around the wrist), with a ceremony that requires the devotee to sit down and perform water sanctification, along with (or without) the singing of *shlokas* (sacred verses).

The efficacy of the site manifests in various instances and this is confirmed by informants. In conversations with female satsangis, I was pointed towards the 'fact' that several miracles had already happened after the performance of abhishek at the site. Sadhna, a full-time volunteer, told me that Abhishek Mandap was so popular precisely *because* it was known that several miracles had already taken place. However, male volunteers such as Jignesh P. rejected the use of the term 'miracle' and emphasised the 'fact' that it was belief/faith, and that because everybody could perform it, abhishek was a truly 'democratised' ritual. According to him, people were by no means looking for miracles. Vipul G. explained that some people would take rituals seriously for selfish reasons such as examinations, happy marriage, personal health improvement or financial matters. In his opinion, this was a very shortsighted and harmful form of devotion (personal conversation, New Delhi, March 2006).[3] He vehemently countered my question as to whether the inclusion of arati and abhishek was for

---

[3] Usually, the *abhishek* does not contain water (as in the Neelkanth Mandap) but *panchamrit* (five sacred substances/nectars): milk, yoghurt, *ghee* (clarified butter), sugar, honey and *kesar-jal* (saffron-soaked water). It is poured over the statue while chanting Vedic *mantras*. After this, the liquid is sanctified, collected and made available for partaking by the devotees (see also www.swaminarayan.org/ rituals/patotsav/ index.htm (accessed 6 July 2007).

entertainment appeal, to draw large crowds: 'Oh no! They are here since the Vedic times, and the Vedic times are still important for today, even though they have been interrupted by the 800 years of Mughal invasion, the British and Christian conversion' (March 2006). What emerges in this interpretation is the continuity of ritual as a 'given' property of intangible cultural heritage.

Historical grandeur and personal involvement are fused here. Pouring water over the idol is about the closest a devotee can get to a deity, and it serves as a very immediate way of expressing care and devotion. This finds reflection in many images depicting the corporeal, and intimate relationship between devotee and deity, where hands almost but never really touch the deity, as if they wanted to caress it tenderly. The use of media such as photography and film by BAPS is remarkably sophisticated and has developed a language that demarcates the *sampradaya* from others. It invites not only by appeal to the intellect but by soothing the senses, and turning even the 'documentation' of a ritual into a special event.

Rituals as Heritage, Catharsis and Helping Hand

Let us take recourse to the 'essentialised' idea of ritual in BAPS worship before we investigate its variations and improvisations as a means of distinction. Ritual is presented almost as if it was the DNA of modern Indians, the 'script' according to which Culture (with a capital 'C'), world and life make sense. One central aim of BAPS, also true of the ACC, is to convert ritual as a signifier of modernity. It is expected that through this, pride, respect and recognition of spiritual people would be restored as opposed to their reputation as social (backward) 'misfits'. A senior BAPS swami who maintains that rituals protect culture and soul, society and individual they writes:

> Rituals represent the bark of a tree. The tree cannot survive long without its bark. Neither can any religion or society (survive) without its rituals. Rituals are gestures and symbols of social, political and religious events of the distant past and are also useful in teaching abstract ideas and concepts ... making them understandable and accessible to the masses ... Rituals are our riches. To renounce them would be to invite cultural poverty and religious ignorance ... Rituals also serve to prevent social disintegration by bringing thousands of people together with a spirit of oneness ... Thus, as an almost complete and holistic nourishment, rituals educate, coordinate and sublimate our lives (Sadhu Vishwamurtidas 2003: 57–58).

The notion evoked here is one of utter importance for rituals of today's times and societies. It plays on the idea of ritual as a healing device, as an intangible cultural heritage that must be preserved and revitalised to prevent societal dilution.

The standard set of rituals referred to earlier reflects a particular process of transformation of religious practice in the context of the experience of modernity and migration. To be sure, BAPS, and thus the ACC, could not be understood without acknowledging the crucial role of the transnational networks and activities of Indians overseas. There is a shift from religious practice and belief to cultural heritage and spirituality as pillars of life conduct and public interest. In his study on the Hindu diaspora, Steve Vertovec maintains that Brahmin-dominated practices have been widely established as a kind of 'canon' for Hindus living abroad, shaping a global religious ecumene: the performance of *puja* (with Sanskrit elements), with arati and *samskaras* (life-cycle rituals), *yagnas* (sacrifices), readings from sacred texts, and massive communal meals and rituals (2000: 53). *Kathas* (recitals of sacred love) too play a central role, even though they introduce non-Brahminical elements. Looked at closely, we find these elements in the philosophy of BAPS too. Besides, the label 'Vedic' is attached to ritual, tradition and culture at the ACC in order to legitimise BAPS as a custodian of Indian (Hindu) Culture. Rituals appropriated from the past affirm some kind of 'hereness' (Kirshenblatt-Gimblett 1998: 153). Rituals make the past come alive as a repertoire of Indianness, as nostalgia without memory (Appadurai 1997). But much more than this, rituals also come to form a heritage through which an Indian way of modernisation and globalisation can be framed and imagined, quite like the heritage discourse of Delhi as a world-class city discussed in Part I of this book.

Besides the 'external' discourse of heritage as resource of indigenous knowledge, rituals also shape narratives of healing, catharsis and conversion. In his study of *guru bhakti* — devotion to a spiritual master — in the context of the Radhasoami faith in north India, Mark Juergensmeyer discusses the relation of this movement to modernity and modern lifestyles (1991: 5). I concur with Katharina Poggendorf-Kakar (2006) in that the popularity of *bhakti* is most probably based on its emphatic, yet passive and relatively simple, devotion for flexible lifestyles requested in today's contexts, as opposed to more complicated and meditation based movements earlier.

As cultural heritage, ritual, then, becomes part of the 'rooted cosmopolitanism' promoted by BAPS in the light of their transnational networks and appearance. Moreover, it turns into a strategy of ethnicity proclamation and distinction, as John Fenton has underlined in his concept of the 'cultural Hindu'. Placing this vis-à-vis the 'religious' Hindu while observing Indian students at an US-American campus, Fenton proposes:

> Hindu ritual survives for them as second-hand celebration of ethnic heritage and as festival (fun and games). In the future, Asian Indian community festivals might also become tourist attractions. In crisis situations some kind of individual or puja sometimes serves these students as an extraordinary coping device (1992: 263).

The writings of BAPS create notions of ideal-typical versions of rituals as a device that ties mind and body, individual and society together amid the challenges and threats of the outside world, purifying and immunising the devotee from the outer world's alleged pollution.

The organisation does not claim to be the leader of the only spiritual movement that leads to 'happiness'. It has, however, produced a host of narratives through which this interpretation is supported. There are several 'conversion' stories and testimonies that reveal the power of Pramukh Swami Maharaj and Lord Swaminarayan that have been even adapted as stage plays (available for sale on DVDs in the souvenir-shops at the temples in London, Gandhinagar and New Delhi). In fact, in conversation, I was told several such stories too. One story, narrated by Vipul G., is that of six Muslim teachers from Pakistan who visited the ACC. Instead of looking only at the theme halls, they insisted on seeing the Abhishek Mandap too. Vipul G. says:

> And they performed it with such dedication! Finally, their devotional feelings could be expressed. When people have a vacuum, devotion can be released. This place releases devotion! After that, they cried, and even we were touched (personal conversation, New Delhi, March 2006).

This is not only an interesting story in that rituals can purportedly transform a person's status but also because it creates the dramatic notion of people whose belief is allegedly suppressed and who, when at a place where they can be 'who they are', find their ultimate peace and self. After narrating this story, Vipul proposes that 'rituals take you over; they create sympathy, they encourage participation.' To him, the experience of *darshan*, seeing the divine, and being seen by it, is central and liminal:

> You look into the eyes of the *murti* — whether in the temple or in the monument does not matter much. And the flow of energies is just amazing. It's a penetrating force, a glimpse of the divine. We simply get charged! We even get glued sometimes, we feel that we just can't get away (personal conversation, New Delhi, March 2006).

In this context, ritual serves as an anchor for soul-searching and the highest source of happiness — another facet of Schulze's *Erlebnisgesellschaft* (see Introduction to this book).

One of the major points on the agenda of BAPS as mentioned earlier is to constitute rituals as vehicles of culture and morals, and to make them socially acceptable and respectable as essential elements of cultural identity. They are brought in tune with modernity, however, without suggesting that this process amounts to westernisation. Thus, rituals are part of a larger discourse on Indian modernity. BAPS promotes the idea that rituals are not only stirred by superstition and miracle but by scientific and rational thinking.[4] In *Perspectives: Inspiring Essays on Life* (2003), available as print and online editions, Sadhu Vishwamurtidas reflects upon the duty of Indians to be proud of their nation and religious beliefs. He suggests that in following a spiritual path and guru, devotees may even become superior to the 'rest' of society. He polarises western secularism and Indian religiosity. In stereotypical and ideologically charged anecdotes, he argues that religious persons have been stigmatised as 'freaks' and 'social misfits' because they do not drink, smoke and have sex freely. In fact, the religious 'freak' is only someone who is 'superstitious, impractical and way behind the times' (Sadhu Vishwamurtidas 2003: 40–41). In the author's view, however, it is the 'mundane' people who are limited by their horizons. They are 'spiritual misfits', opportunists without principles and values, humiliating the religious persons. In another essay, critics of religion (i.e., not only secularists) are bashed — as lacking 'true' knowledge and being ignorant. Thus, we find a polarisation of an Indian modernity that is very well capable of being spiritual and modern versus an ignorant western modernity that views religious rituals as backward. This crude and polemical polarisation of the 'East' and the 'West', the 'good' and the 'bad', 'right' and the 'wrong' is based on an odd essentialisation of culturally distinct identities — surprising insofar as BAPS is a transnational organisation with millions of satsangis who have been/are exposed to 'the West' in one way or another in their everyday work lives. The East–West divide, as Michael Pinches argues, is a ceaseless 'classical' motif of distinction for the new middle classes in Asia, searching for a distinct identity, in particular, differentiated from formerly 'superior' ones. This kind of transnationalism promotes an ethnic chauvinistic cosmopolitanism.

---

[4] This approach can be found in most of the revivalist Hindu movements of the late-nineteenth and early-twentieth century.

Steven Vertovec maintains that modernisation and urbanisation have impacted on traditional caste identities, but not in terms of diluting them. Instead, they have an impact on 'the construction of Hindu religious "orthodoxy"' (Vertovec 2000: 26), one in which parochial identities and traditions give way to more standardised and homogenous ones.[5] As a consequence, what we see is an emergence of an 'ecumenical sort of Hinduism' (Milton Singer cited in Vertovec 2000: 27) which is underlined by the doctrine of *bhakti* as also notions of democratic and egalitarian ideals (see Fuller 1992: 157).

For the formation of an ingroup of satsangis, in the context of their transnational distribution and the experience of globalisation, rituals are perceived as important, too. In the 1990s, the Gujarati community emerged as a 'dominant' minority in terms of large diaspora and political participation as also display of wealth in the public sphere, both in India and abroad. Yet, the Gujaratis have kept relatively stronger communal and local ties both overseas and in India. They even encourage the learning of Gujarati on their webpage for children and through online satsangi exams. In order to achieve this mixing with members of other castes from other regions is often avoided and relations with India upheld through patronage, marriage, business, voluntary organisations, pilgrimage and other ties. Roots here are thus localised in a particular landscape of globalised aboriginality as a 'continuance of corporate caste identities, statuses, endogamy and caste-related custom' (ibid.: 25–26). The nation state plays a marginal role; what matters instead are regionalism and nationhood as the repository of glocal cultural identity.

Like every charismatic religious movement, the stability of the ingroup is crucial, while at the same time, new members are constantly sought in order to spread the movement. Since the late 1990s, BAPS has opened up to swamis and satsangis from several other regions of India. The regional and yet 'sacred' language, Gujarati, in which the texts of Lord Swaminarayan are distributed and studied at satsang meetings, has by now been supplemented with English, Hindi and Punjabi translations. Given the relevance of Gujarati-ness for the transmission of knowledge and culture over decades and centuries, this shift announces drastic changes for the regionally-tied community.

---

[5] A similar difference exists between *shastrik* (scriptural, unchanging, higher form of) and *laukik* ('folk', changing, lower form of) beliefs and practices. See van der Veer in Vertovec (2000: 30).

Several satsangis pointed out in conversation that these changes had come in tandem with the opening of the ACC in Delhi, which underlines BAPS' motivation to shift the centre stage of the nation state, and to promote a more overt global visibility and membership. Satsang exam forms and material are available online, in English and Gujarati. Further changes have taken place in terms of dress code (from *salwar kameez* and *kurta* to *sari* and western suit) and food tastes (from Gujarati cuisine to Punjabi or south Indian, even western fast food).[6] Many satsangis have remained remarkably 'local' in their life conduct, despite their exposure to 'other cultures' vis-à-vis their life overseas. But equally interesting is that fellow satsangis look at them with some amount of concerned empathy, sometimes even slight embarrassment for their reluctance to open up to the 'modern' way of life.

The opening up of the BAPS ideology to a religio-spiritual and national market, by means of the ACC, is an interesting move. It shows that only in doing this, BAPS members became aware of what 'Indianness' (versus Gujarati-ness) could imply. To many, India in this respect was a 'foreign land', quite like the experiences of returning overseas Indians with regard to the real estate market (as described in Part I of this book). Quite suddenly, the members now got involved with national culture in a way they had never done before, 'carried by a transnational network rather than by a territory' (Hannerz 1996: 104).

This also shapes the creation and consumption of rituals. At one end of the spectrum of creating 'pure' rituals (for self-authorisation and ingroup constitution), we find the 'official' face of Hinduism à la BAPS, while on the other end there is the 'popular' rhetoric of the movement. However, as is often the case, the possibility of overlapping and blurring of these ends is always there. 'Official' Hinduism, as Vertovec elaborates:

> can be taken to mean a set of tenets, rites, proscriptions and prescriptions which are promulgated through some institutionalized framework ... which determines orthodoxy and orthopraxy, arranges and administers a variety of socio-religious activities, unusually controls some sort of communication network ... and is often directly involved in religious education through schools and other programmes (Vertovec 2000: 41).

Likewise, he maintains that 'popular' religion can be understood basically as beliefs and practices undertaken or maintained by lay believers: these

---

[6] BAPS lists all its mega-events of the past 20 years in India and abroad in detail at http://www.swaminarayan.org/festivals/ (accessed 28 June 2008).

include orthodox practices undertaken outside "official" auspices ...'
(ibid.: 42). As regards new spiritual movements such as that initiated
by the BAPS, we can even find hybridisation in the form of what I call
'gospelisation' of spiritual life and practice through popular Hinduism. For
instance, staged DVD-testimonies in which a volunteer addresses a large
audience of satsangis is very much in the style of US-televangelism. Some
appearances of spiritual leaders have the character of a stage show, featuring
rap music and tunes reminiscent of the style of Joan Baez, inviting mass
chanting. There are new collective rituals such as 'Fun-o-tsav' (Festival of
Fun in USA), and new rituals are invented, such as 'Get-Well-Soon-prayers'
at hospitals in Delhi and Sydney.[7] NRI youths are taken on a 'holiday camp'
to India where they go on a pilgrimage along the route of Neelkanth's
yatra. Indeed, most of these neologisms are aimed at a young generation of
(almost exclusively) Indians and can be associated with what Vertovec has
called the 'discoization' of Hindu ritual (2000: 17; Milton Singer used the
term 'pop-Hinduism' in similar contexts, see Singer 1972: 4). This might
be of relevance because the reintroduction of religion and spirituality to the
young generation and aspiring middle classes among the diaspora reveals
the transculturality of the phenomenon.

Internally, from the perspective of BAPS satsangis, there is no contradiction in the multiple employments of rituals: Vedic rituals and 'Get-Well-
Soon-prayers' coexist within the same community, without the 'official',
high culture-ritual questioning the 'popular' and vernacular other. It is important to mention I think, however, that the guidelines and rules for the
inclusion and exclusion for what is 'official' and what is 'popular' change
and are negotiated on the basis of differing contexts and perspectives.
The meaning of 'pure' or 'impure', of 'temple' or 'monument', then, depends
on *who* is being addressed and appealed to, and how symbolic and cultural capital are defined in this process. Everything passes, so it seems, as
long as the intention is adequate.

Temples as Spiritual
and Humanitarian Hospitals

'Mandirs, scriptures and sadhus are the three protectors of culture', reads
an online quote in which the classical definition of 'high Sanskrit culture'

---

[7] One addition by the BAPS in their ritual calendar is the introduction of several
festivals related to the spiritual leaders, in order to legitimise the divinisation of
Lord Swaminarayan.

is affirmed and attributed to the 'custodian community' of BAPS.[8] Temples (*mandirs*) are pillars of ritual performance and purity, but much more than that, they are a 'vessel' of Indianness and cultured-ness. The promotion of strong networks of temples, covering India and, successively, expanding across the globe, works like a shield of protection, a topography of castles facing all kinds of challenges and challengers. According to the history of BAPS temples were built by Swaminarayan to revitalise moral values, civility and peace in India, all three allegedly diminishing in the 'dark age' of the eighteenth century. Today, the global network of temples, strongly emphasised in their web presence, is a crucial means of tying the BAPS community together as a moral ecumene, and making a statement of visibility in order to attract confidence among the old and interest among potential new followers. In my view, the ACC is less inherently 'Indian' in terms of a territorial identity but the product of a transnational gaze and cosmopolitan agenda related to 'world-class Indianness' instead. On the one hand, the temples affirm regional identity and privilege it over national identity. On the other, the temples generate a globalised identity, making BAPS members feel at home wherever they go in the world. The temples are thus 'translocal' sites, yet full of 'tradition'. 'Home' could thus, principally, be everywhere (see also Dwyer 2004: 196–97). This is interesting insofar as it presents an identity that seems to be more local and global than national. The global presence of various networks of sites and people, mostly rooted in large urban environs, also points us to the fact that transnationality creates its own rootedness and does not necessarily have to be tied to one site (see also Ong 1999). A feeling of nationality, then, does not always rely on the identification of a geophysical nation state.

Two kinds of temples exist within the global network of BAPS. Accordingly, different rituals of murti worship are conducted. The *shikharbaddha mandir* is usually a traditional stone temple with pinnacle(s) and dome(s), with lifelike painted murtis of Lord Swaminarayan and other spiritual leaders from the *guru-parampara* (line of gurus) who are worshipped with arati five times a day.[9] All rituals and festivals are duly celebrated and sadhus live in an accompanying *haveli* or assembly hall. Before 1995, no *shikharbaddha mandirs* could be found outside of India. Now, there is one each in Atlanta, Chicago, Houston, London and Nairobi (see Plate 8.5). Since 1995, BAPS

---

[8] See http://www.swaminarayan.org/news/2000/11/delhi/index.htm (accessed 5 May 2007).

[9] See also http://www.mandir.org/mandir/concepts.htm (accessed 23 May 2008).

Plate 8.5: The Swaminarayan Hindu temple at Neasden, London (2006).

sadhus have been sent out of the country to supervise the *shikharbaddha mandirs* on a permanent basis (Williams 2001: 197). The *hari mandir*, on the other hand, in the diaspora is often a mundane building, e.g., a house or a factory, converted into a temple. Murtis are worshipped twice a day in these temples, and sadhus do not live next to the temple premises.

In any context of drastic change, be it in the diaspora or in a rapidly changing India, the mandir can come to serve as a harbour of faith, heritage and strength. It is often the only place where the youth gets to practise rituals, learns to appreciate and be proud of India's cultural heritage, and over-come feelings of inferiority and isolation that often come from being a part of a very small, misunderstood minority' among the majority com-munity abroad (ibid.: 164; see also Waghorne 2004). Likewise, the temple and its community serve as a pillar in a society allegedly estranged by modernisation and secularism. In such a case, knowledge of cultural heritage may work as a means of creating distinction and selfhood, or what I term, the 'cultured Hindu'. In this context of turning itself into a custodian community, and the ACC at New Delhi into a heterotopia, BAPS engages in a rewriting and invention of Hindu tradition and history, establishing an alternative 'overseas Indian' modernity. The mandir now becomes a historical and reformist site where all are equal in that they belong to the same moral community of citizen-consumers (Fernandes 2006). BAPS paints the following image of the (Swaminarayan) temple in the eighteenth century:

> [U]niversally accessible. People from all backgrounds and all places came to the mandirs … mass population was given free and regular access to the stories, the epics and the scriptural traditions that was the foundation of their culture. Thus, historically the mandir universalized the knowledge of their scriptures by making that knowledge accessible to everyone.[10]

The temple is defined here as public library, open to all. But we shall see subsequently that this imaginary character of the site as 'publicly-owned' glosses over its very hierarchical nature and move towards privatisation, discrimination and control, underlined by the idea of a moral community. The temple is where personal peace and social unity combine:

> Mandir is a Sanskrit word for where the mind becomes still and the soul floats freely to seek the source of life, peace, joy and comfort. For centuries, the mandir has remained a centre of life — a common community place where people forget their differences and voluntarily unite to serve society.[11]

To be sure, historically speaking, these are claims that have been made earlier. The new forms of temples and sacred monuments for a secular, independent India insist that caste must not count as a means of hierarchical distinction. Instead, new models of civil society and responsibility, heralded by the idea of seva have come to shape and replace previous notions of national identity. It is exactly the principle of equality promoted by advocates of the BAPS' *sampradaya* that has been questioned by scholars such as Makrand Mehta (see Hardiman 1988), since access to religious scriptures and sites has, until Independence, and till recently, been restricted on the basis of caste membership. Only those who belonged to the upper castes had access to temples and scriptures, while lower castes, in particular, Dalits (the so-called 'untouchables') were neither eligible to enter the monuments nor read the sacred texts, or be initiated into the rank of a priest. This was due to a strong belief in the ritual purity and dominance of high-caste members and, accordingly, the polluting force of the low castes. It is only since the last PSM that low-caste Hindus can be initiated into the ranks of a sadhu and mass inter-caste marriages are conducted.

---

[10] See Question 8, http://www.mandir.org/mandir/concepts.htm (accessed 23 May 2008).

[11] See http://www.mandir.org/mandir/concepts.htm (accessed 23 May 2008).

At a time when the secular state has largely withdrawn from religious and welfare duties and tasks, the concept of the temple as a social 'community' centre as viewed by BAPS purportedly takes care of each and everything: it provides spiritual well-being and solidarity; it is a regional centre for humanitarian activities (rehabilitation work during natural disasters, consultation and help with drug addiction and blind superstition addiction and superstition), a centre for arts, dance and crafts, a source of love, peace and harmony.

With this vision of the temple as a haven of humanity and tradition that serves as an ideal site linking deities and people across the globe, the concept of seva emerges as the ideal solution to secularism's disenchanted world. Although BAPS taps into traditional notions of collective work of a community for social and spiritual purposes (seva), they give it a particular 'tone' by turning it into the ideal form of transnational solidarity. The concept of seva can be found in Sikhism and different Hindu sects, and it has enjoyed a remarkable rise in popularity among urban middle-class Indians in the last decade or so, quite like the concept of charity work among the European bourgeoisie. The emphasis on seva could also be understood as an answer to the colonial critique of Hinduism as lacking charity.[12] The spiritual magazine *Life Positive* defines seva as follows: 'Socially-engaged movements that motivate and are motivated by personal and universal responsibility, based on principle of selflessness, non-violence and delete the modern dualism of self and the world'.[13]

Without entering into too much detail as regards the popularity of this kind of charity work, I propose that seva is not just linked to the increasing relevance and popularity of non-governmental organisations in India in the light of the declining welfare state. It is also linked to new modes of distinction and habitus, late-capitalism plus human values — and the notion of 'helping' out in compassion and belongingness, simultaneously celebrating self, life and feeling good (Schulze 1992). Despite its heterogeneity and centrality in the concept of *bhakti*, seva also helps enhance the notion of a transnational moral fraternity of beautiful and happy people of 'New India'. Having said this, it must be added that this is not the view shared by BAPS spokespersons or even the majority of satsangis whose priority is asceticism and loyalty towards the guru.

---

[12] I thank Sophie Hawkins for her reference to the reformist concept of socially-engaged religion.

[13] *Life Positive*, October, p. 14. Sri Sri Ravi Shankar, guru of AOL, maintains: 'Seva is our own inner joy pouring forth into action. It is not compulsory duty or uncomfortable obligation, but a *natural* state of mind' (Jacob 2005).

The idea of the temple as a haven for an ideal modernity has strong undercurrents through transnational networks and activities of Hindus. Vertovec maintains that the 'traditional' temple in India may be crowded by a large number of Hindus. But he argues that these visitors and places are 'known for their lack of group-oriented, participatory or what might be called "congregational" ritual activity' (Vertovec 2000: 126). Instead of being a private act of devotion, visiting the Akshardham Complex becomes a statement and promulgator of cultural knowledge and national confidence. The Monument at the ACC is really more a consequence of the rapid global spread of Indians and their networks through temples in major urban centres such as London, Nairobi and Atlanta. It is a product of the growing confidence of Indians to have religious icons displayed next to other 'world-class' symbols like shopping malls or mega-events. In this course, places of worship have expanded their meaning and form from being sites of ritual devotion and congregation for particular regional, linguistic and caste groups to cultural and social centres that aim at finding consensus about a shared moral consciousness, spiritual practice and engagement in the world.

While in the past many reformist movements have tried to abolish, if not at least sideline, the casteist institution of the temple as well as ritualised idolatry, BAPS has reintroduced them to centre stage. In fact, BAPS activities overseas have succeeded in getting a lot of attention for the splendour of their social service, temples and festivals.[14]

The mandir's function, at least for the BAPS community, is to stabilise and protect what Sadhu Vishwamurtidas, in preceding discussions, calls the 'spiritual person'. In theory, a proper satsangi must visit the temple every day to worship the murtis. On the BAPS website's homepage for children it is even called an 'unforgivable sin' if murtis are not worshipped.[15] Only recently, and due to the fact that temples are not always in proximity to satsangis, *darshan* is also possible — and potentially efficient — through online murti *darshan*. Moreover, non-satsangis may enjoy the BAPS mandir's educational and uplifting power through visits and ritual performances. The mandir continues to stand as an island, kept apart from the 'impure' and chaotic daily routine. Here, people worship daily, celebrate festivals and 'seek shelter in sad times'.[16]

---

[14] Some of the most spectacular Festivals of India hosted by BAPS were in 1991 (Edison, USA), and in 1985 (London).

[15] See http://kids.baps.org/ (accessed 7 May 2007).

[16] See www.mandir.org/mandir/concepts.htm (accessed 31 June 2007).

Many of the rituals hosted in temples resemble feasts of conspicuous consumption. The idea that hard work, regulated life conduct (as opposed to lifestyle) and moral purity result in material and spiritual surplus that can be invested in rituals or temples instead of luxury commodities reflects a positive approach towards capitalism. It legitimises the staging of pompous rituals as morally correct and distinguishes the sect from others who might have less ostentatious performances. Temples and their keepers have often been criticised for creating sites of illegal monopolisation of financial capital, decadent spending of money and restricted access (especially to non-Hindus and Dalits). However, BAPS spokespersons proclaim that materialism in the name of religion, similar to protestant ethics, is nothing to be ashamed of. Instead, material wealth seems to be 'purified' in the light of the 'right' intentions of its possessors. To some extent, this can be partly related to the confidence of the movement as well as the culture of conspicuous consumption and production of the middle-class members attending the rituals. This attitude finds entrance into affluent and extravagant rituals such as Annakut, the first day of the Hindu New Year, when thousands of vegetarian dishes, prepared by female satsangis days in advance, are presented to the murtis at BAPS temples (however, not at the ACC Monument surprisingly) (see Plates 8.4, 8.6). Through the themed display of food, the producers of the dishes could also make individual statements of distinction. At the Annakut festival at the BAPS temple in Delhi in 2006, I found replicas of American hamburgers, pizzas and milk shakes with plastic straws, iced cakes in the shape of the map of India depicting Neelkanth's yatra, next to vegetarian Indian dishes.

This way, the desire to display material wealth and social distinction can be merged with intentional spirituality. Money, in such a context and through the act of the Diwali puja, is transformed into prasad (offering sanctified and returned by the deities), and simultaneously dissociated from its mundane associations such that wealth becomes 'clean'. The particular 'business'-ritual performed at Diwali for traders and businessmen, is called sharda puja. In BAPS shikharbaddha mandirs, 'it is a tradition for swamis to perform the Vedic Sharda Pujan rituals of the devotees' account books.' This seems to make specific sense in the light of the fact that a majority of BAPS followers come from trading and business communities in Gujarat.[17]

Such rituals of conspicuous devotion can easily be mistaken as an arrogant display of wealth. However, there are concerns addressed by critics

---

[17] See http://www.swaminarayan.org/festivals/diwali/index1.htm (accessed 10 November 2007).

Plate 8.6: Display of *prasad* (sanctified food) at the Annakut festival
at the BAPS temple next to the ACC, New Delhi (2006).

that the ACC is a showpiece of capitalist decadence and, thus, dishonest to
that degree. A so-called 'spot-guide' who had kept a diary with comments
about visitors' questions, remarks and behaviour confirmed this view.
She had noticed that one of the most frequently raised concerns was that
the entrance hall to the ACC looked like that of a five-star hotel, and that

the whole site must have cost a fortune — and this too in a country with so much poverty. The answer I often read and heard in return was that the ACC could not have been built in such a short time, even with more money if the driving force were not commitment and devotion. The main contribution that raised the ACC above the status of being 'just another luxurious theme park' was the dedication of the satsangis. Seva, not *paisa* (money), was the motor behind this monumental site, and thus decadence was an unfounded criticism. In response to such queries, the homepage of BAPS, website tackles the issue of material affluence by in fact categorising it as a 'frequently asked question' (FAQ):

> Question: Why build majestic mandirs? Why spend so much money for mandirs?
> Answer: [Government buildings] promote pride in one's country and values, and thus spread a beneficial social message ... [T]he architecture of the mandir also promotes a message that is spiritually and socially beneficial. The architecture of a mandir evokes feelings of purity, devotional fervour, faith, wonder and the splendour of God, and pride in one's culture ... If society admires wealthy people for the massive mansions and palaces that they construct to serve their own selfish needs, should not society admire even more, those people from all backgrounds who selflessly donate to the mandir for the socially beneficial message the mandir's architecture promotes.[18]

In the eyes of the BAPS satsangis, a disciplined life does not necessarily mean that modernity and materialism are sidelined. Rather, they have to be regulated, especially sexual desires and food consumption (see Williams 2001: 164). The mandir functions as a response to what is by definition established as a 'deficient modernity'; it at once 'heals' and 'educates' modern (wo)man's mind and soul.

---

[18] See Question 3, www.swaminarayan.org/faq/mandir.htm (accessed 6 June 2007).

theme park antecedents
and indigenous concepts
of leisure religion

I s the ACC a theme park or a 'real' pilgrimage site? I have maintained earlier that this is a misleading question to ask because the underlying message is that we can have 'either/or' (see Oakes 2006; Lyon 2000). Instead, I argue, the ACC qualifies as both and more. Such a question is as misplaced as the one interrogating the authenticity and depth of feelings and interaction of visitors at the site. However, it does make sense to consider at least certain elements of theme parks and their culturally specific histories to go beyond the façade of this spectacle of religious 'edutainment', the theming of pilgrimage, nationalism and heritage tourism.

According to Bryman, the process of 'Disneyization' is marked by four elements. First, 'theming' gives a storyline to a site, as we already saw in the context of real estate development in the NCR (see Part I). Second, there is a fusion of different practices of consumption, for instance, the consumption of culture and the consumption of goods in a shopping mall. Fused, these become part of an eventful experience. The third element is merchandising, i.e., the creation of logos and goods for the branding of a certain image. In the case of Akshardham, at least to some extent, rituals are part of the merchandising. Fourth, and last, there is the emotional labour involved in visiting and promoting the place. For instance, the full-timers at the ACC invest a high degree of emotional labour in their function as 'translators' and 'guides' for the sake of Lord Swaminarayan and BAPS.

'Disneyization breaks down differences, is depthless, and deals in cultivated nostalgia and in playfulness about reality', maintains David Lyon (2000: 6). This becomes particularly obvious in the ways in which representatives of the ACC claim that the site is a 'world-class' gift to the whole nation, and indeed, to the whole world. They present a romanticised picture of India's heritage, especially the period of Lord Swaminarayan's life and deeds.[1] Furthermore, there is a certain playfulness in the ways in which the Monument is referred to as a temple. Borders between the two are consciously blurred, which has important consequences for visitors. Drawing upon the discussion on the enclaved gaze, as it emerges versus the notion of a vulgar, dangerous and chaotic 'outside' of the megacity, the theme park must be understood as a response to the desire for a culture of civility, order and security — an oasis quite like the romantic vision of the Indian village explored in Part I of this book. Like the urban space, the theme park too is a moralising space of control that excludes and makes invisible that which is forbidden, unpleasant or irritating in various ways. I expand the definition of a theme park and a pilgrimage site by proposing that differences might be diminished in certain ways. However, in some contexts, differences are sharpened as well, especially when it comes to narrative dichotomies of the 'inside' and the 'outside', the 'pure' and the 'polluting', the 'safe' and the 'dangerous'. This has further consequences for the fabric of public spheres.

Michael Sorkin interprets the phenomenon of the theme park and, what he calls, the 'Disneyfication' of society coinciding with the disappearance of the public sphere (1992a: 103). In his view, a theme park is a space in which the narrative is based on the movement of visitors and where one becomes a visitor by observing or gazing at one's own behaviour. Whether this observation of the self through the 'external eye' of social control can be identified as self-reflection with a critical potential can not be explored here. However, the hypothesis is that this external eye is closer to Foucault's notion of the panopticon, i.e., the internalised eye of the prisoner's watchman that classifies, disciplines and controls the individual's (prisoner's) behaviour.

Crossing between Here and There, and Elsewhere

Certainly, the concept of the theme park must not be wholly reduced to Disneyland. There are various antecedents and regional variations, as Terence Young and Robert Riley (2002) in *Theme Park Landscapes* and Anton Clavé (2007) in his comprehensive analysis of *The Global Theme Park Industry* have shown. In general, the theme park has become a metaphor for

---

[1] For instance, there is the narrative of morally dark times in which Swaminarayan grew up, and the messianic light of change he shed on India through his teachings and actions.

modernity and urban life, for the rise of a capitalist, consumer and leisure society. There is a 'social life' to the institutionalisation of spectacle and pleasure. As much as the world fairs have their roots in the baroque *Wunderkammer* or pleasure gardens of sixteenth-century Europe, the theme park also has its roots in amusement fairs, parks of the eighteenth and nineteenth century, and people's exhibitions at zoological gardens such as Hagenbeck in Hamburg. While the *Wunderkammer* were designed for an aristocratic elite that sought to create their own little paradises and exclusive enclaves, the world fairs were opened to the public and became pleasure sites for all kinds of flâneurs and hedonists, exhibiting 'real people'. Besides their ludic, and even carnivalesque, element, they were meant to be curative, educative, inspirational and demonstrative of man's power over nature. The world fairs of the late-nineteenth and early-twentieth century claimed to bring fun, happiness and knowledge to the people, and specialised in the manufacturing of sensations. Another exhibitionary space is that of the 'classical' anthropological museum, with dioramas and taxidermic display, sceneries of animals and 'primitive' people threatened with extinction. The museum, like the anthropology of 1900, thus caters to a highly ambitious moral claim: the idea of the salvage paradigm, the preservation of that what is destined to vanish.

The spiritual or religious theme park is a relatively new addition to this exhibitionary class of public spaces. But the ACC is not the only religious 'theme park' that claims to offer more than consumerist experiences. Holy-Land in Florida, USA, for instance, offers the experience of divine encounter: 'above all, beyond the fun and excitement, we hope that you will see God and His Word exalted'.[2] To some extent, the idea behind this could also be a taxidermic one.

Even though amusement parks and landscape gardens were exported across the globe with colonialism (e.g., into Singapore in the 1920s), the theme park as an industry went global only in the 1990s (see Clavé 2007: 72–92).

Concepts of reality and fantasy or myth are rendered useless if we try to understand the ACC as a place with or without a history. The landscaped theme park is linked to the idea of a mythic origin of a social group, paradisaical or Arcadian in kind, connecting the mundane to the divine. In this context, we can actually talk about the ACC as a *tirtha*, a sacred place where the pilgrim can bridge over the worldly to the sacred sphere. This is indeed

---

[2] See http://www.theholylandexperience.com/abouthle/index.html (accessed 4 July 2008).

what the creators of ACC propose: it is a place where Lord Swaminarayan has descended, and will, possibly, descend again, Messiah-like — an epiphany that associates the visit of ACC with a pilgrimage that enables the pilgrim to meet the divine (see Eck 1998; Michaels 2003).

Possibly, in the context of the ACC, the mythical reality of the new pilgrimage site, leads us to rework our preconceived Cartesian distinctions between the worldly or the mundane on the one hand and the sacred on the other. This constant play with ritual citations at the ACC forms an almost hermetically sealed coat of 'second nature', what Jean Baudrillard called 'simulacrum', i.e., a virtuality that presents itself as 'natural' or 'given': the 'model of a real without origin or reality' (1983: 1–2).[3] This challenges our authority of judging what is real or imagined, what is true and what is false, rendering those differences discursive, at best. The ACC is a continuation of the dream of perfect control of nature in that it shapes our experience into believing that it has always been there.

Indigenising a Foreign Concept

At the ACC, the citations from rituals are derived from a variety of domains — some, for instance, from 'Vedic traditions', some from Christian charismatic movements. Aesthetic and performative means too come from different festive and cultural directions within South Asian popular culture: the tradition of the jhanki (moving tableau paraded at religious processions), the lila (religious drama, folkloric play) (see Sax 1995) and the mela (fair).

Besides traditional concepts of leisure and architecture, the ACC is also based on certain 'foreign' concepts of entertainment and consumption. As argued earlier, BAPS swamis have turned into event managers and specialists. Despite the hefty critique of western materialism within BAPS rhetoric, the swamis who designed the ACC in fact drew upon theme park predecessors: Disney films and theme park sceneries like *Pirates of the Caribbean* (for the Vedic boat-ride) and Disney Land as well as Holy Land in Orlando and Chinese theme parks such as Shenzhen in the province of Guangdong.[4] By talking

---

[3] Thanks to Christoph Wulf for alerting me to Baudrillard's work here.

[4] For the Holy Land theme park in Orlando, USA, see http://www.theholyland experience.com. On Chinese theme parks, see Stanley (2002) and http://www. asia-planet.net/china/splendid-china-shenzhen.htm. In 1985, Marianland was constructed in Texas, USA, another religious, explicitly Catholic, theme park displaying replicas of Lourdes, Fatima, Guadalupe, the Holy Land, and the Vatican; see http://www.marianland.com/marianland.html (accessed 21 August 2007).

to and consulting architects and engineers at the sites, the swamis selected and collected what they found appropriate — or inappropriate — for the theme halls and musical fountain show.

Jignesh P., one of the full-time volunteers of ACC who was involved in the creation of the site for three years and now works as a tour guide for very important guests (VIPs) and an official photographer, explained to me:

> The saints went to all the theme parks in the world and took the best from them for inspiration. But they also chose temple elements from India, for instance, from Konark. One could say that even India served as a theme park for them, as they found inspiration and picked elements from architecture and ritual traditions from the whole subcontinent.[5]

This underlines the glamour and appeal of the ACC to which people are drawn (like tourists) owing to curiosity, a desire for novelty, and a fascination with 'what we Indians have managed to do — and shown the world that we are able that we can do it!' (Ritesh M., personal conversation, ACC, January 2007). Possibly, the intention of the 'producers' behind this, even though not openly articulated, is that the ACC could become a shining emblem for India's worldwide success quite like the spectacular seven-star Hotel Burj al-Arab in Dubai or the heritage monument of Taj Mahal in India.

In fact, tourist organisations specialising in secular as well as pilgrimage tourism are already offering sight-seeing trips to the ACC, branded as heritage tourist and pilgrimage site. The ACC thus falls between clear demarcations of what we might understand as a pilgrimage site, a cultural centre or a tourist spot, and I argue that it consciously does so. Like the 'secular' Birla temples, built by industrialist Birla in the first half of the twentieth century, or the Bharat Mata Mandirs at Varanasi or Haridwar, the ACC invites visitors from all caste, class and religious backgrounds. This can be traced back to the early twentieth century, when claims were made for holy places to be opened to members of all religions and castes.[6]

---

[5] Comment by Jignesh P., one of the thinktanks of the ACC in New Delhi and its predecessor at Gandhinagar, elaborating further that the Monument is a mixture of different styles of temple construction: south Indian (*dravid*), west Indian (the *nagar* temple model from Somnath), east Indian (Bengali and Oriya), and so on.

[6] Mohandas K. Gandhi inaugurated Delhi's Birla temple in 1938. He attended this opening on the condition that people from all castes and creed would be allowed to enter it. A plaque at the temple's entrance welcomes people of all faiths and classes. On the management of religion, see McKean (1996).

Likewise, it is part of a larger agenda of commercialisation, where visiting temples becomes part of a tourist act, of education and nation-building, beyond constraints of a particular religion.

Even though New Delhi is not a pilgrimage site like Haridwar or Varanasi, the twentieth century has brought to it many initiatives of Hindu temple construction. Most groups visiting the ACC combine their trip with other sacred places in Delhi such as the Baha'i Temple (established in 1986, also known as the Lotus Temple), the ISKCON temple complex (founded in 1998 in Delhi) as well as the Chhattarpur temple near Mehrauli in South Delhi. The ACC is not the first 'spiritual theme park' or tourist pilgrimage site in Delhi. There are several places where leisure, entertainment and pilgrimage fuse. For instance, small temples with large statues of deities such as Ganesha or Hanuman, with dioramas depicting scenes from the Ramayana or Mahabharata, and with larger-than-life figures of Mother India, most of which came up in the early 1990s. The ISKCON temple complex and Chhattarpur temple incorporate a few elements of theme park construction.[7] The ISKCON temple complex hosts a museum and offers animated robotic shows depicting episodes from the Bhagavad Gita.[8] Like the ACC, the ISKCON temple was inaugurated by the then Prime Minister Atal B. Vajpayee, and it calls itself the 'Glory of Indian Vedic Cultural Centre' claiming to respond to modern times and needs. The temple has several themed exhibitions, with dioramas depicting battle scenes from the epic Mahabharata, and there are others criticising materialist and western lifestyles. The last scene depicts a mirror cabinet in which apocalyptic visions of capitalism let loose are put on display — problems of drug addiction, violence, pain are the main themes.

All these recent developments must be seen as dynamic continuations of a tradition of edutainment and animated sacred architecture as well as certain performance traditions that fuse spectacle and devotion, folk and classical genres. One such performative element is the *jhanki* tradition, the tableaux or dioramas of specific deities set in a particular mythic narrative or a ritual enactment, and pulled through a city on a procession or exhibited at a fair on the occasion of a special anniversary or ritual festival-cum-parade (see Hansen 2006; Sax 1995). In many cases, devotees approach these

---

[7] On Chhattarpur, see Menon (2005: 110); see also Säävälä (2006) on a Hyderabad theme park.

[8] Hi-tech robotics represent Krishna, Arjuna and Srila Prabhupada, the founder of ISKCON.

figures as deities manifest. The Tulsi Manas temple in Varanasi (established in 1964), dedicated to Lord Ram, hosts an exhibition of moving tableaux that depicts scenes from the Ramayana. During special holidays when large numbers of visitors crowd the site, the exhibition is moved down to the ground floor and expanded by adding other *jhankis* — it is lit up in bright colours, accompanied by songs and narration (personal conversation with the temple-keeper, October 2006). In Amritsar, a Vaishno Devi 'theme park' has come up. Visitors are made to walk through water, squeeze through rock caves, and made to feel that they are embarking on a pilgrimage (personal conversation with Yousuf Saeed, New Delhi, October 2007). Furthermore, there is a temple of the Brahmakumaris at Mount Abu, which can be treated as the previous generation of temples with entertainment, with scenes depicting spiritual themes. In Delhi, several of my conversation partners born in the city remembered and recommended Birla Mandir on Mandir Road, west of the colonial heart of the city. Vipul G., a senior full-time volunteer at the ACC, tells me that as a child he was impressed by the silence of the place:

> This was one of the first temples that came up with the concept of silence. Gita Mandir is a place for both meditation and tourism. Other mandirs only want a crowd (personal conversation, New Delhi, October 2006).

In the past 15 years or so, quite a few sites have come up in north and west India, claiming to be of religio-educational value (educational in the sense that they address the perceived lack of religious knowledge and consciousness as well as national awareness among many Indian citizens from overseas as also India). Such religious tourist sites are created with a fair amount of entertainment value, recalling both Bollywood and Disneyland — for instance, the Bharat Mata Mandirs at Varanasi and Haridwar (see McKean 1996; Ramaswamy 2006). One such example of leisure-cum-religious site with a strong element of Hindu nationalist education is Ram Darshan, in Chitrakut, Uttar Pradesh where the Deendayal Research Institute, affiliated to the Sangh Parivar, has built a complex with a monumental statue of Lord Hanuman shown tearing his chest apart to reveal Lord Ram and his wife Sita. Five theme halls at the site display selected events from the Ramayana using new media technologies, dioramas and more (Herman 2003). The site is presented as a temple, and the habitus is one of pilgrims. Yet, the aim is to instill nationalist fervour, and clearly, a sentiment that is biased to Hindu culture rather than religious pluralism. Chitrakut is part of the sacred topography emerging in the context of the epic Ramayana. It is said that in this forest, Lord Ram, Lakshman and

Sita lived for 11 years during their 14 years of exile. The site is also part of a modern topography of Hindu nationalists to engage in so-called 'reconversion' of *adivasi* (tribals) from Christianity to Hinduism. The region has previously been known for active Christian missionary activities, an agenda now challenged by Hindutva organisations such as the Vishwa Hindu Parishad (VHP).

Another spiritual theme park is Ganga Dham at Haridwar, conceptualised by the famous Sagar family in Bombay, the producers of popular mythological tele-serials such as *Ramayan*, *Krishna* and *Sai Baba*. The theme park is still at the planning stage. For this project the producers envisaged a global set-up for overseas and Indian audiences. The declared aims are noteworthy:

> Develop an infotainment destination targeted at: Children of our country to explain their roots; international visitors; pilgrims having no access to enter-tainment and information. Showcase India's diverse cultural and historical heritage in a manner appealing to all classes and segments without diluting the social ethos. Tremendous scope for extension to Disney type theme parks in Indian metros like Bombay/Delhi and international expansion in tourist places with large NRI populations, such as Mauritius, Bali, Fuji [sic], Los Angeles, London, etc.[9]

Here too, we can see that edutainment and the rhetoric of endless rejuvenation of the imagination is played on.

The dioramas in the theme halls of the ACC might be related to those in the early colonial museums, depicting 'typical' crafts, yoga positions and costumes of India. But they also relate to a very strong performative reli-gious and folk tradition that can still be found in temples and fairs (*mela*). Some of the religious sites are replicas of pilgrimage places elsewhere. They suggest to pilgrims that by visiting the shrine, they simultaneously undertake a journey to a sacred mountain in the Himalayas. However, these spots are rather marginal in terms of the attention they receive, and the grandeur they sport.

The aspect of visual consumption and performance in a theme park are crucial to understand the appeal of the ACC. Different kinds of gaze are at work here, often simultaneously: seeing the divine (*darshan*) and sight-seeing as secular pilgrimage and entertainment. That theme parks are a cultural product of capitalism and urban development implies what was

---

[9] Ganga Dham Haridwar Promotion CD-ROM, 2005.

already argued in Part I, namely, among new social and economic elites, there is a growing desire both for conspicuous consumption (performance) and for space as a reflection of social order. Whether at the condominium or the ACC, the enclave gaze and space is designed to be clean, safe and regulated. Moreover, it seeks to exclude all that might challenge or threaten this safe haven. The theme park provides each visitor with experiences, but it also standardises a particular gaze upon the other visitors and the self, a very intricate interlocking of gazes. This is crucial. Zukin draws upon an interesting point made by architect Charles Moore as early as 1965 who maintained that Disneyland was successful because it offered participation without embarrassment: 'People want to watch and be watched, to stroll through a highly choreographed sequence of collective [prescribed] experiences, to respond emotionally without the risk that something will go wrong' (Zukin 2005: 53). This is relevant when it comes to the self-perception of the visitors at ACC within the larger frames of the domains of the city, region, nation, or even the world.

code-switching
and code-clashing

learly, the main attraction of the ACC is the Monument, located at the
very heart of the Complex. The Monument must be returned to and
looked at repeatedly during the course of a visit to the site. It decorates
the frontpages of souvenir magazines, postcards and posters sold at the souvenir shop. Most of all, it has become a spectacular landmark in Delhi.
Currently, the ACC certainly heads the list of sightseeing items for Indian
tourists and pilgrims, followed by the lotus-shaped Baha'i temple, India
Gate, Chattarpur temple and the Red Fort.

First, the ACC is a theme park: it has a thematic identity (Swaminarayan
and his teachings) that offers lifestyle recreation; it contains several themed
areas; it is organised as a closed space; as a commercial domain (food
and shopping) and 'world-class' facilities such as standards of cleanliness
(see Clavé 2007: 28). Second, the ACC is also a 'true' religious site, and
is even becoming a pilgrimage centre. Finally the ACC is a disciplining
institution. The possible tensions and continuities between these three
features especially with respect to the different registers of authenticity,
taste and distinction will be explored in the following discussion.

The Monument looks like a temple, and is indeed built on the basis of
codes of ancient temple architecture, incorporating temple models from
all over India, such as the Shree Somnath Jyotirling temple in Gujarat,
the Sun temple at Konark in Orissa, and others. It also derives from
other, more contemporary, models of 'secular' temple architecture, for instance Vivekananda Memorial at Kanyakumari, the southernmost tip of
the subcontinent.[1]

Approaching the site, one finds signboards only of 'Akshardham Temple'.
Even articles in brochures and texts in leaflets, as well as the satsangis, refer
to the Monument as a 'temple'. I used this issue several times to engage
visitors and full-timers in conversation about what the monument/temple

[1] Opened in 1970, the memorial honours Swami Vivekananda's concept of national devotion and pride developed in the 1890s. See http://www.rockmemorial.
info (accessed 14 March 2009).

actually was in their opinion. Satsangis working at the site as guides repeatedly emphasised that according to them it did not matter so much whether outsiders identified it with one or the other, as long as they paid respect to both the building and the idols, and preferably, to the ideals of Swaminarayan and BAPS too.

This identification of the temple and the Monument can partly be explained in the context of BAPS' notion of the temple as a spiritual and cultural centre. However, the blurring of borders indicates shifts beyond the concrete territory of the organisation. The ACC sets an example as to how economic liberalisation creates a disciplining society that, despite being impacted by caste, religious or national identities, aspires to emerge as a society of the 'world-class'. Moreover, the ACC functions as an institution through which a complex of disciplinary and power relations is formed, what Tony Bennett called 'exhibitionary complex'. I agree with Bennett that ACC is a place where the crowds:

> become, in seeing themselves from the side of power, both the subjects and objects of knowledge ... interiorizing its gaze as a principle of self-surveillance and, hence, self-regulation (Bennett 1994: 126).

This way, the audience become at once an ordered crowd, part of the spectacle and sight of pleasure. Providing visitors with new and familiar contexts, turning them into both subjects and objects of knowledge, facilitates this. Saloni Mathur and Kavita Singh (2007) have conducted extensive research on the colonial past and museums in contemporary India. They have explored the issue of today's trend of museumisation by religious revivalist and social movements in South Asia, for instance, in the case of a new museum of Sikh heritage or a Dalit museum. For them, the ACC falls into the category of such a move towards museumisation of the kind of groups who are engaged in the attempt to transform their specific religious heritage into national heritage and mainstream culture. Seen in this light, we must understand museumisation as an attempt of particular groups to make themselves visible at a pan-Indian and transnational platform (see Goswamy 1991). It also mirrors the desire to be recognised by others, possibly attract more followers and to cater to the group's self-esteem.

BAPS representatives do exactly this: they blur the boundaries between the temple, the museum and the monument by using the term *garbhagriha* (literally, womb chamber, the *sanctum sanctorum*) for the group of murtis of Lord Swaminarayan, his disciples and other spiritual leaders.[2]

---

[2] See http://www.akshardham.com/photogallery/monument/index.htm (accessed 12 May 2007).

What happens when devotees enter the Monument in the belief that they are, as they are told, in a temple? What changes, if any, are made to the rituals when they move between tourist or leisure attraction and devotional practice? What can be said about consumption and devotion as modes of distinction when we explore the ways in which these rituals are dramatised and defined? In what way does the ACC enable new forms of religious devotion and religious consumption, and to what extent do the two overlap? What kinds of codes are employed and what is expected of the visitors in terms of the labour of competent 'code-switching'? Can we maintain that rituals performed at the Monument are part of a new consumer culture built upon religious rhetoric? We may ask with Lyon as he explores religious consumption, whether this equals relocating to the sphere of leisure as a cultural and spiritual activity (2000: 81).

Max Weber also argued that rituals shape status distinctions (2006: 46). Discipline and self-regulation are key dispositions emerging through ritual performances (Bourdieu 1984). The ritual field through which distinction surfaces at the ACC is complex and multilayered. Like a theme park, it is a highly structured space in which emotions and experiences are charged and controlled.

Let us take a closer look at the performance of arati in the Monument. Before the opening of the ACC, I was told by senior satsangis that no rituals would be performed at the Monument, only at the BAPS temple next door (see Plate 8.4). However, if people insisted on bringing flowers or fruits for the deities they could do so, but nothing whatsoever would be institutionalised from the BAPS' side. Visiting the site a few months after the opening, I was surprised to find a few significant changes. First of all, because of strict security rules, no one was allowed to bring anything but a purse wallet and a water-bottle into the site. But even inside neither flowers nor other objects could be obtained for presenting them to the murtis. The only way of offering devotion other than through prayer is by donation of money. There are dozens of donation boxes and desks spread all over the ACC, and in exchange of a donation slip the visitor receives a pink plastic box filled with prasad at ACC's exit. I was surprised to find that very quickly, arati came to be performed at the Monument twice a day, in the morning just after the main gates of the ACC had opened, and in the evening, around 6 p.m. before the musical fountain would start. Clearly, the evening arati is the more popular of the two because it begins at sunset, at a time when most of the visitors who have just finished a round through the theme halls are about to return home, those who want to witness the musical fountain (Plate 10.1) have just arrived, and people from Delhi and its suburbs come in after work and seek the pleasure of flânerie. It is around the time of sunset

Plate 10.1: Musical Fountain, ACC, New Delhi (2006).
Source: © BAPS, Delhi, Ahmedabad. Used with permission.

and arati that the Monument suddenly starts to glow, first by the setting sun, then as if from within, by means of spectacular lighting.

With respect to the arati in the Monument, a few continuities and differences should be highlighted when comparing it to the arati performed at the temple behind the inner walls of the Complex. There are actually not so many differences between a traditional popular pilgrimage site and the ACC. For instance, out of sheer pragmatism, many popular pilgrimage sites control large crowds by not allowing the pilgrims to circumvent the shrine. At the ACC, whether it is crowded or not, devotees are strictly regulated and held in surveillance with respect to their movement. At the time arati starts, almost every visitor, even if non-Hindu, is requested to worship Lord Swaminarayan.

There are further similarities and differences with an arati in the temple. In the Monument, the murtis of Lord Swaminarayan and his disciples, as well as the deities surrounding them in a circular chamber do not stand behind a door or curtain but constantly reveal themselves to the public. Placed at their feet are metal signboards of their names in Hindi and English. In fact, this is common practice at larger pilgrimage sites where the pilgrims are not expected to know of regional deities. Nevertheless, I observed that at times, the signboards were removed for the puja, indicating a temporal shift from the 'museum' to the 'temple'. The statues would be first fed and given water. Then an audio cassette with a Swaminarayan bhajan (devotional song) would be played. All this would be executed by the two householders dressed in white kurta-pyjamas and a saffron-clad swami would appear only towards the end for the rite of the arati and to ring the puja-bell. While this took place, many visitors would join the performance spontaneously, most of them 'automatically' falling into the praying modus or habitus, imitating what the BAPS satsangis did (singing or clapping), following the gender separation in seating arrangements as enforced by the guides.

The blending of different codes and ways of behaviour required accordingly is tied into the choreography of movement through the Monument. There is a constant shifting between references to cultural heritage and religious practice, one form of action connected with secular consumption, the other with devotional engagement, both closely intertwined. Clearly, the main 'protagonists' of the Monument are the statues of Lord Swaminarayan and his disciples. However, as they face the main entrance, they also face four shrines of the main deities from the Hindu pantheon, altogether eight gods and goddesses. Simultaneously, one can observe people worshipping the statues in the shrines and people whispering to each other while pointing their fingers at some of the carvings in the dome ceiling in admiration. The ACC markets this simultaneity of contemplative devotees and 'cultured Hindus' in brochures and on Internet.[3]

The same can be observed at the gallery of framed 'historical' paintings depicting scenes from Swaminarayan's life. While some people fold their hands once again, assuming that the pictures are sacred, as many framed pictures of deities are, other people carefully study the panels in front of the paintings, written in English and Hindi (first in Hindi only, then followed by an English version). The text is printed against a background that simulates an old manuscript, as if it was a historical document. The text on the panels explains what can be seen. In between this educational 'picture-book' of Swaminarayan's life, the visitor is made to pass through the Hall of Divine Memories. Situated behind the murtis of Swaminarayan and his pupils, this glass case is again surrounded by panels and a red rope to keep visitors at a safe distance. The panels explain that the objects in the memorial box are Swaminarayan's wooden sandals, holy rosary, blessed clothing and auspicious nails, hair, holy thread and asthi (ashes). The items are defined as: 'A testimony of God's Incarnation'. While right after the opening of the ACC in 2005, one could walk directly towards the glass case, a thick red rope surrounded it a few months later, and two guards were permanently placed there to guarantee that no one touched the surface of the case. More than once I observed that guards with annoyed

---

[3] See http://akshardham.com/photogallery/mandir/peoplemoods.htm (accessed 25 August 2008).

faces approach and shout at devotees who are about to touch the glass box or the replicas of Swaminarayan's feet that are embossed in the enormous wooden gates that mark the four cardinal points.

A red rope barrier could soon be found in front of these gates. The embossed emblems are stylised and the sacred replica of Lord Swaminarayan's feet are said to carry 16 symbols of his divinity. They are seen as abodes of God as he descended on earth. In theory, to touch them means to be close to, and be part of, the divine. However, at the ACC touching is prohibited. Keeping visitors at safe distance and regulating their behaviour by means of written or spoken rules is part of the choreography at the ACC. This strategy of distancing is also part of a larger attempt to infantilise and educate the 'uneducated' visitor-devotee — to make them aware of possible mistakes and inadequate behaviour while they are told what to do and what not to do, and establishing BAPS as a legitimate authority or custodian of Hindu culture. Following their routine behaviour at temples, visitors of the Monument become self-conscious and embarrassed by 'making mistakes' and 'misbehaving'.

One more example: along the steps of Narayan Sarovar, the sacred lake that surrounds the Monument almost completely, appeals to authority and authenticity are conveyed through yet another signboard. This panel reads, in Hindi and English: 'Please respect the sanctity of the pond. Do not enter the water. Do not push or rush. Do not walk or sit on the steps.' A female guard especially posted at this spot tells me that visitors also must not run or sit idle, and that it was often the case that some people who considered the site as a leisure garden had be disciplined. I could watch this guard approaching 'misbehaving' visitors, in particular groups of young people, several times. The underlining message is didactic, one of a teacher reminding naturally curious and free-spirited children not to behave 'abnormal'. But only a few people would read the signboards. In many cases, rules were just ignored. Some people clearly preferred to treat the Complex as a romantic tourist site like the Taj Mahal or the backdrop to a Bollywood movie scene, playing in the water as if it was a mundane pond at a stage-set.

Signboards and verbal reminders are effective in creating distance and a patronising hierarchy. For instance, the only places where sitting is allowed are: while waiting for entrance into the theme halls, during arati in the Monument, at the sound and light show in the evening at the musical fountain and on the square in front of the restaurant and the souvenir shop. A senior ACC volunteer maintained: 'We do not want people who come here and think they're visiting a picnic spot!' (see also Coleman 2004: 58–59).

So while there is a conscious slippage between the temple and the monument (as illustrated through the translation of arati from one site to the other), clear rules for 'proper' and 'acceptable' behaviour are imposed. This brings me to the exploration of the various frames in which code-switching, i.e., the conscious usage of different signs for different contexts, and the play of boundaries between different registers of taste and difference takes place. In this course, 'masses' are transformed into citizen-consumer-devotees. This is what code-switching is about: it is a means of establishing social solidarity. In the case of the ACC, this is the solidarity among devotees on the one hand, and cultural elites on the other.

Different Sensories: Cultic Value and Exhibition Value

In their study of museums in an age of religious revivalism in India, Mathur and Singh (2007) have argued that one can observe 'the incursions of the museal mode into the institutions built by a range of religious revival movements' and that 'this blurring of the boundary between museum and shrine is emblematic of the shape-shifting of key cultural institutions in response to the needs of the new cultural economy'. They maintain that in order to promote and stabilise, if not spread, their philosophy, religious institutions today must 'be designed to perform new tasks, to address unfamiliar audiences as well as to consolidate their existing constituencies, to make new claims and to repeat old messages' (ibid.). Possibly the greatest task for BAPS with the ACC was to appeal to both citizens of India and the diverse audiences of NRIs, to create the ACC as the 'world-class' centre of a globalised, sacred Erlebnis-landscape. In this respect, BAPS is not alone, and faces competition against other centres, e.g., ISKCON or the Art of Living Foundation. Hence, there is an overlap of different topographies to which different groups claim access — of sacred pilgrimage sites on the one hand, and leisure and cultural tourism on the other. Involved in the negotiation of taste and difference are at least three groups that claim dominance in the ritual (and ritualising) field that the ACC constitutes, and to some extent they coincide. These are members of BAPS (swamis and satsangis), the emerging middle classes, and the transnational class of Indians.

To be sure, at the ACC we can see the shaping, and partly the clashing, of codes of different kinds of Erlebnis. There is the Erlebnis of a unique authenticity ('Echtheit') by being a connoisseur of concepts and things related to India's as well as BAPS' cultural heritage. And, there is the Erlebnis of experiencing something divine, of being intimately close to and even merge with the divine object by means of ritual. Benjamin's perspective on the history of modernity was one in which 'thin experience' (Erlebnis) suggests givenness and creates immediacy, intimacy and even closure. In this context, Erlebnis is not a historically formative experience. It seems precisely this mediation of immediate experience (eye candy) and transformative experience (spiritual discipline) that has emerged within new religious movements. The sacred is released from its relegation to the private sphere and reintroduced into the moral public sphere. The worldly separation from the divine can thus be overcome while, at the same time, a new form of distinction is introduced: the taste of aesthetics. As emphasised elsewhere, this is an attempt to create an alternative form of secularism and modernity without selling off to ideas of the West.

I suggest that the fusion of ritual object and performance (merging with the divine), and exhibition commodity and heritage knowledge (distancing from the object of observation) can be well analysed with Walter Benjamin's work on the shifts of 'auratic' value and the transformation of the corporeal sensorium in modernity. Particularly in his essay 'The Work of Art in the Age of Mechanical Reproduction', Benjamin develops his discussion of a fundamental shift of ritual, art and aesthetics in reference to the relationship between illusion and reality. The fields of his investigation were world exhibitions and shopping malls, urban restructuring, political changes and economic expansion in the late-nineteenth century, as well as new media technologies such as photography and film of his time, the 1930s. In the 'spectacularisation' of the public Benjamin saw a means of celebrating a 'new' self, emerging from the notions of progress and growth both in the fields of economy and civilisation.

According to Benjamin, the 'aura' of the object changes with the experience of modernity. For Benjamin, the most drastic change of auratic value of an object was figured by its displacement from its foundations in ritual practice and the shift from cult to commodity, from ritual object to fetish with market and exhibition value. Both values create a notion of uniqueness. However, while the first one is marked by the inapproachability of the divine (even we might want to modify this in the context of India, because the concept of *bhakti* allows for the fusing of devotee with deity in the act of worship), the second one suggests a closeness on the basis of its production of taste and consumer value (see Benjamin 1963: 18).

However, I want to suggest, concurring with Bourdieu, that our example shows a more complex structure of a new aura emerging. It requires an expansion of 'cultural capital' in order to navigate between, and negotiate, the different codes imbued in the fields of production. The 'cultic value' is not fully replaced. Instead, our case-study shows that it is entangled with the 'exhibition value', preserving and transmutating traces of fetish and ritual power by merging them with sensation and Erlebnis, two distinct experiences of modernity. Two kinds of gaze are thus blended, sharing the pleasure of looking in spiritual gazing and hedonistic aesthetic consumption.

Following this, the red ropes around the glass case as well as in front of Swaminarayan's feet embossed in the huge gates of the Monument can be conceived of as being employed with the intention to tame the visitors' desire for physical encounter, and transform it instead into a joyous but sensually detached consumption that derives from connoisseurship (e.g., cultural capital). Kajri Jain remarks on this point in Benjamin's work: 'The value of the object now integrally derives from the qualities of its producer, rather than from a transcendent source' (2007: 220), and the commodity gains 'fetish character' (*Fetischcharakter*) that 'naturally' replaces the auratic value. In other words, there is a move away from corporeal seeing (Pinney 2004) to the disembodied gaze of the museum visitor and art connoisseur.[4] What seems relevant, however, is that the emotional appeal of *darshan*, of embodied seeing and feeling the divine, is simultaneously nurtured and policed.

But, likewise, a form of social anxiety and control is enforced that emerges from the fact that two different domains merge under a seemingly identical umbrella, for instance, the performance of a ritual. Yet, these domains, imbued by the cultic and the exhibition value, require the visitor to display a different habitus, to switch codes. Employing strategies of social upgradation of oneself by downgradation of others is a phenomenon of aspiring middle classes versus the 'vulgar' or 'bacchanesque crowd', or what Cross has called 'the middle class … escape from the crowd and distractions of urban space in genteel settings' (2006: 633). The aspect of social anxiety and arrogance is important insofar as it highlights cultural competence as a major status-creating factor, as for instance, choosing the 'right' interior design (see Part I of this book). Taste as a fundamental partner of distinction and status now moves to the centre stage, even in religious practice, as it becomes obvious in the shift from cultic value to exhibition value that familiar things transform into distinctive signs and classified practices. Social anxiety thus becomes a self-stigmatising fear of being branded as ignorant and thus excluded by dominant groups because of certain alleged 'disabilities' to read the signs.

---

[4] According to Pinney, 'corpothetics' is the practice of aesthetics, 'synaesthetic, mobilising all the senses simultaneously' (2004: 19), thus constituting an alternative sphere of seeing as corporeal immediacy vis-à-vis Cartesian perspectivalism.

Museumisation and Aestheticisation

As we have discussed, the Monument is the combination of a temple and a museum. Let me elaborate this further through what can be referred to as the 'temple-museum effect'. In his seminal work on the *Lives of Indian Images*, Richard Davis (1997) observes a similar shift in the context of Indian art exhibitions at places such as the National Gallery in New Delhi. From the perspective of western(ised) museum visitors, Davis maintains, great Indian sculptures had become 'art objects' as opposed to being worshipped and as animate icons hosting the transcendent reality of a deity. Davis alerts us to art historian Svetlana Alpers' concept of the 'museums effect' by which visual and interpretive attentiveness (rather than interaction with the icons by means of worshipping them), come to be the more 'suitable' interaction and behaviour (ibid.: 23; see also 49–50).

In order to heighten the Erlebnis-factor of the visit, several strategies are employed at the ACC that aim at museumisation, aestheticisation and monumentalisation. Along with this come certain 'standards of behaviour' required in order to move comfortably along with the other visitors. The experience of the visit is sought to be heightened by creating both an intimate gaze as well as a panoptic gaze in (and of) the visitors.

There are many occasions at the ACC where the visitor finds him or herself in front of a signboard or a panel: for example, an introduction to the various aspects of the ACC as well as BAPS in the entrance hall, at every major architectural 'item' such as the Peacock Gate (Mayur Dwar) or the circular walkway with elephants selected from fables and mythology (Gajendra Peeth), or in the gallery of paintings narrating scenes from Lord Swaminarayan's life in the Monument. The fact that they are framed in gold and that one must read in order to understand is perhaps a minor, but still an important, detail. It underlines the highly didactic tone of the institution, an emphasis on text, and on text-centred actions. The gold frames and the explanatory panels alert the literate, and even the illiterate, visitor, that something must be studied and acknowledged. I noticed many people who seemed irritated, amused or perplexed at these. I could observe several elderly visitors who folded their hands in devotional respect in front of the paintings. Others would mimic those who seemed to know 'how to behave' in such a quasi-museum context: one must look at the object described, then at the sign and read the text, then again look at the object and contemplate before moving on. Some people would point at the stone ceiling, or the gallery of sculptures, something that seemed worthwhile to point at, thereby underlining one's alleged 'cultured' competence.

This observation is relevant in the context of a question central to ritual studies: Can rituals be a means to the acquisition of specific kinds of knowledge? The regulation of bodily behaviour in rituals and movement through space at the ACC also renders the body visible and transforms the visitor into a consuming and self-monitoring object. In this process of ritualisation, visitors become at once performers and beholders of knowledge and power. We must see that in enforcing particular forms and practices of knowledge, rituals too are used to enact distinction, social constructions that reproduce inequalities based on judgement and taste. Besides appealing to people through the language of familiar rituals and architecture, the intention is also to pave the way for a 'high culture' that fits the desire to belong to the 'world-class' and to have a cosmopolitan flair. The people behind the ACC know that they can convince only when they seem to deliver on this rhetoric. Furthermore, BAPS has its own interests: to project and convey Swaminarayan's philosophy as a healing force and the need for a spiritual leader like PSM, for instance, by creating the desire in people to turn away from addictions of all kinds — materialism and individualism — to turn them into disciplined and morally clean citizen-devotees. This way, the approach of the museum is located in a lineage of public museums from the Victorian era (quite like Benjamin's phantasmagoria-filled arcades of Paris or Berlin around 1880). Part of the museumisation within the exhibitionary complex of the ACC is the transgression and opening up of religion and rite from 'religious aura' (Benjamin 1973) to 'exhibition aura' in which culture and national identity at once can shape (and be shaped by) pilgrimage tourism, cultural and heritage tourism. Moreover, this applies to real estate development.[5] The seemingly familiar is now reintroduced in a different context, brought close to the beholder as at once strange and disembedded, desirable and exotic. We must understand the habitus associated with this new domain as a marker of a 'cultured' person, a person who can read and interact with the museumised items and performances and find pleasure in belonging to the larger beautiful picture and spectacular choreography painted and staged respectively by the ACC. This way, BAPS becomes an educational institution in, and through, which a particular gaze and 'taste' of 'New India' is shaped and policed.

---

[5] The fluidity between the religious and the exhibition aura has been discussed by scholars such as Kirshenblatt-Gimblett who differentiates exhibitions as 'fundamentally theatrical', fragmented and privileging experience in order to create completeness and authenticity (1998: 3; see also MacCannell 1973 on 'staged authenticity'; Balme 1998; Hall 1998).

Simultaneously appealing to the visitors to succumb to the idea of visiting a pilgrimage site, there is also an attempt at the ACC to keep visitors at
a safe distance from the objects of worship by highlighting their exhibition value. The same holds true of BAPS' huge Hari Mandir, the first one
outside India to host its own swamis, opened in 1992 in London. Here
too, signboards are put up everywhere in the temple telling the visitors
to '[p]lease observe spiritual atmosphere by observing silence' or '[t]o
observe the sanctity of the murtis, please do not touch', in Hindi and in
English.[6] The pillars are surrounded by optical fibre glass as if they were
ancient heritage to be protected.

Besides museumisation, aestheticisation is another vital aspect of turning the ACC into a place at which experiences are shaped and transformed
in order to channelise a 'new gaze' upon religion-as-spirituality, as the
foundation for a desirable community and utopian world-view. One
more example to illustrate this is that photography is not permitted
at the site. Pictures are taken and widely, if not excessively, but distributed
by BAPS only. This happens through the media of souvenir postcards, the
photogalleries on the various BAPS' homepages and online rituals. Like the
films in the theme halls and even the IMAX, a picturesque gaze allowing
for monumental and yet intimate feelings gauges the representations.
This kind of discursive viewership is closely linked to what I examined
as 'enclave gaze', in the previous chapters, as well as the 'panoptic gaze'
as the manifestation of a surveying desire and subject. It places fetishised
objects and forms of consumption at the centre stage. Objects turn into
beloved intimate objects to be touched, brought home, and cared for. In
various ways one can dive into a vast material culture of things to collect
and possess, and there is no shortage of aesthetically appealing images
shaping the global imaginary of the new India.

Familiar and everyday rituals too are aestheticised, upgrading a mundane
practice to a 'beautiful' sign, or a sign of (one's) beauty. Visual and corporeal
pleasure and control underline the process of a kind of self-folklorisation
and celebration of 'cultured-ness' predominant at the ACC. The whole site,
including its intangible rituals and material culture, works like a 'mirror-
chamber' through which the visitor-devotee can simultaneously look at
and present itself as the beholder and revitaliser of heritage and tradition,
of 'modernity' and 'progress'.

The transformation from the religious to the cultural–spiritual realm is
particularly important for the perception of those people who are looking

---

[6] Eleven signboards of this kind were present in the London temple when I
visited it in May 2006.

for a new form of practising religion, or spirituality, but by no means do they want to return to 'old-fashioned' ways of performing traditional rituals. They are especially responsive to elements associated with cultural heritage, to 'cultured' Indianness, to aesthetically appealing choreographies that allow the middle-class practitioner to position himself or herself within an upwardly mobile and aspiring social environment. Vipul G., senior full-timer at the ACC maintains:

> The NRIs (Non-Resident Indians) start to rethink their identity when they visit Akshardham. They start to feel proud about being Indian. This is our heritage, our culture: they think when they look at Akshardham. Of course, such people are also there in India, those secular people who don't go to the temple because they think it's not modern! ... Akshardham gives Delhi a boost. It gives values and pride to Hindus. Now they can finally say: look who we are (personal conversation, New Delhi, September 2006)!

In fact, the examples from this section support the hypothesis that the ACC is a 'diaspora-project', made by (and for) people with a 'diaspora gaze' on Indian tradition, heritage and religious practice. On the one hand, this can partly be explained on the basis of NRI-donations. On the other hand, I argue that the diaspora gaze embodies a particular form of what is at once an auto-oriental and occidental gaze that produces spatialisations such as the ACC, and renders India as a fetish of the new cosmopolitan, rediscovering his or her homeland through the eyes of a stranger.

One could even argue that the ACC is a panoramic lens that encourages the domestic Indian audience to gaze at itself through diaspora-eyes, as if they were a museum exhibit, through eyes nostalgically looking for myths of the homeland, longing to preserve tradition, fearing for its loss and thus introducing institutions to re-memorise and experience that which is apparently at the risk of fading. India thus becomes another planet to be discovered, or as Lowenthal argues about the past, a 'foreign country' (1985, 2002). In her book *The Third Eye*, Fatimah Tobing Rony (1996) has referred to film and ethnographic practice of the early-twentieth century as intertwined 'taxidermic practices', viz. strategies to document an allegedly dying race or animal breed by means of recording on audio and audio-visual media and then revitalising the object of inquiry to the extent that it can be mistaken for the original. I suggest that this technique can be transferred to the ACC where a monumentalised 'second nature' of Vedic culture and BAPS' way of life is created as national heritage. What was shaped by the notion of progress and civilisation, of tradition and modernity in the West and the context of colonisation is now re-appropriated and altered by the formerly colonised. Out of this fusion of perspectives evolves a strange mixture of occidental and oriental elements. In the context of the just discussed role of the ritual as the essential ingredient required for modern selves, I want to coin the term 'taxidermic spirituality' for the phenomenon of museumisation and aestheticisation at work here.

Disciplining and Moral Cleanliness

The shaping of the new middle classes as moral citizens has been discussed in Part I. The ACC also encourages the constitution of a moral community of 'citizens'. Both real estate development in an aspiring global city and the ACC and BAPS philosophy promote a highly moralised environment out of which a culture of security and civility can arise — a gated community. References to moral, ritual and physical cleanliness accompany the strategies of museumisation and aestheticisation on various levels. All three enforce each other and can be achieved through discipline, education and spiritual guidance. Many people I spoke to during fieldwork highlighted their admiration of the spotlessness of the ACC ('like Infosys!'), how many garbage bins they had seen there, and how clean and reliable BAPS food in the food-court was. This is an important issue because many high-caste middle class families are reluctant to consume food prepared outside their home and by strangers. This is for health and ritual reasons, for the fear that the food could be 'polluted' or 'polluting'. BAPS food has the reputation of being 'clean' and tasty, and the fact that BAPS full-timers prepare the food, and that it is made with no onions or garlic, underlines concerns with high-caste ritual purity.

Everywhere people sweep the marble floors or are found engaged in repair work. There are no unpleasant smells or dubious corners inviting visitors to secretly dump garbage. Everything seems well looked after. Several informants compared the ACC to the 'Golden Temple' in Amritsar, the most important religious site for Sikhs in India, also known for its spotlessly clean maintenance by devotee-volunteers.

There are various soundscapes addressing and guiding the visitor: informative, religious, educational and entertaining. Directly in front of the Monument, one-minute loudspeaker announcements in English and Hindi inform the visitor about the ACC, the access to the Monument as well as the entrance fee to the theme halls. In the landscaped garden with assorted groups of spiritual and national heroes of India, in-built loudspeaker commentary in Hindi explains their relevance. *Bhajans* can be heard permanently in the arcades surrounding the stepwell. Like the chanting during the second half of arati at the Monument, they are tape-recorded. The musical fountain show in the evening entertains visitors with an explanatory voice-over commentary and quasi-cinematic new age music, with a similar bombastic effect as the sound and music in the IMAX film. In between are areas of controlled silence. People visiting the Monument are instructed to keep their voice low, and that children must not play and run. Silence, here, is certainly a sign of power and distinction. The contemplative mood is one that signifies the 'cultured citizen' or connoisseur as (s)he interacts with high art. But silence is also a symbol of spirituality, moral upliftment and healing. Temples, says Vipul, senior public relations representative at the ACC, are hospitals for the soul. The silence maintained in the Monument is a mark of respect of the devotee for the divine. According to him, temples of other sects do not follow this rule. They want the big crowd, not individual peace. They are unhygienic. Silence thus marks the border between 'serious' and 'selfish', 'high' and 'low', 'authentic' and 'fake' temples and indicates how this becomes visually manifest and emically relevant. Other concepts, besides silence, are discipline and cleanliness, also tropes of modernity and capitalism. A pure soul finds reflection in a well-maintained place of devotion and conduct of life. Again, this mirrors similar fears of the new condominiums discussed in Part I, where chaos and order, dirt and cleanliness, are pathologised. 'Direct impact'-allegories can be found in several fields of the BAPS life conduct, be it related to the consumption of food or television. Vipul explains:

> People like the fact that Akshardham Cultural Complex is clean. They might behave inside, but outside they will immediately throw garbage and spit. But the cleanliness affects them while they're at Akshardham. When you're surrounded by cleanliness, you are clean, when you are surrounded by bad thoughts, you become bad … Over the time, people know this. Nobody would dare to make this place dirty (October 2006)![7]

Most 'traditional' temples did not have an ideal and cared simply for money and mechanical performance of ritual, maintains Vipul. Undoubtedly, one should argue here, many devotees visit even 'noisy' temples and consider them as 'charged' with the divine.

The notion of noisy masses that have to be disciplined and educated is not specific to either BAPS or India but is part of a global and asymmetrical flow of concepts. It emerges wherever old, or even new elites, attempt to differentiate themselves from the allegedly uneducated masses by pointing out their 'unsophisticated' or 'inadequate' behaviour in actual public

---

[7] Observing the BAPS Cultural Festival of India in Edison in 1991, Shukla notes an 'obsessive attention to cleanliness' (1997: 304).

spaces that had become associated with 'public civility' and visibility. One of the basic and very mundane strategies of making people obey the rules is by publicly embarrassing 'uncultured' visitors. By drawing lines between what is regarded as 'appropriate' and 'inappropriate', normal and abnormal behaviour, new alliances between people not belonging to the same kin, caste, region or even sect and religion can be generated.

The ACC is a strange mixture between public and non-public space, a public field shaped by different discourses that shift between notions of a community of strangers and that of the moral brotherhood, between the introduction of religion into the secular sphere and negotiations related to heritage nationalism. Furthermore, the site creates its own categories of the 'inside' and the 'outside'. There are two categories of strangers created here, since most of the people do not know each other in person but are all joined by means of their visit to the site: the cooperative stranger, willing to be disciplined and consequently integrated, in affirming BAPS' legitimising power, and those unable to do so and thus experiencing exclusion. A person lacking the right credentials could expect to be denied entrance, according to the rules and regulations of the public in eighteenth-century England. In fact, the entrance signboards announce that entry to the ACC could be denied by the administration (Plate 10.4).

Compared with Part I of this book that was concerned with urban planning and real estate aesthetics, we may say that while the key motivation there was to belong to the 'world-class' city, in the case of the ACC we find a desire to belong to a 'world-class' spiritual brotherhood and custodian community. The two do not excude but rather complement each other.

Despite a publicly liberal and highly integrating outlook, BAPS websites, for example one addressing specifically children and youth show that there is a strong desire to clearly distinguish between 'us' and 'them', 'inside' and 'outside'.[8] This is done by means of drawing ritual boundaries of pollution and purity. The English-language homepage, written by swamis for (Indian/BAPS) children living all over the world, demarcates certain 'zones' of danger and pollution: the most 'infectious' ones are television, food and touch. The homepage is styled like a scholarly discourse between guru (PSM) and shishya (disciple): the latter asks a brief question and the former responds. Again, this underlines continuity from the classical guru–shishya system of teaching. For instance, the separation of satsang society and worldly society leads to imbalances and questions of prioritisation of

---

[8] See http://www.swaminarayankids.org (accessed 10 July 2007).

different lifestyles and values, particularly for satsang youth. In fictional online dialogues, a Swamishri maintains that 'the more we stay in contact with satsang, the less our friends outside will be able to influence us.[9] The dialogue suggests an essential danger imbued in any kind of exchange with the outside world and the creation of as many activities and institutions in order to provide to the children what every other child might need, only that these are 'BAPS-approved'. There is also a fear of pollution through media consumption, particularly television, alleging a direct impact of the media on the psyche, leading to a weakening of moral values. Finally, food is a great source of pollution through the outside world, and Swamishri warns the fictional youth against eating out: 'If the person cooking our food has a polluted mind with bad thoughts, and we eat the food which that person cooks, our minds, too, become just as polluted.'[10] There is thus a way of reasoning and legitimising a general reluctance to engage with people, places and material culture outside the enclosed enclave of the satsangi community. The fear of pollution from 'bad' thoughts that are transmitted through new media technologies, food and social interaction is at work 'backstage'. The following section explores the tension-filled field of discourse with respect to the notion of the unwelcome stranger and external threats.

Othering and Security

Akshardham is all this: sacred and mundane world, theme park and gated community. There is 'inside time and space' and 'outside time and space', separated by high security (e.g., surveillance cameras everywhere, watch-towers, high walls with barbed-wire and body scans) (Plates 10.2 and 10.3).

There are particular rules to obey in order to legitimise the Monument as a ritual space. But likewise, there are also rules to obey within the secular space of the 'theme park'. Zukin writes about a similar ordering and surveillance at Disney World:

> The landscape of Disney World creates a public culture of civility and security that recalls a world long left behind. There are no guns here, no homeless people, no illegal drink or drugs. Without installing a visibly repressive polit-

---

[9] See http://kids.swaminarayan.org/thingstoknow/74to76.htm#76 (accessed 5 January 2007).

[10] See http://kids.swaminarayan.org/thingstoknow/54to56.htm#56 (accessed 5 January 2007).

Plate 10.2: 'Fortress ACC'. The aesthetics of security and fear, with watchtower, barbed-wire walls and security lights, New Delhi (2006).

Plate 10.3: 'Fortress ACC', allegedly a 'top terrorist target' in New Delhi (March 2006).

ical authority, Disney World imposes order on unruly, heterogeneous populations ... and makes them grateful to be there (Zukin 2005: 52).

This reference to the creation of an alternative world à la Bentham, where
order is established, and every inhabitant is 'grateful to be there' to be part
of this exclusive club culture, is very important when it comes to drawing
parallels to recent developments as regards urbanisation and the shaping
of private and public space (see also Clavé 2007: 191–92).

Let me concretise this in the context of the ACC. An institutional message on the homepage of ACC in New Delhi with respect to the rules and
regulations and rights reserved for visitors reads as follows: 'Behaviour:
Avoid impolite and rude language ... Clothing: Visitors are requested to
wear respectable clothes to respect the dignity of the place.'[11] There is a
conscious play of creating difference (and unity) through a host of strategies: dress and modes of behaviour are the most visible ones, for insiders
as well as outsiders. This becomes evident in the order that all female
volunteers at the ACC in Delhi (not in Gandhinagar) must wear a sari in
red, yellow and white tie-dye style (their male counterparts would wear a
western suit but also white kurta- pyjama), in order to appear with a corporate
identity, recognisably Indian and 'respectable'. Yet, several women told me
that especially in the first months, they felt very uncomfortable, almost as
though they were masquerading. They had been used to wearing Gujarati
style salwaar kameez (knee-length shirt on top of trousers).

The ritualisation of status is imposed through various strategies. There
are, for instance, technologies of surveillance at the ACC that render
the body docile and visible to power. They also make the visitor aware of
the fact that she or he is part of a choreography, caged in a self-monitoring
system of looks (Bennett 1994: 133). One of the small brochures that can
be bought for INR 5 at the entrance gate of ACC reads: 'The Management
reserves all rights to entry', while appealing to the visitors to 'maintain
the peace, dignity and divinity of the complex' suggesting that it is a sacred site. The most drastic way of using dress codes for classification and,
consequently, stigmatisation, could be found at the entrance gates, on huge
signboards explaining what to do, bring in and wear at the ACC: 'Food &
drinks, spitting and eating chewing-gum are not permitted in the premises'. The same signboard also communicates that 'Burkhas & Lungis are
not allowed' (Plate 10.4).

---

[11] See http://www.akshardham.com/visitorinfo/index.htm (accessed 12 May
2007).

SWAMINARAYAN
Akshardham
NEW DELHI

GUIDELINES FOR VISITORS

ENTRY TO AKSHARDHAM CULTURAL COMPLEX IS FREE
THERE IS A NOMINAL FEE ONLY FOR THE EXHIBITIONS

- ALL VISITORS ARE REQUESTED TO PASS THROUGH SECURITY
  CHECK
- SMALL LADIES WALLET (6"X4") IS ALLOWED IN THE COMPLEX
  (also available at cloakroom for use of visitors at a refundable deposit of Rs. 20/-)
- PLEASE DEPOSIT ALL VALUABLE ITEMS IN THE CLOAKROOM

NOT ALLOWED

- PHOTOGRAPHY & VIDEOGRAPHY IS NOT PERMITTED IN THE PREMISES
- FOOD & DRINKS, SPITTING & EATING CHEWING-GUM ARE
  NOT PERMITTED IN THE PREMISES
- IMPOLITE & RUDE LANGUAGE WILL NOT BE ACCEPTED

DRESS CODE

Shorts & Skirts shorter than knee length are not permitted
Burkhas & Lungis are not allowed
However under such circumstances, you are required to make use of
Suitable Wrappers available at the Security-Plaza at
a refundable deposit of Rs. 100/-

PLEASE HELP TO KEEP THE COMPLEX NEAT & CLEAN

MANAGEMENT RESERVES THE RIGHT OF ADMISSION & THE RIGHT TO AMEND WITHOUT PRIOR NOTICE
THANK YOU FOR YOUR KIND CO-OPERATION

Plate 10.4: A signboard at the entrance to ACC, New Delhi (2006).

It is crucial to draw attention to the collapsing fields of classification here. On the one hand the ban on chewing-gum may be a pragmatic injunction that reminds of 'world-class cities' such as Singapore, where spitting in public is forbidden. Chewing-gum reflects westernisation; gum is associated with America. Lastly, this association is also a comment about class and habitus: it might refer to having 'vulgar' habits, or to mean 'common' or 'lower class'. But even worse, on the other hand, listing the *burkha* in the same breath reduces the Muslim to an object of undesirability.

This kept me wondering: what is being referred to by the classifiers of chewing-gum and how, simultaneously, could the *burkha* sneak into these rules and regulations? Are these images not part of a larger claim over the 'cultural appropriation of public space', strategies of cultural models of inclusion and exclusion, 'giving (or denying) distinctive groups access to the same public space' (Zukin 2005: 286)? How did the imperative to ban *burkhas* — and with them, people — from the Complex find legitimacy and become a means of controlling the site as well as increasing the desire to have such control? Was this restriction related to an already familiar anti-Islamic ethnic stereotype and global imaginary that is now pulled into the realm of leisure-based religion? Can the conclusion from this 'legislation' be that only good and clean people may enter, and if so, how are the distinctions made?

I asked one of the key spokespersons of the ACC in a personal conversation why *burkhas* and *lungis* were not allowed in the premises? The answer was revealing in many ways: Vipul said that my question was clearly based on a misreading, and that the *burkha* was in fact allowed in. But, those clad in them were not allowed to cover themselves completely. They would have to permit that they were checked by a female security guard. This seems like an appropriation of a global rhetoric of security as burqas and veils are currently widely debated, for instance when it comes to wearing them in government services, at university campuses or for passport identification. Underlining this desire for visibility is a moral stance, as Vipul further elaborates: 'We expect this from them; that the gaze is open and direct', for otherwise, it would harm the sacred atmosphere. Furthermore, there were security reasons: what if a man was behind the burqa?! What if he was a terrorist?! 'Any devotee will understand this', maintains Vipul. And what about the *lungi*, a long cloth worn by men as a piece of garment, wrapped around their hips, sometimes short, above knee-length, sometimes below? *Lungi*, argued Vipul, was 'obscene' [sic]; it was not good for the ladies to see male legs and not appropriate for men to walk like this. A female volunteer told me that 'you should see what these people from Haryana look like!', again creating distinction through the maintenance of moralistic purity borders by means of clothes, and adding regional (people from Haryana are often considered 'low' class) to religious stereotype. The *lungi*, in north India, is associated with Muslims as well as 'uneducated' farmers from Haryana. Even though in theory the appeal of visiting the ACC is for members of all religions, in practice there is a policy of creating distance and awareness against potential 'threats' from the outside world. In this context, the Muslim stereotype features as a recurring narrative element and enforces the creation of a 'panoptic gaze' and surveillance apparatus.

Even the approach and entrance to Akshardham are part of a ritualised choreography of spectacle, surveillance and control. The closer one gets towards the ACC, the stronger becomes the idea of how vast, lush and magnificent this area is. Likewise, its appearance almost as a modern fortress becomes evident: the external wall is about 4–5 metres high, with metal spikes on top, and watchtowers every few 100 metres are positioned within the compound along the wall. A strip of sand then stretches towards the next wall behind which the ACC entertainment compound and the parking area begins. On seeing this, in fact, I was reminded of the former wall between East and West Germany, and the border strip between Mexico and the USA (Plate 10.3). I would argue that this association is part of the strategy to heighten the perception that one is coming close to another country, utopia, and that in the context of today's terrorist attacks, these security measures seem more than reasonable. As Vipul maintains:

> Delhi is a hot spot. Akshardham and the Metro are on the top hit list of terrorists. We want people to know that they are safe. Akshardham gives Delhi a boost. It gives values and pride to Hindus (personal conversation, New Delhi, March 2006).

The clear demarcation of the 'inside' and the 'outside' is relevant for various reasons and based on binary oppositions: for one, it suggests that the 'outside' is potentially insecure and the 'inside' is a safe haven. Second, the 'protection belt' surrounding the ACC reminds us of an escalation in the creation of protection zones in the light of international and national terrorism. The 'real' threat is manifold and located at political, economic and religious levels. The Indian Parliament was attacked by terrorists in December 2001; New Delhi's popular shopping areas witnessed several bomb explosions on Diwali in 2005, the height of the annual shopping season; and the Akshardham Monument in Gandhinagar was attacked in autumn 2002, allegedly by Islamic terrorists.[12] In September 2002, 'terrorists' who had entered Akshardham Complex in Gujarat shot 33 people. Rumours are that this was a well-planned conspiracy by clerics and terrorist groups (from Riyadh) to avenge the killings of Muslims during the post-Godhra communal carnage of February 2002. The terrorists were shot at the site; the case was never completely solved. Following this event, fears were spread that temples all across India were in danger and should be better protected by the state. Priests should be allowed to carry guns. In the aftermath, a high protection wall was pulled up at Gandhinagar's Akshardham Complex, and national army forces were stationed in watchtowers. As a result, access to the site became a security hassle and number of visitors has gone down quite drastically since the attack. At the same time, critics have raised the point that the fear of another attack also highlighted the 'importance' of Hindu temples and other magnificent sites as symbolic markers and 'UPS' (unique selling point) for Akshardham and Delhi. 'People like this kind of tension as if they were part of an action movie', argues journalist Lalit L., 'It's a thrill to think that something of national and even international interest might happen while they're at the site.'[13]

The question of marking new prestigious objects such as the ACC as a top terrorist target speaks not only about India's engagement with terrorism but reflects a global tendency that demands the control of public liberties and public space more than ever before. In particular post-9/11, it legitimises the establishment of ubiquitous regimes of control and surveillance, with reference to London, New York or Madrid.[14] Bomb blasts in public places

[12] Opinions vary and sufficient evidence is still lacking for many: for some, the attackers were revenging the pogroms against Muslims in spring 2002, for others they supported Kashmir's cause for independence. See also http://www.onlinevolunteers.org/gujarat/news/temple (accessed 12 May 2007).

[13] Safety for holy places is a great concern since 2001. In 2005, the Sikh Gurdwara Management Committee decided to install closed-circuit television cameras around the Harmandir Complex in Amritsar and has since announced adding more security due to attacks on other religious areas in India.

[14] Sikh Dharma in New Mexico, for instance, is a new age group that has come up with Akal Security, one of the nation's fastest-growing security companies, benefiting from a surge in post-9/11 business: 'With 12,000 employees and over $1 billion in federal contracts, Akal specializes in protecting vital and sensitive government sites ... Equally important are a number of non-profit ventures also owned by Sikh Dharma. The biggest of these is the 3HO Foundation, with the name standing for Healthy, Happy and Holy Organization', specialising in Kundalini Yoga (see Wayne 2004). I thank Sophie Hawkins for this information.

in New Delhi on 13 August 2008 have only heightened the demand for more security and rigid control systems. The ritual of surveillance and security controls finds much acceptance for the sake of 'safety' and 'global importance'.

Visiting the ACC is clearly framed as a liminal experience, a ritual act. Approaching ACC's entrance, one has to leave everything behind, like in a purification ritual. The only things allowed in are money-purses and bottled water. This transgression has a liminal quality. To many, including me, the security checks are a rhetorical means of executing power over the visitors: the more anxious the visitors feel, the more peace and spirituality they feel they need.

Surveillance is a major construction principle of a site like the ACC (see Legnaro and Birenheide 2005: 43). Body searches, high walls and watchtowers are not enough: dozens of small black surveillance cameras have been placed all over the ACC, even within the Monument. This kind of panopticism can be understood as the condition of modernity and postmodernity. This kind of informal control is based on the suggestion of a threat from the outside turning inwards, of distrust against an anonymous other, a subject–object relationship between the controllers (BAPS) and the controlled (visitors). The security measurements increase the feeling of the intimate inside versus the anonymity of the outside — you do not know whom to trust; potentially anybody could be a terrorist (especially Muslims).

Another institution that helps us understand the mechanisms of the ACC is the panopticon. The panopticon educates and uplifts its occupants by being at once a form of pedagogic instruction as well as disciplinary gaze: 'It works as a machine that transforms the selfish bourgeois into a citoyen' (Oettermann 1980: 35; translation mine). According to Jeremy Bentham, the father of the panopticon, this architectural principle could improve moral and hygiene, and reduce public burdens and other problems of current society (Foucault 1977). The ACC is, in some respects, a cousin of Foucault's panopticon, developed in *Discipline and Punish* (1977), the incarnation of the bourgeois gaze (Oettermann 1980: 38), in its attempt to create a 'better' world and society. Instead of the tower overshadowing the cells of Bentham's panopticon, the ACC has installed dozens of small video cameras that transmit the movement of each and every visitor into a room below the site. Foucault proposed that the external gaze of surveillance is internalised by the person watched (even if he or she is not watched), and translated into a self-regulatory habitus: 'The prisoner in the Panopticon is perpetually trapped by visibility. There is no place to hide' (Gaonkar and McCarthy 1994: 562).

In fact, visitors at the ACC are not aware of the CCTV's presence. Through surveillance cameras the panoptic technology of power is electronically extended. But the notion of being watched is enforced by the omnipresent figure of the guard. All over the ACC, guards watch the movement of visitors, asking them to refrain from sitting down where they must not sit, from running, writing, speaking loudly, and so on. One begins to become aware of the presence of a constant gaze of surveillance, right from entering the site through the security control. The gaze of surveillance is immediately inverted and the inherent suspicion produces mixed feelings of vulnerability, irritation and guilt. The ACC works on similar levels like the panopticon in that it emphasises control as moral rectitude by claiming that Vedic philosophy and Lord Swaminarayan's philosophy bring people closer to happiness and makes them realise their essential humanity and humbleness.

Ritualising the Panoramic and Panoptic Gaze

Like many elements discussed here, print and audio-visual media, architectural sites and exhibitions provide a panoramic view of what it means to be 'global' and 'world-class'. The panorama is an invention of the nineteenth century and reflects the desire to represent (glorious or shocking) moments in history (starting from Greek antiquity), an expansive European economy, a growing confidence and urge for visibility and conspicuous consumption by a bourgeois public. Both panorama and panopticon result from capitalist society, the dominance of capital, and the 'dialectic of the bourgeois gaze' incarnate (Oettermann 1980: 38). These two elements are dominant parts of the ACC's choreography and rhetoric.

The 'modern selves' that surface in a place like the ACC, are to a large extent invoked through the use of ritual as a rhetorical device and a highly aesthetic means, often communicated by the latest technological devices (e.g., animated robotics and Internet). Rituals and cited elements of a whole range of rituals or rites that can be found at the ACC and that in fact make up the 'felt' fabric of the place, are meant to ritualise a culture-specific panoptic and panoramic gaze and experience in the visitors. In fact, the ACC in many ways is an inherently 'modern' institution in that it functions like a panopticon — disciplining and educating 'citizens' of a new age and a 'new modernity'. The site absorbs the nation state and national history and transforms it into a new utopian vision of India and of Indianness and I shall argue subsequently that this is done by following the lines of an already established discourse — that of Hindutva as a way of life (Brosius 2005). The 'cultural complex' I am speaking about uses a range of ritual prescriptions that cultivate and ritualise notions of a selfhood that seems better equipped to engage with and manage the imperatives of modernity, a self that leads a more balanced, holistic, pure and happy life but is constantly threatened by the fabric of the 'outside world'.[15] The notion of the spiritual leader also turns him into a watchman in the panopticon's tower, while his followers, and even visitors of the ACC, become 'inmates', internalising the gaze of control as if it was naturally theirs.

The ACC is a conglomeration of ritual sites, practices, and 'imaginaries': there are orthodox rituals, mostly executed for the exclusive eyes of the 'in-group' of satsangis and available online or on DVD, there are transformed rituals, readymade for mass identification and performance, and there are 'edutaining' rituals where, nevertheless, dissatisfaction may arise from shifting codes. Rituals are used to appeal to the idea of a Hindu cultural heritage, rooted in the ancient Vedic civilisation; there are rituals that suggest 'home', 'purity', 'self-awareness', and rituals are employed for distinction and differentiation of 'others' (marking 'uncultured' visitors). I have examined several examples connected to the role of rituals and ritualisation as a normative, regulating, disciplining and discriminating force. The rituals and forms of ritualising we find linked to an institution like the ACC can be read as attempts or strategies to bring stability into the enormous changes occurring within India as well as on a global scale, linked to transnational movements and communities (and to a new national confidence).

They display strategies of monumentalisation, historicisation, aestheticisation, commodification and standardisation, and generate what Lieven de Cauter has called 'panoramic ecstasy', that is the synthesis of the panopticon for surveillance and the panorama for survey, both marking the disciplinary society and the spectacular society respectively (Cauter 1993: 3). The key argument is that the stages on which panopticon and panorama came to be put on display at world fairs and the like around 1900, narrated the 'desire to visualize progress itself' (ibid.: 6). I consider this performative gaze as highly relevant for the new spaces, sites, desires and experiences that shape and are shaped by contemporary urban middle class society in India. Ritual space, ritual and ritualisation help the makers of the ACC to establish a platform on which notions of Indian identity and religious practices can not only be preserved but also promoted as ideal-typical models in a disenchanted, imbalanced modernity, with a highly heterogeneous society — promoted to the largest possible denominator of audiences.

---

[15] Thanks to William Sax for this input on the 'healing' powers of rituals in modernity.

This requires extreme mechanisms of opening up on one level (largely done through use of extensive and diverse media) — creating what I propose to be 'flat rituals', coined after Thomas Friedman's book *The World is Flat* (2005). In this view, we could perceive 'flat rituals' as rituals that are not deeply rooted in a special locality and can thus be comfortably transferred to another locality and social context. Transnational rituals are such rituals that show a great flexibility and mobility in this context. They can be practised everywhere, at great ease, and appeal to a large and diverse crowd who can utilise them instantly.

At the ACC, rituals too are woven into the spatial narrative and flow of the compound, structuring physical movement, ways of engaging and experiences of the visitors. They have to appeal to international, transnational, and materialistically-oriented audiences, to members of different religions, sects, castes and geographical regions. The rituals on offer at the ACC are widely used by members of various Hindu sects, especially to those following the *bhakti* tradition of devotion that emphasises a highly sensuous and intimate relationship between the devotee and the deity (albeit, and this is vital, having recognised the guru as a mediator between the individual and the divine). The rituals are not complicated to perform and if needed, various employees, either guides or *grihasthas* at the site, provide help. The devotee requires no special competence, as long as she or he follows the rules. I argue that the 'flatness' and the aesthetic, almost film-like, grandeur to which the ritual performances appeal and in which they are embedded render them successful as performances invoking ideas of stability, substance and power.

Simultaneously, closure is at work in and through rituals. By no means is everybody allowed in! A relatively rigid system of purity and pollution (e.g., of sex and food), control and order is established that makes clear distinctions between those who have the 'right gaze', attitude and habitus and those who do not. I propose that the visitors at the ACC are made conscious of their action in such a way that they begin observing themselves as if they watched through an external eye, rendering themselves as both part of a spectacle and docile, disciplined mass.

Controlling Media Flows

I would argue that without the sophisticated use of event management, the construction of spectacular sites in urbanised environments and the production and circulation of new media technologies, BAPS would not exist the way it does. All three enable the organisation to become globally visible, and 'close' or approachable, as a group with 'ethnicity' and 'cultural heritage'. One may even get the impression that in times of the World Wide Web, each and everyone can become a Hindu or a member of the BAPS *sampradaya* with a mouse-click, thus rendering traditional rules of status by birth impotent.

In order to gain credibility and authority the ACC depends on various means of visibility and performance. The religious specialists and event 'managers' of the ACC have created a two-fold strategy of performative representation through media. The desire for visibility, and thus recognition, is rooted in a bewildering paradox. On the one hand, there is a grand desire to be seen, always accessible, to *be* by being visible. Myriad pictures of the ACC and BAPS float around, in the galleries of the main Internet webpages, on shelves of the souvenir shop, as postcard, poster, calendar, picture book, pencil, alarm clock, fridge magnets, mouse pad, to mention only a few. The Monument, Lord Swaminarayan and PSM clearly lead the list of mass-reproduced fetishes or 'authentic replicas' (Oakes 2006). One can download a film clip of the Dedication Ceremony, ACC, November 2005; other films documenting mega-rituals conducted by PSM are also available on You Tube.[16] On the other hand, there is a very strict control and monopoly over image-production and circulation in that a ban has been imposed on taking pictures as souvenirs. Moreover, not even an official site map is available. This is an interesting attempt to counter the global decentralisation of image-production through the ubiquity and omnipraxy of digital cameras, mobile phones and even satellite photography. With one exception, all images produced of ACC, are issued from and copyrighted by the BAPS head office at Ahmedabad in Gujarat. Every image is officially approved by the senior members before it is allowed to leave the head office.

Let me elaborate on the first point: the ubiquity of images. Each day, 'murti darshan' (ritual of visually encountering the deity), hosted from the homepage of the BAPS temple in London, presents the visitor with a glimpse of one or a set of statues from one of the more than 700 BAPS temples around the world. Lord Swaminarayan and his disciples, some-times accompanied by deities Krishna and Radha, are carefully dressed in different costumes according to season or the actual ritual event.[17]

---

[16] The video clips of the opening ceremony can be downloaded at http://akshardham.com/whatisakdm/index.htm (accessed 30 July 2009).

[17] See http://www.mandir.org/murtidarshan/index.php (accessed 12 May 2007).

Important rituals performed, predominantly by PSM, are also documented and exhibited online, allowing the devotee to accompany the spiritual leader and witness other activities of the vast transnational and highly flexible community across the globe, no matter where he or she is at that moment in time. Vistors to the webpage can click on religious songs, download speeches of PSM, listen to traditional and regional Gujarati hymns such as *thal*, *doon*, and *arti* or upload personal prayers to be recited by priests at an actual temple ritual elsewhere. This media presence — with wide internet access — allows the shaping of an intimacy that is almost impossible to recreate with another medium.[18] Such multi-locality can only be provided through a medium like the Internet, which generates a monumentalisation of 'synergetic' seeing and identification, and heightens the notion of a globalised imagined community of a kind that Benedict Anderson could not envisage when he wrote *Imagined Communities* (1991 [1983]). The effects of 'virtual devotion' and 'witness' also heighten the experience of participating in a sublime sacred event or a moment of great historical relevance for India's heritage. Somehow, the 'myth of return' to the homeland seems to have arrived in as much as the new media deliver the homeland, even more 'authentic', at the migrants' doorstep. Even 'Gujaratiness' can be nurtured through the Internet.

The idea that images can generate (transnational) community networking and attachment to the sect has not been treated with consistence. The early days of the Internet were met by critical distance. Raymond Williams writes:

> One of the early internet sites contained beautiful pictures of images in a popular Swaminarayan temple, but it contained the warning that the images could not be used for darshan in exactly the same way as the images in the temple. Virtual images do not possess the powerful presence of god that was instilled in dedication; hence, they give no darshan (Williams 2001: 194; see also Little 1995).

This reminds one of Sophie Hawkins' study of online devotion in the case of Satya Sai Baba (Hawkins 1999) or John Little's ethnography (1995) of the restriction of free flows of video cassettes of the teachings of a spiritual guru: he describes how the showing of the cassettes without religious framing (specific time, place, congregation, appearance of the devotees) was not

---

[18] See http://www.akshardham.com/makingofakdm/index.htm (accessed 12 May 2007).

permitted and said to be ineffective. Similarly, such control of the 'ritual stance' is sought by BAPS, too. Today, this approach is almost reversed and in the section for online devotion one can now read the following:

> Daily Murti Darshan is uploaded at 8.15 am daily (BST) after the *shangar arati*. This is today's Darshan if you were to visit the BAPS Shri Swaminarayan Mandir, Neasden, London. For close-up *murti darshan* of Shri Harikrishna Maharaj, Bhagwan Swaminarayan and Sri Ghanshyam Maharaj, please click on the respective images.[19]

This suggests that one can actually engage in ritual seeing with the murtis displayed on the site. It also points to the fact that authenticity (of ritual action and intention) does not lie solely in the media. Nor can it possibly be enforced through a particular kind of media. Webmasters of two BAPS homepages confirmed that by now, the organisation is aware of the role played by the Internet in the shaping of a well-oiled transnational network and consciousness. They also emphasise that the websites are mainly used for information.[20] Special functions for children's edutainment, a Gujarati language course for youth, and tests on the 'sacred scriptures' and teachings of Lord Swaminarayan, can be found in English, Hindi and Gujarati. Satsang exams have been offered since 1972 by BAPS in India and rest of the world and serve the internal, regional connectedness of the community as well as the outwardly image of being a 'custodian community' of Vedic heritage.[21]

In terms of practices of representation, BAPS' stance towards mono-polising photography has changed in one instance. At the ACC, photography is not permitted. But due to complaints from various sides, partly related to the fact that souvenir photography is a must both for leisure tourism and pilgrimage, a high-tech photostudio was set up in 2006, facing the Monument. Now, one can have a digital photo taken at the fairly high cost of INR 90 (c. €1.50). While the monopolisation of images of rituals or sites may be related to the desire to keep control over the *sampradaya*'s representation, and to ensure a canonisation of a very specifc iconography, the fear of cameras may also be credited to heightened anxiety over the alleged threat of terrorism. In the past years, since 9/11, a few large, conventional temples started to restrict visitors against

---

[19] http://www.mandir.org/murtidarshan/index.php (accessed 20 August 2009).

[20] E-mail exchanges with BAPS webmasters (London, Ahmedabad) were held in May–July 2008.

[21] See www.swaminarayan.org/satsangexams/index.htm (accessed 22 August 2009).

bringing cameras into the temple compounds. As a matter of fact, the ACC has an even more urgent reason for being cautious because of its history — a terrorist attack on Akshardham in Gandhinagar in 2002.

Particularly through mass media like the Internet, BAPS presents itself as a provider of (and for) everything. There are online receipts for food that can be offered to the deities, invitation cards for auspicious occasions, astrologically auspicious times for the performance of rituals such as marriage, the buying of account books on Diwali (annual online calendar), and so forth. One can order items for daily *puja* ('one's personal appointment with God'), buy books, magazines, CD-ROMs and DVDs of BAPS-mega-events, discourses by the spiritual leader, or gift items.[22]

BAPS' relationship towards mass media is ambivalent. The paradox lies in the desire to remain unique by controlling its visualisation and monopolising the circulation of images on the one hand, and on the other, to have a ubiquitous, 'almighty' global presence and thus become a leader in the process of shaping a global imaginary of 'world-class spirituality'.

---

[22] See www.swaminarayan.org/publications (accessed 12 May 2007).

critics and sceptics

A monumental site such as the ACC also receives criticism from various quarters. There are many environmentalists, urban planners and housing activists who disapprove of the ways in which land that belonged to the protected strip of river embankment was appropriated by the ACC. However, the Supreme Court of India and the Delhi High Court have underlined the legitimacy of its construction; the latest court decision to this effect was taken in July 2009. For the opponents, the construction of ACC is but the beginning of a radical and brutal urban transformation of the city of New Delhi, towards commercialisation and privatisation of public space, enforcing yet another form of social discrimination through spatial segregation. Many voices have articulated concerns about the growing aggression of the upper middle classes against 'illegal' housing of the poor in the light of revamping urban space for 'world-classification' (see Appadurai 2006; Batra and Mehra 2006b; Baviskar 2003; Chatterjee 2003). Another concern is the rising real estate prices in neighbourhoods close to Metro stations or prime sites like the ACC.

On a less political level, there are other concerns. Here, I want to consider individual visitors' remarks about their experience of the ACC. Security and danger are prominent topics, addressing the growing awareness of Delhi's citizens, and even people worldwide, that security controls in urban hubs have become part and parcel of everyday life and a hassle for individuals' movement. Some feel that for the sake of 'security', personal rights are restricted and even altered. Several non-satsangis I spoke to strongly opposed the rigid security measures taken at the entrance. They felt that instead of inviting them BAPS was patronising, intimidating and even harassing visitors. Some saw an attitude of both arrogance and insecurity in the offensive emphasis on security measures and restriction of movement. Online discussions, too, carry a few critical responses. Responding to the question whether 'photography (is) allowed in Akshardham Temple', a netizen describes his/her perception on Yahoo India:

> I'm just back from the temple ... Photography is not allowed so I did not carry my camera ... but I say guys they treat you real bad ... indeed like 'atankvadi'

[terrorist] ... One of the guys thought the SOS sorbitrate tablets and the semi daonil tablets I was carrying were some kind of a button explosive/detonator ... made me get rid of them before I was allowed in.[1]

Despite the discomfort, however, as in today's security controls at airports, visitors of the ACC, on the whole, have come to get used to the procedure and might even feel that it attributes more importance to the site and to themselves.

One of the often-raised points in conversations is that the ACC is a camouflage — under the surface of new-found spirituality and happiness lies a religious luxury shopping mall (on the terminology, see Martikainen 2001). Many argue that the place is 'empty', 'lifeless and meaningless', even 'cold'. Mrs Khanna, an elderly lady, and Gandhian, from South Delhi says: 'It's all very neat and clean, like an art gallery, really efficient. But there is no soul, you don't find any devotion!' (personal conversation, March 2006). Neetu K. argues that 'the only reason why people visit Akshardham is because of the musical fountain. They say they're better than the ones in Singapore' (personal conversation, October 2006). Sushmita S., Professor at Jawaharlal Nehru University, who visited the place with her students, states:

There is certainly a fascination with monumentalisation, aestheticisation and historicisation. The weird thing is that people talk about it a lot. That creates a hype and huge expectations and draws lots of people to the site. You constantly hear about the place, it almost seems as if everybody had been there, but then, the site seems so empty, lifeless, and Lord Swaminarayan so 'faceless', empty of personality, individuality — like an empty shell. I have seen people yawning in the exhibition halls, saying that there was too much indoctrination, too many stories just of Him, too long, and too packed with multimedia effect. True, there is not such a dramatic enacting of heaven and hell as there is with ISKCON — that clearly works on a shock and polarisation basis. But there are other means of making people want to belong to the *sanstha*. Tourists, also foreign tourists, like it. They find it an ideal place to 'learn' about India, her architecture, her culture. They enjoy the fact that it's grand, that it's easily digestible (personal conversation, New Delhi, October 2006).

We saw earlier that visitors come to the ACC with different expectations and competencies. In conversation with both strangers and friends I learnt

---

[1] See http://in.answers.yahoo.com/question/index?qid=20070327215337AAxAReo (accessed 27 July 2007).

that their irritation does not stop with security control. They feel 'over-guided', and finally exhausted, not having been able to withdraw from the scenery and reflect: 'The fact that these people are constantly trying to engage you, to guide you, to show you what this and that is, make it such a boring, arrogant and redundant place. They want to teach you all the time, it's so annoying', says Ravi A. (personal conversation, October 2006). Some visitors found that the emphasis on the BAPS ideology was exaggerated, particularly, in the theme halls. Instead, they were more attracted by the special effects and scenery of the dioramas.

It is, however, interesting to consider the other side too, especially the ordinary volunteers working at the ACC. One of my key sources here was a woman volunteer who worked as a spot-guide in the entrance hall. With her, I had several conversations about the different questions asked and comments made by visitors. I asked her first what her overall impression was about visitors' concerns. According to her, the most frequently made comments were related to the cleanliness and professional appearance of the place. But there were visitors who would lament about the 'five-star' aesthetics of the site, for instance, the entrance hall. She says: 'How can they [the visitors] criticise that the entrance hall looks like the lobby of a luxury hotel?! They should know that this is what *havelis* [traditional mansions from western India] were built like!' Now, even though there are elements of *haveli*-architecture in the entrance hall at Delhi, as well as the assembly hall of the Swaminarayan temple in London and in Mumbai, they are part and parcel of entertainment or heritage architecture, relating less to 'authentic heritage' than to 'new urbanism'.[2] These architectural elements are part of a vernacular neoliberal impression management tailored to the needs and interests of BAPS, presenting the organisation, at once, as wealthy and traditional.

What the spot-guide emphasised too was how little people actually knew about Swaminarayan, and how they showed little interest, visiting the site only for the 'spectacle value'. Quite a few visitors would even display disrespect against Swaminarayan and laugh about him. They could

---

[2] They cater to what Denslagen and Gutschow (2005) have termed 'architectural imitations', i.e., reinvented and altered architectural traditions in a new context. This could also be related to touristic production of recognisable items. Edensor in his study on the Taj Mahal writes: 'Through place-marketing and the construction of tourist attractions, potted historical narratives are produced ... and the standards required appear to conform to particular notions of convenience, comfort and consumability' (1998: 12).

also not believe that the ACC had been built in only five years. What was a great surprise to them was the selfless attitude of the volunteers, both in the construction of the Complex and the voluntary service performed by them as guides, assuming that the ACC was predominantly a commercial undertaking: 'People did not trust us when we said that we do this for free, that we do not ask for money' (personal conversation, October 2006).

Not as many people as expected by the PR-department of the ACC visit the theme halls, probably because they take too much time and money. The musical fountain and the court in front of the restaurant are the favourites. Possibly, this is because there is no other place where people can sit and chat and where they can move about without being controlled. One can guage the popularity of this venue especially on a weekend and even more so in the evening, during and after sunset, when the whole site is emerged in spectacular lighting and when it is cooler. Because these sites are free (even INR 10 for parking and INR 20 for the musical fountain are not too much), people come for an evening stroll or for a snack with family and friends. That way, flânerie might also be understood as a strategy of circumventing or at least marginalising BAPS' attempts to control the 'masses'.

Let me close this chapter with another ethnographic vignette. I want to refer to a conversation with Suresh, an upper middle-class friend of mine, and a journalist. In February 2006, we managed to get hold of tickets for a mega-event of new age spirituality, the Shivaratri festival. Sri Sri Ravi Shankar, the spiritual head of Art of Living, performed the ritual addressed to Lord Shiva on the grounds of the envisaged Commonwealth Games village right opposite the ACC. Upon arrival, I thought that we were attending a pop concert instead: thousands of people had flocked from all over New Delhi, even beyond, dressed in their best clothes, passing the first security check, the commercial stands of banks and entrepreneurs selling religious devices, and then another control post. We were seated in front of a large stage, crowned by a throne-like chair at the centre, with several video screens, and meditation music blaring from the loudspeakers. The ritual was part of an entire event-choreography, including chanting of hymns and meditation.

Soon afterwards, we started to talk about the efficacy of these new global movements. Suresh argued that the Hindu middle classes had until recently more or less withdrawn from the practice of religion as such. In his view, this was a rather unfortunate development that occurred for various reasons and over a long period. Such a development propelled a feeling of inferiority and backwardness in religious people, first in the British colony and then in the post-independence secular state of India. With people like Ravi Shankar and with sites like the ACC, this attitude has, however, changed. The message is simple, appealing especially to the 'cosmopolitans' (Suresh uses the term himself). They would be not as profound as what more demanding and less media-savvy gurus would ask of their followers. Yet, they would be more attractive. For Suresh, this was clearly a middle- and upper-class movement: 'Look at the ways in which banks and other organisations use Art of Living as a projection screen for their advertising!' We passed by a stall — the Bank of Punjab announces its release of a credit card honouring 50 years of AOL, with a picture of Sri Sri Ravi Shankar and his Bangalore *ashram* in the background. Suresh maintained that these segments of society, previously ashamed of showing their religious feelings in public because it was percieved as 'backward', have now come to join spiritual movements having declared religiosity and spirituality to be *en vogue*, 'beautifying' the body and soul. To Suresh the most important thing was that 'traditions, through those people, are now preserved and safeguarded, traditions that had been denigrated and ridiculed by those people who now cherish and support them, because of modernity. They all put great significance in tradition.' Did such a mega-event not have negative consequences on the 'authenticity' of religious traditions? The answer was simple: All those congregations where *puja* is performed and the Vedas recited are 'good events and good for the country', no matter whether they appear as pop concerts or not. Shivaratri had not been performed in north India in public for a long time. Now, Sri Sri Ravi Shankar has given new meaning to it, he has revived it. Such a spiritual movement fills a void that people feel, especially in urban India: 'It's a form of touching, that binds you beyond the limits of economic and family bonds, like those *bhajans* and hymns they performed on the stage,' said Suresh, referring to the fact that Ravi Shankar has indeed appropriated hymn-based music into his repertoire of multicultural devotional songs. Upon returning from the event, my host Lalita G. confirmed the 'good vibrations' at a community like AOL: 'some of my friends are serious followers of AOL, they are all young, sexy, affluent. The Gospel-atmosphere gets them, it's cool to swing along — and I enjoy it too, and actually, why not?!' (personal conversation, New Delhi, February 2006). It looks as if the young generation in India's megacities privileges religious events and sites which have a globalised touch about them. 'How many people go to the temple these days?' posed Suresh, 'Hardly anyone! Temples are poorly maintained. This is why Akshardham

Cultural Complex is such an ideal model for what the temple could be.' Ravi Shankar revitalised rituals; he translated them into a language people are willing to listen to. In that sense, the mega-ritual is only a reflection of the understanding that religious devotion has become meaningful once again, often under the name of spiritualism, i.e., less dogmatic belief that is open to members of different sects and religions. Suresh appreciated the fact that this day had now become a significant day in the Hindu calendar again, like in the old days: 'We had lost the awareness of these days. It is heartening to see that 10,000 people from Delhi have made the effort to come and attend the event, to participate in such a puja. This links them up with so many traditions that have survived for thousands of years. This understanding has to be revived in the people.' This, argued Suresh, was what AOL and BAPS were about.

The observation connects various issues that were of relevance in this part of the study: the growing popularity of religious practice or 'new age spirituality' among members of the urban middle classes and trans-national classes, without being instantly associated with Hindu nationalism. The emergence of a popular discourse of spirituality in the context of neoliberalism is interesting to look at because it enables us to explore the importance religion has in the secular, modern, and globalised domain (see Carrette and King 2005). It opens up the field of agency, of visitors-as-consumers, of religious experts as event managers, of the shifts and tensions between the 'cultic', and the 'exhibition' value that marks the experience of modernity by means of creating particular forms of Erlebnis, and registers of taste and distinction. The ethnographic example also alerts us to the new status and recognition of rituals in the shaping of urban modern lifestyles, after an alleged phase of stagnation, if not repression. What Suresh seems to suggest is that in the light of 'India Shining', religious values and traditions are revitalised, and with them, concepts of essentialised Indianness. In his view, new media- and mass-events and sites such as the Shivaratri ritual and the ACC are the new locus of the emergence of a global national awakening of Indians, and that in (and with) them, the Indians become a moral community that can be rooted in tradition in spite of their possible lives in the diaspora. If we believe Suresh, India shows us how neoliberalisation enables a better, more beautiful, life.

Conclusion

The ACC reflects a new confidence of the urban middle classes in India, a new confidence of marginal religious groups such as BAPS that have managed to become pioneers in rooted cosmopolitanism by building strong transnational networks and regional associations. It addresses a new form of 'cultural citizenship' through which people can aspire to be both globally and nationally confident, and religiously humble, without being traditionally backward. However, this new identity requests persons to be willing to acquire, and adapt to, a new aesthetics and a life conduct that is presented as morally superior, utopian and holistic.

The idea that the new space of the ACC represents a society of equals is misleading; the ACC shows that there are strict rules of social and ritual segregation, and that the idea of liberalisation is tied up with rigid control and surveillance. India and Indianness, as well as the ideology of Swaminarayan, are 'exoticised' and fetishised in order to fit the overarching capitalist world-view of leisure and consumption. This does by no means indicate a politically neutral discourse — underlining the production of celebration at the ACC are tensions arising from the symbolic struggle for status and dominance, polarisation of religious lifestyles and world-views (Islam versus other religions, East versus West), the desire to regulate and survey public domains and discourses to such an extent that they are rendered disciplined and controlled. Quite similar to the rhetoric of real estate development explored in the previous chapters, we can find a polarisation of the 'inside' and the 'outside' (according to metaphors such as 'orderly' and 'threatening') that creates in the beholders of the images and visitors of the ACC the desire to live in an enclave world, or at least, to give its existence — and ideological foundation — legitimacy. This way, the ACC becomes part and parcel of a privatisation and enclave-creation in the urban space of India. However, religious practice and consumerism at the ACC cannot be isolated from the attempts to gentrify urban space through real estate development, and shape new social and economic elites in a highly structured and moralised environment.

André Béteille explores the option of a culturally specific resurgence of religious movements as carriers of such voluntary action. He notes that possibly the only field in which Indians 'show initiative in voluntary action' is in religious matters, be it the organisation of a festival, a rite of passage, or, as I would add here, the display of national and cultural pride in history in the case of the ACC. Religious activity, argues Béteille, 'is one extensive and significant domain of social action in which (Indians) show genuine initiative, mutuality, and self-reliance' (2005b: 453). He holds that 'the ease with which help and support can be mobilized in India in the organization of a religious event is remarkable' (ibid.). This also applies to the construction of temples, which has even increased despite (or because?) of India's secularisation. Yet, Béteille is cautious about this development:

> How far do religious movements and assemblies for moral, ethical, and spiritual discourses contribute to the formation of civil society? ... I remain sceptical about what religious assemblies and religious movements can contribute directly to the formation of civil society, although their indirect contribution may be extremely valuable. Civil society requires the *separation* of open and secular institutions from the institutions of kinship and religion, although it does not require the exclusion of the latter from society as a whole (Béteille 2005b: 455).[3]

This concern is definitely shared by those critics of the ACC who maintain that it produces even wider gaps between the 'world-class' and the 'rest' of Indian society, and it does not help create civil society. Instead of arguing that the ACC is either a 'theme park' or a pilgrimage site, I have maintained that it is both, and more. This way, I would also argue that the ACC could be a place in which certain aspects of an alternative civil society may emerge. Simultaneously, however, there is also the danger of locking such an option out by means of regimes of strict regulation and categorisation. Religion and secularism do not exclude each other any longer. What surfaces at the ACC is the formation of a national heritage that is consciously different from western secularism, in which a modern form of religion is promoted that appeals to the emerging middle and transnational classes. It helps invoking the idea of Indians as a moral community that is tied to 'India Shining', and to the notion of 'rooted' cosmopolitanism and cultured Indianness. India, in this process, turns into a 'foreign land', or a distant planet, that invites discovery. We can thus witness a form of nation-building cum spiritual awakening and self-cultivation where the project of modernity is Indianised and in return globalised (for instance, through a network of 'world-class temples' and 'world-class festivals').

We must understand the ACC as a contested site filled with 'competing discourses' and different kinds of experiences offered and perceived: as pseudo-events or as miracle, as simulacra and hyper-reality on the one hand and as a *tirtha* (sacred crossing-point where the divine can be encountered), on the other. As a consequence, the idea of 'communitas', even though

---

[3] Pavan Varma too, has criticised that the care of the self inscribed in Hinduism as 'personal salvation' does not include 'contracts' with people outside kinship and family, especially nation or civil society (1998: 124). On the sacralisation of the self, see Heelas (1996).

projected in many ways on various occasions within BAPS topography, is a shining emblem. As for audiences, I suggested that we have to, first of all, differentiate between the 'in-group' (a heterogeneous mixture of followers, in terms of age, birthplace, language, residence, etc.) and the 'out-group', i.e., large anonymous and heterogeneous audiences. The latter may comprise domestic and international tourists of different regional, ethnic and religious origin, Indians living abroad and members of other nationalities. The BAPS tries to establish spiritual and moral authority of Swaminarayan Hinduism, and Lord Swaminarayan and spiritual leader Pramukh Swami Maharaj as divine and legitimate leaders of a new society. It tries to be cosmopolitan by incorporating and mainstreaming a highly provincialised (Gujarati) identity, addressing partial (Indian) audiences that have the exposure and experience of living abroad and who are, to some extent, comfortable with the idea of being part of a cosmopolitan community that rediscovers Indian tradition, history and spirituality.

BAPS does so by employing a set of different ritual categories that move between deep devotional sentiment and entertainment (edutainment). I suggest classifying them according to the experience they purport to transmit or encourage: 'pure ritual', 'feel-good or lifestyle rituals', thus conflating the two concepts that Steven Vertovec (2000) differentiated as 'orthodox' and 'popular' Hinduism. These enable different kinds of engagement (flat/deep) and cater to different audiences: satsangis, villagers, urban educated Indians, NRIs, and members of other religions. I argue that with each group, the rituals — as a rhetorical device — make different statements of distinction about who belongs to the 'world-class with a nationalist touch'. I take this to be an important issue in contemporary India, but perhaps also on a more global, transnational scale, where rituals and ritual spaces — also through media spaces — allow agents to 'rework' notions of tradition and modernity, stability and dynamics, authenticity and authority, selfhood and society for themselves. A key attempt is to create ecumenical mainstream official Hinduism, to tap into heritage discourses (as it is often the concern of a minority group to claim legitimacy) and to make itself glamorously visible. Yet to me, the ACC is a modern disciplining institution, both a panopticon and a panorama. It enforces a ritualised, enclaved gaze and instrumentalises rituals and ritual space in order to authorise Swaminarayan Hinduism as a global way of life and create 'modern' Hindu selves. It proves that religion is central to negotiations of (alternative) modernities, and that the borders between 'religious' and 'secular' rituals are extremely fuzzy.

Under this surface, the site wants to impose even more: the importance of temples, rituals and devotion in modern times. It wants to legitimise itself as an ambassador for moral values and spiritual knowledge, and the necessity to have a spiritual guru who guides the individual beyond the materialistic world towards enlightenment. Akshardham is an ambitious heterotopia: a living paradise on earth, a reflection of an Arcadian past, a statement of national pride à la India Shining and international recognition of being 'world-class'. It is also the attempt of a minor religious group with remarkable economic wealth and transnational presence to shape and have power over the definition of the experience of modernity and national discourse: 'Akshardham Temple … is one of the wonders of the modern world, and the wonders of modern India'.[4] Its confidence is predominantly a disguise for cultural arrogance.

By means of analysing rites and rituals, ritual space and ritual agents one thing becomes obvious: what Louis Dumont has attributed to India as her pillars, and what was thought to be eliminated with India's initiation into 'modernity', remains a strong force of socialisation and change even today, namely, (ritual) hierarchy and purity. However, this is possibly a result of growing class divisions instead of caste divisions. While reformist movements of the colonial era attempted to diminish the prominent role of the temple and idolatry because they understood them as indicators of backwardness, segregation and fragmentation of society as well as the (Hindu) nation, in fact, my case-study reveals that both mandir (temple) and murti (divine image) have moved to the centre stage. In fact, they do so with great pomp, propagating Swaminarayan Hinduism as a religion (and 'cure') for all, readymade for (relatively easy) consumption. However, it is quite clear that the emphasis on modernity and equality is only one layer of the reality; simultaneously, and even complementing it, strategies of exclusion and discrimination turn the Akshardham Monument and its 'inhabitants' into yet another hermetically sealed-off enclave — quite in the spirit of the vacuum-packed glamorous condominiums and shopping malls of Delhi's new neighbours Ghaziabad (especially Indirapuram) and Gurgaon.

---

[4] See http://www.swaminarayan.org (accessed 22 August 2009).

PART III

๛

'Masti! Masti!' Managing Love, Romance and Beauty

The mushrooming of event management companies and the high visibility of their bosses as party kings and queens confirms this [change of urban India]. The new ism is undoubtedly epicurism ... now as the great middle class gets on board in its pursuit of *la dolce vita*. Any occasion — birthdays ... thread ceremonies, contract-clinchers, anniversaries, silver anniversaries, gold anniversaries, mother's day, dog's day, whatever — is a *cause celebre*. Anything for a celebration. Enjoy is the new buzzword (Jain 2001).

This quote underlines a key motif of this part: the rich infrastructure of lifestyle, leisure and event management that has emerged with economic liberalisation since the 1990s, and boomed since the early 2000s. It points towards the key inhabitants of the new 'service sector', the lifestyle experts ('kings and queens') and their customers, the 'great middle class', attempting to join the bandwagon of pleasure and celebration of consumption and lifestyle at any cost. It also highlights the production of reasons for the celebration and display of fun and wealth by means of new rituals like birthdays, or, I would add, Valentine's Day. Joy, fun, or *masti* mark the rhetoric of the aspiring middle classes' culture of celebration (of itself). *Masti*, a term originally used to express intense enjoyment or intoxication of the senses, has been derived from devotional (Sufi) songs and translated into the world of material pleasures, predominantly in north India, quite like 'Erlebnis' à la Schulze (1992).

This section primarily deals with the creation of new spaces and sites of pleasure and consumption, some of which have been explored in the previous chapters of this book. While the first Part focused much on the imaginary of the 'world-class' city in real estate advertising and urban planning, and the second part discussed a particular site (the Akshardham Cultural Complex) that captures the global imaginary of redefining spirituality, compatible with modern lifestyle, this part engages in the experience, promotion and management of the Self as the locus of pleasure and a 'good life'. It does so by presenting material on weddings, beauty and spirituality.

These three domains are strongly related to new urban lifestyles in India, and are intrinsically glocal, i.e., they are informed by globalised notions of 'wedding', 'beauty', 'spiritual well-being' while simultaneously generating standardised concepts from 'Indian traditions'. The majority of empirical data presented here has been collected in New Delhi. At one time, compared to Mumbai or Bangalore, New Delhi used to fall behind when it came to nightlife and leisure culture. However, since the turn of the millennium, this is changing, partly due to the growing presence of BPO professionals and other service sectors emerging in Delhi and the NCR. In this course, government employees, who once dominated India's capital, have been pushed aside. Cafés and lounge bars, a multicultural culinary landscape, shopping malls and cineplexes with food-courts have carved a stage for more pro-active members of the new middle classes, marking their (partial) transformation from the 'couch potato' to the 'mall rat'. The times of video evenings in the living-room seem outdated, and since the introduction of the cineplex, which restricts access to those who can pay at least INR 100 (€ 1.60), the middle class now prefers family visits to popular Indian and foreign movies outside. Another example: while in the late 1990s, most of the bars serving alcoholic drinks had a rather bad reputation, and were primarily visited by middle-aged men wanting to get drunk, today a variety of cocktails and Indian wines can be enjoyed in stylish surroundings that appeal to both women and men of 'class'. There used to be only a few places where one could go and 'chat', where passing time was part of the pleasure of hanging out. Today, there are plenty of cafés that enable young affluent middle class youth to mingle informally, read newspaper, surf the Internet, or play chess, inviting professional employees to sit for one or two 'after-work' drinks, and housewives to chat with their power-walking or yoga friend. Ten years ago, 'fitness' was hardly heard of, and was either too exclusive or associated with the traditional martial art of wrestling practised by a particular group of males dedicating physical exercise to the divine monkey king Hanuman. Today, Hanuman has transmutated into an American wrestler, and 'workout factories' and 'fitness centres' are mushrooming in localities with high density of corporate offices and upper middle class neighbourhoods. Women, too, are increasingly joining their local gym. Until the late 1990s, women would primarily visit beauty parlours available in every local market. These parlours mostly consisted of two rooms, not more, filled with the smell of nail polish, hair dye and perfume, with high-pitched women's voices accompanied by 'filmi' songs. One step behind the synthetic curtain — and one was in another *purdah* (female enclosure), removed from the sounds and smells of the street. Now, day spas and beauty clinics engage in grooming female and male bodies and souls, offering beauticians and masseurs, with an air-conditioned room for each client.

All these examples give only glimpses of the topography of emerging everyday leisure life of a megacity like Delhi. They underline crucial shifts within the 'public' and the 'private', subjectivity and moral community, and the notion of pleasure as a privilege and duty of caring for 'the self'.

Aspirational Consumerism
as 'Progress through Pleasure'

Anthropologists and sociologists sometimes criticise the new middle class in India as hypocritical agents and, at worst, passive victims of capitalism (e.g., Gupta 2000). However, William Mazzarella's notion of 'aspirational consumerism' (2003) throws new light on the discussion of conspicuous consumption. He does not confine consumerism to unreflected and manipulated activities of morally corrupt dupes. Instead, Mazzarella's ethnography of advertisement and globalisation in neoliberal India underlines the emergence of a new form of subjectivity and agency in the light of economic liberalisation. Though he does not deny that consumerism is highly discursive and hedonistic, he foregrounds pleasure and individuality as opposed to state-governed notions of citizenship as duty and sacrifice. One of his key arguments is that with the market liberalisation in the 1990s, the power of the state over the imagination of its citizens (idolised as dutiful and selfless) was shifted to the margins. Taking the example of sexuality, he elaborates how the dogma of family planning (including forced sterilisation; see Tarlo 2003) and planned development considered (and, as a consequence, rejected) the desire of citizens for consumption as a sign of a bourgeois lifestyle. This was done so in favour of the citizens' duty to engage in nation-building. This logic is drastically reversed in the 1990s. The citizen transforms into a consumer whose duty is to ensure nation-building through the economic growth of the liberalised market. The body is no longer a site of production (or sterilisation towards the national task of birth control) but a source and stage of pleasure, where the relationship between the 'official' and 'popular', or vernacular notions of sexuality and pleasure change with the advent of economic liberalisation (see Srivastava 2006). Along with these comes intimacy, which is, quite like the desire for solitude discussed in Part I of this book, a new concept of modern subjectivity. Moreover, consumption transforms from vice into virtue. Mazzarella defines this shift as 'progress through pleasure' (2003: 101). The desiring self replaces the demanding state, without rendering it obsolete. According to Mazzarella, aspirational consumerism:

> promised to link the particularity of individual consumer desire with universal progress, imagined at once as material and aesthetic … it offered to mediate between the particularity of local or national 'culture' and a global repertoire of images (ibid.).

To legitimise this shift, the goal of consumption-as-pleasure is connected to a noble charitable cause, bound by values and good intentions. Consumerism can thus remain a morally loaded activity, even dediated to nation-building. Acknowledging the importance of aesthetics and media in this shaping of new subjectivities, this section of the book moves beyond advertising and explores the multimedia exhibitionary and performative aspects of aspirational consumerism. This is in tune with Liechty who holds that middle-classness is not a *state* but a *process*; it must be performed, narrated and put on display in order to become. Many narratives and media are cited in this context, for instance, Bombay commercial cinema. But even the pleasure of consumption, of patchwork religiosity, is linked to regimes of self-regulation and self-surveillance. The desire, if not the duty, to participate in, and live the 'good life' is promoted in lifestyle magazines, advertising hoardings and television shows. It creates a globalised imaginary that suggests equal access and choice for all aspirants. Yet, despite the alleged intimacy and closeness of these goals, everyday lives and practices reveal the ambivalence of open access and equality, the controlling and restricted forces of consumption, pleasure and the celebration of self.

Selling Know-How: The New 'Caste' of Pleasure-Managers

An increasingly relevant part of the new event-culture and topography that shapes with the new middle classes in neoliberal urban India is the infrastructure of service providers referring to themselves as 'experts'. These 'expressive specialists' (Hannerz 1996: 139) address, and at the same time create, the desires and needs of people to look after and celebrate themselves as 'lifestyle-flâneurs'. Particularly to the new aspirants of the 'world-class' lifestyle, they seem unavoidable, for they transform, and make use of, culture as capital. The new profession of lifestyle-managers appears to have taken over the function and importance of the religious specialist, the pandit, while the lifestyle magazines replace the sacred scriptures as 'handbooks' for life guidance.

This part discusses a range of new lifestyle-experts and environments that have come to provide their (attested) expertise to the shaping of well-being and pleasure to affluent middle class consumers. In the next two chapters, I explore case-studies related to the expanding infrastructure of the wedding industry and the wellness/beauty industry. At its centre stage is the concept of conspicuous consumption as part of the economy and performance of material wealth and excess, on the one hand, and a means of drawing borders based on distinction in order to negotiate the concept of the 'world-class', on the other. Weddings, beauty and wellness feature centrally in lifestyle media, narratives and performances, and they must be understood as signifiers of the new identifications and subjectivities (Shields 1992a; see also Ngai 2003: 473) as well as 'sets of practices and attitudes' that differentiate people (Chaney 1996: 4–5), even within the 'same' class. The experts and their domains help elaborate strategies of differentiation, create and frame both pleasure and discipline, both of which are key elements of modern societies. Lifestyle is structured by, and at the same time structures, consumption practices and social relationships. I argue that the aspiring middle classes' dream of self-transformation and a 'good life' in neoliberal India is made accessible by the wedding and the wellness industry and their 'representatives'. Moreover, these two domains of the new pleasure industry are based on rigid forms of control of the self and others. The consumer-citizen is thus both a flâneur practising a mobile gaze and is an object of panoptic surveillance (see Parts I and II of this book), whose life conduct is entangled with an almost threatening idea of permanent success, wellness and happiness. Ritual, heritage, leisure and exhibition are important concepts to understand this ambiguity of lifestyle politics in neoliberal India.

Consumption has become a crucial practice as regards the constitution of culture, status and distinction in late-capitalist societies. Since late-capitalism indicates a radical shift from production to consumption and celebration of lifestyles, consumption has become the motor of modernity and agency throughout the world: 'It not only indexes wealth, health, and vitality, but it also constitutes a privileged site for the fabrication of self and society, of culture and identity' (Comaroff and Comaroff 2000 in Ngai 2003: 470). Moreover, scholars have highlighted that despite the possible practical value of a commodity it is more important that both producer and buyer know how to weave it into the larger scripts of performative display of wealth and lifestyle. For instance, it does not suffice to possess a wine bar in order to 'belong to class'. One must know how and when to use it, and in style. Only then can a commodity become a status-marker and -maker. However, it can quickly transform into a 'status-unmaker' when its owners lack the competence of knowing how to use it. This is why, as Rahul M., designer of bars for private and official purposes in South Delhi reveals, he offers customers intensive courses in the etiquette of bar usage and alcohol consumption: 'They know that it is "in" to have a bar in the living-room. But, they don't want to fail in front of their guests by choosing the wrong wine, the wrong glass and the wrong snacks' (personal conversation, April 2005). The underlining fear of public embarrassment, of failing to convince, is not to be underestimated.

Liechty employs the very useful metaphor of the middle classes' 'dance' to explore middle class culture as practice, production or performance 'that brings together host of competing cultural assets, consumer demands, and media influences into a performance of cultural life that is by its nature complex, halting, unstable, and in periodic need of "redoing"' (2003: 4). The different industries related to lifestyle and wellness introduced in this chapter, are connected to what Liechty calls, 'the ways that people manage these narratives of modernity — stories of being and becoming modern that people tell, and that tell people', and how much the global and the local thus shape in tandem (ibid.: 251). The performative elements of consumption practices are emphasised by Uberoi as she explores the dynamics of weddings:

> [W]hat is the use of wealth unless it is spent, and spent conspicuously? But in weddings now, as in all else, the crucial question from the perspective of social reckoning is not only *how much* is spent, though size certainly does matter, but in *what way* it is spent — a question of *taste* (2008: 233–34).

In the Introduction to this book, I discussed the new middle classes' confidence about participating in India's progress and rise. This confidence is simultaneously paired with the fear of falling, of experiencing the dark side of economic liberalisation. The awareness that confidence and anxiety are intertwined was articulated time and again by many of my informants. These experiences of modernity's ambiguity relate us to Schulze's idea of Erlebnis as a central element of the project 'Live Your Life!' where risk, responsibility and insecurity play a part too. Moreover, the imperative of happiness and suitability is tied closely with the dilemma of having to be happy, and mirrored in Appadurai's notion of the 'agonized drama of leisure' (1997: 207).

One of the strategies to overcome this insecurity is to claim custody over taste and cultural capital such as to downgrade aspiring groups trying to 'join the bandwagon' in order to exclude them. Here, distinction is a strategy that operates with the categories of 'respectable' and 'old rich' versus 'new rich', 'sophisticated' versus 'low' or even 'bad' taste, 'educated' versus so-called 'parvenus', upstarts or 'uncultured' people.[1] Let me give an example. Malika S., an upper class wedding designer, on being asked what her 'worst' theme wedding had been, described this:

---

[1] About the use of the term 'parvenus', hypocrite or pretender, in the context of Egypt's economic liberalisation in Cairo, see also Abaza (2001: 116).

My husband and I were invited to this theme party entitled 'A Touch of Turquoise'. You know, colours are an in-theme these days and guests were asked to respond to the theme. My husband sported a turquoise tie and I wore a turquoise *dupatta*.[2] But listen to this, you simply won't believe it! Upon arrival, we discovered that EVERYTHING was in this colour and that guests and hosts were completely covered in turquoise! What a taste! We almost fainted and left the party soon (personal conversation, New Delhi, January 2007).

From reading between the lines, I gathered that the hosts and many of the guests were probably members of the 'new rich'. But it seemed as if their financial capital could not hide their lack of cultural capital — of taste. The just cited quote clearly demarcates those as parvenus who have money but no taste ('they') from those 'old rich' with money and taste ('us'). It restricts access to those aspiring to belong to class, on the basis of birth and cultural capital, a strategy that complicates the concept of class as free of other concepts such as one's lineage, caste or regional descent.

For this study, besides ethnographic material collected through conversations with middle class informants in Delhi and research in lifestyle magazines, I rely on data gathered from interviews with experts from the domains of bridal, wellness and spirituality marketing.[3] Most of these experts started their business less than ten years ago and some of them have done so with great success. They cater to the seemingly new needs of the predominantly new rich — most of all, their desire for visibility and recognition, status improvement/stability and pleasure. The new specialists sell their competence to 'teach' lifestyle and taste to bring order into the unstructured world of choices. Members of the affluent middle classes aspiring to belong to the 'world-class', increasingly, rely on such expertise, either by hiring a consultant or by referring to the growing market of print media and TV-programmes. They do so for various reasons: lack of free time and resources that are needed for the right display of both material possessions and cultural taste. The desire to be talked about and the fear of making an inappropriate or unsuitable choice leads many families

---

[2] This is a shawl worn by women dressed in *salwaar kameez*, to cover their shoulders.

[3] Some of the popular bridal magazines are *Celebrating Vivaha*, *Asian Bride*, *Asian Wedding*, *Femina Bridal*, available at prices ranging between INR 50 and INR 150 (€0.90–3.00). Asian Bride magazines from the UK are also for sale in India, however, at a much higher rate (c. €5–10). There is even an *Asian Groom* magazine published from England. See also Oza (2006) and Reddy (2006) for their analyses of gender and advertisement in neoliberal India.

and persons to approach a lifestyle expert, or, for example, a wedding planner. These new specialists gain more attention these days because lifestyle magazines, TV-shows and everyday conversations use them to get access to the 'stars' of the glamour world. Most of my informants from the professional domains of real estate marketing, event marketing or wedding organisations highlighted that people today wanted 'complete solutions' and convenient packages: everything must be readymade for instant consumption, easily accessible among a whole range of choices, be it weight loss programmes or grooming during pre-marriage and post-marriage times. Further, if taste can not be developed sufficiently, the expert may as well help to develop strategies of hiding the lack thereof to minimise public embarrassment. This results in to an on-going loop of self-control.

It is only by seeing the coexistence of all these visual, narrative and performative genres and agents that we can understand the creation of 'middle-classness' as a cultural practice and the imaginary of a 'good life'. The 'experts' promise support and relief in solving the riddle of the 'good' and 'beautiful' life by catering to the individual domains of, or fusing, physical, spiritual and mental wellness and bringing it into a well-balanced relationship with material lifestyle and individual aspirations. The next chapter explores further as to how the wedding industry shapes the new event-culture and how event-society evolves through particular aesthetics, choreographies and management expertise.

'for whom the bell rings': arranging marriage

Here in India, weddings are meant to be grand, meant to be big. Weddings, in fact, are the biggest celebration of a person's life. The size and scale of your wedding determines your pecking order in society … But suppose, you can't quite manage an Antwerp or Bali wedding and a French chateau is totally out of the reckoning: you can always create a Venice in Goa, a Rajasthani fort in Mumbai or a tropical forest in Delhi. As disposable incomes grow healthier, more couples than ever are opting for professional planners to see them through their weddings rather than depending on the sage advice of uncles and aunts who would otherwise have pitched to help with wedding preparations … Today, you too can have your own version of the big fat Indian wedding (Menon 2007)!

In many ways, this quote from an author of a special bridal issue of the women's magazine *Femina* encapsulates the theme of this chapter's section: everyone wants a 'big fat Indian wedding' and is prepared to enter a spiral of immense competition in order for the event to be recognised as such. While weddings (*vivaha*) are certainly important as a key life-cycle ritual, the idea that they are the biggest celebration of a single person's life is rather new, and part of a shared imaginary of a largely urbanised and educated audience. To be sure, a 'traditional' wedding does not celebrate the individual. It underlines an asymmetrical inter-caste alliance and exchange between two families in which the bride is 'given' to the groom (*kanya daan*, i.e., the gift of the virgin to the in-laws, the purest of all gifts; see Raheja 1988; see also Michaels 2004: 111–30). During the ceremony, highly complicated family relationships are enacted with caution, almost as if explosive substances were mixed carefully. Who interacts with whom, who gives and who receives gifts, who eats what kind of food and when, is crucial for the efficacy of the ritual and the fortune of the relationship between the families, not the individuals (Kolenda 1984: 104–7).

The combination of weddings, status-definition and spending money is nothing new. Traditional weddings have long been a key stage of conspicuous consumption, and thereby the generation of symbolic capital.

What is new in the themed weddings explored here is their emphasis on scale and pomp, on new glocal aesthetics and taste. What is new is the celebration of class, not so much caste (even though caste has not been rendered invalid!). What is new is the focus on the romantic love between two individuals and sexualised, fit, beautiful bodies (predominantly that of the bride). The face of the bride is not veiled but every inch of her light skin beams with happiness; her eyes do not look down in a gesture of modesty and chastity, burdened by the weight of leaving her home for a new place. Instead, they smile with life, impatiently awaiting the new flat that would need furnishing after returning from honeymoon. The wedding, as it is promoted by wedding designers and lifestyle media, is no longer a quasi-mechanical ritual procedure headed by a priest and conducted around a sacred fire-place (*homa*, if it is a Hindu wedding according to Vedic rituals, around which the couple walks, performing *saptapadi*, the rite of seven steps; see Kolenda 1984: 106–7). Instead, it has become an event, a theme park, an action film of romance (see Plate 12.1). The family remains in the background while the wedding planner has taken over. And if the budget does not allow hiring a wedding designer, a host of media assist the bridal couple and their relatives and friends to design one à la carte. To be sure, the 'Indian wedding' has been standardised and tailored to the conditions of 'modern' lifestyles. But the argument that, due to westernisation, the

Plate 12.1: A hoarding promoting a wedding photographer, Gurgaon (2006).

Source: Photograph by R. S. Iyer.

wedding (of an affluent middle class or upper class family) has been reduced to a few hours of ritual is only partly true. The ritual frames have been shifted instead. While the wedding ceremony itself, with the priest conducting the ritual of marrying the groom and the bride, might have undergone substantial shortening, the number of events leading up to the wedding have been expanded. The 'standard' length of a middle-class wedding in Delhi, and even other urbanised areas in north India, is seven to ten days. Ten different sacred and mundane ceremonies make up the list of 'items' to be included in a wedding plan. This prospect suffocates many family members, especially if the proposed wedding partners live in nuclear family set-ups and follow modern work life, which means that they work six days a week, probably ten hours per day. Weddings of the arrived urban middle class are as much a financial risk as weddings in non-urban India. Even though the groom or the bride might be earning a monthly salary of INR 30,000 or even 100,000 (€550–1,800) and even more, the expenditure of the wedding may well leave the bride's family financially challenged, if not broke, for quite some time.[1]

There are, of course, many styles and themes of weddings possible to choose from. But it is crucial that a 'good' wedding displays a 'cultured' background filled with both knowledge of the world and of India. Earlier, I have emphasised the aspirational claim to status displayed by the new middle classes by accumulating cultural knowledge about important places, historical periods and lifestyles from around the world (see Chapter 4 of this book). Such capital provides evidence of a person's cosmopolitan knowledge. Like the colonial exhibitions and world fairs of the nineteenth and early twentieth century, the 'big fat Indian wedding' mirrors similar motivations, on a more individual level. The quote cited at the start of this chapter (Menon 2007) mentions a wedding at 'a French chateau' and thus refers the initiated reader to one of the spectacular 'weddings of the century', namely that of industrialist and multi-millionaire Lakshmi Mittal's

---

[1] The average American wedding costs about $26,327. Indian wedding budgets feed on rapidly growing salaries and an ever-increasing number of high net-worth individuals, remittances by NRIs and a strong inflow of investments in India. The *Hindustan Times* reports that the total value of the wedding industry in the year 2005 was US$11 billion, growing by 25 per cent per year. The budget of an average Indian wedding is between US$4,000 and 400,000; the minimum spent on a middle-class wedding is US$34,000 (Das 2005). See also 'Bigger, Fatter Weddings' *Hindustan Times*, 13 January 2007.

daughter at Versailles in 2004. Undoubtedly, this wedding set an example for other ambitious big fat Indian weddings, with or without French chateau or Kylie Minogue invited as an 'item'-dancer. But what I consider almost as important are the signs sent to the international community: India has now reached, if not overtaken, western standards of the 'world-class'. The breathtaking choreographical display of wealth by millionaires like Mittal or the Ambani brothers has reversed the Orientalist gaze by surpassing tales of Arabian Nights and subverts ethnocentric and colonial stereotypes of world order at once (Plate 12.2). Even in the shadowlines of these gigantic mega media events, smaller 'big fat weddings' herald a similar confidence — one of belonging to 'world-class' India.

The claims to 'big fat Indian weddings' are made by members of the aspiring or arrived middle classes, while the actual budgets of what is referred to can be thought of being paid only by the very rich Indians. With a similar appetite but a much smaller budget, these tiny fantasy lands often appear pretentious and embarrassing, stuck between imagination and real-time budgets. This is possibly what Madhu Jain meant when she argued that in the course of the hype around event management and celebration-culture, the 'great middle class gets on board in its pursuit of *la dolce vita*'. Even to incorporate the world in a wedding at home, by reconstructing Venice in Goa or the American President's White House in South Delhi requires more than what a member of the upper middle classes will be able to pay for. But no matter whether the budget is sufficient or not, the dreams of self-transformation are dreamt by all. And in this course, the notion of Indianness becomes an exotic export good availed of in such a way that spurs ideas of a new, fascinating discovery. It is — at least to some extent — an auto-orientalist cosmopolitanism through which the beholder looks at his or her own culture through a different, and in this case, neocolonial lens.

The majority of scholarship about rituals and popular culture in contemporary India, at least until recently, associates the first with redundant boredom and the latter with kitsch and inauthentic trash. In the context of economic liberalisation in India,

Plate 12.2: Newspaper advertisement for themed royal weddings by Sariska Travels (2005).

however, life cycle rituals have partly become lifestyle rituals and constitute an important domain of scholarly research on contemporary change, globalisation and gender issues in popular culture. The first time I heard an Indian speaking about an Indian wedding was with respect to commercial cinema from Bombay, in the 1990s: 'If you want to know what an Indian wedding is like, watch a Hindi movie! Both are equally long and noisy.' This was not exactly a compliment for either occasion and even associated a kind of low-class vulgarity or lack of taste and sophistication with the remarkable style, sound and size of both. During my postgraduate year at the School of Oriental and African Studies in London, I came to watch Hum Aapke Hain Koun...?! (directed by Sooraj R. Barjatya, 1994), and shortly after, Dilwale Dulhania Le Jaenge (The Brave-Hearted will take the Bride, also DDLJ, directed by Aditya Chopra, 1995) in overcrowded movie halls in West London, both known for their dramatic, romantic wedding narratives, and for their celebration of middle class dreams.[2] Little did I know that I would be studying both topics later in my life (and that I would choose one song from DDLJ for my own wedding). There is an extra portion of big emotions, lightness as well as weight of possible impossibilities in the Indian melodrama that nurtures the senses, and in particular those seeking a language for what is often unspeakable. Scholars like Sudhir Kakar (1989), Rosie Thomas (1995) and Rachel Dwyer (2000) have contributed much to this discussion, and how film and social reality and imagination enhance each other. Since the early 2000s, a lot has changed in middle-class weddings in terms of their choreography and marketing. Today, the worlds of film, Page 3 news, and traditional weddings have come to overlap in multitudinal ways and are constantly cross-referencing each other. In addition, the self-portrayal of Indians, though still highly stereotypical, follows the 'ethnic chic' (Tarlo 1996), thereby challenging the western styled suit and white dress as signifiers of culturedness. Indian wedding planners have non-Indian clients, too, who largely get married outside the Hindu wedding season in winter. In conversation, a wedding planner from Delhi illuminated this trend. According to him: 'The West has lost its capacity to celebrate, to create spectacles, to be enchanted. Now people turn towards India to have fun.' Masti — joy and pleasure — dominate the sensories of the booming wedding industry, confirming Mazzarella's argument about national progress through pleasure (2003).

---

[2] I want to thank Rachel Dwyer and Christopher Pinney here for sharing their knowledge of, and passion for, Indian commercial films with me while I studied at SOAS in 1995–96.

With the boom in the wedding industry in India, often termed as 'the fastest growing sunshine industry', of the early millennium, the wedding planner and the wedding designer emerged as new specialists of lifestyle desires. 'Weddings have become the single most visible expression of a person's social standing and wealth, an expression that is both acceptable and expected', says image consultant Dilip Cherian, who heads Perfect Relations, a leading Indian PR company (Das 2005). The scale of urban middle-class weddings in their orientation towards theme weddings of the elite, drawing upon tourism and heritage as cultural repertoires, is worthwhile to examine. According to sociologist Krishna Kumar, the Indian urban middle classes' concern with marriage is almost 'obsessive' (cited in Uberoi 2006: 291) and works as a source of social prestige.

That today's marriage is a platform for status claims is not new; it has always been a matter of a variety of social interests and ritual regulations, in north or in south India. However, what is new is that caste is no longer the key status-marker or maker for a Hindu marriage. The frontpage of an *India Today* special issue on 'Netrimony' postulates: 'Forget horoscopes. Ignore caste' (Datta 2008). As opposed to entering marriages arranged by parents, astrologers and families, youths now seem to throw all rules overboard and make their own search and choice, finally even managing to convince their parents to agree to their decision on their partner for life (ibid.). Uberoi postulates that class location now determines 'habits of mind and lifestyle more than regional, caste, religious, linguistic affiliations' (2006: 22) and that festivals, rituals, marriage, have become 'insignia of Indian ethnic identity' (ibid.: 28), both in India as well as among NRIs all over the world.[3] If true, this would be a revolution against the conservative brahminic codes of ritual behaviour, where marriage is a means of 'control of reproduction' and where the most persistent rule in north India (and Nepal) is that a marriage should be undertaken within the same caste (however, outside one's own kinship group, joint family and neighbourhood; see Michaels 2004: 121). To call this rebellion would be misleading. Marriage candidates might have become smarter in choosing their future partner, and have more choice at their hands due to online marriage portals. But surveys have shown that '64 per cent men in Delhi favour intra-caste marriage' and most urban youths want their parents' blessings as regards their choice (Datta 2008: 74). When I asked wedding planner Vijay A. whether caste still mattered for marriage decisions, he confirmed that it was: 'Why should

---

[3] Sara Dickey contends that both caste and class shape today's identities and interactions in urban households in south India (2000: 464).

one have an arranged marriage otherwise?! Only love marriages would mix caste. But after the age of 25–26, caste would not really matter any more — as long as you get married at all!' (personal conversation, October 2007). Despite many claims by sociologists and anthropologists that the concepts of joint family and arranged marriage are declining because of urbanisation, modernisation and westernisation, this assumption is wrong: surveys have shown that especially in urban habitats, even as many as 90 per cent of the young people privilege arranged marriage over romantic love (Rastogi 2007: 5). In many cases this has little to do with belief in caste as a ritual identity but functions rather as an emotional strategy of dealing with the flip side of mobility in the contemporary world. Psychologist Jasmeet K. from South Delhi tells me that this is 'because the youth does not want to take full responsibility for such a big step in their life. They want to take no risk! Instead, they want a "security-cover" such as the decision of the parents. If the marriage fails, they will be able to blame them, instead of being blamed by the family' (personal conversation, New Delhi, March 2005). She adds:

> Hardly any people come and see me if they're from an arranged marriage background. These people know anyway that it's all about compromising, right from the start! It's those people who entered a love marriage who come and see me. This is also because people from such marriages do not have much social and emotional security to fall back onto when their relation breaks up (Jasmeet K, personal conversation, New Delhi, March 2005).

Surveys have found that 70 per cent of divorces take place among people who entered a love marriage and are below the age of 35, a figure that has increased by 30 per cent since 2000. One of the most frequently given reasons is stress and that the wives are unhappy with their husbands. The rise in divorces is also due to the fact that women are more financially independent and often have to face much less social stigmatisation than before.[4] Thus, it can be said at the same time that a growing number of people, mainly in big metros, also choose not to marry at all. However, unmarried people are still considered as 'sociophobic' and 'spinsters'. Homosexuality is still stigmatised despite Delhi High Court's recent ruling allowing for its unexpected decriminalisation. And while the joint family in its 'arche-typical' sociological form — of members of different generations being assembled in one household — is certainly fragmenting, and nuclear families — capable of reacting to the modern demands of

---

[4] See 'Singles-Survey', The Week, 23(13), 27 February 2005.

flexibility and mobility — are becoming standard, the joint family as a 'structure of consciousness' and 'code of conduct' (Uberoi 2006: 286) is still very much intact.

In this chapter, I focus not so much on the changing role of women in the mass media, indigenous conceptions of interrelatedness or specific constructions of familial personhood.[5] Instead, I foreground weddings as a stage for the display of 'world-class' lifestyle and Erlebnis, and as they are imagined and communicated by lifestyle experts such as wedding planners. The wedding industry is vast and specialises in the creation of pleasure and desire, distinction and status, the marketing of travel destinations and culinary and other sensuous experiences, status, style and etiquette. The worlds of romantic love as a neoliberal moral economy, of tourism and commercial film, are closely intertwined here, helping social agents to 'invent tradition' filled with morals and value. That way, the wedding ceremony is perceived as a moral economy of the middle classes as they imagine and project themselves vis-à-vis other elites in India and abroad. If at all, then, we explore the categories of the family, or the woman and sexuality, it is in order to discuss them as units of production, distribution and consumption of cosmopolitan middle-classness.

The Wedding Industry, Cosmopolitanism and Heritage Production

Claims to cosmopolitanism surface even in the seemingly traditional terrain of marriage, as a marker of both 'rooted nationalism' and the 'world-class'. It is affirmed, along with the concept of heritage, as a conservative attitude towards preservation and a repertoire of 'Indianness'. In this process, a kind of 'soft' Hindu cultural nationalism is generated, through which mainstream culture and lifestyle habits can be foreshadowed. In her study of the middle classes in Hyderabad, Säävälä maintains that there is a 'growing need of the new middle classes to engage in Hindu practices' for social distinction. However, these practices are neither chosen according to one's caste identities nor are they inherited (Säävälä 2003: 245). Instead, she argues, 'hierarchy remains, but is transformed through new interpretations in which auspiciousness has become culturally pivotal' (ibid.). The affirmation of 'Hindu practices' as markers of Hindu/Indianness underlines that culture is turned into a resource to shape status and reproduce inequality (see also Rao and Walton 2004).

---

[5] On the subject of gender, liberalisation and media, see Fernandes (2006), Munshi (2001), Oza (2006), Reddy (2006), Sreenivas (2003).

The wedding industry, in particular the new elements of wedding choreography according to themes and entertainment as well as luxury destination weddings, rely heavily on evocations of heritage, converting locations into tourist destinations and rituals into staged performances. There are many overlaps with heritage tourism. In fact, both wedding and tourist industry draw heavily upon regional and ethnic stereotypes that sport a vibrant inter-visuality, from colonial photography to Republic Day parades and other paraphernalia of the Indian state to song and dance scenes in Hindi films (see Plates 12.3, 12.4, 12.5).[6]

The bridal industry, states Patricia Uberoi, is all about the making of class, ethnic identity, gender, and family relations (2008). Even though these notions are fluid, the role of the bride has probably changed the least, and is still confined by concepts of chastity and devotion to the husband. What is considered to be suitable or appropriate is highlighted in the following example. Ashok S., Senior Manager at one of India's leading marketing and consultancy agencies with its head office in Gurgaon, tells me that while weddings in the 1980s and 1990s, would even sport western suits for the groom and guests, therefore documenting their cosmopolitan attitude, this was hardly fashionable today anymore. Today, 'trend-conscious' people wear 'ethnic' dress of royal and historical background, in mostly Punjabi or Rajasthani style with long and beautifully embroidered coats. Historical costumes from nineteenth-century north India have a strong impact, especially since block-busters like *Devdas* (directed by Sanjay Leela Bhansali, 2002). Rajasthani 'folk style', too, has been 'gentrified', for example, with films like *Lagaan* (Tax, directed by Ashutosh Gowariker, 2001). Moreover, elements appropriated from religious practices are no longer perceived as auspicious Hindu items in the

Plate 12.3: Stamp from India, entitled 'Bride-Bengal' (1980).

---

[6] See Aumweddings, 'Rituals and Customs: An Authentic Guide', http://www.aumweddings.com (accessed 17 July 2008). Other online services providing packaged weddings and honeymoon trips are Exotic Indian Weddings, http://www.exoticindianweddings.com (accessed 22 August 2009), and Indian Wedding Planners, http://www.indianweddingplanners.com (accessed 22 August 2009). To a large extent, these services cater to NRIs and members of the affluent middle class in India.

first degree but become part and parcel of a material culture and circulation system that define a social value instead. In this context, Hindu rituals become scripts for new narratives with an ethnic highlight. Most of all, while the marriage rite of the couple by a *pandit* (priest) would have absorbed most of the time in a 'traditional' wedding, today the fact that choreographies last over several days, involving elements that have become independent 'items', such as the engagement, the *sangeet*, or the reception, clearly show a relativisation of the key rite in favour of other modes of entertainment.[7]

Plate 12.4: 'Indian Bride', popular bazaar print, Delhi (2006).

Previously, only the weddings of the upper class, senior politicians and royals would count more than hundred guests from a variety of regional, religious and caste backgrounds, while traditional weddings kept to themselves, i.e., within a regional compound of 'face-to-face' contacts. Today, a middle-class wedding event might add up to 500 guests and involve a host of diverse participants. The latest 'fashion' for so-called A-grade weddings is to clad the wedding *mandap* (pavilion) in orchids from Thailand and Swarovski jewellery, to fly in Bollywood film stars, or prominent personalities from the West, for instance, Bill Clinton. What has remained more or less

Plate 12.5: Frontpage of bridal magazine *Wedding Affair* 7(4) (2006).

the same, however, is that at conservative urbanised high-caste, upper-class weddings, no alcohol is served on the day of the ritual ceremony itself, that for the wedding rite, groom and bride wear traditional dresses, and that a *pandit* is called to perform the wedding rite according to an auspicious date and time.[8]

---

[7] *Sangeet* refers to the pre-wedding gathering of the family, accompanied by celebration through singing, dancing and story-telling.

[8] The caste- and class-specific requirements here demand more research in terms of urban contexts. Moreover, there are many weddings, e.g., in the Himalayan region, that request alcohol even at the ritual occasion — thus, it is not always a taboo.

Today, western elements are still — and maybe more than ever before — indices of a cosmopolitan mindset and lifestyle. But 'the West' is somewhat exoticised and thus both distanced and appropriated, for instance in the case of the Chatwal wedding in 2006, when the Carnival in Venice was introduced as a theme in one of the functions. Although this could also be seen as a form of westernisation, I would argue that the citation from a 'western tradition' is a statement of post-colonial mimicry, quite like the architectural montaged history in Delhi's condominiums (see Chapter 4 of this book).

Heritage tourism and destination weddings, including honeymoon trips, have become a key segment of the tourist industry, be it royal weddings in Rajasthan or beach weddings in Kerala or Goa. And they have come to mark a new topography of taste and status in the light of economic liberalisation. Chhaparia (2006) reports:

> In a bid to cash-in on the marriage fervour, a host of states — spread across the length and breadth of India — are now offering to play wedding planners for well-heeled Indians and foreigners … 'Ancient palaces, heritage hotels, colourful traditions and the *shahi* costumes are the main attractions,' says Rajasthan tourism minister Usha Punia. 'Cities like Jaipur and Udaipur, which have big palaces, heritage hotels, serve as perfect venues. Add to that camels, elephants and ethnic jewelleries, and they make Rajasthan a hot destination for royal weddings' … [O]thers like Uttaranchal and Goa are hardselling their natural beauty to woo the wedding party.

Both the auto-orientalism (Mazzarella 2003: 138–45) and the occidentalism in Indian middle- and upper-class weddings projected as events for the new colonial maharajas reflected in this quote are interesting. These lines remind us of real estate advertising, discussed in Part I of this book, where a similar nostalgia was evoked. The wedding industry also shows that the regional states too now move in as wedding planners and designers, in competition with each other, quite like the global cities competing for 'world-classness'. They often do so in alliance with the expanding tourist industry that responds to the growing aspirations of Indian citizens to travel.

Here, Ashok S.'s remarks about the young Indian middle class are revealing. The senior manager works for a major consultancy agency in Gurgaon that tracks national consumer aspirations. He tells me that this is a 'young India' in terms of economic liberalisation and lifestyle aspirations: 'India in that sense is virgin land in the context of lifestyle, in the search of a global identity.' This search operates through the concept of the global citizen or

Indianness, argues Ashok S. and has in the past few years generated a new kind of national chauvinism. There is a strong feeling of pride to be Indian today, awareness that no longer is 'being Indian' somewhat 'wrong' and embarrassing. Instead, he says:

> Being Indian is the most important issue! Right now, the atmosphere is of a pioneering spirit like the one in the US in the nineteenth century. The kids ask themselves: Why should I junk India?! These Indians believe that they are Europeans or Americans sitting in Asia rather than being Asians (personal conversation, Gurgaon, March 2006).

These Indians, according to Ashok S., are the rays of hope for India. And he goes on to mention the 'Chatwal' wedding describing it as an anti-climax. In his view, people like the Chatwals should not be treated like kings when they are sought by the CBI for corruption, and when they declare to be bankrupt but waste money at the same time:

> Vikram Chatwal's father [the owner of the hotel empire in NY] invested in India for chauvinist reasons. Many people really don't get it that those people abuse India, and they are even getting pampered here for less money, wasting it and showing off, with big mansions, shopping, and showmakers. I have disgust for them (ibid.)!

Disgust and disrespect are probably the extreme versions for the ambivalent stance of Indians within India vis-à-vis their fellows overseas. A whole 'genre' of narratives circulates about the allegedly inadequate, pompous, arrogant attitude of overseas Indians who 'made it' abroad and show off in front of fellow domestic Indians when back in India. In many conversations, I overheard stories of NRI-specific decadence, for instance, of people who built mansions in their hometown but lived in them only for a few weeks, when they came to India for their children's holidays, to 'familiarise' them with the motherland. Or, they tried to show off (but failed to convince with) their purported knowledge of, and membership to the 'world-class' lifestyle and ethos or 'Indianness'. This ambiguity is another interesting and yet not enough studied source of inter-communal cultural conflict.

Negotiating Bridal Authenticity

In her ethnography of bridal photography in Taiwan, Bonnie Adrian (2003) points towards a fascinating paradox within the 'dream industry', in particular, with respect to bridal photographers and entrepreneurs. She argues that while bridal photographs are completely staged and thus could be referred to as lacking authenticity, everybody is aware that 'the photos are full of authentic social value and meaning' (ibid.: 21). Refer-ring to Daniel Miller's work on consumption, Adrian maintains that the anthropology of material culture can no longer claim that commodity and gift are essentially different, on the basis of assigning the stigma of being inauthentic and meaningless to the first and the power of the authentic and meaningful to the latter. In fact, however, the two are intertwined (ibid.: 19). Likewise, I would argue, the consumer culture linked to the wedding industry in India or elsewhere is certainly made up of formulaic codes but not of alienated goods. The bride is commodified to the extent that she becomes an expression of social desire and beauty. Yet, she may find that all of those processes and forces actually cater towards her personal aspirations and pleasure. This creative potential of the sphere of consumption has been highlighted by various scholar, with respect to different com-modities and media (Friedman 1994; Mazzarella 2003). The leisure industry, and in particular, the print culture of magazines, has had a vital impact on the structuring of subjectivity and pleasure, gender and modernity, much before the 'official' advent of economic liberalisation in India in the 1990s. Consumption has shaped a new public space in which social, moral and cultural values as well as identities could be negotiated. Similarly, in this case, arranged marriage, love marriage and respective identities can be negotiated.

Possibly, more than other life-cycle rituals, the wedding constructs identities in a very complex manner and offers itself ideally for appropriation by lifestyle experts and event planners. The professionalisation of organisation and standardisation of the wedding have grown with the urbanisation and change in work culture and lifestyles of Indians. Increasingly, thus, the wedding shifts from the hands of the families of the (to-be-wed) couple into the hands of non-religious specialists who engage in offering a 'total wedding package' (Goldstein-Gidoni 2000: 39).

Notions of love and romance that have found entrance into current wedding rhetoric, for instance, were shaped in the colonial context, both in appropriation of a model of loving partnership as well as against strictly moral and patronising tones of colonial rulers towards 'Indian society' (see Sreenivas 2003). To be sure, the notion of liberalised sexuality emerges in the context of an educated middle-class formation, on the one hand, and is thrown out of the backdoor by a bourgeois ideology that aims at disciplining female sexuality by means of (male) codes of honour, on the other (see Kakar 1989).

There is a strong ambiguity among different segments of the middle classes about the style of the 'big fat Indian wedding' as it has emerged since the beginning of this millennium. One opinion that is shared widely is that the celebration of such a key ritual in elaborate ways demonstrates a revitalisation of tradition. Further, people opine that these elaborate Indian traditional celebrations show that Indians are 'water-proof' against westernisation.[9] Critics of this view claim that such lavish weddings are simply 'graceless' and underline the superficial agenda of the new rich: 'Where weddings were once *celebrated*, today they are *performed*' (see Das 2005; emphasis added). Both perspectives highlight the concept of 'essential' cultural building blocks that can be either revived as heritage or abused by people lacking the cultural capital to appreciate culture the way 'it is'. The juxtaposed opinions also underline the very mono-dimensional local notion of authenticity. Punita S., one of the key wedding planners in this case-study, emphasised that the latest trend of upper class weddings was to leave all the materialist pomp aside and go 'back to the olden days' where, according to her, 'love and bonding prevailed'. Punita who married into a family belonging to the 'old class' in New Delhi has become a wedding planner not for financial profit but as a kind of charity — to ease the pain and stress of wedding preparations on the wedding hosts and the couple. She holds that while the 'wow'-effect might be there in a grand Mittal or Chatwal wedding, emotional warmth and memory — the most important things that stays — may not necessarily be included in them! The fact that the 'old rich' turn the public spectacle into a classical, simple and 'authentic' rite in which the bonding of family relations is central is clearly a means of distinction.

Punita's claim to concentrate on the wedding rite instead of the extravaganaza of the decor and preparations is reflected in the special edition of the bridal journal *Celebrate Vivaha*: 'In the sanctified environment of rich Indian rituals and heartwarming customs, so much happens. The atmosphere is blessed and family bonds are revoked.'[10] Surely, neither a wedding designer nor money can buy emotional warmth. But this nostalgia without actual memory, essentialising rituals as containers, may not necessarily lead to the desired efforts, too.

---

[9] See Dipanker Gupta on 'westoxication' (2004: 11–31).

[10] See *Celebrating Vivaha* 4(2): 217, 2002. This trend is in tune with, and possibly stirred by, 'clean' family movies such as *Kabhie Khushi Kabhie Gham* ('Sometimes Happy, Sometimes Sad', aka 'The Indian Family', directed by Karan Johar, 2001); see Brosius and Yazgi (2007); Krueger (2004).

Setting Wedding Trends

Who sets the pace for wedding trends and why, thus shaping taste and distinction? Why do Indians overseas and their perspectives on 'Planet India' as the homeland of dream weddings have such an impact on this matter? In one of our conversations, wedding planner Tarun tells me about different categories of weddings. A-grade weddings are those which 'grab the headlines' because of the fame of their hosts, their exorbitant choreography and list of prominent guests. B-grade weddings are expensive events of the upper middle class. Finally, a C-grade wedding is a 'routine and traditional occasion'. Tarun goes on to give an example of an A-grade wedding: the invitation cards are designed by eminent artist M. F. Husain, and presented in a silver box or embellished with crystals. Another example is from the print media: a recent Delhi wedding had 51 *pandits* chanting the mantras of the wedding rite in unison, thus creating what was called a 'different spiritual dimension' (see Menon 2007). All three categories, according to Tarun, may employ wedding designers.

In setting the pace for weddings to follow, three mega-weddings have been groundbreaking in the past few years. The owner of the Sahara business group got his two sons married on Valentine's Day in 2004; Lakshmi Mittal, steel industry baron from London rented parts of the Versailles castle near Paris for his daughter's wedding in 2004; and restaurant and hotel owner Chatwal from New York staged the wedding of his son in 2006.[11] These weddings caught the attention of international and national media and became a benchmark for the new style in event-wedding choreography a well as an affirmation of the 'brand' of 'India Shining' in which tradition and modernity, arranged and romantic love marriage could be harmoniously fused. The new affluence and astonishing confidence imbued in these three instances that displayed material wealth in ways that recession-struck Europe had not witnessed in a long time has certainly led to a revision of the stereotype of India as a land of poverty and apathy into that of fairy-

---

[11] Eleven thousand guests attended the Sahara wedding in Lucknow, from key politicians and Bollywood stars to national-level cricket players. 'The bill for the candles alone came to $250,000', writes a BBC-reporter, 'a 100-piece orchestra was flown in from the UK while 50 acrobats and stage artistes from eastern Europe performed and 140,000 meals were given to the poor'; see 'India Mega-Wedding Justifies Hype', http://news.bbc.co.uk/2/hi/south_asia/3479773.stm (22 August 2009). Mittal is said to have shelled out over £30 million to host his daughter Vanisha's engagement and wedding celebration. The Chatwal wedding was turned into the docudrama *The Great Indian Wedding* by Discovery Channel.

tale rulers and great riches. The world suddenly seemed to lie at the feet of these millionaires, and India, and many saw this as a sign of changing tides. With the staging of these 'new maharajas', fantasy and reality merged once again, shaping the on-going power of colonial travel writing and photography. Moreover, these 'mediatised' events helped reinforce the cliché of the 'big fat Indian wedding' and the 'wedding-obsessed nation' to redefine tradition and employing it as a means of claiming status. Media attention is crucial for every family that aims at increasing their social prestige and gaining the status of a B-grade wedding, for instance, through the attendance of politicians, businesspeople and stars from the world of films or fashion. While placing the personal and intimate occasion of two people getting married to each other on the centre stage, it emerges that the contract is actually made between their two families. Moreover, it is a welcome occasion to display wealth and increase personal charisma by being associated with glamour, fame, power and money. This is why there was more talk about Lakshmi Mittal's wealth than his daughter in person at the wedding. Lakshmi Mittal did not only receive the status of the 'Person of the Year', and came to top the Forbes list of richest people in the world as Number 5. He also came to be known as a loving father prepared to host the most expensive wedding ever, leaving us puzzled as to whose celebration it actually was.[12]

It is here where the themed wedding and the destination wedding began their career. The week-long wedding festivities of investment-banker Vikram Chatwal and ex-model Priya Sachdev included a masked 'fantasy party' à la Carnival of Venice at the palace-city Udaipur in Rajasthan, as well as a 'Queenie and Raja party' in Mumbai. The wedding planner from New Delhi ensured that the painted elephant, 50,000 kg of flowers from Bangkok and Amsterdam, three chartered jets and 70 private cars arrived at the right time to transport and surprise the over 1,000 guests. For one of the events, in order to have the Rajasthani theme as 'authentic' as possible, the wedding venue of a five star hotel was transformed into a Rajasthani village. Folk artists performed traditional dances and guests had been instructed to dress in Rajasthani outfits. This underlines what Uberoi remarked about the fact that festivals, rituals and marriage have become 'insignia of Indian ethnic identity' (2006: 28). It also reminds us of those voices critical of the auto-orientalist stereotype of India reproduced here.

---

[12] *Financial Times*, 2006. See also http://southasianoutlook.com/issues/topical/mittal_wedding.html (accessed 7 February 2007).

Reverse Orientalism and Occidentalism

Today's middle-class weddings have become entangled with the expanding domestic and international tourism and heritage industry. Through them, 'the West' and India are rendered as a spectacle, archives for the costume balls of the aspiring elites. Moreover, both weddings and tourism display a modern tendency for society itself to be rendered as a spectacle. By their means, the new Indian middle classes can take a look at, and experience, themselves as exotic and spectacular props as if they were partaking in a great exhibition, show or festival. In their search for 'authentic Indianness' middle-class Indians create a patchwork that is presented as if it was 'real'. Heritage as a 'mode of cultural production' (Kirshenblatt-Gimblett 1998: 149) is turned into a theme park through which an imagined past and a homogenous cultural identity are staged for a global audience. In this process, the familiar becomes strange and the strange becomes familiar. '[A] hallmark of heritage productions — perhaps their defining feature — is precisely the foreignness of the "tradition" to its context of presentation' (ibid.: 157). This new context in which the performance occurs is because of the new performers, choreographers or event managers and the audi-ence. The outcome is what I have elsewhere called 'internalised orientalism' (Brosius 2005), i.e., the self-conception of (middle-class) Indians along the lines of Orientalist projections. In this context, Indianness becomes at once the source and product of power and knowledge through staging and exoticising. It is important, however, to mention that it is in this way that cosmopolitan status is claimed. Orientalist ideas or images, then, become global commodities, part of a global imaginary, through which value is traded, transformed and translated. In this form of capital accumulation, for instance, 'ethnic chic' is not a signifier of national identity any longer, but of 'world-class' cosmopolitanism. In fact, it turns into a marker of global competency. In this, the wedding industry, like ethnic advertising, takes up a 'mediating position in regard to ... the relationship between aspirational consumerism, aesthetic community, social distinction, and cultural identity' (Mazzarella 2003: 139), tying the global to the local. Consequently, hosts of the 'big fat Indian weddings' display both symbolic and cultural capital (at a great cost of material capital) in the new glocal consumer economy, thus constituting themselves as progressively traditional.

Another aspect of internalised orientalism as regards the wedding in-dustry is that there appears a change of quality in its commodities by which value and meaning are further negotiated. This has been discussed with reference to Walter Benjamin earlier, as a paradigmatic oscillation between 'cultic value' and 'exhibition value'. For instance, the performance of *puja* in a temple can now be seen to transmutate into an ethnic commodity and cultural value, as much as the chaste bride transforms into an erotic fetish.

The wedding industry also underlines that neoliberal consumerism in India produces new forms of occidentalist stereotypes: the 'West' is rendered exotic and can thus be 'Othered', and distanced. It is both a repertoire for the new maharajas and a shield against critique, in particular when it comes to the cliché that crucial social values and institutions are forever deteriorating, if not already lost. On the level of cultural identity thus, we can find a reverse colonialism at work. The fascination with high-class heritage at wedding events shows the shaping of an idea of India Shining as a new empire that now, for a change, reverses the order and imports the world, quite like the world fairs in Europe and the USA in the age of late-capitalist empire: pre-wedding ceremonies have everything from female Russian bar tenders to middle eastern belly dancers and UK-bred DJs. The more exotic a wedding, the more status the organiser and host can accumulate. Tarun L., who runs his own wedding company, argues that people with money want to display it, choosing the wedding as the best means to do so without running the risk of being called selfish (personal conversation, New Delhi, October 2006).

What can we say about the possible changes occurring with key life-cycle rituals such as weddings, when they take place in the context of a socio-economic shift such as economic liberalisation? It is easily pronounced that globalisation leads to commodification and standardisation. To some extent, this might even be true: the 'Indian' wedding is subject to standard-ised, 'fashionable' choreographies and tastes that have been appropriated from media flows such as cinema, television or international lifestyle magazines, from ethnic flows such as migration, from urbanisation and the pragmatics of economic factors such as work conditions.

All the wedding designers I spoke to in 2006–7 told me that 'Bollywood' is a very important narrative as well as aesthetic genre according to which weddings in a city such as Delhi are meant to take place, not just because of the glory of the stardom and recent weddings of filmstars but also because of the depiction of excessive celebration of family values and traditions as well as the, at once, chaste and exoticised body of the bride. The wedding planners set the tone for matters such as fashion design (often the bride is made to look like one of the heroines of a Bollywood movie, such as Aishwarya Rai in the blockbuster *Devdas* (directed by Sanjay Leela Bhansali, 2002), spatial and dance choreography, and for the ways in which the com-plementary wedding photographer and video-*wallah* (hired filmmaker), depicts the ceremony as an event (see Sengupta 1999).

The Desiring Gaze of the NRI

For some, the wedding has become a symbol not only marking social relations and financial status but also a declaration of transnational patriotism and ethnic stereotypification ('internalised Orientalism'). This has been argued earlier, when Ashok S. elaborated on the new confidence of Indian middle-class youth, and described the inappropriate behaviour of Indians returning from overseas, for instance. Young Indian nationals are now taking a fresh look at 'traditional' India, turning its culture into the property and repository of a heritage exhibition and performance, making it an extension of new consumer culture. In this context, a central and ever-growing category of wedding-event clients and trendsetters are the NRIs. The Delhi Times, a supplement of the newspaper The Times of India, that predominantly reports about 'society' events such as exhibition and restaurant openings, business fairs, and weddings, projects the wedding of New York hotelier Chatwal's son Vikram with 'Delhi party girl' and model Priya Sachdev on Valentine's Day in 2006 as a marker of affirmation of India's self-esteem. The event is said to have spread the 'India everywhere-mood', a feel-good factor metaphor related to the rhetoric of 'India Shining'. India, it seems, is now recognised abroad, and even by those who had once left the country, often in the expectation that they will find better lifestyles elsewhere. The Indians overseas are the 'new heroes' and diplomats of India abroad as also back in India. Delhi Times cites Vikram saying: 'Oh wow, this is such fun. I just love the magic around Indian weddings.' Given that he and his fiancée had been part of an elaborate choreographed wedding, the magic is possibly a rather hollow declaration of Vikram's awakening to India. The couple's wedding sangeet took place at a farmhouse at a venue between South Delhi and Gurgaon, with the 'who's who' from Mumbai, Delhi and New York. The bride's father says, about his son-in-law's initiation into 'Indianness': 'I strongly feel that it's very important to understand one's roots. Becoming an Indian, Vikram needs to see and feel the country, its culture, tradition and its diversity. In Rajasthan, he saw how kings lived, in Delhi he gets to discern the cosmopolitan flavour of an international city, just like New York is.'[13] Whether Mr Sachdev meant what he said or not, the interview excerpt reveals the rhetoric of more than a romantic commitment to Priya Sachdev. It is in fact a statement claiming the national identity of the NRI as a 'cultured Hindu' in the making. The wedding is a liminal state in which Vikram is transformed into an authentic Indian groom, exotic foreigner and elite citizen discovering 'Planet India' at a package wedding.

---

[13] Delhi Times, Times of India, 20 February 2006, p. 2.

Some wedding planners organise NRI-weddings abroad, for instance in Dubai, Singapore or Canada. Others specialise on choreographing an NRI-wedding in India. Interestingly, several wedding planners I spoke to emphasised that NRIs in particular wanted very traditional weddings and had an almost old-fashioned idea of 'Indian traditions'. At the same time, I also heard, sometimes even from the same wedding planner, that NRIs no longer possessed any sense of their roots and tradition and thus made completely unreasonable, unsophisticated and even disrespectful demands — for instance, to have alcohol served and belly dancers perform at the central wedding ceremony. For them, then, the wedding planner accomplishes the crucial function of helping to avoid making mistakes of the kind that could — in the worst-case scenario — upset the sentiments of the local Indians, or go against the classical taste of the observing elite whose approval is crucial to the act of status-positioning as 'world-class'. Avi from Aumweddings maintains that overseas Indians, who return only for their wedding celebrations, do this because, to them, at least some key events in life must be authentic and should take place in the 'motherland' (personal conversation, New Delhi, September 2006). But they would not consider living in India, thus using it predominantly as a stage. Avi claims that he returned to India from the UK when he realised that the:

> NRI community and their children need something to bond them with their heritage. India is in fashion and everything Indian is being adopted by the world, a wedding in India followed by a honeymoon gives you a chance to experience your roots and realise why you are part of the most beloved country in the world.[14]

Moreover, he remarks that the NRIs are often 'people who could not make it big in India. Now, they want the "roots"-feeling and implant that in their children too'. The wedding is thus one of the ties that bind persons and groups into families and countries transnationally. Among many local Indians there is great ambiguity towards NRIs, and this surfaces particularly in the context of mega-events such as weddings. Many Indians feel that NRIs have let down the country and her underdeveloped economy, and chosen the easy way out. Now that India is 'shining', they argue, NRIs rediscover India, pretending they were never unfaithful. The critique of the Chatwal wedding, then, has to be seen in that light. Many film stories about the returning Indian paint a transformation of the NRI from pariah and traitor

---

[14] See www.aumweddings.com/about-aum-wedding/html (accessed 3 August 2007).

to the hero. However, in the context of this chapter, it seems that the notion is far more complex and it must therefore be highlighted that the NRI who 'made it' according to the American dream does not necessarily fulfil the expectations of the 'Indian dream'.

Making (Middle-Class) Dreams Come True: Wedding Planners

The wedding industry in India is not unique; there are global counterparts with remarkable similarities and yet differences too, whether in the USA or in Japan. Before the advent of the wedding planner in India, there was the bride's father, there were aunts and uncles, people who rented tents, wedding brass bands who played songs for the *baraat's* (groom's party's) procession, with the groom on a white horse leaving for the bride's house. There were beauty parlours, *mehndi* (henna) artists, food caterers, photographers and possibly some classical musicians for the ladies' *sangeet*.[15] Further, there was a priest who would come to conduct the marriage rite. But there was no one to do the organisational work of creating an overall choreography. Much has changed since. Aspirations of the new middle classes as well as the 'new' rich to demonstrate their affluence and to mark status are stirred by the ever-expanding global consumer market, by a large network of transnational connections as well as the media landscape, in particular, satellite television and Bombay cinema's genre of the 'clean' family movie (see Brosius 2005; Uberoi 2006). Nuclear households and flexible careers for both men and women have increased the necessity to operate within efficient time frames. The wedding planner exists to design and coordinate clients' dreams and aspirations.[16] To present the work of wedding designers, three wedding planners from Delhi have been chosen and are portrayed briefly as follows.

Avi A. from Aumweddings

> So if you are a couple willing to get married in Palaces, it's no more a Dream with all that regal hospitality and charm, it's not a dream anymore.[17]

---

[15] Interestingly, food catering indicates the fact that the previous caution about ritual pollution through *kacha* (impure) food has been sidelined in favour of practicality and status — many weddings serve at least four to five different cuisines from across the world — the more, the better.

[16] In 2004, charges for a wedding designer could range from INR 50,000 to 500,000 (€900–9,000; see Bhumika 2004).

[17] See www.aumweddings.com (accessed 4 June 2007).

Plate 12.6: 'Palace Wedding Theme' by wedding planner Aumweddings.

Source: http://www.aumtours.com/weddings/palace-wedding.html
(accessed 19 September 2008).

This slogan comes from a wedding event company called Aumweddings. Its head office is in New Delhi, close to the New Delhi railway station with a partner office in Vancouver, Canada. Aumweddings is a transnationally active organisation, pragmatically tied to a travel agency and a chain of hotels. The term 'pragmatic' fits insofar as one of Aumweddings' key specialities is the organisation of destination weddings to Goa and Kerala (beach weddings), as well as Rajasthan (palace weddings) and farmhouse events (see Plate 12.6).[18] They offer 'designer weddings', 'honeymoon tours' and overseas Indian weddings.[19] This makes the overlap of booming industries such as tourism, wedding and wellness explicit. As weddings of

---

[18] The concept of the farmhouse is related to formerly agricultural land in the vicinity of New Delhi that has now come to be sold or rented to the upper middle class and expatriates. Most 'farmhouses' are illegally-built luxury residential compounds. Some are rented out for exclusive events such as weddings (at prices starting from INR 30,000 per event, i.e., €550).

[19] About 65,000 Indians celebrated their honeymoon abroad in the year 2007–8, which makes Indians the largest segment of honeymooners in the world (*India Today*, 22 August 2007, p. 37).

the aspiring and affluent middle classes are increasingly valued according to their 'exotic' and 'unique' set-up, the same applies to the honeymoon destinations and other activities related to aspiring lifestyles.[20]

According to Avi A., the acting Director of Aumweddings, now in his late-20s, who lived in the UK most of his life, the outsourcing of weddings to special locations has become a major trend in affluent segments of Indian society. On the one hand, he holds, this is partly based on a felt lack of time and energy to be spent on the occasion. On the other, it results from the expansion of middle-class weddings into mega-events that re-quire expertise with respect to exotic settings, costumes or decorations. Many 'ordinary' families would not even know what is needed for a wed-ding that could become the talk of the town, or at least, the neighbour-hood. The only points of reference for them are the media-hyped weddings of Page-3 VVIPs ('very very important people').

Aumweddings promotes itself by naming clients who belong to the alleged 'high society' of cosmopolitans, viz., internationally renowned fashion designers, Indian filmstars, wealthy businessmen, overseas Indians as well as Europeans and North Americans. More than 100 people work for Aumweddings, ranging from engineers, architects and artisans to designers. The themes it offers concern the exotic touch of cosmopolitan-ism and the 'world-class': there are events called '*An Evening in Paris*' as well as Japanese and Moroccan theme weddings. Quite a few themes have been chosen because of popular Hindi films from the 1970s or 1990s, in which the lovers-to-be or the married couple visits spectacular tourist sites around the world. According to Avi, currently the most popular themes are the heritage Rajasthani palace wedding and the Goa beach wedding.[21] The genre of the palace wedding is tailored for members of each

---

[20] Among the most popular destinations for newly-wed middle class couples are Goa and Kerala in India as well as Mauritius, the Maldives, Malaysia, Thailand and Europe. While in 2004, a package tour for two days to Goa would cost around INR 20,000 (€360), an international trip could cost approximately INR 50,000 or more (€900 plus). Lower middle class couples would choose Kathmandu or Colombo (see Trehan 2004).

[21] The film *An Evening in Paris* narrates the story of a newly-wed couple on their honeymoon through Europe (directed by S. Samantha, 1967). Even 'modern' elements such as a DJ or reception at a nightclub, are possible now and enjoyed. But they are clearly dominated by traditional and folk elements and events. Only 20 per cent of the weddings organised by Aumweddings were staged at a beach. Almost 80 per cent were in favour of palace sites, explains Avi, the company manager.

and every religion; elephants, horses and camels 'are used to give a touch of regalia' so that the guests experience what it is like to be a member of a royal family for a day. One can dine with a maharaja, join a gala lunch or dinner with the theme of 'Desert', 'Market' or 'Village' life: 'To add up the ambience, local Folk performers, dancers and musicians, Snake Charmers, Puppet Shows ... could be integrated very conveniently.'[22] To increase the exotic and quasi-colonial touch, the exhibition and Erlebnis-value, there is entertainment for the guests too: elephant polo, camel safari or an exclusive dinner in the sand dunes of Jaisalmer. Avi adds: 'We also offer them trips where they can take wine and cheese into the desert!' The theme weddings follow the same pattern as the colonial exhibitions of the nineteenth century. Simultaneously, they include elements in their weddings that are also frequently used in public performances of state governments (e.g., Republic Day parade, regional folk shows, heritage festivals, shows at visits of international prominent figures and conferences).

The fascination of temporarily becoming someone else has become a marketing strategy, irrespective of the social and regional background of the customers. Dressing up as someone else underlines the liminality of this modern event in the context of 'aspirational consumption' as performance, and has an almost carnivalesque flavour, quite like a set from a photostudio (Pinney 1997). Other weddings by the entrepreneur are readymade to such an extent that bride and groom slip into clothes made available to them: for instance, at the Kerala wedding, that includes a dhoti (long cloth worn by men around the waist) a white shirt with white shawl for the groom and a silk sari and costume jewellery for the bride. The programme of such a wedding almost, and possibly consciously, sounds more like a tourist agenda:

> Day 2: Breakfast. By 9 am, the groom's family is taken to the Siva temple to get the Nuptial Chain blessed ... Wedding sadhya (feast) on banana leaves follows [the marriage rite]. Afternoon at leisure. Evening 6:00–7:30: performance by dance troupe showing the classical dance forms of Kerala. Day 3: Visits to the local area and a farewell Dinner.[23]

---

[22] See www.aumweddings.com/indian-wedding-overseas.html (accessed 4 June 2007).

[23] See http://indianweddings.swagattours.com/keralaweddings.html (accessed 2 December 2009). Weddings in Udaipur, Rajasthan, are promoted as a romantic highlight, set in world-class hotel chains as 'the perfect choice for a Fairytale Wedding', www.aumtours.com/weddings/rajasthan-wedding-tour.html#exotic (accessed 4 June 2007).

What makes people go for such an extensive and even excessive undertaking like this is the desire for prestige. Such a modern wedding is not only a matter of getting two people married and surely it has never exclusively been so anywhere in the world. Yet, the wedding industry's recent and rapid development proves that a wedding is also an exercise in conspicuous consumption, in the display of 'know-how' and status. For customers with smaller budgets, Aumweddings offers a range of 'second-class' palaces. The best prices are available outside the wedding season, in the months of February and March one could even get a reduction of 30–40 per cent. However, Avi also acknowledges that hardly any traditional family that goes for an arranged marriage would opt for this period as it is considered inauspicious, and it is unlikely for an astrologer to proclaim this as the best time of tying the knot. The case differs with love marriages that are not always obliged to follow these rules of ritual purity.

Both overseas Indians and westerners approach Aumweddings to plan a 'typical' wedding in India. As of yet, explains Avi, more Indians overseas than non-Indians seek his expertise. But he reckons that it is only a matter of time until the Indian wedding is as popular abroad as Bollywood. To hold a wedding in Rajasthani style, his customers must be willing to spend approximately US$350 per person for the entire wedding. Given the fact that 400–500 guests might attend the occasion, the cost for a wedding could amount to US$175,000. Like other wedding designers I talked to, Avi mentions the unbelievable amounts of money some Indians would earn and be willing to spend these days. This 'Gold Rush'-atmosphere, i.e., the notion that much could be earned in India if one only searched at the right places, also impacts lifestyles. Avi maintains that besides lavish wedding celebrations, there are parties at people's own or rented farmhouses almost every weekend in New Delhi. Possibly, assuming that I would associate extreme wealth with inapproachability and snobbery, he adds: 'You can have lots of fun with rich people' (personal conversation, New Delhi, September 2007). To be sure, this is another rhetoric of distinction, through which Avi speaks of the proximity to 'the rich' and presents them as 'nice people' as if he had to challenge an often-projected view of 'the rich' as unapproachable.

When I asked Avi as to whether he thought of this wedding event boom as temporary, his answer was to the contrary. At any rate, he optimistically maintained, India would continue to shine for all those people (who invest in weddings today) at least until the Commonwealth Games in 2010 and even beyond that when the Cricket World Cup takes place in 2011; then, the Asian Games in 2014. To him this was a guarantee for constant inflow of money into a city such as New Delhi, both in forms of private and public investment, generating a superfluity of events, needs and experts.

Vijay A. from Moment Makers

Vijay A. from Moment Makers in South Delhi explains that it is only since the last two to three years that people are willing to spend so much more money for a wedding, be it on decor, food or entertainment extras. They would easily spend anything from INR 30 lakh to INR 100 crore (€5,300– 180,000). Among north Indians, Punjabis and 'Banias' would spend the most, and overseas Indians rank second.[24] Vijay wonders whether this could be due to the fact that life abroad is 'much tougher — there are no servants, and one is not used to a spectacular lifestyle' (personal conversation, New Delhi, October 2006) — but he is not sure. According to Vijay, big (or rich) clients often have "world-class" taste, also because of their exposure to the world by travelling, having friends, or living abroad: 'These kinds of people', says Vijay, 'really want to be involved in the detailed planning of their wedding, they have ideas, even if they are over the top, and expect you to fulfil them' (ibid.).

In Vijay's view, the 'big fat Indian wedding' is a trend clearly related to the phenomenon of 'India Shining'. Sitting behind a glass desk in an impressive office, with plenty of space and colour, with photographs of film and television stars performing at different occasions, Vijay explains that before this boom, there might have been a wedding brass band but hardly ever a performance by a pop singer and definitely no grand choreographies. The bride and her women guests would have danced and sung at the *sangeet* and the *mehndi* event. 'This has changed', says Vijay, 'Indians have a tendency to show off anyway, but this is so much more open now. The maximum amount people spend in India is on the wedding, a car and their house.' Weddings from the south are still more 'modest' and conservative. According to Vijay, event management at weddings derives from big corporate houses importing celebrities and stars to their functions in the late 1990s. The wedding extravaganzas of families like Sahara, Mittal and Chatwal followed this. Today, every 'good' Indian family would do at least five to seven functions per wedding. Celebrities are an important component in this chain of events. Vijay adds, with a smile, that he and his company profit from this desire to display wealth.

Vijay's company, set up in 1997 but catering towards wedding management only since a few years, specialises in both wedding entertainment

---

[24] Vijay translates 'Banias' as 'Jains'. Predominately, traders (from Gujarat) are associated with this term.

and corporate events. They organise Bollywood concerts abroad, 'item girls' (dance performers), Hindi or Punjabi pop singers, qawwalis and rock bands as well as international dance troupes with Russian belly dancers for a host of private and corporate events. For weddings, special effects such as a cage raised by a huge crane that lifts bride and groom onto the wedding stage, comedy shows, or a gala celebration with Bollywood star(let)s and other prominent figures from the television world, are roped in.

Punita S., the Private Entrepreneur

Being in control of the wedding right from the beginning is one of the wedding designer's most difficult tasks. He or she shares this responsibility with the bride who is 'tested' by the new in-laws and many relatives and friends as to whether she has the competence to become a good homemaker, daughter-in-law, wife and mother.

It is through her own joint family that Punita got into writing about wedding planning a few years ago, as she explains. The family Punita married into belongs to one of those with 'old money' — living in the most expensive part of New Delhi, in a colonial bungalow surrounded by a lush garden, guards keeping trespassers from entering the small street that leads into the residence. This family has preserved the property and confidence of a wealthy clan over generations. Every year, they host generous garden parties to celebrate the coming of summer, where a band would play, alcoholic beverages and different kinds of food are served, tables and chairs spread across the vast lawn. After she married into this large family, says Punita, there were all those marriages of other family members, and family friends, to be organised. Passionately writing down every little detail, making suggestions for improvement and alteration, Punita came up with a whole notebook about what can go wrong and what worked well at a wedding. A well-known publishing house turned the notebook into a costly, glossy coffee table book. The next book she wants to do is about making lists for holidays, shopping, birthday parties, and so forth She says: 'My motto is get organised, this makes life so much more easy!' This is quite in tune with a growing desire among consumers of any kind in India to 'do it yourself', a movement that derives from the USA and the UK and represents a trend towards creating regimes of regulation in order to avoid disorder and mistakes.

The worst outcome of this is someone wanting to be in total control of the self and the environment. There are suggestions that the control taken by women over their own or others' weddings is part of an empowerment, while the feeling of lacking control prevails in their everyday life, and the pressure of the in-laws on her to 'function' according to their expectations puts her on the verge of constant failure. This also seems to be a pheno-menon deriving from the fact that women in urbanised habitats are in-creasingly independent in terms of working and having their own income. On the verge of being married, for many, this, however, means the exemp-tion from such independent spaces. They turn into 'Bridezillas', a term coined by US-American Gail Dunson, referring to a new category of person, that of the soon-to-wed women who magnify the idea that weddings are their 'day'. The euphemism is a combination of *bride* and *Godzilla*, a mutant dinosaur of the US-sci-fi culture of the 1950s. They harass members of their family and bridal party, make greedy demands and break all rules of respect to ensure that they are the single most important persons, until they are married. The control obsession and perfectionism that drives them makes them go as far as asking overweight friends and members of family to lose weight in order not to 'spoil' the photographs!

In our conversation, Punita referred to the pressure on all family members, sometimes continuing for six months or more. People would usually have nervous breakdowns after the marriage. For the bride-to-be and her closest associates — the mother and her girl friends — this is 'her day', when she stands in the limelight, proving the appropriateness of her womanhood. Future brides often stop working up to half a year before the wedding in order to fully concentrate on the wedding preparations. In this context, Indian brides, might turn into 'bridezillas' as well for they are aware of the ritual attention given to the bride as the representative of transition. With the wedding being more a chain of events, often with particular themes, than simply a rite, the bride must be able to appear perfect in each frame. This brings me to the details of a theme wedding and its proximity to the structure of a theme park as a site at which taste and sensations are manufactured and an alternative world is shaped that generates inauthenticity as normality.

Shaping a Taste of Exotica and Erotica

The choice of subject or theme, the appropriateness of the choreography and occasion, the rules of display and performance are important for the impression management of a wedding designer, and the wedding hosts. If we follow Bourdieu (1984), both designers and customers navigate between various levels of legitimacy and repertoires of cultural goods and 'cultivated' taste. There is, for instance, what is considered to be 'high' and 'low' culture (e.g., classical music, folk performance), cosmopolitan and local fashions (e.g., dancefloor and DJ, carnival of Venice, ethnic chic), main-stream and individual taste. Stories about exotic items and spectacular choreographies of unique theme weddings circulate in many social circles in New Delhi. They evaluate as to whether a choreographic item displayed 'vulgar' or 'good' taste, and are relevant in the context of negotiating taste, value and status. Global and local imaginaries are fused, or held against each other, in order to shape or challenge cosmopolitanism.

Sushmita S., one of my friends in Delhi, told me about a wedding reception hosted at the spectacular heritage hotel Neemrana, a palace in Rajasthan.[25] By now, many theme weddings are hosted at heritage sites such as this fifteenth-century fort-palace. Through these, the bridal couple as well as the guests are provided with an experience of 'living royal past'. However, the theme of that very pre-marital event apparently was 'Moulin Rouge'. Sushmita described how the female guests appeared dressed up as if they were characters from *Moulin Rouge*, the Hollywood film that repeatedly draws upon Bollywood aesthetics and is known for its extravagant erotic accessories and decadent moral unwinding around a tragic love story (directed by Baz Luhrmann, 2001). Guests at the wedding reception in Rajasthan apparently appeared clad in such skimpy outfits and danced to the tunes of *bhangra* and western music. Even if this was just a rumour, the fact that outsiders imagine an event and its guests this way reveals the attraction of a themed wedding as a projection screen for fantasies or anxieties such as the moral panic about a class losing its purported chastity. In this context, we can argue with Liechty that 'a fundamental part of the middle-class cultural project is precisely to *circulate* these tales of modern propriety and impropriety' (2003: 251).

As we could see so far, mundane and spiritual both offer themselves for exploitation to the world of entertainment, especially if they explore the grey zone between love and sexuality. Vijay A. from Moment Makers tells me what his most impressively managed event was:

> Clearly this year's highlight was spiritual wedding theme. We staged the performance of two television stars enacting Radha and Krishna accompanied by eighty classical dancers depicting various *raslila* dances on five stages that surrounded the key stage.[26] The Vedas were recited by 111 pandits, along with 21 *shankh* [conch] players in specially tailored dresses. The dancers played Holi with 400 kg of loose rose petals (personal conversation, New Delhi, October 2006).[27]

---

[25] Neemrana is an exclusive initiative that restores heritage sites all over India, clearly responding to the thriving tourist and event industry in India and abroad. See also Menon (2005: 116–19).

[26] Today, Radha and Krishna are the idealised divine forms of the erotic couple and romantic love.

[27] Holi is a major north Indian festival celebrated with colours and often with worship of Hindu deities Krishna and Radha.

Less spectacular themes in terms of the narrative but nevertheless simi-larly grand sites and details, through which the idea of being special and global imaginaries are communicated, find entrance into wedding man-agement. *Mehndi* ceremonies, where female guests and bride traditionally get together before the wedding and have their hands and feet delicately painted with *mehndi*, turn into ceremonies combining 'Madonna-inspired tattoos, tarot card reading and lounge atmosphere' (Atul L., personal conversation, New Delhi, January 2007).[28] 'Mexican theme' events present swing doors, horse saddles, a bar, guns and rifles, plenty of tequila bottles, painted cacti on the walls and service staff wearing ponchos and straw hats. The 'Goa theme' could have palm trees, fishing nets, food counters as boats, and a Hawaiian dress code. Wedding designer Nitin Raichura recre-ates Roman palaces and Egyptian pyramids for some customers (see Menon 2007: 32). Moreover, wedding event management can involve wedding themes such as 'Temples of India' (complemented by Indian drums and ritual chants of pandits), 'floral themes' (where an elegant trio or quartet provides classical western music), 'Royal Victorian theme' (with a pianist), 'Prince Edward theme' (accompanied, interestingly, by jazz music).[29] These eclectic geographies are used to tickle the guest's senses at cocktail party functions. Opinions about the popularity of certain themes, however, vary from one wedding designer to another, with Rajasthan ranking highest in popularity.

If a customer is not interested in renting an actual (but expensive) site such as a palace, stage-sets are often used instead. One man, recalls Avi A. from Aumweddings, had the White House in Washington D.C. replicated in his farm in South Delhi, for the wedding of his daughter. Furthermore, Avi tells me that high pavilions upto two floors can be built by his designers and engineers. The most interesting design to him, in this context, was that of the 'Heaven and Hell'. The customers wanted the guests to walk into hell, situated on the ground floor, where alcoholic drinks were served and cigarettes could be smoked, accompanied by club and belly dancing. Heaven was located upstairs, where the invitee would find himself or herself surrounded by light, statues of Hindu deities, and classical music, in 'a spiritual setting' (Avi A., personal conversation, New Delhi, September 2006). Again, this would not be used at the auspicious wedding ceremony

---

[28] *Mehndi* is a thick henna paste which, after having been kept on the skin for several hours, leaves dark tattoo-like traces on the skin.

[29] See http://www.soundofmusicindia.com/themes_concepts.html (accessed 1 August 2007).

but for the more flexible reception or engagement. Avi further recalls a pavilion decorated in 'Egyptian style' for an Egyptian theme party. All the waiters and dancers were dressed up as pharaohs, and guests had to climb up an artificial pyramid to reach the bar in order to get a drink.

These examples underline the playful and mimetic alterations of foreign and exotic elements into 'aboriginal cosmopolitan rhetoric'. Can we call this 'vulgar cosmopolitanism' because, as so many critics of such mass spectacles argue, this is not any better than high tourism in Goa, Phuket or Mallorca? I refrain from answering this question, even though it seems important to point out the heterogeneity of the concept of cosmopolitanism and its accessibility to a wide range of aspirants to the 'world-class'. A similar pastiche method of cutting and pasting has already been explored in the context of residential housing advertisements in Chapter 4 of this book, when the concept of 'Punjabi Baroque' is discussed, as a means of symbolic status accumulation.

Pre- and Post-Marital Pleasures and Fears

Consumer exhibitions and fairs as well as the print lifestyle media are important sites at which taste is shaped and status negotiated for important ritual events like weddings. The consumer market is the key playground at which pleasures, and fears (of failing), related to weddings are tested and generated. Economic liberalisation has had a major impact on this domain. It is no longer an exception to see foreign luxury brands wooing Indian customers, in particular, at sites where special events such as weddings are advertised. Celebrating Vivaha, for instance, is a bridal exhibition held annually in New Delhi, where Indian fashion designers can be found next to cosmetic brands by Christian Dior, tourist banners from India as well as travel agencies from Australia, Switzerland and Malaysia offer exotic wedding and honeymoon destinations, and shops feature the latest wedding gift: chocolates from Luxemburg. Wedding planners and shows like Bridal Asia or Celebrating Vivaha are so successful that they are now exported to countries with strong South Asian communities, for instance, the USA, the UK and the Middle East (in India often referred to as 'West Asia').[30]

For three consecutive days I conducted participatory observation and informal interviews at Bridal Asia, one of the largest themed consumer

---

[30] In 2004, *Celebrating Vivaha* hosted 80 Indian and international brands and was visited by more than 120,000 people. Transactions worth INR 6 crore (c. €105,000) were made at the exhibition (see Trehan 2004).

fairs on wedding fashion, jewellery and other designed luxury items, hosted at a five star hotel in New Delhi in January 2006. Predominantly, mothers visited the show with their daughters and brides-to-be, as well as girlfriends. Rarely would a male member of the family or even the fiancé accompany his partner. Bridal Asia is only one of several events through which the new lifestyles of the new middle classes are marketed and, in fact, constituted because they are made available for consumption and imagination, and where taste and etiquette feature centrally. Here, I refer to the definition of consumption as a creative engagement and Erlebnis, not just as passive reception. It is here where the performance of cultural capital is, and thus I heard conversations about what to wear for the Rajasthani theme-reception and who could be wearing what and how to stand out by wearing something 'different'. At such an occasion, invited guests as well as brides-to-be can start imagining and getting a feel of the 'real' event, where outfits are tried out, ideas are collected, budgets made and one's personal taste is acclimatise with the latest fashion. Pre-wedding shopping is a central social occasion, mainly for the bride and her family and friends. Even from abroad, mothers and daughters come to major cities like New Delhi to shop for the wedding, at the Karol Bagh market, Sarojini Nagar, Lajpat Nagar or Old Delhi, to mention just a few. They do so, on the one hand, because the range of choice is much wider and the prices lower than in the West. On the other hand, this is a consumption and holiday trip for female members of the family that allows them to bond once again before the daughter leaves the household.

The new infrastructure responds quickly and the consumer fairs and bridal magazines are but two domains in which this becomes obvious. In this context, themed shopping malls related to weddings have also emerged. The message in the colour brochure of the Omaxe 'Wedding Mall', India's first theme mall reads:

> Marriages have always been an important part of the Indian way of life. Symbolising the auspicious merging of two destinies, in a way it's a grand celebration of life itself. In our culture, a wedding has always been an occasion for a mega-celebration. But the last few years have seen it growing exponentially in its sheer scape and extent. The reasons are not too far to seek. Fuelled by a formidable spending power and exposure to international lifestyle trends, Indians are getting more and more imaginative when it comes to organising a wedding. No more is it a household affair, managed by the others. From wedding planners to theme marriages, it has travelled full circle ... It's time for the Wedding Mall.

Furthermore, a sales manager at Omaxe explains that the mall will feature a honeymoon tour operator, decor specialists, floral arrangements, service providers for printing wedding cards, wedding bands, ladies *sangeet*, *pujas*, beauty and slimming centres, a banquet hall for weddings, completely catering to pre- and post-wedding needs (Sanjeev S., personal conversation, New Delhi, October 2005).

The expanding and eclectic consumption economy spills over into weddings of the middle classes where bridal magazines teach wedding hosts to organise return gifts and souvenirs for the guests and the weddings guests to treat the bride and the groom with a 'special surprise'. Once again, cosmopolitanism can be claimed in the mixing of the exotic, neo colonial and national folklore. Wedding planner Tarun tells me that wedding websites on the Internet and bridal magazines advertise wooden African masks, Raja–Rani sets, Victorian-style book marks, rustic baskets with sweets (ranging from INR 100 to 5,000) for the hosts who wished to gift and embroidered bags, porcelain statues of Hindu deities, French shepardesses (starting from INR 1,000), framed pictures, usually gold-plated, of saints, gods and so forth, for the guests who might want to gift the couple.

Bridal magazines are not just about shopping, preparations and the celebration of the wedding day. They also introduce the urban bride and groom to tabooed themes such as lovemaking, impotency and jealousy. Some even advise the bride to get pre-marital sex counselling; others suggest 'outdoor sex' and 'sex in the shower', if the first attraction has paled.[31] In the chaos of wedding preparations and family negotiations, the desires and fears of the married couple are usually marginalised. These have in fact not really mattered much until recently, unless with respect to reproduction. Intimacy, romance, pleasure and trust, are largely talked about only since economic liberalisation. The issues are addressed by conservative bridal and lifestyle magazines, sometimes with a surprising openness (Plates 12.7 and 12.8).[32]

As several authors, in particular, Patricia Uberoi (2006), have shown, these magazines also familiarise the future bride with possible hiccups after marriage. While the general message to the young women is 'how to learn to adjust' as a daughter-in-law and wife, or how to keep the romance going by means of affection, compromise and understanding, anxieties and problems are discussed too (Uberoi 2006: 217–47).

---

[31] 'Steam up your Sex Life', *Wedding Affair*, 2008, 9(6): 158–59.

[32] Not much scholarly literature has been published on the topic of sexuality in India (leaving aside Shobhaa De's novels); see Dwyer (2000, 2006); Kakar (1989); Orsini (2006).

Plate 12.7: Staged intimacy: Designer wear brand Diwan Saheb's advertisement projecting the wedding night as a relaxed, friendly event (2005).

Central themes are aphrodisiacs as well as means of contraception, childlessness, coping with giving up work after marriage and infidelity.[33] The themes addressed in the print media show how closely changing habits, lifestyles, gender-roles, consumption and morals are intertwined. How what is availed and spoken of is really translated into people's lives, is another issue. In other words, for sex on the sofa one needs a sofa and solitude, for love at the beach one needs to afford a trip to Thailand, and so on. Intimacy as a quality factor of marriage is a new concept. It introduces the notion that the pleasure of being together, of getting to know each other, as a ceaseless process of self-discovery, and looking after more than two families, children and a household are subjects that have moved into lifestyle magazines. Moreover, the element of erotic stimulation and pleasure within a marriage allows for a new language of romance. It moves beyond what Sanjay Srivastava (2009) has termed 'footpath pornography' (in the context of the affluent middle classes to be complemented by

---

[33] See, for instance *Celebrating Vivaha* 3(3), 2002. Pre-marital counselling is available in megacities like Delhi. Singles can talk and inform themselves about sexuality, career, family planning or even breaking-up. Clinical psychologists and marriage counsellors offer the service with offices in modern hospitals like the Escorts and Max Healthcare.

Plate 12.8: Erotic underwear (2006).

Source: *Indiawali Brides*, October–November, p. 97.

glossy erotic magazines) or what author Shobhaa De has thematised time and again in her novels on extramarital love affairs, underlining the often raised assumption that marriage is for reproduction and affairs are for real pleasure. Today, formerly exotic (and erotic) luxury goods are more easily available and expand the consumer market in India. But if we believe the vernacular and English press, the ease with which problems and pleasures of marital sexual lives are addressed, does not mirror in the everyday lives of those actually involved.

The Difference between 'Old' and 'New' Taste

One designer of exclusive wedding costumes at Bridal Asia related the following to me when I asked her about the role the slogan of 'India Shining' has played in the rise of conspicuous consumption and celebration of wealth, even among the middle classes: 'We know how to sell ourselves better now. But you must understand that India has *always* been shining, not only now!' Actually, it did not become clear what kind of 'shining' she referred to until she differentiated between those people who come to inherit money over generations, and in tandem, are 'cultured'. These are the so-called 'old rich', anxious about drawing clear borders between themselves and the aspiring middle classes. In their eyes, these 'parvenus' fall behind in good taste and etiquette. Moreover, those 'old rich' people will know how to *celebrate* a wedding and the 'new rich' can only *perform* it. Quite a few wedding event designers affirmed this impression in conversation. (For the 'old rich', for instance, serving alcohol was never a problem because they belonged to a cosmopolitan class where drinking was not necessarily associated with unsophisticated behaviour or a lack of a particular kind of cultural capital.) So how are distinctions made between the 'new rich' and the 'old rich' when it comes to weddings?

Vulgarity is a key characteristic for which both the aspiring middle classes as well as the old rich blame each other. But, vulgarity is relational, as Liechty remarks:

> What constitutes this sense of middle-classness is not necessarily a common lifestyle or a uniform set of values but rather a shared project of locating oneself in a new and legitimate space between two devalued social poles. This space is one separated both from the 'vulgar' lives of the national elite ... and from a lower class trapped in equally vulgar lifestyles of 'tradition' and poverty ... The experience of middle-classness lies in this uneasy relationship with 'the modern', one of both emulation and distancing (2003: 67).

This indicates that the new middle classes claim to be within the limits of taste and suitability while the upper class and the lower class do not. Top down, many comments are made about the fact that the aspiring classes go beyond the limits of taste by imitating the rich and famous unprofessionally, just to show off. Even though to some extent, this might be true, then why is the decadent display of wealth among the elite not criticised? Barbara Kirshenblatt-Gimblett argues:

> [t]aste distinguishes those who make the distinctions. This is what makes bad taste so coherent as a category. Indeed, it is a mark of good taste — part of its mystification — that, according to the etiquette books, it never calls attention to itself except in the breach (1998: 260).

This classification is reflected in the following example from my ethnographic field. Instead of a forcefully 'special' and often pompous wedding, Punita S. promotes the concept of the simple 'home wedding ceremony' without consulting a professional wedding event-manager:

> This is an approach I have taken voluntarily. It's about going back to 'the olden days', where there is love, warmth, care. All this is sidelined when a wedding designer is appointed even for the ceremony at home. The important thing of a wedding is that everybody has to be involved; this brings the family together, once again. You have to make them feel how important the wedding is and their involvement in it. Today, a lot of unhappiness is leveraged. Love is getting lost (personal conversation, New Delhi, January 2007).

Punita's underlined suggestion associated with the comment that the 'old rich' discover the 'deep' meaning of a 'simple' wedding (which possibly still means spending a lot but not showing it) is that the 'new rich' do not have the competence to be modest and thus hide that they are 'climbers'. Her idealisation of the bondedness of families in 'olden days' reveals at once a nostalgic and a romantic gaze as well as an element of patronising dogma.

The rhetoric of nostalgia has a very pragmatic and mundane reason: moral distinction. On the one hand, the ability not to show off, to restrain oneself from conspicuous consumption, is a strategy of the social elite. To control one's material wealth means that one is a step ahead of those people who inherit wealth and must show it. On the other hand, the nostalgic emphasis on an imagined past, the 'olden days', might be better understood in the context of the seemingly growing upward mobility of members of lower castes and classes due to economic liberalisation and implementation of reservation politics that led to a politicisation and increasing confidence of social movements. This upward mobility that started to take off in the late-1980s, challenges the monopolies of high caste Indians and other elites.

The other side of the coin is that the new rich imitate the old rich in a way that sometimes blurs the two as if they were equals. However, the 'old rich' were not particularly keen on being identified with the 'new rich' and did not recognise the cultural capital of the new rich. Thus, the demand to return to 'simplicity' has strong moral undertones and can at least to some extent be explained in Kirshenblatt-Gimblett's thoughts about the relationship between taste, status and distinction: 'The civilizing process is directed towards self-restraint' (1998: 261). This means, according to the rules of the 'old rich', and in order to remain different from the aspiring middle classes, financial capital must be paired with cultural capital. Kirshenblatt-Gimblett even suggests avoiding using the dichotomy of 'good taste' and 'bad taste' and replacing it with 'classic' and 'grotesque': 'the grotesque is about paradox, ambivalence, mixture'; it is potentially dangerous and thus has to be distanced (ibid.: 264–65). Good or classic taste is imbued with moral attitudes, clarity, truth and honesty: 'Good taste is cultural capital masquerading as the natural attribute of an elite' (ibid.: 278). It is largely in this context that we must understand Punita's appeal to simplicity, where social distinctions emerge as moral distinctions.

The chapter explored how central life-cycle rituals such as weddings have come to be transformed into an industry based on economic liberalisation and the emergence of aspiring middle classes who aim at marking status, distinction and culture. Weddings have become celebrations of conspicuous consumption, and a means of what Mazzarella has termed 'progress through pleasure'; the duty of the post-Fordist citizen is less to produce and more to consume. As an aspect of theming life(style), the wedding is a highly structured event through which consumption and experiences are fetishised and controlled. The themed wedding foregrounds leisure and the wedding rite is turned into an item within this choreography.

The notion of the cosmopolitan is constituted through one's ability to 'stage the world' in one event, through playful mimesis, to impress by citing from a range of visual and performative registers that prove one's cultural competence and taste. For this, specialists are needed, for instance, wedding planners, who have the task to coordinate increasingly more expansive events and ensure that the appropriate means are selected in order to impress. However, the case-study has also explored how class distinctions are made along the basis of 'failed' displays of taste (vulgarity), of moralistic undertones as to the selection of themes, and a turn towards snobbery through recalling simplicity that is packaged as 'back to the olden days of a simple wedding'. This way, control and discipline of the modern society are enforced through the lens of cultural heritage and pleasure as duty.

'all you need is wellness' and a good body

> For a bride, her wedding day is like walking the red carpet. It's her big moment, when countless eyes are watching her every move. And every bride wants to look her absolute best. But reaching that stage requires preparation and dedication. Because you don't want your audience, much less the bridegroom, to notice flabby arms, dark circles under the eyes or love handles (Srinivasa 2007).

This quote from *Savy*, a lifestyle magazine, bridges the gap between the wedding and the beauty or fitness industries, underlining how closely these are connected and how much pressure is exerted on aspiring candidates in terms of performance and the fear of losing credibility. The beautiful and the fit body have moved to the centre stage in the feel-good ideology promoted in neoliberal urban India. The first time I encountered the passion and disgust aligned with the physical body (not the divine!) of worldly India was in 1996, when the first Miss World contest was hosted in the country and became a contested issue in various media (Butcher 2003; Runkle 2004). A highly moral debate was led about the commodification of the female body, the question as to whether the display of so much skin was not blasphemic, and whether the ideal Indian body should really look like the ones of the thin Indian models.

A survey on the debates and publications on gender concepts and market economies in South Asia is beyond the scope of the discussion here (see Fernandes 2006; Osella and Osella 2006; Oza 2006). Since 1996, whenever I have visited Delhi for fieldwork, the wellness and beauty industry seem to have boomed remarkably, manifest in the rising numbers of fitness centres, golf courses, wellness centres such as day spas, spirituality, beauty and wellness fairs and health and beauty magazines. Both men and women of the new urban middle classes show a great concern with being up to the latest standard of wellness programmes and physical fitness. While Lodhi Gardens in South Delhi used to be a place where romantic couples went for a walk, and families enjoyed a day out with a picnic on the lawns of the heritage site, nowadays the park is flooded with power-walkers and joggers of all age groups at sunset and in the mornings. Wellness-gurus have combined the idea of the body as a temple with that as a signifier of affluent, beautiful lifestyle and happiness. The need to appear well-groomed and physically attractive has assumed greater importance in the last decade, not just for women, but for men as well. The thin body has replaced the plump, round body, previously identified with wealth. A beautiful body is now a happy body. Beauty, thus, is part of a moral discourse revolving around the experience of modernity (Munshi 2001).

The dynamics and demands of modern life cause more people to turn towards professionals for treatments that improve and maintain their physical looks. The beauty business is one of the fastest growing industries in India, with a growth rate of 25 per cent, with the herbal and ayurvedic industry even growing at 40 per cent. Part of the growth is indebted to the media coverage and event management of Miss India and Miss World contests since the late-1990s. International attention has come to focus on India as a country of authentic heritage and beauty. At the same time, the notion of global beauty standards have created controversial but influential debates about female features and virtues that emerge when a global 'world' standard and a national(ist) register meet. One key attention has been to communicate that the Indian woman can be both chaste and sexually seductive.[1] Here, as Reddy argues: '"The beautiful" exists as a space of social mobility, of ascendancy into a leisure class' (2006: 66), in which middle-class women in particular have to bridge the wide gap between being at once a symbol of sacrifice and of progress, of being an attractive bride, housewife, dedicated homemaker and a financially independent and career-oriented businesswoman. Furthermore, on the level of representation, we find a discourse in which orientalism and occidentalism are played out against each other in such a way that they almost overlap by means of mimicry.

Another booming industry is that of wellness. In many ways, it overlaps with the beauty industry but not in all respects. The fact that today even a state or central government can profit from the boom of the wellness industry by taxing and patenting it, has led to the promotion of new infrastructure of 'indigenous' health and medicine, based on yoga, ayurveda, homeopathy and so forth. A government initiative in 2005 constituted a committee of yoga experts researching and classifying yoga positions

---

[1] In her exploration of the iconography of women in the women and lifestyle magazine *Femina*, Reddy argues that a particular Hindu middle-class consumer identity is celebrated (2006: 64; see also Oza 2006; Mazzarella 2003; Munshi 2001 and Rajagopal 2001b).

across India, going back to the ancient scriptures. This initiative sought to prevent non-Indians or even Indians overseas from monopolising and abusing indigenous knowledge and practices and making profit without acknowledging the intellectual and cultural copyright 'India' holds on these resources and forms of capital. More than a decade ago, this would have been unthinkable. However, in the light of the profit-gaining wellness and spirituality market, the perspective has changed. The same holds true of the awareness of symbolic and cultural capital among middle and upper classes. Some argue that the growth in the wellness market in India is four-dimensional and comes from changes in consumers' lifestyle, their desire for better health, and their desire to avoid high costs of illness as well as the importance of healthy food. At the same time, middle-class Indians are exposed to fast food culture and multicultural cuisine coming from the West. Obesity, even among children, has come to be a big issue within the new and established middle classes. The new codes and regulations for a 'good life' appeal to specific forms of physical and mental wellness and beauty. Even though they are presented as 'natural' and 'liberalising', I argue that at least to some extent, they reflect the panoptic gaze of the emerging pleasure-driven disciplinary society.

Inner and Outer Beauty

With respect to beauty care, external beauty care and internal wellness must be differentiated, even though the two seem to overlap at times. The beauty parlour, a ubiquitous institution of the old and the new middle classes, falls under the first category. In order to underline the shifts taking place through the more recent introduction of the wellness or spa centre, it is necessary to take a look at the beauty parlour first. An institution that can be traced back to the 1970s, it can be found even in small towns and is a common means of beautifying middle-class women, preparing them for ritual occasions such as a special festival or a wedding, where the hair is done up, and the body of the bride treated with oil, turmeric and henna. But the parlour also functions for the regular, more mundane manicure, treatment of skin and hair, where even a massage is possible. Despite the fact that there are very different kinds of beauty parlours in terms of size, price and customers, the most common parlour is primarily made up of one room, either located in a residential area or a small bazaar, often simply separated from the pavement or street outside by a curtain or a door with tinted glass. Waiting and served customers are usually seated in the same room and are entertained by means of film or lifestyle magazines or even a small television screen showing film songs. For many women, the classical local beauty parlour serves as a social centre too, where they gather and exchange news, where they are among themselves, in a family-free space, where weddings can be envisaged and criticised, husbands and mothers-in-law cribbed about, and so forth. Many women know each other here, and as one owner of a beauty parlour at South Delhi's Khan Market tells me:

> At home, these women are normally not listened to. Here, they feel that they're being taken serious and they appreciate that. They can talk about their husbands, in-laws, marriage preparations or a show they have watched on TV (Sonia L., personal conversation, October 2005).

In some ways, then, a beauty parlour is also a wellness centre for the psyche insofar as most customers also come to communicate and engage with each other. Depending on the location, treatments are usually tailored for the purses of the lower middle classes, with a hair cut costing around INR 150–400 (€3–7.50).[2]

Interestingly, the parameters are still the same in the context of the relatively recent emergence of the wellness industry. Yet, several things are distinctly different. The spa and wellness culture, too, underlines particularly upper class women's desire to treat themselves to something special and acknowledge their own needs and desires. But it emphasises exclusiveness, 'world-class' standards, and contemplative atmosphere with meditation music for relaxation, individual seclusion rather than group entertainment, Bollywood film music and everyday conversations.

Miriya C., former employee of a five star wellness hotel close to the sacred city of Rishikesh in the Himalayas, and now independent entrepreneur dealing with traditional perfume essences, proposes that the difference lies in the emphasis on 'external' beauty in beauty parlours (that cater, to a large extent, to middle classes and lower middle classes) and that on 'internal' beauty' in the spa. In her view, this recent concern with inner beauty is linked to a new status consciousness and many upper-class women would consider a beauty parlour as 'ordinary' and 'low class'. In their case, the beautician would be asked to come home or they would visit one of the exquisite beauty parlours in a five star hotel. A spa or wellness club, offers a new experience for men and women who care about belonging to class and are willing to pay at least five times more for half-a-day than an

---

[2] The monthly salary of an employee in a beauty parlour is only around INR 3,000 (c. €54). Nowadays, women of the affluent middle classes get special training at institutes such as VLCC after which they might aspire to a sufficiently higher salary.

all-round treatment at a beauty parlour. Wellness clubs are marketed with the label of holistic lifestyle and international, or 'world-class' quality. They can be found at five star hotels, exclusive malls or affluent neighbourhoods.

Interestingly, Miriya maintains, yoga, ayurveda and aromatherapy once left India through the backdoor, 'because nobody was interested in this "old-fashioned" stuff. Middle-class people were even embarrassed about these practices, as much as they were about Bollywood films'. They were first carried and imported to Europe and the Americas by western and Indian health 'gurus' in the 1970s and 1980s. In the late 1990s, they returned to India, through the front door. Upon their successful arrival, yoga and ayurveda were celebrated and further marketed as exclusively 'Indian' items and heritage export goods, as if they had never left their homeland.

> The bane of a developing country like India is that it's not very confident about itself, resulting in blind imitation of the West. We didn't wake up to the beneficial properties of ayurveda or meditation till the West acknowledged it. The East has always served as a powerhouse of knowledge and wisdom to the world, while the West has packaged and marketed, and actually popularized the Eastern knowledge with immense success (Bharat Thakur, in Nair and Sharma 2005: 3).

This statement by yoga practitioner and author Bharat Thakur reflects the idea of an on-going colonisation, which is certainly legitimate in the context of issues such as genetically modified seeds for agriculture. Moreover, it is imbued with a simplified and orientalist dichotomy of the 'West' as the aggressive agent and the 'East' as the passive victim. Finally, this victimisation is aimed at being counter-balanced by a nationalist undertone that foregrounds cultural difference, as opposed to highlighting entanglements and transculturality, by essentialising the 'West' as superior in terms of exploitation and the 'East' as superior in terms of spiritual knowledge. Sri Sri Ravi Shankar, spiritual leader of AOL, makes similar homogenising and essentialist claims about the centrality of thought in ancient 'Indian society' as he maintains (and he is not alone in doing so):

> We have a very long tradition of wellness. Our association with wellness has been intertwined with our evolution as a society. Also, we have a very deep philosophy in this country which is unparalleled (Jacob 2005).

Let us return to the beauty parlour for further differentiation of the various concepts of beauty, also to show that the stereotypes just mentioned do not hold credible in this light. The Indian beauty parlour is, argues Miriya, not necessarily related to a modern and western beauty concept.

Along with its social function, it has a more pragmatic, 'corpothetic' side without a focus on stimulating all the senses and enhancing the long-lasting comfort of the soul. The senses of smell and touch are not considered as particularly important for the treatment. In the context of spas, however, smell, meditative music, silence, touch and aroma are absolutely crucial.

Miriya argues that women who went to the beauty parlour did not do it to *feel* good but to *look* good, to show beautiful features, for special occasions. Nowadays, she maintains, the celebration of the *beautiful self* — beyond the surface has moved increasingly to the centre stage — at least in rhetoric. There is an interesting twist in the emphasis on 'feeling' and 'looking' good. The first relates to a subjective awareness of one's own self. This is particularly relevant for the shaping of personal identity. The latter is pointed towards fetishisation for an external beholder, most probably the gaze of the husband, or a wedding party.

The borders between the beauty parlour and the spa and wellness culture are not very clear. Much more research must go into this public/private domain in which gender identities, notions of health and the body are constituted. However, some examples will underline the shifts and parallels between the two in the early days of the beauty industry in India. Here, I shall focus on three women who made it big by marketing beauty and identity for the affluent middle class and elite Indians in the country and overseas. One of them, Shahnaz Husain, is a brand in herself, an institution in the Indian world of beauty and womanhood. Husain can be considered the 'grand dame' of wellness culture in India, opening up an international market of external beauty and herbal care business. Husain is known for having said: 'I do not sell products. I sell an entire civilization in a jar'. She set out with a beauty salon in her private house in Delhi in 1977 and has since then been a trendsetter as regards beauty parlours and now ayurvedic massage salons. In 2002, the Shahnaz Husain Group, based in New Delhi, was worth $100 million. It employed about 4,200 people in 650 salons spread across 104 countries. In 1996, Husain opened an ayurvedic centre (for the upper class). Other representatives of the 'new woman' are Blossom Kochhar and Vandana Luthra. Kochhar, an entrepreneur who set up a chain of beauty parlours in north India in the late-1980s, contributed to the re-import of the concept of aromatherapy to India. Vandana Luthra started her beauty empire Vandana Luthra Curls and Curves (VLCC) in 1989 in South Delhi and now runs fitness 'factories', day spas, health food cafes and beauty schools in India and abroad.[3]

---

[3] Here, people can be trained to become photo or movie stylists, hair colour or perm specialists, cosmetology instructors, image consultants and product distributors.

Marketing the Pleasure of Wellness

As of today, despite the differing institutions of the beauty parlour and the wellness centre, physical wellness and spiritual wellness are largely marketed together, as they are everywhere in the world, and find enthusiastic response among both middle-class housewives and businesswomen.

This is also related to the intensified circulation of (and access to) global ideas and images of beauty and a good life. Before economic liberalisation in 1991, there was one major Indian beauty brand, Lakmé. Whenever people went abroad, they would bring western goods back with them, mostly as an affirmation of their cosmopolitan status. With television, new western brands became available in the media domain and in specialised shops (Butcher 1999, 2003). Today, the market has opened up a space for choice, new desires and beauty concepts. The development of the spa resort is an interesting case to look at in this context. The spa resort is a status-related space for privileged women. As opposed to the beauty parlour, the spa requires customers to spend at least one day under the supervision of specialists of all kinds. According to Miriya C., this privilege is marked by the confidence of a woman to say, 'I need that time for myself', without being stigmatised as abnormally individualistic. Having worked at the first Indian spa hotels in the late-1990s, Miriya explains that 'this kind of looking for one's self by going to a spa does not necessarily have to show at the surface. It is rather a part of a whole idea of lifestyle and status, a part of a larger search for one's well-being'.

Miriya laughs as she admits that before spiritual wellness became a key foundation of lifestyle designs by the upper and aspiring middle classes in the early years of the new millennium, people would not even consider talking openly about yoga, aromatherapy or ayurvedic massage. It was considered an 'ordinary' habit practised in particular by members of the older generation who used to do their *pranam*, or *surya pranam* (meditation techniques) on the terrace of their apartment or in a park early in the morning. With a few exceptions, this was practised without reference to 'great masters' or gurus. The marketing of spiritual personalities such as Baba Ramdev or Sri Sri Ravi Shankar had not yet begun. To a great extent, spiritual television programmes and religious channels like Aastha contributed to this new form of connecting wellness as status and prestige to such gurus who were able to bridge the desire for a cosmopolitan spirituality with physical health and financial wealth.

In the beginning, the concept of spiritual wellness at a five star spa resort like Ananda in Rishikesh, where Miriya worked, sold at the domestic level only because it had been successful at the international level first. While in

the year 2000, about 70 per cent of the customers at Ananda were international tourists and business people, today's balance is equal, if not lean-
ing more towards the domestic side. When Ananda, a converted palace
of a local maharaja, opened in 1999, Miriya narrates, the sacred town of
Rishikesh by the river Ganga, close to Haridwar, was not at all a marketable
site. Not many members of the affluent middle classes and the upper
classes were interested in going to yoga *ashrams* for meditation because the
city was associated with dirt and dust, with uncomfortable and low-key
accommodation and no 'world-class' facilities. Spirituality and wellness
had still not been converted into a lifestyle market commodity. Only by
means of inviting international and domestic media persons to stay at the
new hotel for free and report about Ananda did the 'wave' slowly take
up momentum. For quite some time, Ananda was the only five star hotel
in Uttaranchal. Today, many *ashrams* have upgraded their facilities and
even offer air-conditioned rooms for affluent guests. International yoga
festivals are hosted annually and pilgrimage as such has become more
comfortable.

The concept of the spa resort goes back to the turn of the century, where
health resorts ('Kurorte') like Baden-Baden in Germany offered hot springs,
healthy air, relaxation and medical treatment for the upper segments of
societies in Europe, be they from Russia, France, Austria or elsewhere.
The notion of spiritual and physical relaxation and rejuvenation is a new
addition to this old concept. Why did this change take place? Miriya proposes that such concepts are doing well now, worldwide and in India,
because lifestyles are so hectic, and even family holidays are stressful for
some people. Altogether, the idea of going on a holiday, i.e., an activity
confined to leisure, is new among the middle classes in India. One might
have set out for a pilgrimage but to go somewhere just to 'relax' and sit
idle was an unconventional thought and practice, as much as the idea of
solitude examined in Part I of this book.

Leisure and consumption come in tandem. Spa customers have to be
willing to pay: in 2009, the cost for a double deluxe room for one day at
Ananda was US$490 plus. With a recommended standard stay of five to
seven days, this adds up to US$ 2,500–3,500 per person. This basic rate
includes yoga, walks, sightseeing in Rishikesh, teachings about ayurvedic
cooking by the chef himself and lectures about lifestyle changes. There is
also a spa consultation; the director welcomes the guests with an
introduction to the concept of Ananda; customer's programmes are tailored
to individual needs, depending on whether the primary interest is to lose
weight, relax from work and everyday hassles, or improve one's inner and
outer beauty. However, despite the fact that almost a week is necessary to

gain utmost profit from the visit in terms of relaxation and rejuvenation, most Indians, says Miriya, stay for only two to three days, mostly weekends. Her guess is that after five days, most customers would not know what to do any more and get bored. To them, leisure means going to shopping malls, nightclubs or bars, in short, to be entertained. But this kind of stimulation cannot be found at Ananda and even in Rishikesh, at a one-day excursion site for pilgrims from Haridwar or hippies to hang out with gurus in the various *ashrams*. So why should guests at the spa pay for boredom (solitude)?! For a few years, Ananda had no clocks and televisions in the rooms, and did not permit the consumption of alcohol or cigarettes. Now all this has been introduced in hotel rooms following customers' requests. Meal portions were small, due to health reasons. Miriya recalls that people would complain time and again, asking her and other members of the staff why they had to pay so much money if they got 'so little' in return, and if there was so little to do, there should at least be enough food. Furthermore, male guests, often on a business trip, would often expect that sex workers were included in the overall concept of their personal wellness, especially since Ananda offered 'Thai massage'.

It took Ananda almost four years until people in India started appreciating the concept of 'less is more' and that the quality of the place as an environment was what mattered. One difference with the traditional beauty parlour is in fact that people employed in spas and wellness centres undergo special training for customer care and friendliness as part of a marketing strategy. This is something not necessarily expected and delivered in a beauty parlour, where functionality and pragmatism provide good but fast service. The usual way of making a customer feel good in a parlour was to allow her to 'release steam', to gossip, and so forth. 'At the spa, one is king or queen for a day, and treated accordingly', says Miriya, 'and employees fall over themselves to please you'. Service-orientedness certainly is a crucial element of global lifestyles as is the conscious marketing of Indian heritage as an exotic selling point to both international and domestic customers. This is underlined in the following quote from an Ananda advertisement:

> The first Indian spa, Ananda, located in Rishikesh at the sacred river Ganges … brought an Indian concept to the Indian people. It was marketed as a spiritual spa, and sold itself as a place where one could experience something essentially exotic, new and yet 'indigenous'. Set in the palace estate of the Maharaja of Tehri Garhwal, it offers a 'healing-heritage experience'; meditation areas, yoga pavilions, hydrotherapy rooms, etc.[4]

---

[4] See www.anandaspa.com (accessed 17 February 2007).

The relevance of theming also becomes evident in this domain. But who cares about such a deluxe model of wellness? The feel-good factor at a spa like Ananda is clearly evident in the social groups that visit the place: besides work professionals from managerial levels of various business sectors, husbands may send their wives, paying them for a special treat, something equivalent to a shopping event, proposes Geeta M., a middle-class housewife and informant from Delhi. Surprisingly, not many Ananda guests would treat Rishikesh as a pilgrimage site even though quite a few guests use the opportunity to visit the river Ganga at Haridwar for a bath in the sacred waters or use the tourist bus to attend an evening arati by the river, listen to the *bhajans* and return to the spa for dinner. Miriya also points out the upper middle class concept of 'bonding karenge', of grooming bonds that might be neglected in everyday life. For instance, mothers visit the spa resorts with their daughters; and children invite their parents for a weekend trip, as a gift. The gift is the bonding, as well as the time spent together at the site. Thus, in many ways, the spa is perceived as a way to lead a 'better and beautiful life', to have a time out and away from everyday life, 'to be'.[5]

In 2004, after she had been stationed at a branch of the Oberoi chain in Mumbai, and after getting married, Miriya decided that the service sector was not her way of life. She resigned from her job, despite a reasonable salary and recognition from co-workers and guests. She chose to be independent and in charge of her own schedule, to use some of her previously established connections with other service providers and even colleagues, and the opportunities given by the new economy's growth. With a lot of effort and care, Miriya set up her own small business, creating a brand of natural aroma oils as an indigenous alternative to perfumes. This in itself is significant for a whole segment of the professional and younger generation: economic liberalisation opened up a whole world for people with creative

---

[5] The latest trend in Delhi are day spas, where one can go for a day, and can avoid long journeys to get to a place like Ananda. There are independent facilities, as the one set up by VLCC and there are some associated with five star hotels, along with beauty parlours, health and fitness clubs. 'For the stressed out, the time pressed and the bone weary, a spa break is the trendy way to relax in a hurry' (Kaul 2005: 61). On offer are 'items' such as aromatherapy, detoxification, fango body treatment, ayurvedic treatment, reflexology, Swedish and Thai massage, and so forth. Spas can be found in the metros, at tourist and wedding destinations such as Rajasthan, Goa or Kerala.

ideas, for people with disposable income, ready to mortgage, or take a bank loan. She also trusted the fact that the young generation is gradually more conscious about buying 'natural' and Indian goods that are good for both individual health and environment. This was a new development, Miriya explains, because until even the late-1990s, people would not appreciate 'things Indian' and instantly privileged imported goods.

This is interesting in terms of the shifting frames of taste and distinction. As of today, Indian luxury goods have entered the domestic and even international market; fashion designers have taken over western boutiques and orientalist dreams with exquisite materials. Indian spirituality and ayurveda has created a strong self-consciousness that smoothly bridges the gap between tradition and modernity, East and West. 'Made in India' has become a brand quite like 'India Shining'. The more rustic and traditional the branding of ethnic cosmetics, the better is the marketing. Simplicity, again, turns into a marker of luxury.

> Talking about luxury and luxury products, it's not such a new concept in India after all. We, *as a nation*, have always been consumers of luxury products. The maharajas and moghuls of yore led an opulent life. The plush interiors of their palatial houses, their gem-studded attires, the jewels and fancy jewellery, in fact the entire ambience spelt luxury and royalty. Today, the same behaviour pattern has come full circle (Rahman 2006: 73).

The difference is that many of the old maharajas and maharanis are now impoverished and have been substituted by the new royal class of the affluent middle classes and their culture of consumption and display. The concept of the beautiful body sits paradoxically between the colonial fantasy of the exotic and the progressive modern.

Beautiful Body, World-Class Body

> Privacy and tranquility to shed the cares of the world while we pamper your body, mind & soul, with our invigorating treatments. A Spa rediscovers essential sensory pleasures — the pleasure of touch, the aroma of exotic oils wafting the air and more. Feel your muscles being kneaded and the tension sweep away from your body as you drift off to soothing music and enter a realm of blissful happiness and total relaxation. VLCC offers a tranquil escape from hectic city life through its Spa, which is dedicated to complete client satisfaction ... We have mastered the art of wellness for the body, mind and soul.[6]

---

[6] See http://www.vlcc.co.in/vlcc-spa.html (accessed 21 August 2007).

VLCC is another successful institution concerned with marketing beauty and wellness in New Delhi to affluent middle-class women and men. This is a domain with high-level confidence and anxiety among customers, and where 'experts' promise to generate all-round confidence. Using people's insecurities, they also claim to solve lifestyle problems. Yet, sometimes they even provide the problems, it seems, by articulating issues that have not been considered problematic before.

VLCC advertises with the slogan 'Discover a New You' and calls itself 'India's largest and most sought-after slimming, beauty and fitness brand' with its head office in Gurgaon and several centres in New Delhi, all over India and, most recently also in Dubai. This is in tune with a growing awareness that the beauty market in the United Arab Emirates is largely untapped but is quickly adapting to global standards. The competition for this market is growing: in 2006, Shahnaz Husain's beauty empire announced its intentions to expand to the Arabian and even European market, in particular with spa and herbal beauty care products.[7] The 'VLCC brand' promotes 'a totally new health and beauty experience' based on 'world-class scientific and tailor-made fitness and beauty services'.[8] It promises customers to improve their confidence and make them fit for the demands of the professional globalised world. VLCC also markets its own products for the skin, hair and body on the basis of ayurvedic remedies. It could be considered as a fusion of the classical beauty parlour with elements from the wellness market and US-American fitness centres. Its motto: 'Be stress free, relax and feel positive inside, feel good to look good'.[9] Underneath the surface of the 'easy-going' lies a whole machinery of self-monitoring, management and discipline.

After several failed attempts, I got to meet Ritu D., Public Relations manager of VLCC, shortly before Diwali in 2006. The company's head office is a white-washed villa at the outskirts of Gurgaon. Ritu's office was packed with food and wine baskets and other Diwali presents for customers. It was quite clear that Ritu's priorities were set towards conducting a friendly conversation with me within the constraints of a viable time-span. Time is money. Between phone calls and queries from her employees, Ritu responded to my questions. I was curious about her opinion about the 'new Indian woman', especially, in what way she thought that women's

---

[7] Times News Network, 31 January 2006.
[8] See http://www.vlcc.co.in (accessed 21 July 2007).
[9] See http://www.vlcc.co.in/html/faq.htm# (accessed 20 February 2007).

roles had changed drastically and whether VLCC was part of this shift. She highlighted women's independence from men's income, and the need of a woman to:

> feel strong, be in control of life and manage herself, her family and to take care of herself and her personality. This is a new thing for women now, that they also, additionally running a family, manage their own professional work, and look great (Ritu D., personal conversation, Gurgaon, 2006)!

Ritu maintained that 'there is a new confidence in today's women, linked to the notion of new India, the making of a new woman!' The aim, she argued, was 'that you feel good from within' and VLCC ensured that the soul was taken care of first, only then the body: 'We are a solution-provider'. Ritu looked puzzled when I asked her about the difference between beauty parlour and VLCC: 'We are certainly not a beauty parlour! We provide wellness, we are a wellness institute! The beauty parlour only provides "RBS".' This clearly showed my ignorance and I had to be instructed that 'RBS' stands for 'regular beauty service'. Unlike a parlour, professional specialists at VLCC look into a customer's problem from a scientific side, and do not restrict themselves to cover it with make-up. 'We follow an inside-out-approach, not vice versa', emphasised Ritu, maintaining that the new Indian woman was grateful for such a service because it is her own decision to look after herself, not some external occasion or pressure that requires her to look beautiful:

> Previously, the Indian woman was good when she satisfied everybody and everything. Now she can even be economically independent. It is accepted that she must not only be a homemaker, even though that itself is a wonderful challenge and tremendously fulfilling to be a wife and a mother! But now she can take time out for herself, take liberties and not feel bad about this (ibid.).

VLCC, argued Ritu, was a place looking after women with the philosophy that marriage was not a means to an end. To be sure, this sounds impressive but unrealistic and even ideological in the light of ground realities. The idea behind this institution is that women can handle everything as long as their body is in good shape. Many middle-class women I spoke to during fieldwork emphasised how hard it was to uphold both the image of the devoted and sacrificing housewife, daughter-in-law and mother and the successful and independent businesswoman. Suneeta S. is such an example. Even though her family profited from her salary as she was working as a travel agent from home, the expectations from her to cater to the needs of her husband and mother-in-law made her feel suffocated:

'I don't want to be a homemaker only. I need my independence. At least some physical exercise. Why don't they accept that?! Otherwise I'll freak out.' Whenever she wanted to take time off in order to do something for herself, for example her evening walks in Lodhi Gardens, her husband accused her of having become very selfish and possibly even seeing another man. At some stage, Suneeta even consumed anti-depressants because she felt trapped in a cycle of control and surveillance by her in-laws.

Control and surveillance are a continuing topic even in the context of 'wellness'. A less emphatic face of the institution surfaces when Ritu talked about VLCC's 'unique selling point': slimming. She maintained that there was a market for slimming programmes because new India had 'no more tolerance for ugly people'. The pleasure of looking after the body is also a pressure that demands discipline and consensus as regards international beauty standards. Ritu told me that multinational corporations in Delhi and Bangalore offer their employees special deals and credit-points if they look after their body and health at a place like VLCC:

> Overweight people are not welcome any longer. When you face the world, you have to meet the global standard! You must be in good shape, that's your responsibility! Ugly people are really somewhat ... You must also look hygienic! You must be world-class (Ritu D., personal conversation, Gurgaon, 2006)!

Through this facet, the previously declared economic independence of the 'new woman' is suddenly overshadowed by the subtle panoptic social control, internalised and reproduced as 'care of the self'. No status without submitting to particular rules and discipline.

Coming back to Ritu's comment about the beauty parlour, while the parlour transforms the woman only temporarily and often for particular occasions only, the body according to VLCC corporate culture now has to be constantly 'in a good shape'. VLCC thus mirrors the transformation of the woman's body festishised for a more private gaze (e.g., of the husband) to a body cult in which the body is rendered beautiful for a global gaze and for 'aspirational luxury consumption' (Mazzarella 2003: 98). If Mazzarella could rightfully claim that the new middle classes now celebrate (national) progress through the pleasure of the consumer (instead of the duty of the citizen), and that pleasure dominates sacrifice as self-fulfilment (ibid.: 101), Ritu's statement mentioned earlier seems to indicate that sacrifice is still a virtue. However, it has shifted from the level of the family or the state to that of the global consumer market: 'to meet the global standard, you must be in good shape'.

With the slimming industry as VLCC's biggest asset, workout factories have been set up in Bangalore, Delhi and Gurgaon. Its growth is almost 50 per cent per year, and the majority of customers are people working in the corporate and service sectors. The market seems to be growing fast: 50 per cent of urban women above the age of 35 are said to have unhealthy body shapes, and according to western standards, 45 per cent of urban males, 55 per cent of females, and 40 per cent of children in Delhi are obese (see Datta 2006: 32).

Theming, as a narrative and performative way of framing consumption and pleasure, features in this domain as well. Even in a modern institution like VLCC, traditional rituals play an important role. For instance, *karva chauth* — a ritual expressed in a vow (*vrat*) by which the married woman fasts (abstaining even from water) from morning till moon-rise in order to secure her husband's well-being — is one of the several rituals that are marketed 'in a big way'. Women observe the ritual to present themselves as good, beautiful and faithful wives. This indicates an important shift: the wife as guarantor of prosperity, incarnated in the goddess Lakshmi, traditionally plump and round because this was associated with wealth, turns into an erotic object, aligned with western notions of being thin as being sexy.[10] The *karva chauth* package addresses middle-class women in order to bond them with VLCC, explains Ritu's assistant Meena. VLCC also offers special packages to make women come to the day spa, for instance to have henna applied (*mehndi*) on their hands or/and feet for special occasions such as weddings or Diwali (Hindu New Year): 'Young girls and housewives can come to the spa in groups and have a great day out'. Other day spas offer bridal packages for INR 6,000 onwards per day.[11]

However, slimming is still the most successful item offered by VLCC. Beauty services and personal care currently witness a huge expansion. This is a holistic approach, 'head-to-toe-care'. It is a new thing that people want to look good, to celebrate, to have their 'feel-good thing' and to do it properly — and constantly. The packaging of special events has become an activity offered around the year, designed by experts, and advertised in the print media as well as through personally sent out invitation cards to the regular customers. The VLCC spa in South Delhi offers massage using 'Cleopatra's elixir' while the international spa market offers 'special packages' ranging from US$2,500 for three days (Banyan Tree Resort, Indonesia) to US$350 per night (Royal Park Evian, Switzerland).

---

[10] I am grateful to William Sax for outlining this shift to me.

[11] This is approximately €55. See *Asia Spa*, September–October 2005, p. 103.

On the one hand, rituals serve as stages for social control and on the other as self-fashioning tools and display of financial and cultural capital. Katharina Poggendorf-Kakar cites the example of *karva chauth* among middle-class women in New Delhi (2002: 97–109). Her studies underline the importance of using a ritual as a narrative and stage for the performance of love, beauty and wealth (see Poggendorf-Kakar 2001). One way of legitimising the conspicuous display of wealth is that on *karva chauth* a woman should appear as a goddess glowing with inner and outer beauty. With respect to this topic, it is interesting to re-read M. N. Srinivas's article 'The Changing Position of Indian Woman' (1977). To him, rituals always have a direct reference to the pursuit of secular ends and he takes *vratas* (optional rituals mostly performed by women) as an example to underline this claim. Rituals, argues Srinivas:

> provide women with occasions for socialising with their peers and superiors, and for showing off the family's wealth, clothing and jewellery. During the last few decades in particular, the economic, political and status dimensions of ritual have become increasingly conspicuous (ibid.: 229).

Moreover, he adds: 'Feminine preoccupation with ritual provides them with power over men' (ibid.). Finally, the man depends on his wife to perform rituals in his and his family's favour. The quote underlines, first, that Hindus have been practising conspicuous consumption even before economic liberalisation. Yet, in the 1990s, the practices have spread by means of westernisation and Sanskritisation to social groups that had not emerged as a class in the 1970s. Second, the statement shows the various ways of continuity in the practices of employing traditional rituals as markers of social and power relations. This holds especially true in the different forms in which they are offered, and appreciated, by women consumers in the modern beauty and wellness industry.

Conclusion

In *Die Erlebnisgesellschaft* (The Society of Sensual Experience), Gerhard Schulze observes the production of a constant surplus of desires and fears as people search for happiness in a growing consumer society like Germany, placing sensuous experience at the centre stage of their everyday worlds. The promise of happiness is not located in a distant past any longer, available only through renunciation, asceticism, careful conduct, hard work and so on, but its fulfilment in the instant present and by constantly comparing oneself with others (Schulze 1992: 14).

Yet, Schulze also alerts us to the fact that the desire to experience happiness — in the light of so many opportunities and choices — creates insecurities and disappointment, and rigid regimes of control and surveillance. Responsibilities are shifted and oscillate between the domains within and outside the individual life-sphere: friends and family, leisure and romance, on the one hand, and the state, social organisations, or lifestyle experts trained in spiritual, psychological and physical guidance, on the other. The previous example of wedding planners has shown how much the meaning of life is defined by means of subjective experiences, linked to a beautiful, interesting, fascinating, and pleasant life and the recent affirmation of arranged marriage in urban habitats as a romantic undertaking. Moreover, Schulze proposes that many of our concerns and actions are now centred on the imperative of life being 'valuable' only when it can be experienced with a pleasure related to the self ('Erlebe Dein Leben!'; 1992: 34). The 'livability' of life is a result of an incredible expansion of opportunities to act in and upon one's life, irrespective of one's social position. The 'project' or rather, the 'manifest' of the beautiful life affects the ways in which we perceive body, mind and soul, imbuing it with increasing desire of the 'care of the self'. All this is also a result of a growing capability of choice and self-reflexivity of the experience-oriented person, the on-going production, circulation and evaluation of thoughts related to one's actions and desires, the varied opportunities and actual outcomes of those on one's life. Schulze defines the 'beautiful life' as something that results from self-reflexivity, from a complicated process through which a person attempts to manipulate circumstances in such a way that the consequential reaction to it is that something (or oneself) is perceived as beautiful. At the same time, a beautiful life is never taken for granted, constantly at risk, while consensus about the criteria that make it is contested and fluid.

The pleasure of having a beautiful mind, body and life can transform into a high pressure for aspiring members of the 'world-class': a subtle machinery of self-surveillance and self-control is generated by the beauty and wellness industry that reveal the almost threatening idea of permanent wellness. Beauty and wellness almost become a moral duty. The beauty industry also indicates a shift from the beauty parlour as a public space to the wellness centre as yet another enclavic domain through which experiences are structured by means of theming. Having spare time, going on a honeymoon and family holiday are new phenomena in the Indian middle class. This requires careful yet effective 'socialising' and monitoring by institutions like a spa hotel or the new infrastructure of event managers and experts for important occasions by which status can be claimed and marked. In this, the wedding industry functions very much along the lines of the discourses discussed in Chapter 1, where I proposed that residential housing becomes a lifestyle statement, where the world is seamlessly and almost eclectically collected and inserted into the exhibitionary complex of events à la 'India Shining', as part of a cultural repertoire of cosmopolitan Indianness. At the same time, continuous pressures are generated by means of quantifying status through taste. Vulgarity of the lower classes as well as the elite, noble simplicity and relentless conspicuous waste are both monitored and paraded as part of a strategy of distinction and for this, experts as well as print and audio-visual media are required. They mark the seemingly borderless universe of categories through which the middle classes navigate in terms of life-cycle rituals and beauty culture. This way, Bryman's thesis of life's 'Disneyisation' can also be applied to the Indian context, however, with specific markers of post-coloniality such as auto-orientalism and occidentalism. Once more, cosmopolitanism emerges as a strategy of enclave-construction, distancing and self-disciplining, as opposed to opening up.

conclusion: 'indianising' modernity

In spring 2008, a friend and colleague, an Indian citizen who had moved to the USA to take up an academic position at a university there, visited me at Heidelberg. She had lived in India off and on and had just returned from research in Delhi when we met again. We discussed the topic of Indian media when she argued that somehow she felt very nostalgic about the Nehruvian era, wanting India to return to those days when people were more down-to-earth and modest and less shrill. She referred to a common friend of ours, who had just delivered a keynote lecture at a conference, where he coined the term the 'ugly Indian'. What culminated in this vignette on what India has become since economic liberalisation was a certain view of 'India Shining' as something that had moved out of control, characterised with a shrill, pompous, uncultivated and over-confident rhetoric. This discussion accompanies me until today, and makes me think about my idea of India, of East Delhi's 'India Shining' and the India of Old Delhi's *galis*. Without wanting to conclude this book in a sea of moralistic prophecies about 'India's path' between Nehru and Infosys, economic liberalisation and global meltdown, I take this anecdote to underline the emerging criticism, not of the return of the 'old rich' but of those observing the bandwagon as it spins, higher and faster. A book revolving around the lifestyles and aspirations of the new middle classes in neoliberal India cannot but generalise, to some extent, the heterogeneous fabric of this growing segment of Indian society. The case-studies may not necessarily represent mainstream (Hindu) middle-class attitudes and aspirations. But they mark ventures and trends, mostly in the context of urbanisation and transnational networks, that underline the shaping and changing of status and taste among these groups, and give a body to the concept of the 'world-class'. To be sure, the price to be paid by the aspirants to 'belong to class' is high and class has become a trap that cannot be escaped from. Commenting on Nepal's new middle class, Liechty has argued that no one can 'afford not to participate in the new consumer economy' (2003: 250), and this also holds true 'in spite of the ambivalence, moral hesitation, and even anger that many people express toward the unstable and constantly expanding realm of goods and images'

(Liechty 2003: 250). Many of my informants have come to experience this with respect to the ambiguity of 'India Shining', not so stark in terms of 'light' and 'darkness', 'climbing up' and 'falling behind' but through varying shades, speed and temperatures. Let me return to Neetu K., mentioned in the Introduction to this book. Neetu criticised the conspicuous waste of money on occasions like Diwali, New Year and Valentine's Day, when people shell out thousands of rupees for a Chanel scarf, Swarovski items, or a flat-screen television as gifts:

> Tell me, why do people need Louis Vuitton bags for INR 200,000 as presents for Diwali? That's perverse! At the same time, cultural values are flushed down the toilet. We have really become uncivilized. Where is India Shining? There is no India Shining (personal conversation, October 2006)!

Despite criticising the 'uncultured' economies of consumption, my informant played the game himself, shelling out extravagant presents to customers and leading a relatively luxurious lifestyle at the verge of bankruptcy. According to Neetu, religion has fallen prey to commodification too. Spiritual specialists like TV gurus Ramdev and Sri Sri Ravi Shankar have become marketing specialists, and places like the ACC are artificial showpieces of a global city, with no spirituality whatsoever. The sandwiched position of the middle classes leads to the drawing of more rigid borders to keep socially and economically lower, but upwardly mobile, groups out. Distrust of strangers in the public sphere is an often-discussed theme now, and efforts are made to define the intangible markers of trust and betrayal in times of drastic change. A dominant fear among the new middle classes resulting from the myth that globalisation's fruits of wealth would trickle down and reach everyone, is that of revenge by those who cannot participate in India's economic growth: 'One day, the masses will get disillusioned and come to murder and rob the upper classes. This is bound to happen. You can't trust these people any more!' argued Neetu and admitted that they now lock their bedroom doors at night lest the servants ever attacked them, one of the key themes of Aravind Adiga's bestseller *The White Tiger* (2008). The underlining message, of course, is that 'established' dependences and loyalties, old values and status positions are not respected any longer.

One cannot but notice the deep disillusionment in Neetu's views about the role of the middle classes in the backdrop of India's economic growth, and the bitterness of in fact not having made it into the ranks of those he actually criticises. Moreover, Neetu felt let down by the promise of the 'Indian dream': if merit was the key to success, why was the door still locked? Why did his business partners betray him? Why have others been privileged despite a market that promises to work according to the system of equality and quality? Reflected in Neetu's comments are aspects of what Schulze has called *Erlebniskultur*, the notion that a liberalised market promises fair treatment to all participants alike. It requests from them, quasi in return, that they fulfil their 'duty' to produce and experience instant happiness. According to Schulze, the critique of consumption is part of a strategy to challenge felt or experienced injustice, betrayal and unhappiness (1992: 60). Neetu's unfulfilled aspirations are products of modernisation and globalisation fantasies of unbound mobility (Pinches 1999) as well as the myth of free and equal competition in capitalism (Robinson and Goodman 1996: 2) that reveals its illegitimacy in cases like this one.

This study of the emergence and contestation of new imaginaries, aesthetic practices and values of India's rising middle class ties together ethnographies of places, media, people and events. The case-studies explored the imaginary of India's new global visibility and confidence that surface in ideas, spaces and practices of urban and transnational lifestyles or 'citytainment' through real estate advertising, new religious and cultural leisure parks, theme weddings, and the beauty and fitness industry. All of these imaginaries are particularly relevant for the various negotiations that evolve around the idea of a globalised emerging India that, despite its new and shining appearance, is purportedly rooted in and is retranslating ancient traditions, religious practices, national and cultural heritage. In this context, aspirations and forms of distinction, sensuous pleasures and experiences generated through particular events, spaces and media, play a major role. The notions of tradition, religion, national and cultural heritage are packaged and circulated in new ways and along new routes and topographies, across global and local domains, by means of the transnational mobility of media, people, images and concepts. They shape what seems decisive for the creation of prestige and status for new middle classes: cultural capital and competence. Very often, however, they fall back on already established concepts and patterns (e.g., caste and region) that are appropriated and altered according to the new contexts (class). Therefore, it is crucial to understand that this movement does not take place only from 'A' to 'B'. Instead, it travels in circular and multidirectional ways and coinciding in time.

These entangled developments do not take place in a neutral space but are connected to various desires, hopes and fears that relate us to everyday worlds of their bearers. On the one hand, the book addresses the enthusiasm of 'New India' conveyed through many of my conversations with informants and by a variety of new media that have come to populate the landscape of popular culture in urban India and abroad in the diaspora. On the other hand, the various case-studies highlight that the rhetoric of status aspirations is coupled with an underlining and on-going anxiety of slipping, failing and falling, for instance, through inappropriate behaviour and taste. The study also indicates how new specialists move in to fill, and sometimes even enhance, the imagined gap of lacking the necessary know-how required to belong to class. The various ethnographies, thus, examine how this is constituted and negotiated on different levels, be it on the spatial, the performative or even an imagined level. Key domains inquired are those of spatial segregation and themed urban planning, religious–spiritual consumption, the creation of modern subjectivities through spectacular rituals (weddings) and bodies (wellness and beauty).

The introduction of the concept of wellness to India, for example, was met by the fact that leisure and care through solitude and 'doing nothing' as strategies of revitalising the self, and paying substantial sums for it was new to many members of the aspiring as also upper middle classes. This holds true for the introduction of the concept of romantic intimacy, or the skinny body as a statement of 'world-class' status and beauty consciousness (while in the traditional context the chubby body was privileged as sign of wealth, prestige and fertile sexuality).

The key metaphors of 'New India', the 'Indian Way' or 'India Unbound' refer to foundational notions of a 'superior ancient civilisation' and 'natural distinctiveness of India' that surface even more strongly in the context of globalisation where they relate to protection or revitalisation. The result is a 'glocalised' cultural heritage packaged predominantly for professional urban and transnational Indians who allegedly 'deserve' to belong to the 'world-class'. Each chapter in this book focuses on the ways in which a global and yet genuinely 'Indian' lifestyle shapes, and is shaped by, the new infrastructure of experts and mass media to evoke and legitimise notions of a 'good' and 'beautiful' life, a new sense of freedom (also from the obligation of uplifting India's poor and being loyal to the state as promoted under four decades of planned socialist economy), and of happiness and prosperity as foundation stones of a 'good life'. The underlining agenda is that neoliberalism develops the new middle classes as a moral and moralising community. Thereby, not only new hopes and possibilities but also new fears and risks play into the creation of cosmopolitan 'world-class' and Indianness. These subjectivities impact on the ways in which tradition and modernity are played out against each other and attributed with meaning in a constant effort to 'Indianise' modernity and cosmopolitanise Indianness.

How 'Indian' are Cosmopolitan Indians?

The notion of being cosmopolitan draws borders between groups: (a) between Indians living in India and those overseas, (b) between 'first class' and 'third class' citizens in cities such as Delhi, and (c) between Indians and non-Indians. While the first two categories work along the lines of 'being cultured', the last one does so on the basis of orientalist and occidentalist stereotypes. All three generate the notion of cosmopolitanism in alliance with defining the fabric of 'Indianness'. In this process, 'tradition' is transferred into the domain of (predominantly Hindu) cultural heritage. To know what cultural heritage and 'world-class' lifestyle are and how to perform them is part of the challenge for members of the new middle classes and in doing so they often compete with, and find opposition from, the 'old' middle and upper classes. The contest for being cosmopolitan is thus a contest of distinction and a matter of perspective. Despite the fact that regional differences are often highlighted (as with Gujarat in Part II, or ethnic types of wedding in Part III), the definition of varieties follows very much the same principle as it has in the process of nation-building and 'unity in diversity' throughout the twentieth century. Moreover, given the on-going references to 'experts' of all kinds and to custodian communities keeping an eye on 'Indian heritage', it is remarkable how little differentiation surfaced in conversations. While distinction, and difference, are sought to be exercised by displaying knowledge of what the 'original' and the 'authentic' elements of a ritual like a wedding are, the reasons for doing so were rarely given. And, if so, they sounded surprisingly similar.

The reasons for accumulating cultural capital from a local and globalised imaginary based on the notions of cultural heritage vary. The question as to how much 'Indianness' is possible *despite* modernisation and globalisation may put us on the wrong track. It presumes the acceptance of a primordial identity ('Indianness') that is challenged by 'foreign' influences. It does not acknowledge, on the one hand, the essentially transcultural and transnational fabric of cosmopolitanism, and on the other, it turns a blind eye to the fact that cosmopolitanism can also be the opposite of what it suggests: open and integrative. Globalised Indianness now has to be tied into the concept of class as a category loaded with new meaning: the promise of a good life. The concept of class might be relatively new for large sections of Indian society — bringing along substantial changes due to other forms of socialisation, mobility and flexibility. At the same time, traditional concepts such as that of the extended family or the centrality of religion in public life remain remarkably stable and are even further strengthened and modified. This is true, for instance, of arranged marriage in urban and transnational habitats, or the role of religion in the creation of a modern national identity. Family, caste and religion still play a vital role in education, residential environments and for life-cycle rituals despite the privileging of merit over birth for life-conduct and upward mobility. In a stagnant way, caste also plays a major role in electoral politics, reservation politics and social movements. Yet, what Milton Singer called 'Sanskritised Hinduism', carries on to dominate the imaginary landscape of 'New India' when it comes to the shaping of values and cultural heritage. Cosmopolitanism, then, is the competence to incorporate western elements in one's Indian repertoire, and to know which mixture is the most suitable and 'cultured' one. For this, lifestyle and life-conduct specialists of all kinds compete for the most credible solution. Often, the results are both 'auto-orientalist' and occidentalist, as in the case of the Chatwal or the Mittal wedding. I referred to this as neocolonial mimicry, combined with an enclaved, a panoptic or a panoramic gaze. In many ways, these enclaved and panoramic perspectives are underlined by a certain nostalgia and distance that characterise the view of diasporic Indians on 'planet India'. This was discussed, for instance, in the context of the religious transnational movement of BAPS (Part II), the concept of the 'big fat Indian wedding' (Part III) or the desires created by real estate developers in order to appeal to NRIs (Part I).

The fact that 'authentic' Indianness is partially contested by Indians who either live abroad or have enjoyed western education and lifestyle makes the distinction between 'global' and 'local' a very complex one. It sheds light on the fact that a seemingly 'genuine' identity is made up of multiple perspectives. While in some cases, NRIs were wooed (such as for real estate investment as we saw in Part I), they were seen as misrepresenting India in others (as in the case of NRI weddings in India). Such entanglements require constant re-adjustment of relations and point us towards the ambivalence and highly discursive field of identity production as regards the meaning given to purported dichotomies such as 'East' and 'West', 'foreign' and 'indigenous', 'self' and 'other', 'us' and 'them'. The notion of 'Indianness' is imbued with the enclaved gaze of the other who looks at India as if it was a foreign country, distanced through the instrument of the telescope through which (s)he observes a scene at a proscenium or a zoo. Parallel to the enclaved gaze, we have to consider the force-field of the panoptic gaze, that is the self-monitoring and self-regulating gaze of new middle class consumers as they compete for cultural capital in new environments that generate new demands, challenged by other agents.

In many discussions, cosmopolitanism is a term associated with a globalised way of life, less oriented on national identity than transcultural competence and cultural translation. It relates to persons aspiring to and accumulating moral values, cultural and economic forms of capital that generate a 'world citizenry'. Lifestyle experts or event managers cater towards notions of cosmopolitan Indianness, and so does the new urban and media-based infrastructure in which they operate. Cosmopolitan Indians compartmentalise their identities and ways of life: by, for example, being 'western' in their work attitude and 'Indian' at home. Cosmopolitan Indianness thus takes different shapes and is imbued with different meaning depending on the context where it is ought to be played out. Several chapters in this book have thus employed and highlighted the metaphor of 'spiritual awakening' to one's 'true' identity (Indianness) which is seminal in helping one to respond to global challenges. This may take the shape of initiation rituals through which a person, allegedly alienated from one's 'roots', becomes aware of one's relevance and position within the domain of Indian tradition (without losing cosmopolitan capital). For instance, a ritual performed at the religious leisure site of the ACC becomes a healing device as well as a means of purification from modernity's purported alienation and pollution, and an arena for the congregation of a global ecumene of satsangis. A theme wedding may revitalise Indian cultural roots in an estranged son or daughter of the motherland and communicate India's great tradition to a larger audience.

The three parts of this book present different facets of a complex modernisation process in which tradition becomes re-appropriated and created in (and through) the spectre of the world-class and cosmopolitanism — with a clear and deep focus on entertainment consumption and media in images, architectural environments and performances. Aesthetics and sensuous experience (Erlebnis) are crucial for the idea of cosmopolitanism and the world-class to become social facts, and vice versa, to feed into and create new desires, experiences and imaginaries.

The question here is, thus, not so much whether or not Indians are westernised in the course of modernisation and globalisation. In many ways, the concepts of 'Indianness' or the 'indigenous' may be utterly misleading because other categories of identification are as significant, e.g., gender or class. Further, even 'indigeneous' as a criterion of authenticity must be considered as being caught up in multiple and historically deep transcultural entanglements and power discourses. So, the more crucial insight lies in distinguishing between different shades of modernity, a constant transgressing, pulling and pushing of borders in which agents actively seek to position themselves and claim ownership over cosmopolitan Indianness in this dense and wide field of modernity. So, the performance of middle-classness must be treated in several ways here. Many forms of consumption — beyond the limits of the accumulation of goods and cultural capital — are related to the display of such knowledge and are essentially performative. However, the conditions as to how one arrives at a judgement about 'culturedness' vary and leave space for different interpretations as also varying assignments of efficiency (e.g., taste versus vulgarity, competence versus ignorance).

There are many challenges to the concept of a western modernisation package, highlighting that modernisation is diffused from a geographical and enlightened centre to its margins. The rituals and temples of BAPS, for instance, may be conceived of as 'alternative worlds' and 'helping hand' for those who seek refuge from the 'dark sides' of modernisation and westernisation, especially, individual alienation and loneliness, fragmentation of society and emotional greed. This allows for the idealisation of an 'Indian' identity which, in turn, is prefigured upon all that the west appears to be lacking: it is presented as caring and holistic, mostly through the projection of the functioning extended family and spiritual brotherhood (satsangis and *sampradaya*), part of both a global ecumene and a local neighbourhood/community. Underlying this projection is an on-going moral/ising discourse about values, tradition and culture, predominantly based on an East–West divide. This book, however, highlights the multi-locality and distributed agency of modernisation, whereby cultural identity and territory can no longer be identified, and where transnationality and transculturality should be examined instead (see Appadurai 1997; Friedman 2004; Gupta and Ferguson 1997; Ong 1999).

In all these negotiations evolving with respect to 'India Shining', glocalisation — like cosmopolitanism — must be understood as an attempt to improve one's position in a field of discourse that is both transnational and local, modern and traditional, elite and popular. It compels us to rethink the notion that a single locale may be constitutive for globalised identity-creation and to work instead with several and simultaneously existing localities or (semi-)public spheres.

Old and New, Global and Local

The question of how to define status by drawing upon 'old' or 'new' patterns and practices is central to the search for cosmopolitan Indianness. Again, there are no given and clear-cut borders between tradition and modernity, global and local, but in each instance shifting and oscillating movements that force us to examine each case of translation and transfer. For example, one ritual in different contexts or different sets of rituals may be developed by BAPS to appeal to a heterogeneous audience, for example, old and new potential members, tourists and pilgrims, overseas and local Indians. Thus, notions of 'official' and 'popular' Hinduism as well as the idea of a situational hierarchisation of rituals are important tools to differentiate the mimetic alteration and interpretation of the 'old' and the 'new'.

Upon coming closer, we also see that the 'new', the 'foreign', or the 'other', are often quickly fused with older patterns of cultural practice and traditional life. There is great flexibility in assigning 'foreignness' and 'sameness' to cultural products and practices. Consequently, what is included or excluded often appears somewhat arbitrary but is in fact a conscious indexing of meaning in a specific context. In fact, several examples have shown how western concepts were 'Indianised', or how practices previously rejected as old-fashioned and outdated (such as Ayurveda) are re-imported through western lifestyle institutions and media. Furthermore, a genre such as commercial film, often stamped as vulgar kitsch by westernised elites in India before the 1990s, has now become an industry through which a glocalised medium (film) turns into a global item and consumption practice. I denote this 're-globalisation', an important addition to the otherwise often mono-directional concept of globalisation and glocalisation. Instead of weakening identity, the new means of cultural production and performance are strengthening modern, glocal Indianness. This becomes clear in the case of the ACC where elements from the model of a theme park as well as museum, both phenomena of modern and urban societies, are appropriated into traditional concepts of worship and religious entertainment and, for instance, in fact generate religious commodity fetish. The result — ACC — is a new means of distinction for (and control of) experiences and aspirations of urban 'modern selves'. But the domain is essentially consumer-oriented and based on the principles of spectacle and leisure enjoyment and what I discuss as 'exhibition value'. Despite the fact that rituals at the ACC look old, they are actually new means of distinction within the frames of class and leisure. Because of the mobility of images, goods, people and ideas across borders, it is difficult to hold on to the idea that the local is stronger than the global because the two are more entangled than it is sometimes acknowledged or evident.

Transgression is at work in many instances. At times, tradition dresses up as modern and the modern as tradition. New social networks are created through economic liberalisation, complementing and challenging those related to caste and kin or family, yet without rendering them meaningless.

In this course, new social types emerge in the urban and modern habitat: the leisure flâneur and cultural connoisseur, the lifestyle expert, the (business, fitness, and school) friend, the event manager or spiritual professional. Along with the new social types arise new practices: poaching (of environments) and hanging out at public places of consumption, enjoying solitude and caring (or worrying) for the self, wellness and fitness activities, destination tourism, weddings, and so forth. New places too, have emerged, and by no means are they replicas of a western 'original' even though western spatial models may have influenced them. This is what makes the city such an important site of investigation. Theories of globalisation have largely ignored such processes. The anthropological challenge is to examine what is said to be new and what is old, what changes and what remains, or seems to remain, stable. Besides the concepts of caste and family as key markers of solidarity and loyalty, tradition and stability, certain spatial forms of social segregation in urban India can be traced back to older manifestations of social spatialisation, such as the local neighbourhood, the colonial city, or the post-Partition resettlement colony. Even now, public space shared by and accessible to all citizens alike is not attributed with much positive meaning. Instead, it has to be bridged (in order to get from A to B, or C, and back again), monitored, ordered, and at times, 'cleaned' from unwanted and disturbing sites and sights. This is where the distinction between 'first-class citizens' and 'third-class populations' manifests most drastically, particularly, in the case of real estate development and slum demolitions.

Before economic liberalisation, many of these practices were accessible abroad and only to members of the social and economic elite. 'World-class' lifestyle and conspicuous consumption were considered as morally decadent and inadequate for socialist India. Emerging or 'unbound' India is marked by a shift from the ideal of sacrificing individual aspirations for the improvement of the nation as a collective to the celebration of individual aspirations in the context of the extended family and closer, individually chosen transnational networks — what can be viewed as the new moral imperative of 'enjoying your life' and (national) 'progress through pleasure'. Even pleasure must be 'learnt', and class given a 'face' and a 'body'. As one of my informants, a senior marketing salesman from Gurgaon told me: 'Consumer society in India is virgin land. Everything has to be learnt and done from scratch'. This is indeed a key factor of modernisation and globalisation in India: the structuring of experience by means of developing and institutionalising cultural repertoires (heritage, popular culture, religious practice), specialists (lifestyle experts, event managers) and places at which this heterogeneous experience can be made available for consumption (malls, leisure parks, residential sites, films). Caste, religion and extended family are one means through which this structuring is generated. While they might become marginal in some contexts (e.g., caste for a career in the service sectors and multinational corporations), they gain new meaning in others (e.g., arranged marriage in urban milieus). It must be clear, however, that the privileging of consumption and class does not equal the dilution of culture and the homogenisation of identities. Moreover, it is a new form of identity construction and arena of class conflict and inequality, in which distinction then becomes the major force of positioning within the field of discourse and social spatialisation, as discussed, for instance, in the context of making and unmaking 'first'- and 'third'-class citizens.

'Feel-good' Life: The Ambiguities of Pleasure, Experience and Taste

Even in the shadow of the economic meltdown, which has led to the slowest GDP growth in six years (at 5.3 per cent), and with individual consumption and the real estate market at a record low (down by 50 per cent), there is a strong belief that promulgates the vision of India rejuvenating faster than other countries hit by the crisis (see Mishra 2009). The case studies presented in this book — all collected before the global economic crisis in 2008 — underline that the experience of modernity is a highly ambivalent one. It opens doors and options for some on the one hand; it may close them and open others, towards unexpected directions and different perspectives, on the other. Many studies on globalisation, and even public opinion-making, in India in the 1990s can be defined as being associated with certain moral fears. In the first years of economic liberalisation, especially, the fear of loss, standardisation and dilution of culture and tradition, of being once again colonised, of invasion and alienation, was particularly strong. It was strongly promoted by mass media and shared by social agents from a wide spectrum of Indian society, ranging and even oscillating between right-wing organisations and leftist groups. The fear of loss of identity and self-esteem has now, however, been widely replaced by the 'feel-good' and 'India Shining' enthusiasm that evolved in the early years of the millennium and was coupled with a new form of globalised patriotism. Members of the middle and upper classes realised that a lot was to gain from economic liberalisation as also from the concept of India as a global powerhouse. The gains were manifold: financially, socially, symbolically and culturally. To be sure, discussions about alleged failures of western modernity and the fear of repeating them certainly continue to exist. But they have shifted and become somewhat milder and more differentiated. They show a rise in of confidence (if not chauvinist superiority) and growth of agency in terms of strategies of engaging with 'westernisation'. Thus, it becomes clear that, like modernisation, westernisation is a discursive strategy rather than a given force. Modernity, then, is not just a form of enchantment but a condition in (and through) which cultural translations take place in multiple and performative forms.

A key concept in the context of 'India Shining' was the so-called 'feel-good factor', paired with associations of the 'Gold Rush' and the Indianised 'American Dream'. It must be emphasised, nevertheless that while the significant changes of lifestyle and selfhood occured, during the 1990s consumption and pleasure industries have existed before this dramatic shift, active at local and global levels. However, they did not affect such wide and new audiences and rather belonged to a small section of the social and economic elite of cosmopolitan Indians. Furthermore, other forms of consumption and leisure have to be positioned in the lineage of religious and devotional entertainment and economic market forces that were connected to religious practice even in pre-colonial times. As much as there are drastic changes, there are continuities in social hierarchies, religious practices and mundane performances related to the display and construction of status too. With economic liberalisation in the 1990s, the changes and possibilities suddenly seemed more sensuously and ubiquitously available.

The 'feel-good factor' suggests that with economic liberalisation came subjective experiences such as stability, optimism, the pleasure to both consume and 'be' Indian by contributing to its progress through consumption. Yet various parts of the case-studies emphasise as to what extent pleasure and sensuous experiences are highly discursive, monitoring and even disciplining a person's behaviour (and imagination). Further, they highlight that the felt obligation to be modern or world-class only if one 'felt good' leads to various pressures and frustrations, to code-switching and code-clashing. I only want to refer, here, to the example of the ACC that appeals to both devotees and heritage-connoisseurs and in fact, seems to prioritise the 'cultured Hindu' who places her or his devotion in the light of (trans)national progress. To what extent the blurring and switching between registers is successful is difficult to say. While on the one hand it could be suggested that the code-switching is a statement of resilience (against the previously characterised monoliths of nationalism and/or globalisation), on the other it could be an indication of a dangerous fragmentation such that people are more inclined to be manipulated by forces of culturalist conservatism.[1]

Different qualities of pleasure are differentiated in this study. For instance, the Erlebnis at the ACC seems to be the mediation of 'thin', immediate experience of the consumption spectacle, and 'thick' transformative experience through the spiritual discipline that together attract the visitors and followers of new religious movements, shaping notions of authenticity even beyond that domain. This also implies a shift from the corpothetic gaze within the domain of cultic value to the rather disembodied gaze of the museum visitor, even while appropriating and policing the emotional appeal of *darshan*. But while there is a constant and conscious slippage between the boundaries between the temple and the monument as illustrated through the ritual of arati, different codes are applied to the visitors (devotee versus connoisseur) to regulate the boundaries of acceptable and appropriate behaviour. This becomes clear in the monitoring of movement and behaviour within the compound of the Monument and Abhishek Mandap vis-à-vis the consumption spaces of the restaurant and the souvenir 'mall'. The ACC's popularity speaks and responds to a very real sense of alienation, both within and outside India. With the 'taxidermic practice' of exhibiting Vedic culture as if it was still alive, the ACC functions as a crash course in cultural heritage for the culturally alienated but aspiring Indians. This shapes what I have called 'taxidermic spirituality', i.e., a notion of how 'appropriate' religious behaviour ought to look like in order to create the impression that it is authentic. Surveying and enjoying oneself are closely tied to each other (see Bennett 1994; Schulze 1992). At the same time, there is a shift from participation to reverence, for instance, with the various injunctions: to be silent, to respect the deities, divine spaces, rituals, etc. This collapses our notions of the sacred and the mundane ordinarily viewed as essentially polarised and exclusive. The sacred is now released from its relegation to the private domain and reintroduced into the moral public sphere of transnational nationalism. The worldly separation from the divine can now be overcome, while simultaneously a new form of distinction emerges: the taste of aesthetics and the knowledge of religion as cultural heritage.

The transnational ecumenical movement BAPS is inspired by global capitalism, multinational corporations and the notion of the world-class.

---

[1] I owe this suggestion to Sophie Hawkins in a personal conversation, October 2007.

This also includes the creation of a global enclave gaze in that devotees and visitors are made cautious about the dangers and threats to their (religion's and physical) security: security control, CCTV and warnings as well as the internal structure of the ACC celebrate the site's importance by calling upon the global fear of terrorist attacks, and the interplay of religion and fundamentalism. Devotees and visitors are made to feel anxious in order to create in them both the desire for physical and spiritual security and safety. This enforces a panoptic gaze, one that justifies extreme security measurements by suggesting potential threats from outsiders/ Others (e.g., Islam). But the panoptic gaze goes beyond the imaginary of terrorism. It seeks to educate the citizens of 'India Unbound' to execute self-discipline through moralising narratives of the 'good' cosmopolitan Indian, the educated connoisseur of Indian culture, the devotee-consumer, on the one hand, and vulgar parvenus, on the other. Urban planning and leisure architecture support this gaze.

The aspiration to climb up the social and economic ladder, and the fear of failing to perform, falling out of the web of enthusiastic growth and losing out by being 'uncultured' leads to a range of strategies through which the middle classes practice distinction and difference, thereby calling upon a variety of spaces and places, events, performances and media. Prosperity, pleasure and freedom to consume and, thus, become is a new concept within India's society, a concept based on the duty to live and experience a 'good life'. This requires permanent engagement and updating with lifestyle trends. These are communicated in (and through) lifestyle media (e.g., magazines, advertisement), lifestyle experts (wedding planners, beauty experts, priests as event managers), and sites. Conflicts arise with the need to acquire 'know-how'. They derive from difficulties of translation and transfer from one domain into another, caused by an insecurity that is based on the lack of knowing who the middle class is, what the 'world-class' actually means, and by unmarked or unannounced code-switching and code-clashing. The continuous negotiation and manoeuvering between imagined and actual worlds, East and West, tradition and modernity, and in this context, also global and local domains, is the underlining and often invisible and subtle force that causes these conflicts.

Probably the most difficult task is to ignore the sea of poverty in which these islands of good lifestyle swim. This is done by the constitution of an enclave gaze, a gaze that creates comfort and confidence among those executing it — one that legitimises inclusion and exclusion, that creates new means of distinction and thus differentiation of 'Others', for instance, citizens and populations (see Chatterjee 2003). It also generates a gaze of surveillance and panoptic control. 'Belonging to the world-class' implies on-going negotiations of drawing and monitoring borders through the definition of allegedly appropriate behaviour and adequate lifestyle. This is done in the light of evaluating what is 'Indian' and what is not, or how something non-Indian could be translated into something specifically Indian. The chapters of this book examine this process of contestation of the authentic and the cosmopolitan Indian as it appears in different contexts and different degrees, sometimes even in the light of completely different frames of reference. As I have argued, consumption is more than the accumulation of goods: it is the accumulation and conspicuous display of cultural capital in order to claim access to, and ownership over, status. This, cultural citizenship is a form of market-driven citizenship, fuelled by a future-oriented nostalgia and search for heritage as living repertoire (taxidermy). We saw this surface in the appeal to NRIs to 'touch the roots' of their childhood days in real estate advertisement, the 'exoticising' and orientalising rhetoric in the Chatwal wedding and the NRIs' purported search for roots, norms and values of an idealised transnational and national community (as extended family).

The enclaved gaze also demarcates certain forms of globalised capital and Hindutva as a sign of glocal provincialism, that is imbued with an inverted look that does not seek to transgress and open up but to stabilise borders by ostensibly promoting openness by quoting 'from abroad' (see Varma 2004: 81). This leads to a strengthening of conservative forces that operate through the imaginary force of fragmentation and danger. Underlining these notions are concepts of those who create disorder and danger that pollute the physical and mental environment of the world-class citizens. The discourses legitimise a moral and/or physical distancing from those allegedly threatening elements as well as strategies executed against them — be it 'illegal' slum-dwellers or western lifestyles and the constant threat of Islamic terrorism, all of which are said to weaken the city's reputation and the nation's economy. The threat of terrorism in public sites of cities across the Indian subcontinent has recently gained momentum and new anxieties, with attacks in Ahmedabad, Delhi and other cities in 2008, enforcing demands for new laws to 'protect' the citizenry.

One key strategy of defining borders and values of the world-class, or creating relations and meaning, is that of 'theming' and 'heritagisation'. The case-studies examined several of these 'themes', such as history, nature and patriotism. One of the most appealing themes is that of 'Dubaisation', namely, the creation of a 'simcity' — a simulated city with no origin(al) (see Soja 2000), an urban simulacrum that seems to function without any embeddedness in its direct environment but with manifold references to historical and civilisational 'success-stories' (Egyptian pyramids, Roman and Italian Empire, colonial architecture, world cities like Paris, New York and London). 'Dubaisation' also underlines the on-going competition between cities claiming 'world-class' status on a global scale, yet with the shift of wealth and prestige to cities and countries that have formerly not competed for 'world-class' status. Tied to this is the heritagisation of urban space and architecture, the gentrification of a locality for tourist and business purposes, such as in the case of Old Delhi and Connaught Place in New Delhi. But heritagisation as a means of distinction can also be found in the ethnic chic theme weddings, or the dramatisation of westernisation as well as receptions of wedding rituals in the diaspora. There is also a trend towards heritagisation of lifestyle in the ways 'ancient' traditions such as *vaastu* and Feng Shui are translated into residential architecture, wellness treatments, and so forth. Along with this comes a strong tendency to package culture in a way that I have called 'museumisation': NRIs rediscover their ancestral land, and Indianness, as exotic and empowering fetish. In the course of this, Indian heritage is turned as a museum exhibit. By way of museumisation or heritagisation, religion can be marketed as a substantial pillar of national identity, and even as a modernisation tool. Heritage shows that religion, dressed up as subjective spirituality, can be modern and appealing: religion, rituals, temples are said to create values that enable cosmopolitan Indians to move confidently in modern habitats. Moreover, defining heritage is a means of differentiating the Indian from western secularism.

The theming of lifestyle, media and urban spaces is a means of providing experiences of 'Indianised' modernity. Whether or not we as anthropologists consider these as copies or originals, as authentic or fake, is not at stake here. What is interesting, however, is in what way these sensuous experiences (Erlebnis) of a good life are linked to particular forms of new control and surveillance of modern selves. The pleasure of having a beautiful mind, body and life can thus transform into a pressure for all those aspiring to belong to the 'world-class': a subtle machinery of self-surveillance and self-disciplining is generated by the beauty and wellness industry that reveal the nearly threatening idea of permanent wellness. Beauty and wellness almost become another regime of control and surveillance, and a moral duty associated with care of the self as an obligation to please others.

The Qualities of Place

Ever so often has globalisation been criticised as creating 'placelessness', deterritorialising or uprooting and alienating people from their 'origin'. Notions of a disenchanted or homeless mind, unable to cope with the varied influences of modernisation and globalisation are, however, increasingly challenged by anthropologists and social historians. For instance, Appadurai (1997) underlines locality as a relational and contextual category rather than a given territorial unit. Ong (1999) argues for the agency of 'global nomads' in finding creative and constructive answers to cultural globalisation. This study has explored various qualities of places at which cosmopolitan Indianness is constituted, made available for experience, but simultaneously also negotiated and even questioned.

The concept of the 'global city' brings in a host of spatial qualities and histories (as discussed in Part I), turning New Delhi into a 'thick' carpet of space and places, localities and histories, all of which are highly contested and regulated, and often emerged in reference or competition to each other. A city like Delhi, aspiring to be a 'world-class' event generates different spatial stages for the experience and performance of its 'valuable' citizens. Real estate advertising functions like a cloth spread across a city that is not yet what the advertisements promise: hoardings, posters, construction sites and the myth of residential housing qualities add to the idea that a better world is at reach, ready to emerge phoenix-like.

But what about its inhabitants? If we follow the definition of the cosmopolitan as a world citizen, we would conclude that the cosmopolitan does not need a home in a constant location at which (s)he must be rooted. Yet, most narratives and images of the cosmopolitan Indian suggest a deep yearning for having a homely place. The quality of these places has changed insofar as a homely place can now be replicated (e.g., the transnational temple), does not need to have a history (e.g., condominium), and can be communicated and re-invoked by new media technologies and imagined communities. What kind of a neighbourhood and social attachments these new condominiums create has not yet been examined. Different registers of coding capital (e.g., ritual hierarchies) generate different qualities of place. Places are in competition with each other, be they megacities competing for 'world-class' status or leisure sites competing for visitors. To be sure, displacement is not really an issue in times of higher mobility of people and goods unless we talk about the displacement of 'illegal' slum-dwellers or the growth of the informal sector. Cosmopolitan communities and global enclavic tribes are no longer bound to a particular site but to multiple sites, with multiple loyalties. In this light, the relationship between centre and periphery is increasingly difficult to pinpoint. And as an 'authentic' imaginary place, India is constantly reshaped by those claiming custody over her heritage, be they local or overseas Indians, beyond the geophysical location, in transnational networks.

New identities in the process of being imagined and shaped require new spaces in (and stages on) which they can be manifested, visualised, converted from imagination into actuality and vice versa. New spatial aesthetics, residential, leisure and commercial spaces such as gated communities, malls or leisure parks, are among the sites spearheading the exposure and performance of 'world-class' identities. Again, in the light of the concept of glocalisation, it can be argued that the relationship between new and old, global and local, indigenous and foreign is a very delicate one. Our understanding of glocal imaginaries of contemporary urban and middle class India is complicated by the fact that mass mediation and mass migration entangle global and local, popular and elite, centre and periphery even further. What seems to be genuinely Indian and traditional may be brand new and European or American of origin, and vice versa. One example is the gated community as part-Indian *pol* (urban neighbourhood in industrialised Gujarat), part-European Garden City, part-colonial civil lines. Another example is the ACC, where western concepts of the theme park have been applied but not always obviously, and where shifts of taste-making and taste-shaping can be studied in the context of traditional rituals and ritual sites. At the same time, we also cannot talk about a complete westernisation à la Disney: Indian concepts of pilgrimage and sacred geographies, entertainment and spectacle surface too. Above that new spatial forms are generated, linked to the desires, networks and activities of transnational communities. Again, the ACC is such a case, where the temple becomes a quasi-public place, purportedly open to all members of Indian and even global society, informed by the crucial role of the overseas temple as a social centre and a place of the display and revitalisation of cultural heritage. Partly rooted in Hindu revivalist movements of the nineteenth and early-twentieth century, partly the result of overseas migration, the ACC is both local and global. But this is also a good case in place to demonstrate that the global and the local do not really work in dichotomies but have to be understood as constantly and historically entangled through circular flows and not clearly distinguishable as separate entities. The transnational temple network enables distributed agency to be orchestrated and monitored by means of a global ecumene and cultural economy, shaping an imagined community that goes beyond the nation (Anderson 1991). The overseas institution of the temple is then reintroduced into the Indian context, however, through the eyes of the enclaved gaze of the NRI, as a multinational corporation plus pilgrimage site. The diaspora comes home and brings with it a different understanding of cultural citizenship and Indianness — one where efficiency and efficacy are given expression through the double-meaning of cleanliness (of morals, mind and place). It is also where the habitus of the 'modern persona' undergoes constant monitoring and disciplining of the self and the other, what Bennett (1994), speaking about the role of exhibition as the relation of a complex of disciplinary and power relations through which the body is rendered docile, calls the 'exhibition complex'. The ACC thus becomes the 'site for a sight', a place both to see and to be seen from. The network of 'world-class' religious sites pushes the ACC beyond the topography of a sacred geography that is tailored upon the physical body of India. This way it can be compared to the network of global cities, even though the cultural and nation-specific context must not be sidelined and rather seen as problematic in that they are intrinsically interwoven and shifting forces within the same field.

Both religion and nation have entered a global domain in which they start competing with each other for members of all kinds through the concept of culture, using spectacle and media technologies. The most evident strategy is by promoting a rhetoric of 'world-class' habitus and an organisational apparatus and appearance that often reminds one more of a multinational corporation than a genuinely local set-up. Having said this, the ACC cannot be defined as an exclusively middle-class site; this would be counterproductive to the BAPS's sectarian programme and ideals. Instead, it attempts to be equally important to members of lower classes and castes who it also tries to persuade, beyond the sectarian agenda, to aspire to become cultural citizens and global Indians, and accumulate the appropriate spiritualised-cultured behaviour. It also celebrates and reformulates regional identities and associations, especially Gujaratiness. The ACC is a new place based on old patterns: it fuses concepts of pilgrimage and post-colonial leisure, tourism and heritage, communal politics and nationalism, regional, national and transnational identities. The case-studies have revealed that the 'world-class' must be considered in the light of such magnified regional identities, as in the imagined desire of the NRI to return to his or her childhood memories, the confidence of the sectarian transnational network of Gujaratis, destination weddings and ethnic chic.

What spaces like this have in common is that they might refer to their role as democratic motors of national identity and pride. However, they also generate a selective and exclusive notion of who belongs to that society of glocal Indians, constantly appealing to fears of insecurity, instability, downward mobility and threat that comes from elements positioned outside first and world-class citizenship. This legitimises their exclusion, stigmatisation and constant surveillance.

Theme parks and gated communities, as two examples from the chain of case-studies presented here, are the forerunners of the cities and transnational networks of the future. They compel us to reconsider the relationship between global and local, private and public, elite and popular, national and transnational, thereby showing that those relations are neither mono-dimensional nor based on either/or solutions. As showcases of 'India Rising' or 'India Unbound' they challenge our notions of authenticity, or 'real' and 'unreal' experiences based on an original. 'India Shining', as a glocal trope, creates moralising utopias and panopticons of new national and transnational identities, and fills us with hopes and anxieties about the future of a vernacular cosmopolitan modernity.

GLOSSARY

❦

abhishek (Skt. *abhiṣeka*)	Ritual washing
adivasi	Tribals
Annakut (Skt. *annakūṭa*)	The first day of the Hindu New Year festival at the ACC
arati (Skt. *āratī*)	Worship of a Hindu deity at dawn or sunrise with light from wicks soaked in ghee (purified butter) or camphor
ashram	Village-like spiritual community
basti (H. *bastī*)	Squatter settlement
bhajan (Skt. *bhajana*)	Devotional song, mostly performed in congregation
bhakti (Skt.)	Devotional movements in Hindu religiosity
Bharat Uday	India Shining (BJP campaign, 2003–4)
burkha (Arab. *burqa*)	An enveloping outer garment worn by Muslim women
chal murti	Movable icon of the deity hosted in a temple
dalit	'Untouchables' or 'outcastes' within the caste ideology, said to be ritually impure
darbar	Court
darshan (Skt. *darśana*)	Reciprocated 'vision' of the divine or deity
deshbakti (Skt. *deśabhakti*)	Devoted service for the country
feng shui	Chinese teaching of harmonising architecture
grihastha (Skt. *gṛhastha*)	Married householder
guru (Skt.)	(Spiritual) teacher
hindutva (Skt.)	'Hinduness' as a way of life, nationalist movement
homa (Skt.)	Fire sacrifice
jhañki (H. *jhāṅkī*)	Moving tableau paraded at religious processions
kalash (Skt. *kalaśa*)	Sacred vessel or pot
karva chauth (H.)	Ritual in which the married woman fasts from morning till moon-rise in order to secure her husband's well-being

lila (Skt. līlā)	Religious drama, folkloristic play
lungi (H. luṅgī)	A male garment worn around the waist
mandap (Skt. maṇḍapa)	Pillared outdoor hall or pavilion
mandir (Skt. mandīra)	Temple
mehndi	A thick henna paste, typically applied on hands and feet
mela (Skt. melā)	Fair
mohalla	Traditional neighbourhood (Mughal origin)
murti (Skt. mūrti)	Idol, statue
panchayat (H. pañcāyat)	Local assembly and level of governance
pandit (Skt. paṇḍita)	Teacher, priest
parampara (Skt. paramparā)	Succession of teachers and disciples
parikrama (Skt.)	Sacred circumambulation
pol	Traditional neighbourhood in Gujarat
prasad (Skt. prasāda)	A gift offered to a deity and then returned to the offerer
puja (Skt. pūjā)	Worship of a deity
reiki	Spiritual healing method by means of hands
rishi (Skt. ṛṣi)	Seer
sadhu (Skt. sādhu)	Ascetic
sampradaya	Spiritual/religious congregation
sangeet (Skt. saṅgīta)	Pre-marital gathering of family, accompanied by singing and storytelling
sanskriti (Skt. saṃskṛti)	Culture, tradition
saptapadi (Skt. saptapadī)	'Seven steps', a sub-ritual at the Hindu marriage
satsang	Devotional gathering
satsangi	Member of a religious fellowship or satsang among the Swaminarayan movement
seva (Skt. sevā)	Service, voluntary work; paving the way to good virtue/karma
sevak (H. sevaka)	The agent who carries out seva or service
swami (Skt. svāmin)	Honorific title of a guru or religious leader
vaastu	Ancient architectural tradition related to holistic living
vivaha (Skt. vivāha)	Marriage
yatra (Skt. yātrā)	Procession, pilgrimage

BIBLIOGRAPHY

Primary Sources

Print Media

LIFESTYLE AND NEWS MAGAZINES (2002–8)

Asia Spa India (Lifestyle Magazine, Wellness Monthly)
Wellness (Lifestyle Magazine, Wellness Quarterly)
The Eternal Solutions: The Wellness Magazine (Lifestyle Magazine, Wellness Monthly)
Life Positive (Lifestyle Magazine, Spiritual Monthly)
Outlook (Weekly News Magazine)
India Today (News Weekly, plus Travel Plus, Home and Buyer's Guide Special Issues)
RealtyPlus – India's First Real Estate Monthly (Real Estate Magazine)
Savy (Lifestyle Magazine)
Society Interiors (Lifestyle Magazine)
Society (Lifestyle Magazine)
Life Matterz (Lifestyle Magazine Quarterly)
Lifestyle Trends (Lifestyle Magazine)
Femina (Womens' Lifestyle Magazine)
Good Housekeeping (Womens' Lifestyle Magazine)
Women's Era (Lifestyle Magazine)
New Woman (Lifestyle Magazine, Monthly)
Celebrating Vivaha (Wedding Lifestyle Magazine)
Indiawali Brides (Wedding Lifestyle Magazine)
Wedding Affair (Wedding Lifestyle Magazine)

REAL ESTATE NEWSPAPER ADVERTISEMENTS (New Delhi editions):

Times of India
Hindustan Times
The Tribune
The Indian Express

BAPS/ACC BROCHURES AND PAMPHLETS

ACC Inauguration Brochure, New Delhi, Swaminarayan Bliss, November–December 2005

Swaminarayan Akshardham: Making & Experience, New Delhi 2006
Mandir: Shri Swaminarayan Mandir, Neasden, London 1995
Aksharbrahma Gunatitanand Swami, Pictorial Booklet, 2006
Vachanamrut Handbook (Insights into Bhagwan Swaminarayan's Teachings) by
    Sadhu Mukundcharandas, Swaminarayan Aksharpith, Amdavad 2004
The Role of Guru in Religious Traditions of the World, ed. N. M. Kansara and
    Jyotindra Dave, Swaminarayan Aksharpith, Amdavad 2005
Basic Concets of Swaminarayan Satsang by Sashu Vivekjivandas and Sadhu
    Amrutvijaydas, Swaminarayan Aksharpith, Amdavad 2002
Swaminarayan Sampraday by Sadhu Mukundcharandas, Swaminarayan Aksharpith,
    Amdavad 2002
Kishore Satsanga Prarambha by K. Dave, Swaminarayan Aksharpith, Amdavad
    1997 (2003)

Films/Documentation Material

BAPS and Akshardham Cultural Complex (DVDs):

Swaminarayan Akshardham New Delhi, Dedication Ceremony 2005–6
Mandir: A Labour of Love. London 2004
Golden Anniversary Celebration, Gandhinagar
Inauguration Rituals for ACC Opening (1–4), 2005
Sanskruti: A Mega Cultural Event, USA 2004
Sahaj Anand: Celebrating 50 Memorable Years of BAPS UK (The most magical
    show on earth), 2004
Sagar Arts: Ganga Dham Haridwar Promotion CD-ROM, 2005

New Age

Art of Living: One World Family Silver Jubilee Celebrations 2006
Bridal Industry
Aum Designer Weddings & Wedding Art, Information material on CD-ROM

Real Estate Development

Rosedale — Touch your Origin, Complementary DVD for the PBD 2007
Greater Noida. It's Just Full of Opportunities! Complementary DVD for the PBD
    2007
Assotech Elegante Deluxe Edition (2006)
Eros City Developers, Rosewood City, Gurgaon Grand Mansions II Brochure (normal
    and deluxe editions, 2005–6)

Secondary Sources

Abaza, Mona. 2001. Shopping Malls, Consumer Culture and the Reshaping of Public
    Space in Egypt. *Theory, Culture & Society* 18(5): 97–122.

Abbas, Ackbar. 2000. Cosmopolitan De-Scriptions: Shanghai and Hong Kong. *Public Culture* 12(3): 769–86.

Adiga, Aravind. 2008. *The White Tiger*. London: Atlantic Books.

Adrian, Bonnie. 2003. *Framing the Bride: Globalizing Beauty and Romance in Taiwan's Bridal Industry*. Berkeley: University of California Press.

Ahmad, Imtiaz and Helmut Reifeld (eds). 2001. *Middle Class Values in India and Western Europe*. New Delhi: Social Science Press, DK Publishers, Adenauer Foundation.

Ahuja, S. K. 2005. Slowdown on Mall Street. *Hindustan Times*, 25 March.

Allen, Jonathan. 2006. The Disney Touch at a Hindu Temple. *New York Times*, 6 August.

Anderson, Benedict. 1991 (1983). *Imagined Communities: Reflection on the Origin and Spread of Nationalism*. London: Verso.

Appadurai, Arjun (ed.). 1986. *The Social Life of Things: Commodities in Cultural Perspective*. Cambridge: Cambridge University Press.

———. 1990. Disjuncture and Difference in the Global Cultural Economy. *Public Culture* 2(1): 1–24.

———. 1997(1996). *Modernity at Large: Cultural Dimensions of Globalization*. New Delhi: Oxford University Press.

———. 2000. Grassroots Globalization and the Research Imagination. *Public Culture* 12(1): 1–19.

———. 2004a. The Capacity to Aspire: Culture and the Terms of Recognition, in Vijayendra Rao and Michael Walton (eds), *Culture and Public Action*, 59–84. New Delhi: Permanent Black.

———. 2004b. Public Culture, in Veena Das (ed.), *Handbook of Indian Sociology*, 257–74. New Delhi: Oxford University Press.

———. 2006. Spectral Housing and Urban Cleansing: Notes on Millennial Mumbai. *Public Culture (Special Issue on Cosmopolitanism)*: 12(3): 627–51.

Appadurai, Arjun and Carol Breckenridge. 1988. Why Public Culture? *Public Culture* 1(1): 5–9.

———. 1995. Public Modernity in India, in Carol Breckenridge (ed.), *Consuming Modernity: Public Culture in a South Asian World*, 1–22. Minneapolis: University of Minnesota Press.

Appadurai, Arjun and James Holston. 1996. Cities and Citizenship. *Public Culture* 8(2): 187–204.

Arthurs, Alberta. 2003. Social Imaginaries and Global Realities. *Public Culture* 15(3): 579–86.

Assayag, Jackie and Christopher J. Fuller (eds). 2005. *Globalizing India: Perspectives from Below*. London: Anthem Press.

Babb, Lawrence A. 1981. Glancing: Visual Interaction in Hinduism. *Journal of Anthropological Research* 37: 387–401.

Badone, Ellen and Sharon Roseman. 2004. Approaches to the Anthropology of Pilgrimage and Tourism, in Ellen Badone and Sharon Roseman (eds), *Intersecting Journeys: The Anthropology of Pilgrimage and Tourism*, 1–23. Chicago: University of Illinois Press.

Balme, Christopher B. 1998. Staging the Pacific: Framing Authenticity in Performances for Tourists at the Polynesian Cultural Center. *Theatre Journal* 50(1): 53–70.

Barker, Kim. 2006. Luxury Market in India on Rise. *Chicago Tribune*, 29 November.

Baruah, Nishiraj. 2005. Gone Cold in Gurgaon. *Hindustan Times*, 10 March, p. 1.

Basu, Kaushik (ed.). 2004. *India's Emerging Economy: Performance and Prospects in the 1990s and Beyond*. New Delhi: Oxford University Press.

Batra, Lalit. 2005. Vanishing Livelihoods in a 'Global' Metropolis, in Dunu Roy and Lalit Batra (eds), *Draft Delhi Master Plan 2021*, 22–30. New Delhi: Hazards Centre.

Batra, Lalit and Diya Mehra. 2006a. Das neoliberale Delhi: Der blick vom trümmerfeld eines planierten slums [Neoliberal Delhi: A View from the Devastated Field of a Removed Slum] in Ravi Ahuja and Christiane Brosius (eds), *Mumbai Delhi Kolkata: Annäherungen an Die Megastädte Indiens*, 157–72. Heidelberg: Draupadi.

———. 2006b. The Demolition of Slums and the Production of Neoliberal Space in Delhi. Unpublished paper.

Baudrillard, Jean. 1983. *Simulations*. New York: Semiotext(e).

———. 1996. Disneyworld Company. *Liberation*, 4 March.

Baviskar, Amita. 2003. Between Violence and Desire: Space, Power and Identity in the Making of Metropolitan Delhi. *International Social Science Journal* 55: 89–98.

Beck, Ulrich. 2004. The Truth of Others: A Cosmopolitan Approach. *Common Knowledge* 10(3): 430–49.

Bell, Catherine. 1992. *Ritual Theory, Ritual Practice*. New York: Oxford University Press.

Benedict, Burton. 1983. *The Anthropology of World Fairs*. London: The Lowie Museum of Anthropology.

Benjamin, Walter. 1963 (1935). *Das kunstwerk im zeitalter seiner technischen reproduzierbarkeit* [The Work of Art in the Age of Mechanical Reproduction]. Frankfurt am Main: Suhrkamp.

———. 1973 (1955). The Work of Art in the Age of Mechanical Reproduction, in Hannah Arendt (ed.), *Illuminations*, 211–44. London: Fontana Press.

———. 1999 (1939). Paris, Capital of the Nineteenth Century: Exposé of 1939, in Rolf Tiedemann (ed.), *The Arcades Project*, 15–26. Cambridge, MA: Belknap Press.

Bennett, Tony. 1994. The Exhibitionary Complex, in Nicholas Dirks, Geoff Eley and Sherry B. Ortner (eds), *Culture/Power/History: A Reader in Contemporary Social Theory*, 123–54. Princeton, NJ: Princeton University Press.

Béteille, André. 2001. The Social Character of the Indian Middle Class, in Imtiaz Ahmad and Helmut Reifeld (eds), *Middle Class Values*, 73–85. New Delhi: Social Science Press.

———. 2005a. *Anti-Utopia: Essential Writings of André Béteille*, ed. Dipankar Gupta. New Delhi: Oxford University Press.

———. 2005b (2000). Civil Society and the Good Society, in Dipankar Gupta (ed.), *Anti-Utopia: Essential Writings of André Béteille*, 437–58. New Delhi: Oxford University Press.

Bhabha, Homi. 1986. The Other Question: Difference, Discrimination and the Discourse of Colonialism in Francis Barker et al. (eds), *Literature, Politics and Theory*, 148–72. London: Methuen.

Bhandari, Vivek. 2006. Civil Society and the Predicament of Multiple Publics. *Comparative Studies of South Asia, Africa and the Middle East* 26(1): 36–50.

Bhargava, Rajeev. 2005. Introduction, in Rajeev Bhargava and Helmut Reifeld (eds), *Civil Society, Public Sphere and Citizenship*, 13–57. New Delhi: Sage Publications.

Bharucha, Ruzbeh. 2006. *Yamuna Gently Weeps: A Journey into the Yamuna Pushta Slum Demolitions*. New Delhi: Sainathann Communications.

Bhatia, B. M. 1994. *India's Middle Class Role in Nation-Building*. Delhi: Konark Publishers.

Bhatia, Gautam. 1994. *Punjabi Baroque: And Other Memories of Architecture*. New Delhi: Penguin.

Bhumika, K. 2004. The Big Fat Indian Wedding. *The Hindu*, 17 August (special supplement).

Bhupta, Malini. 2005a. Mall Mania. *India Today*, 7 November, 4(44): 10–17.

———. 2005b. Mills and Doom. *India Today*, 4 April, 4(13), http://www.indiatoday.com/itoday/20050404/states.html (accessed 30 October 2009).

———. 2007. Plastic Power. *India Today*, 31 December, 6(52): 213–15.

Blakely, Edward and Mary Gail Snyder. 1997. *Fortress America: Gated Communities in the United States*. Washington, DC: Brookings Institution Press and Lincoln Institute of Land Policy.

Bobb, Dilip. 2005. Living It Up. *India Today*, 28 August, 4(33): 34–36.

———. 2007. The Great Indian Globetrotter. *India Today* (Tourism Special).

Bourdieu, Pierre. 1984. *Distinction: A Social Critique of the Judgement of Taste*. London: Routledge.

———. 1993. *The Field of Cultural Production: Essays on Art and Literature*, ed. Randal Johnson. Oxford: Polity Press.

Brah, Avtar. 1996. *Cartographies of Diaspora: Contesting Identities*. London: Routledge.

Breckenridge, Carol (ed.). 1995. *Consuming Modernity: Public Culture in a South Asian World*. Minneapolis: University of Minnesota Press.

Brosius, Christiane. 2005. *Empowering Visions: The Politics of Representation in Hindu Nationalism*. London: Anthem Press.

———. 2008. The Enclaved Gaze: Exploring the Visual Culture of 'World Class-Living' in Urban India. *MARG*, Special Issue 'India's Popular Culture: Iconic Spaces and Fluid Images', ed. Jyotindra Jain, Mumbai: 114–25.

Brosius, Christiane and Melissa Butcher (eds). 1999. *Image Journeys: Audio-Visual Media and Cultural Change in India*. New Delhi: Sage Publications.

Brosius, Christiane and Nicholas Yazgi. 2007. Is There No Place Like Home? Contesting Cinematographic Constructions of Indian Diasporic Experiences. *Contributions to Indian Sociology* 41(3): 353–84.

Brown, Julie. 2001. *Making Culture Visible: The Public Display of Photographs at Fairs, Expositions and Exhibitions in the United States, 1847–1900*. Amsterdam: Harwood Academic Publishers.

Bryman, Alan. 2004. *Disneyization of Society*. London: Sage Publications.

Buck-Morss, Susan. 1989. *The Dialectics of Seeing: Walter Benjamin and the Arcades Project*. Cambridge, MA: MIT Press.

Butcher, Melissa 1999. Parallel Texts: The Body and Television in India, in Christiane Brosivs and Melissa Butcher (eds), *Image Journeys: Cultural Change and Audio Visual Media in India*. New Delhi: Sage Publications.

———. 2003. *Transnational Television, Cultural Identity and Change: When Star Came to India*. New Delhi: Sage Publications.

Butcher, Melissa and Selvaraj Velayutham (eds). 2009. *Dissent and Cultural Resistance in Asia's Cities*. London: Routledge.

Caldeira, Teresa. 2000. *City of Walls: Crime, Segregation, and Citizenship in Sao Paolo*. Berkeley: University of California Press.

———. 2005 (1996). Fortified Enclaves: The New Urban Segregation, in Jan Lin and Christopher Mele (eds), *The Urban Sociology Reader*, 327–45. London: Routledge.

Calhoun, Craig J. 2002a. The Class Consciousness of Frequent Travellers: Towards a Critique of Actually Existing Cosmopolitanism, in Steven Vertovec and Robin Cohen (eds), *Conceiving Cosmopolitanism. Theory, Context and Practice*, 86–109. Oxford: Oxford University Press.

———. 2002b. Imagining Solidarity: Cosmopolitanism, Constitutional Patriotism, and the Public Sphere. *Public Culture* 14(1): 147–71.

Carrette, Jeremy and Richard King. 2005. *Selling Spirituality: The Silent Takeover of Religion*. London: Routledge.

Cauter, Lieven de. 1993. The Panoramic Ecstasy: On World Exhibitions and the Disintegration of Experience. *Theory, Culture & Society* 10(1): 1–23.

Chaney, David. 1996. *Lifestyles: Key Ideas*. London: Routledge.

Chatterjee, Partha. 1993. *The Nation and its Fragments: Colonial and Postcolonial Histories*. Princeton: Princeton University Press.

———. 2003. Are Indian Cities Becoming Bourgeois at Last?, in Indira Chandrasekhar and Peter C. Seel (eds), *Body.City: Siting Contemporary Culture in India*, 170–85. New Delhi: Tulika Books.

Cheah, Pheng and Bruce Robbins (eds). 1998. *Cosmopolitics: Thinking and Feeling Beyond the Nation*. Minneapolis: University of Minnesota Press.

Chhaparia, Parul. 2006. States Bet on Big, Fat Indian Wedding. *The Times of India*, 2 September.

Clavé, S. Anton. 2007. *The Global Theme Park Industry*. Wallingford, UK: CABI.

Clifford, James. 1997. *Routes: Travel and Translation in the Late Twentieth Century*. Harvard: Harvard University Press.

Coleman, Simon. 2004. From England's Nazareth to Sweden's Jerusalem: Movement, (Virtual) Landscapes and Pilgrimage, in Simon Coleman and John Eade (eds), *Reframing Pilgrimage*, 45–68. London: Routledge.

Coleman, Simon and John Eade. 2004a. Introduction: Reframing Pilgrimage, in Simon Coleman and John Eade (eds), *Reframing Pilgrimage: Cultures in Motion*, 1–24. London: Routledge.

——— (eds). 2004b. *Reframing Pilgrimage: Cultures in Motion*. London: Routledge.

Comaroff, Jean and John L. Comaroff. 2000. Millennial Capitalism: First Thoughts on a Second Coming. *Public Culture* 12(2): 291–343.

Conrad, Sebastian and Shalini Randeria. 2002. Geteilte geschichten: Europa in einer postkolonialen welt [Shared Histories: Europe in a Postcolonial World] in Sebastian Conrad and Shalini Randeria (eds), *Jenseits des eurozentrismus: Postkoloniale perspektiven in den geschichts- und kulturwissenschaften* [Beyond Eurocentrism: Postcolonial Perspectives in the Humanities], 9–49. Frankfurt: Campus Velag.

Crary, Jonathan. 1990. *Techniques of the Observer: On Vision and Modernity in the Nineteenth Century*. Cambridge, MA: MIT Press.

Cross, Gary. 2006. Crowds and Leisure: Thinking Comparatively across the 20th Century. *Journal of Social History* 39(3): 631–50.

Crouch, David. 1999. *Leisure/Tourism Geographies*. London: Routledge.

Cunningham, Douglas. 2005. A Theme Park Built for One: The New Ubanism vs. Disney Design in *The Truman Show*. *Critical Survey* 17(1): 109–30.

Das, Anupreeta. 2005. Middle-Class India Plows New Wealth into Big Weddings. *Christian Science Monitor*, 29 September, http://www.csmonitor.com/2005/0929/p01s04-wosc.html (accessed 12 September 2008).

Das, Gurcharan. 2002 (2000). *India Unbound: From Independence to the Global Information Age*. New Delhi: Penguin.

Das, Veena. 1980. The Mythological Film and Its Framework of Meaning: An Analysis of *Jai Santoshi Ma*. *India International Quarterly* 8(1): 43–56.

———. 1993. Der anthropologische diskurs über Indien: Die vernunft und ihr anderes [The Anthropological Discourse on India: Reason and its Other], in Eberhard Berg and Martin Fuchs (eds), *Kultur, soziale praxis, text: Die krise der repräsentation* [Culture, Social Practice, Text: The Crisis of Representation], 402–25. Frankfurt: Suhrkamp.

Das Gupta, M. 2007. Mall Mania and All That Jazz. *Hindustan Times*, 15 January, p. 2.

Dasgupta, Rana. 2006. Living with the Commonwealth Games, 11 August, www.bbc.co.uk/freethinkingworld/2006/08/living_with_the_commonwealth_g.shtml (accessed 8 April 2008).

Datta, Damayanti. 2006. The Weight of a Nation. *India Today*, 10 April, V(14): 28–35.

———. 2008. Netrimony. *India Today*, 17 March, 33(12): 66–74.

David, Stephen and Sandeep Unnithan. 2005. The World is Calling: India Controls 44 per cent of Global Outsourcing. *India Today*, 22 August.

Davis, Mike. 1992a. Fortress Los Angeles: The Militarization of Urban Space, in Michael Sorkin (ed.), *Variations on a Theme Park: The New American City and the End of Public Space*, 154–80. New York: Hill and Wang.

———. 1992b. *City of Quartz: Excavating the Future in Los Angeles*. New York: Vintage Books.

———. 2004. Planet of Slums: Urban Involution and the Informal Proletariat. *New Left Review* 26: 92–124.

———. 2005. Sinister Paradise: Does the Road to the Future End at Dubai? http://www.tomdispatch.com/post/5807/mike_davis_on_a_paradise_built_on_oil (accessed 22 August 2009),

Davis, Richard. 1997. *Lives of Indian Images*. Princeton: Princeton University Press.

Dawson, Ashley and Brent Hayes Edwards. 2005. Introduction: Global Cities of the South. *Social Text* 22(4): 1–7.

Delanty, Gerard (ed.). 2006. *Europe and Asia Beyond East and West*. London: Routledge.

Denslagen, Wim and Niels Gutschow (eds). 2005. *Architectural Imitations: Reproductions and Pastiches in East and West*. Maastricht: Shaker Publishing.

Deshpande, Satish. 2003. *Contemporary India: A Sociological View*. New Delhi: Penguin.

———. 2004. Modernization, in Veena Das (ed.), *Handbook of Indian Sociology*, 172–202. New Delhi: Oxford University Press.

Dickey, Sara. 2000. Permeable Homes: Domestic Service, Household Space, and the Vulnerability of Class Boundaries in Urban India. *American Ethnologist* 27(2): 462–89.

Dickey, Sara. 2002. Anjali's Prospects: Class Mobility in Urban India, in Diane Mines and Sarah Lamb (eds), *Everyday Life in South Asia*, 214–26. Bloomington/Indianapolis: Indiana University Press.

Dirks, Nicholas, Geoff Eley and Sherry B. Ortner (eds). 1994. *Culture/Power/History: A Reader in Contemporary Social Theory*. Princeton: Princeton University Press.

Doshi, Harish. 1974. *Traditional Neighbourhood in a Modern City*. New Delhi: Abhinav Publications.

Dupont, Veronique. 2000. Spatial and Demographic Growth of Delhi since 1947 and the Main Migration Flows, in Veronique Dupont, Emma Tarlo and Denis Vidal (eds), *Delhi: Urban Space and Human Destinies*, 229–40. Delhi: Manohar.

———. 2005. The Idea of a New Chic Delhi through Publicity Hype, in Romi Khosla (ed.), *The Idea of Delhi*, 78–93. Mumbai: Marg Publications.

Dwyer, Rachel. 2000. *All you Want is Money, All you Need is Love: Sex and Romance in Modern India*. London: Cassell.

———. 2004. The Swaminarayan Movement, in Knut Jacobsen and Pratap Kumar (eds), *South Asians in the Diaspora: Histories and Religious Traditions*, 180–202. Leiden, Boston: Brill.

———. 2006. Kiss or Tell? Declaring Love in Hindi Films, in Francesca Orsini (ed.), *Love in South Asia: A Cultural History*, 289–302. Cambridge: Cambridge University Press.

Eck, Diana. 1981. *Darshan: Seeing the Divine Image in India*. Chambersburg: Anima.

———. 1998. The Imagined Landscape: Patterns in the Construction of Hindu Sacred Geography. *Contributions to Indian Sociology* 32(2): 165–88.

Edensor, Tim. 1998. *Tourists at the Taj: Performance and Meaning at a Symbolic Site*. London: Routledge.

Ewen, Stuart. 1988. *All Consuming Images: The Politics of Style in Contemporary Culture*. New York: Basic Books.

Falzon, Mark-Anthony. 2005. *Cosmopolitan Connections: The Sindhi Diaspora 1860–2000*. Delhi: Oxford University Press.

Featherstone, Mike. 2002. Cosmopolis. *Theory, Culture & Society* 19(1–2): 1–16.

Fenton, John. 1992. Academic Study of Religions and Asian Indian-American College Students, in Raymond B. Williams (ed.), *A Sacred Thread*, 258–77. Chambersburg: Anima.

Fernandes, Leela. 2000. Nationalising 'the Global': Media Images, Cultural Politics and the Middle Class in India. *Media, Culture & Society* 22(5): 611–28.

———. 2006. *India's New Middle Class: Democratic Politics in an Era of Economic Reform.* Minneapolis: University of Minnesota Press.

Fisher, Melissa S. and Greg Downey (eds). 2006. *Frontiers of Capital: Ethnographic Reflections on the New Economy.* Durham: Duke University Press.

Foucault, Michel. 1977 (1975). *Discipline and Punish: The Birth of the Prison.* London: Penguin.

Freitag, Sandria. 1989. *Collective Action and Community: Public Arenas and the Emergence of Communalism in North India.* Berkeley: Cambridge University Press.

Friedman, Jonathan (ed.). 1994. *Consumption and Identity.* Amsterdam: Harwood Academic Publishers.

Friedman, Jonathan. 2004. Globalization, Transnationalization, and Migration: Ideologies and Realities of Global Transformation, in Jonathan Friedman and Shalini Randeria (eds), *Worlds on the Move: Globalization, Migration and Cultural Security*, 63–90. London and New York: I. B. Tauris.

Friedmann, J. and G. Wolff. 1982. World City Formation: An Agenda for Research and Action. *International Journal of Urban and Regional Research* 6(3): 309–44.

Friedman, Thomas. 2005. *The World is Flat: A Brief History of the Twenty-First Century.* New York: Farrar, Straus, Reese and Giroux.

Froystad, Kathinka. 2003. Master–Servant Relations and the Domestic Reproduction of Caste in Northern India. *Ethnos* 68(1): 73–94.

———. 2005. *Blended Boundaries: Caste, Class, and Shifting Faces of 'Hinduness' in a North Indian City.* New Delhi: Oxford University Press.

Fuller, Christopher. 1992. *The Camphor Flame: Popular Hinduism and Society in India.* Princeton, NJ: Princeton University Press.

Fuller, Christopher J. and Haripriya Narasimhan. 2007. Information Technology Professionals and the New-Rich Middle Class in Chennai (Madras). *Modern Asian Studies* 41(1): 121–50.

Gandhi, Mohandas K. 1966. *The Collected Works of Mahatma Gandhi*, vol. XXI. Delhi: Government of India.

———. 1982. *The Collected Works of Mahatma Gandhi*, vol. LXXXVI. Delhi: Government of India.

Ganguly, Shailaja. 2002. The Spirit of Gen X. *Life Positive*, April, 11(4), http://www.lifepositive.com/archives/archives2002.html (accessed 12 September 2008).

Ganguly-Scrase, Ruchira and Timothy J. Scrase. 2009. *Globalisation and the Middle Classes in India: The Social and Cultural Impact of Neoliberal Reforms.* London: Routledge.

Gaonkar, Dilip Parameshwar. 2001. *Alternative Modernities.* Durham: Duke University Press.

———. 2002. Toward New Imaginaries: An Introduction. *Public Culture* 14(1): 1–19.

Gaonkar, Dilip Parameshwar and Robert J. McCarthy. 1994. Panopticism and Publicity: Bentham's Quest for Transparency. *Public Culture* 6(3): 547–75.

Gellner, David. 1982. Max Weber, Capitalism and the Religion of India. *Sociology* 16(4): 526–43.

Gentleman, Amelia. 2006. Letter from India: India Can't Wait to Put the 'Super' before the 'Power'. *International Herald Tribune*, 23 November.

———. 2007. Real India Seeps into Gated Villas. *Observer* (London), 26 August.

Gill, Rajesh (ed.). 2005. *State, Market and Civil Society: Issues and Interface.* Jaipur: Rawat Publications.

Glasze, Georg, Chris Webster and Klaus Frantz (eds). 2006. *Private Cities: Global and Local Perspectives.* London: Routledge.

Goel, Vijay. 2003. *Delhi: The Emperor's City: Rediscovering Chandni Chowk and its Environs.* New Delhi: Lustre Press.

Gokulsing, Moti and Wimal Dissanayake (eds). 2009. *Popular Culture in a Globalised India.* London: Routledge.

Goldstein-Gidoni, Ofra. 2000. The Production of Tradition and Culture in the Japanese Wedding Enterprise. ETHNOS 65(1): 33–55.

Gooptu, Nandini. 2001. *The Politics of the Urban Poor in Early Twentieth Century India.* Cambridge: Cambridge University Press.

Goswamy, B. N. 1991. Another Past, Another Context: Exhibiting Art Abroad, in Steven Lavine and Ivan Karp (eds), *Exhibiting Cultures: The Poetics and Politics of Museum Display*, 68–78. Washington and London: Smithsonian Institution Press.

Gottdiener, Mark. 2001. *The Theming of America: American Dreams, Media Fantasies, and Themed Environment.* Boulder: Westview Press.

Gupta, Dipankar. 2000. *Mistaken Modernity: India between Worlds.* New Delhi: Harper Collins.

———. 2004. Social Stratification, in Veena Das (ed.), *Handbook of Indian Sociology*, 120–41. New Delhi: Oxford University Press.

———. 2006. Is This the Master Plan? *Hindustan Times*, 27 September, p. 12.

Gupta, Navina. 2006. Delhi nach der teilung Indiens: Zur flüchtlingsgeschichte einer megastadt [Delhi after Partition: On the Migration History of a Megacity], in Ravi Ahuja and Christiane Brosius (eds), *Mumbai–Delhi–Kolkata: Annäherungen an die megastädte Indiens* [Mumbai–Delhi–Kolkata: Approaches to India's Megacities] 143–56. Heidelberg: Draupadi.

Gupta, Shruti. 2006. Home Truths: How to Procure a Dream Home. *India Today* (Buyer's Guide), July–September, pp. 50–55.

Gupta, Akhil, and James Ferguson (eds). 1997. *Anthropological Locations: Boundaries and Grounds of a Field Science.* Berkeley: University of California Press.

Habermas, Jürgen. 1989 (1962). *The Structural Transformation of the Public Sphere: An Inquiry into a Category of Bourgeois Society.* Cambridge: The MIT Press.

Hall, Stuart. 1997. The Local and the Global: Globalization and Ethnicity, in Anthony King (ed.), *Culture, Globalization and the World System*, 19–40. Minneapolis: University of Minnesota Press.

Hall, Stuart. 1998. *Representation: Cultural Representations and Signifying Practices.* London, Thousand Oaks: Sage Publications.

Hannerz, Ulf. 1980. *Exploring the City: Inquiries toward an Urban Anthropology*. New York: Columbia University Press.

Hannerz, Ulf. 1992. *Cultural Complexity: Studies in the Social Organization of Meaning*. New York: Columbia University Press.

———. 1993. The Cultural Role of World Cities, in Anthony Cohen and K. Fukui (eds), *Humanizing the City: Social Contexts of Urban Life at the Turn of the Millennium*, 69–83. Edinburgh: Edinburgh University Press.

———. 1996. *Transnational Connections: Culture, People, Places*. London: Routledge.

Hansen, Kathryn. 2006. Ritual Enactments in a Hindi 'Mythological': Betab's *Mahabharat* in Parsi Theatre. *Economic and Political Weekly*, 2 December: 4985–91.

Hardiman, David. 1988. Class Base of Swaminarayan Sect. *Economic Political Weekly*, 10 September: 1907–12.

Hardt, Michael. 1995. The Withering of Civil Society. *Social Text* 45: 27–44.

Harvey, David. 1987. Flexible Accumulation through Urbanization: Reflections on 'Post-Modernism' in the American City. *Antipode* 19(3): 260–86.

———. 1989. *The Condition of Postmodernity: An Enquiry into the Origins of Cultural Change*. Oxford: Blackwell.

———. 2000. Cosmopolitanism and the Banality of Geographical Evils. *Public Culture* 12(2): 529–64.

Hasan, Zoya. 2001. Changing Political Orientations of the Middle Classes in India, in Imtiaz Ahmad and Helmut Reifeld (eds), *Middle Class Values*, 152–70. New Delhi: Social Science Press.

Hassenpflug, Dieter. 2008. *Der urbane code chinas* [China's Urban Code]. Boston: Birkhäuser.

Hawkins, Sophie. 1999. Bordering Realism: The Aesthetics of Sai Baba's Mediated Universe, in Christiane Brosius and Melissa Butcher (eds), *Image Journeys: Audio-Visual Media and Cultural Change in India*, 139–63. New Delhi, Thousand Oaks, London: Sage Publications.

Hazards Centre. 2006a. *Delhi Fact Sheet 1*. New Delhi: Hazards Centre.

———. 2006b. *Delhi Fact Sheet 8*. New Delhi: Hazards Centre.

Heelas, Paul. 1996. *New Age Movement: The Celebration of the Self and the Sacralization of Modernity (The New Age Movement: Religion, Culture and Society in the Age of Post Modernity)*. Oxford: Blackwell.

Heelas, Paul and Linda Woodhead (eds). 2005. *The Spiritual Revolution: Why Religion is Giving Way to Spirituality*. Oxford: Blackwell.

Heitzman, James. 2004. *Network City: Planning the Information Society in Bangalore*. New York: Oxford University Press.

———. 2008. *The City in South Asia*. London: Routledge.

Herman, Phyllis. 2003. Remaking Rama for the Modern Sightseer: It's a Small Hindu World After All. *South Asian Popular Culture* 1(2): 125–40.

Heryanto, Ariel. 1999. The Years of Living Luxuriously: Identity Politics of Indonesia's New Rich, in Michael Pinches (ed.), *Culture and Privilege in Capitalist Asia*, 159–87. London: Routledge.

Hoover, Stewart. 1988. *Mass Media Religion: The Social Sources of the Electronic Church, Communication and Human Values*. Newbury Park: Sage Publications.

Hoover, Stuart and Knut Lundby (eds). 1997. *Rethinking Media, Religion, and Culture*. London, Thousand Oaks, New Delhi: Sage Publications.

Horshield, Peter. 1984. *Religious Television: The American Experience*. New York: Longman.

Hussain, Shabana. 2009. DDA to Buy 333 Flats in Games Village for Rs 700 cr. Livemint.com, 11 May.

Ihlau, Olaf. 2006. *Weltmacht Indien* [World Power India]. München: Siedler Verlag.

Inden, Ronald. 1999. Transnational Class, Erotic Arcadia and Commercial Utopia in Hindi Films, in Christiane Brosius and Melissa Butcher (eds), *Image Journeys*, 41–66. New Delhi: Sage Publications.

India Brand Equity Foundation. 2005. India's Middle Class Dream Takes Shape: Economic Indicators, *India Brand Equity Foundation* (Gurgaon), February, p. 6.

Indian Troops Storm Hindu Temple. *CBS News*, 25 September 2005.

Jacob, Apana. 2005. Seva as Sadhana. *Life Positive*, October, pp. 73–76.

Jaffrelot, Christophe and Peter van der Veer (eds). 2008. *Patterns of Middle Class Consumption in India and China*. New Delhi: Sage Publications.

Jain, Jyotindra. 2009. Curating Culture, Curating Territory: Religio-Political Mobility in India, in Gayatin Sinha (ed.), *Art and Visual Culture in India: 1857–2007*. Mumbai: Marg Publications.

Jain, Kajri. 2007. *Gods in the Bazaar: The Economies of Indian Calendar Art*. Durham and London: Duke University Press.

Jain, Madhu. 2001. The Good Life. *Seminar 501*, May (Special Issue), 'Culturescape', http://www.india-seminar.com/2001/501/501%20madhu%20jain.htm (accessed on 29 August 2008).

Jha, Prem Shankar. 2002. *The Perilous Road to the Market: The Political Economy of Reform in Russia, India and China*. New Delhi: Rupa & Co.

Jodhka, Surinder. 2002. Nation and Village: Images of Rural India in Gandhi, Nehru and Ambedkar. *Economic and Political Weekly*, 10 August: 3343–53.

Johnson, Randal. 1993. Pierre Bourdieu on Art, Literature and Culture, in Randal Johnson (ed.), *The Field of Cultural Production: Essays on Art and Literature*, 1–25. Cambridge, Oxford: Polity Press.

Juergensmeyer, Mark. 1991. *Radhasoami Reality: The Logic of a Modern Faith*. Princeton: Princeton University Press.

———. 1992. A New International Religion: Radhasoami, in Raymond B. Williams (ed.), *A Sacred Thread: Modern Transmission of Hindu Traditions in India and Abroad*, 278–99. Chambersburg: Anima.

Juluri, Vamsee. 2004. *Becoming a Global Audience: Longing and Belonging in Indian Music Television*. New Delhi: Orient Longman.

Just, Tobias, Maren Väth and Hry Chin. 2006. Baustelle Indien: Perspektiven für die indischen immobilienmärkte [Construction-site India: Perspectives for the Indian Real Estate Markets], in Hans-Joachim Frank (ed.), *Indien spezial aktuelle themen 351*, 28. Frankfurt: Deutsche Bank.

Kackar, Sunitha Dasappa. 2005. Mpd-2021 and the Vision of a 'Slum-Free' Delhi, in Dunu Roy and Lalit Batra (eds), *Draft Delhi Master Plan 2021*, 15–21. New Delhi: Hazards Centre.

Kakar, Sudhir. 1989. *Intimate Relations: Exploring Indian Sexuality*. New Delhi: Penguin.
———. 2006. The Elastic Indian. *India Today*, 15–21 August, V(33): 38–44.
Kalam, Abdul. 2005. The Akshardham Experience. *About Hinduism*, 7 November. http://hinduism.about.com/od/akshardhamtemple/a/akshardhamdelhi.htm (accessed 15 June 2009).
Karir, Rohit. 2005. Live Life Egyptian-Size. *The Times of India*, 19 February.
Kaul, Vatsala. 2005. Spahhh. *India Empire*, 61–64, http://www.indiaempire.com/v2/magazine/2004/Oct/lifestyle-spa.html (accessed 30 October 2009).
Kaul, Sanjay. 2006. Middle Class in Politics. *Civil Society* (New Delhi).
Kaur, Raminder. 2003. *Performative Politics and the Cultures of Hinduism: Public Uses of Religion in Western India*, New Delhi: Permanent Black.
Kaviraj, Sudipta. 1997. Filth and the Public Sphere: Concepts and Practices About Space in Calcutta. *Public Culture* 10(1): 83–113.
Keith, Michael. 2005. *After the Cosmopolitan? Multicultural Identities and the Future of Racism*. London: Routledge.
Khilnani, Sunil. 1997. *The Idea of India*. London: Hamish Hamilton.
King, Anthony (ed.). 1980. *Buildings and Society: Essays on the Social Development of the Built Environment*. London, Boston and Henley: Routledge & Kegan Paul.
King, Anthony. 1990. Architecture, Capital and the Globalization of Culture. *Theory Culture Society* 7: 397–411.
———. 1995. Re-Presenting World Cities: Cultural Theory/Social Practice, in Paul Knox and Peter Taylor (eds), *World Cities in a World System*, 215–31. Cambridge: Cambridge University Press.
Kirshenblatt-Gimblett, Barbara. 1998. *Destination Culture: Tourism, Museums, and Heritage*. Berkeley: University of California Press.
Kolenda, Pauline. 1984. Woman as Tribute, Woman as Flower: Images of 'Woman' in Weddings in North and South India. *American Ethnologist* 11(1): 98–117.
Koppikar, Smruti. 2005. Pick It up, Break It Down. *Outlook*, 21 March.
Kosambi, Meera. 1993. Colonial Urban Transformation in India, in M. Hasan and N. Gupta (eds), *India's Colonial Encounter*, 203–35. Delhi: Manohar.
Kulkarni, Rajesh. 2006a. Creating Wealth for the Global Indian. *Realty Plus: The Real Estate Review*, December, 3(4): 30–41.
———. 2006b. Foreign Buyers, NRIs Fuel Goa Realty Boom. *Realty Plus: The Real Estate Review*, February, 2(5): 44–46.
———. 2006c. Viva La Goa! *Realty Plus: The Real Estate Review*, February, 2(5): 76–78.
Kumar, Krishan. 1997. Home: The Promise and Predicament of Private Life at the End of the Twentieth Century, in Jeff Weintraub and Krishan Kumar (eds), *Public and Private in Thought and Practice*, 204–36. Chicago and London: University of Chicago Press.
Krueger, Oliver. 2004. 'It's All About Loving your Parents': The Reflection of Tradition, Modernity and Rituals in Popular Indian Movies. *Marburg Journal of Religion* 9(1), September, http://web.uni-marburg.de/religionswissenschaft/ journal/ mjr/ pdf/2004/krueger2004.pdf (accessed 27 June 2009).

Lak, Daniel. 2005. *Mantras of Change: Reporting India in a Time of Flux.* New Delhi: Penguin, Viking.

Lefèbvre, Henri. 1991 (1974). *The Production of Space,* trans. N. Donaldson-Smith. Oxford: Basil Blackwell.

Legnaro, Aldo and Almut Birenheide. 2005. *Stätten der späten moderne: Reiseführer durch bahnhöfe, shopping malls, Disneyland Paris* [Sites of Late Modernity: A Trvel Guide through Railway Stations, Shopping Malls and Disneyland Paris]. Wiesbaden: VS Verlag für Sozialwissenschaften.

Lennevig, Michael. 1988. *Godwatching: Viewer, Religion and Television.* London: Libbey.

Lentz, Sebastian and Peter Lindner. 2003. Privatisierung des öffentlichen raumes: Soziale segregation und geschlossene wohnviertel Moskaus [Privatisation of Public Space: Social Segregation and Enclosed Residential Neighbourhoods in Moscow]. *Geographische Rundschau* 55: 50–57.

Liechty, Mark. 2003. *Suitably Modern: Making Middle-Class Culture in a New Consumer Society.* Princeton: Princeton University Press.

Little, John. 1995. Video Vacana: Swadhyaya and Sacred Tapes, in Lawrence A. Babb and Susan Wadley (eds), *Media and the Transformation of Religion in South Asia,* 254–84. Pennsylvania: University of Pennsylvania Press.

Low, Setha. 2004. *Behind the Gates: Life, Security, and the Pursuit of Happiness in Fortress America.* London: Routledge.

Lowenthal, David. 1985. *The Past Is a Foreign Country.* Cambridge: Cambridge University Press.

———. 2002. The Past as a Theme Park, in Terence Young and Robert Riley (eds), *Theme Park Landscapes. Antecedents and Variations,* 11–24. Washington: Dumbarton Oaks.

Luce, Edward. 2007. *In Spite of the Gods: The Strange Rise of Modern India.* New York: Doubleday, Random House.

Lyon, David. 2000. *Jesus in Disneyland: Religion in Postmodern Times.* Cambridge: Polity.

Maar, Christa and Hubert Burda (eds). 2004. *Iconic Turn: Die Neue Macht der Bilder.* Köln: DuMont.

MacCannell, Dean. 1973. Staged Authenticity: Arrangements of Social Space in Tourist Settings. *The American Journal of Sociology,* November, 79(3): 589–603.

Maharaj, Pramukh Swami. 2006. Introduction, in Pramukh Swami Maharaj (ed.), *Swaminarayan Akshardham: Making & Experience,* 8–9. Amdavad: Swaminarayan Aksharpith.

Maitra, Pushkar and Ranjan Ray. 2004. Household Characteristics and Living Standards: Evidence from India, in Mita Bhattacharya, Russell Smyth and Marika Vicziany (eds), *South Asia in the Era of Globalization: Trade, Industrialization and Welfare,* 165–94. New York: Nova Science Publishers.

Mall to Combine Heritage and Modernity. *Reality Plus: The Real Estate Review,* September 2006, 3(1): 132.

Mann, Michael. 2006. Metamorphosen einer metropole: 1911–1977 [Metamorphosis of a Metropolis, 1911–1977], in Ravi Ahuja and Christiane Brosius (eds), *Mumbai–Delhi–Kolkata: Annäherungen an die megastädte Indiens* [Mumbai–Delhi–Kolkata: Approaches to India's Megacities], 127–42. Heidelberg: Draupadi.

Manuel, Peter. 1993. *Cassette Culture: Popular Music and Technology in North India*. Chicago: University of Chicago Press.

Martikainen, Tuomas. 2001. Religion and Consumer Culture. *Tidsskrift for kirke, religion og samfunn (Journal of Church, Religion and Society)* 14(2): 111–25.

Masselos, Jim. 1991. Appropriating Urban Space: Social Constructs of Bombay in the Times of the Raj. *South Asia* 14(1): 33–64.

———. 1996. Migration and Urban Identity: Bombay's Famine Refugees in the Nineteenth Century, in Sujata Patel and Alice Thorner (eds), *Bombay: Mosaic of Modern Culture*, 25–58. New Delhi: Oxford University Press.

———. 2007. *The City in Action: Bombay Struggles for Power*. New Delhi: Oxford University Press.

Massey, Doreen. 1995. Double Articulation: A Place in the World, in Angelika Bammer (ed.), *Displacements: Cultural Identities in Question*, 110–24. Bloomington and Indianapolis: Indiana University Press.

Mathur, Saloni and Kavita Singh. 2007. Reincarnations of the Museum: The Museum in an Age of Religious Revivalism, in Vishakha N. Desai and Michael Ann Holly (eds), *Asian Art History: Towards the 21st Century*, 149–68. Williamstown, MA: Clark Art Institute.

Mayaram, Shail (ed.). 2009. *The Other Global City*. London: Routledge.

Mazzarella, William. 2003. *Shoveling Smoke: Advertising and Globalization in Contemporary India*. Durham: Duke University Press.

———. 2005. Indian Middle Class, in Rachel Dwyer (ed.), *South Asia Keywords*, http://www.soas.ac.uk/southasianstudies/keywords/24808.pdf. London: The School of Oriental and African Studies.

Mbembe, Achille. 2004. Aesthetics of Superfluity. *Public Culture* 16(3): 373–405.

McCarthy, Paul. 1994. *Postmodern Desire: Learning from India*. New Delhi: Promilla & Co.

McKean, Lise. 1996. *Divine Enterprise: Gurus and the Hindu Nationalist Movement*. Chicago: University of Chicago Press.

McKenzie, Evan. 2006. The Dynamics of Privatopia: Private Residential Governance in the USA, in Georg Glasze, Chris Webster and Klaus Frantz (eds), *Private Cities: Global and Local Perspectives*, 9–30. London: Routledge.

McKinsey & Company 2003. *Vision Mumbai: Transforming Mumbai into a World-Class City: A Summary of Recommendations*. Mumbai: McKinsey and Bombay First.

Mele, Christopher and Jan Lin (eds). 2005. *The Urban Sociology Reader*. London: Routledge.

Menon, Krishna. 1997. Imagining the Indian City. *Economic and Political Weekly*, 15 November: 2932–36.

———. 2000. The Contemporary Architecture of Delhi: The Role of the State as Middleman, in Veronique Dupont, Emma Tarlo and Denis Vidal (eds), *Delhi: Urban Space and Human Destinies*, 143–56. Delhi: Manohar.

———. 2005. Inventive Mimesis in New Delhi: The Temples of Chhattarpur, in Wim Denslagen and Niels Gutschow (eds), *Architectural Imitations: Reproductions and Pastiches in East and West*, 98–123. Maastricht: Shaker Publishing.

Menon, Krishna. 2006. Demolitions and Urban Planning. *The Times of India*, 3 April.
————. n.d. Who Plans Our Cities? Unpublished paper.
Menon, Jayashree. 2007. Wedding Vows. *Femina Bridal Book*, pp. 24–40.
Meyer, Birgit and Annelies Moors (eds). 2006. *Religion, Media, and the Public Sphere*. Bloomington and Indianapolis: Indiana University Press.
Michaels, Axel. 2003. Tírtha: Orte der transzendenz in hinduistischen texten, ritualen und karten [Tirtha: Sites of Transcendence in Hindu Texts, Rituals and Maps], in Gerhard Oberhammer and Marcus Schmücker (eds), *Mythisierung der transzendenz als entwurf ihrer erfahrung*, 349–80. Vienna: Österreichische Akademie der Wissenschaften.
————. 2004. *Hinduism: Past and Present*. Princeton: Princeton University Press.
Miller, Daniel. 1991 (1987). *Material Culture and Mass Consumption: Social Archaeology*. Oxford: Basil Blackwell.
Miller, David (ed.). 1995. *Worlds Apart: Modernity Through the Prism of the Local*. London: Routledge.
Mishra, Asit R. 2009. Slowest GDP Growth in Six Years at 5.3%. *Mint, Hindustan Times*, 3(51), 28 February.
Mishra, B. B. 1961. *The Indian Middle Classes: Their Growth in Modern Times*. London: Oxford University Press.
Mitchener, John. 1992. *Guru: The Search for Enlightenment*. Delhi: Viking.
Mohamed, Nader. 2006. India: Hot Destination for Foreign Developers. *Realty Plus: The Real Estate Review*, September, 3(1): 94.
MoneyLIFE. 2007. The 5 Hottest Lifestyle Stocks, 17 January, http://in.rediff.com/money/2007/jan/17stocks.htm (accessed 30 October 2009).
Mookerjee, Debraj. 2007. It's More than 'Just Hopping'. *Celebrating Vivaha* 6(3): 48–49.
Morris, Brian. 2001. Architectures of Entertainment, in David Holmes (ed.), *Virtual Globalization: Virtual Spaces/Tourist Spaces*, 205–19. London: Routledge.
Mukhopadhyay, Partha. 2006. Whither Urban Renewal? *Economic and Political Weekly*, 11 March: 879–84.
Müller, Harald. 2006. *Weltmacht Indien: Wie uns der rasante aufstieg herausfordert* [World Power India: How the Dramatic Rise Challenges us]. Frankfurt am Main: Fischer Verlag.
Munshi, Shoma. 2001. Marvellous Me: The Beauty Industry and the Construction of the 'Modern' Indian Woman, in Shoma Munshi (ed.), *Images of the 'Modern Woman' in Asia: Global Media, Local Meanings*, 78–93. Richmond: Amazon Press.
Munshi, Surendra. 1988. Max Weber on India: An Introductory Critique. *Contributions to Indian Sociology* 22: 1–34.
Nair, Manoj and Rajeshwari Sharma. 2005. Bulle Shah Beckons. *The Economic Times*, 3 July, p. 3.
Naisbit, J. 1996. *Megatrends Asia: The Eight Asian Megatrends that are Changing the World*. London: Nicholas Bradley.
Nandy, Ashis. 2001. *An Ambiguous Journey to the City: The Village and the Other Odd Ruins of the Self in Indian Imagination*. New Delhi: Oxford University Press.

Narayanan, Harini. 2006. Der schein Delhis: Die luftdicht verpackte welt der shopping malls [India Shining: The Hermetically Packed World of Shopping Malls], in Ravi Ahuja and Christiane Brosius (eds), *Mumbai–Delhi–Kolkata. Annäherungen an die megastädte Indiens* [Mumbai–Delhi–Kolkata: Approaches to India's Megacities], 157–72. Heidelberg: Draupadi.

National Council for Applied Economic Research (NCAER). 2005. The Great Indian Middle Class: A Survey of 2004. *The Billionaire Club*, November, p. 43.

Ngai, Pun. 2003. Subsumption or Consumption? The Phantom of Consumer Revolution in 'Globalizing' China. *Cultural Anthropology* 18(4): 469–92.

Nilekani, Rohini. 2006. Planning for Cities of the Future. *The Hindu*, 18 October, p. 11.

Oakes, Tim. 2006. The Village as Theme Park: Mimesis and Authenticity in Chinese Tourism, in Tim Oakes and Louisa Schein (eds), *Translocal China: Linkages, Identities, and the Reimagining of Space*, 166–92. London: Routledge.

Oettermann, Stephan. 1980. *Das panorama: Die geschichte eines massenmediums* [The Panorama: On the History of a Mass Media]. Frankfurt am Main: Syndikat.

O'Guinn, Thomas and Russell Belk. 1989. Heaven on Earth: Consumption at Heritage Village, USA. *Journal of Consumer Research* 16: 227–38.

Oldenburg, Veena. 1984. *The Making of Colonial Lucknow, 1856–1877*. Princeton: Princeton University Press.

Ong, Aihwa. 1999. *Flexible Citizenship: The Cultural Logics of Transnationality*. Durham and London: Duke University Press.

Orsini, Francesca (ed.). 2006. *Love in South Asia: A Cultural History*. Cambridge: Cambridge University Press.

Osella, Filippo and Caroline Osella. 1998. Friendship and Flirting: Micro-Politics in Kerala, South India. *Journal of the Royal Anthropological Institute* 4(2): 189–207.

———. 2006. *Men and Masculinities in South India*. London: Anthem Press.

Otnes, Cele and Elizabeth Pleck. 2003. *Cinderella Dreams: The Allure of the Lavish Wedding*. Berkeley: University of California Press.

Oza, Rupal. 2006. *The Making of Neoliberal India: Nationalism, Gender and the Paradoxes of Globalization*. New Delhi: Women Unlimited/Kali for Women.

Patel, Sujata and Kushal Deb (eds). 2006. *Urban Studies*. New Delhi: Oxford University Press.

Pinches, Michael. 1999. Cultural Relations, Class and the New Rich of Asia, in Michael Pinches (ed.), *Culture and Privilege in Capitalist Asia*, 1–55. London: Routledge.

Pinney, Christopher. 1997. *Camera Indica: The Social Life of Indian Photographs*. London: Reaktion Books.

———. 2004. *Photos of the Gods: The Printed Images and Political Struggle in India*. New Delhi: Oxford University Press.

———. 2005. Political Campaigns: The Political Economy of Gloss. *Bidoun* (Icons) 5: 87–89.

Poggendorf-Kakar, Katharina. 2001. Middle-Class Formation and the Cultural Construction of Gender in Urban India, in Imtiaz Ahmad and Helmut Reifeld (eds), *Middle Class Values*, 125–39. New Delhi: Social Science Press.

Poggendorf-Kakar, Katharina. 2002. *Hindu-Frauen zwischen tradition und moderne: Religiöse veränderungen der indischen mittelschicht im städtischen umfeld* [Hindu Women between Tradition and Modernity: Religious Changes among the Urban Middle Class in India]. Stuttgart/Weimar: Metzler.

―――. 2006. Adaption, reinterpretation, interdependenz: Postmoderne religiosität am beispiel der Sathya Sai Baba-bewegung [Adaptation, Reinterpretation, Interdependency: Postmodern Religiosity in the Case of the Sathya Sai Baba Movement], in Michael Bergunder (ed.), *Westliche formen des hinduismus in Deutschland*, 68–89. Halle: Verlag der Franckeschen Stiftungen zu Halle.

Pollock, Sheldon, Homi K. Bhabha, Carol A. Breckenridge and Dipesh Chakravarty. 2000. Cosmopolitanisms. *Public Culture* 12(3): 577–89.

Possamai, Adam. 2005. *Religion and Popular Culture: A Hyper-Real Testament*. New York: P.I.E.-Peter Lang.

Prasad, A. 2001. *Consumption Behaviour in India*. New Delhi: Reliance.

Pratt, Mary Louise. 1992. *Imperial Eyes: Travel Writing and Transculturation*. London: Routledge.

Prem, Kamala. 2006a. Feng Shui: Power That Helps Create Wealth. *Realty Plus: The Real Estate Review*, September, 3(1): 124.

―――. 2006b. Tame Heat Energy. *Realty Plus: The Real Estate Review*, February, 2(5): 66.

Punathambekar, Aswin. 2005. Bollywood in the Indian–American Diaspora: Mediating a Transitive Logic of Cultural Citizenship. *International Journal of Cultural Studies* 8(2): 151–73.

Purie, Aroon. 2005. From the Editor-in-Chief. *India Today*, 16–22 August, IV(33): 1.

Raheja, Gloria Goodwin. 1988. *The Poison in the Gift: Ritual, Prestation, and the Dominant Caste in a North Indian Village*. Chicago: University of Chicago Press.

Rahman, Azera. 2006. For 'Millionaires' Only. *Realty Plus: The Real Estate Review*, November, 3(3): 72–74.

Rajagopal, Arvind. 2001a. *Politics after Television: Hindu Nationalism and the Reshaping of the Public in India*. Cambridge: Cambridge University Press.

―――. 2001b. Thinking About the New Indian Middle Class: Gender, Advertising and Politics in an Age of Globalisation, in Rajeswari Sunder Rajan (ed.), *Signposts*, 57–99. New Brunswick: Rutgers University Press.

Rajan, Gita and Shailja Sharma. 2006. New Cosmopolitanisms: South Asians in the United States at the Turn of the Twenty-First Century, in Gita Rajan and Shailja Sharma (eds), *New Cosmopolitanisms: South Asians in the US*, 1–36. Stanford, CA: Stanford University Press.

Raman, Anuradha. 2009. Dignity in Cities. *Outlook*, 15 June.

Ramaswamy, Sumathi. 2006. Enshrining the Map of India: Cartography, Nationalism and the Politics of Deity in Varanasi, in Martin Ganeszle and Jörg Gengnagel (eds), *Visualizing Space in Banaras: Images, Maps, and the Practice of Representation*, 165–90. Wiesbaden: Harrassowitz Verlag.

Ramu, Gaddehosur N. 1989. *Women, Work and Marriage in Urban India: A Study of Dual and Single-Earner Couples*. New Delhi: Sage Publications.

Rao, Vijayendra and Michael Walton. 2004. Culture and Public Action: Relationality, Equality of Agency, and Development, in Viyajendra Rao and Michael Walton (eds), *Culture and Public Action*, 3–36. New Delhi: Permanent Black.

Rastogi, Tavishi Paitandy. 2007. Shaadi No. 1. *Hindustan Times*, 14 January, pp. 4–8.

Ravindran, K. T. 2000. A State of Siege. *Frontline*, 9–22 December, 17(25): 116–18.

Reddy, Vanita. 2006. The Nationalization of the Global Indian Woman: Geographies of Beauty in *Femina*. *South Asian Popular Culture* 4(1): 61–85.

Reeve, Man Richard. 1995. *Urban Design and Places of Spectacle: Social Control as an Aspect of the Design and Management of Mundane Leisure Space in Contemporary British Context*. Oxford: Brooks University Press.

Richter, Rudolf. 2005. *Die lebensstilgesellschaft* [Lifestyle Society]. Wiesbaden: VS Verlag für Sozialwissenschaften.

Roberts, John Michael. 2005. Let the Mob Speak! *Historical Materialism* 13(4): 373–88.

Robertson, Roland. 1995. Glocalizations: Time–Space and Homogeneity–Heterogeneity, in Scott Lash, Roland Robertson and Mike Featherstone (eds), *Global Modernities*, 25–44. London: Sage Publications.

Robinson, Richard and David Goodman. 1996. The New Rich in Asia: Economic Development, Social Status and Political Consciousness, in David Goodman and Richard Robinson (eds), *The New Rich in Asia: Mobile Phones, McDonald's and Middle Class Revolution*, 1–18. London: Routledge.

Rony, Fatimah Tobing. 1996. *The Third Eye: Race, Cinema, and Ethnographic Spectacle*. Durham: Duke University Press.

Roy, Aindrila Basu. 2006. The Game Story. *India Today Buyer's Guide* 1(1): 46–48.

Roy, Dunu. 2005a. Introducing the Draft Master Plan for Delhi-2021, in Dunu Roy and Lalit Batra (eds), *Draft Delhi Master Plan 2010*, 7–9. New Delhi: Hazards Centre.

———. 2005b. Trading in a World Class City, in Dunu Roy (ed.), *Draft Delhi Master Plan 2010*, 31–32. New Delhi: Hazards Centre.

Roy, Srirupa. 2007. *Beyond Belief: India and the Politics of Postcolonial Nationalism*. Durham: Duke University Press.

Runkle, Susan. 2004, Making 'Miss India': Constructing Gender, Power and the Nation. *South Asian Popular Culture* 2(2), 145–59.

Sadhu Swayamprakashdas. 2005. *Swaminarayan Bliss*, Special Inauguration Issue 28(11–12). Ahmedabad: Swaminarayan Aksharpith.

Sadhu Vishwamurtidas. 2003. *Perspectives: Inspiring Essays on Life*. Amdavad: Swaminarayan Aksharpith.

Saran, Rohit. 2005. How Long Will the Party Last? *India Today*, 28 November, pp. 18–23, http://www.indiatoday.com/itoday/20051128/states.html (accessed 30 October 2009).

Sarkar, Sumit. 1997. The City Imagined: Calcutta of the Nineteenth and Early Twentieth Centuries, in Sumit Sarkar (ed.), *Writing Social History*, 159–85. New Delhi: Oxford University Press.

Sassen, Saskia (ed.). 1996. Whose City Is It? Globalization and the Formation of New Claims. *Public Culture* 8: 205–23.

Sassen, Saskia (ed.). 2001a. *The Global City: New York, London, Tokyo.* Princeton, NJ: Princeton University Press.

———. 2001b. The Global City: Strategic Site/New Frontier. *Seminar* 503 (*Special Issue on Globalisation*).

———. 2002. *Global Networks, Linked Cities.* New York: Routledge.

Säävälä, Minna. 2001. Low Caste but Middle-Class: Some Religious Strategies for Middle-Class Identification in Hyderabad. *Contributions to Indian Sociology* 35(3): 293–318.

———. 2003. Auspicious Hindu Houses: The New Middle Classes in Hyderabad, India. *Social Anthropology* 11(2): 231–47.

———. 2006. Entangled in the Imagination: New Middle Class Apprehensions in an Indian Theme Park. *Ethnos* 71(3): 390–414.

Sax, William S. (ed.). 1995. *The Gods at Play: Lila in South Asia.* New York: Oxford University Press.

———. 2002. *Dancing the Self: Personhood and Performance in the Pandav Lila of Garhwal.* New York: Oxford University Press

Schiffauer, Werner. 1997. Zur logik von kulturellen strömungen in grossstädten [On the Logic of Cultural Flows in Metropolises], in *Fremde in der Stadt: Zehn essays über kultur und differenz*, 92–127. Frankfurt am Main: Suhrkamp.

———. 2004. Cosmopolitans Are Cosmopolitans: On the Relevance of Local Identification in Globalizing Society, in Jonathan Friedman and Shalini Randeria (eds), *Worlds on the Move: Globalization, Migration, and Cultural Security*, 91–102. London, New York: IB Tauris.

Schramm, Katharina. 2004. Coming Home to the Motherland: Pilgrimage Tourism in Ghana, in Simon Coleman and John Eade (eds), *Reframing Pilgrimage: Cultures in Motion*, 133–49. London: Routledge.

Schulze, Gerhard. 1992. *Die erlebnisgesellschaft* [The Society of Sensuous Experience]. Frankfurt am Main: Campus Verlag.

Sengupta, Shuddhabrata. 1999. Vision Mixing: Marriage-Video-Film and the Video-Walla's Images of Life, in Christiane Brosius and Melissa Butcher (eds), *Image Journeys: Audio-Visual Media and Cultural Change in India*, 279–307. New Delhi: Sage Publications.

Shah, Ghanshyam. 1990. Middle Class Movements, *Social Movements in India: A Review of the Literature*, 161–80. New Delhi: Sage Publications.

Sharma, Aruna. 2006. A Dirge for Delhi? *Hindustan Times*, 28 September, p. 12.

Sharma, Kalpana. 2006. Can a Slum Become a World Class Township? *The Hindu*, 6 October, p. 10.

Sharma, Sanjukta. 2005. Forget Shanghai, Mumbai Is Headed for Disaster. *Tehelka*, 9 April.

Sharpe, Jenny. 2005. Gender, Nation, and Globalization in Monsoon Wedding and Dilwale Dulhania Le Jayenge. *Meridians: Feminism, Race, Transnationalism*, 6(1), 58–81.

Shatkin, G. 2007. Global Cities of the South: Emerging Perspectives on Growth and Inequality. *Cities* 24(1): 1–15.

Shields, Rob (ed.). 1992a. *Lifestyle Shopping: The Subject of Consumption.* London: Routledge.

Shields, Rob (ed.). 1992b. Spaces for the Subject of Consumption, in Rob Shields (ed.), *Lifestyle Shopping: The Subject of Consumption*, 1–19. London: Routledge.

Shukla, Sandhia. 1997. Building Diaspora and Nation: The 1991 'Cultural Festival of India'. *Cultural Studies* 11(2): 296–315.

Shukla, Amitabh. 2007. Old Plan for a New Yamuna. *Hindustan Times*, 15 January, p. 7.

Siebel, Walter and Jan Wehrheim. 2006. Security and the Urban Public Sphere. *German Policy Studies* 3(1): 19–46.

Simha, Rakesh. 2004. Unkorking the Good Times. *India Empire*, October, pp. 74–75.

Simmel, Georg. 1995 (1903). Die grossstädte und das geistesleben [Cities and Mental Life], *Aufsätze und abhandlungen 1901–1908*, Frankfurt am Main: Suhrkamp.

Simpson, Daniel. 2006. Dubai: Investors' Heaven. *Realty Plus: The Real Estate Review*, 3(1): 36–38.

Singer, Milton. 1972. *When a Great Tradition Modernizes: An Anthropological Approach to Indian Civilization*. Chicago and London: University of Chicago Press.

Singh, Gurinder. 2006. Real Estate: Boom or Burst. *Indian Observer*, 1–15 September, pp. 8–14.

Singh, Kavita. Forthcoming. Temple of Eternal Return: The Swaminarayan Akshardhan Complex in Delhi. *Artibus Asiae*.

Singh, Vijay. 2007. *Master Plan for Delhi: With the Perspective for the Year 2021*. New Delhi: Rupa & Co.

Smith, Michael Peter. 2001. *Transnational Urbanism: Locating Globalization*. Malden and Oxford: Blackwell Publishers.

Soja, Edward. 2000. *Postmetropolis: Critical Studies of Cities and Regions*. Oxford: Blackwell.

Sonwalkar, Prasun. 2004. A Campaign That Lost Sheen. *The Hindu*, 3 October.

Sorkin, Michael (ed.). 1992a. *Variations on a Theme Park: The New American City and the End of Public Space*. New York: Hill & Wang.

———. 1992b. Wir seh'n uns in Disneyland [We'll Meet Again in Disneyland], *Zeitschrift für architektur und städtebau*, December, 114 & 115: 100–110.

Sreenivas, Mytheli. 2003. Emotion, Identity, and the Female Subject: Tamil Women's Magazines in Colonial India, 1890–1940. *Journal of Women's History* 14(4): 59–82.

Srinivas, M. N. 1971. *Social Change in Modern India*. Berkeley: University of California Press.

———. 1977. The Changing Position of Indian Women. *Man* 12(2): 221–38.

———. 1987. The Indian Village: Myth and Reality, in M. N. Srinivas (ed.), *The Dominant Caste and Other Essays*. Delhi: Oxford University Press.

Srinivas, Smriti. 2008. *In the Presence of Sai Baba: Body, City and Memory in a Global Religious Movement*. Leiden, Boston: Brill.

Srinivasa, Kavitha. 2007. Body Beautiful. *Savy*, October, p. 64.

Srivastava, Sanjay. 2006. *Passionate Modernity: Sexuality, Class, and Consumption in India*. New Delhi: Routledge.

———. 2009. Urban Spaces, Disney-Divinity and Moral Middle Classes in Delhi. *Economic and Political Weehly*, 27 June: 338–45.

Stanley, Nick. 2002. Chinese Theme Parks and National Identity, in Terence Young and Robert Riley (eds), *Theme Park Landscapes: Antecedents and Variations*, 269–90. Washington, DC: Dumbarton Oaks, Research Library & Collections.

Stevenson, Deborah. 2003. *Cities and Urban Cultures*. Maidenhead, Philadelphia: Open University Press.

Swami Brahmviharidas. 1992. The Evolution of Swaminarayan Festivals: Internal and External Transmission of Traditions, in Raymond B. Williams (ed.), *A Sacred Thread*, 200–208. Chambersburg: Anima.

Swami Vivekjivandas. 1992. Swaminarayan Temples and Rituals: Views of Sadhus — A Tale of Two Temples: London and Amdavad, in Raymond B. Williams (ed.), *A Sacred Thread*, 191–99. Chambersburg: Anima.

Tankha, Rajkumare. 2006. Noida Draws up Games Plan. *Hindustan Times*, 28 September, p. 6.

Tarlo, Emma. 1996. *Clothing Matters: Dress and Identity in India*. Chicago: University of Chicago.

———. 2003. *Unsettling Memories: Narratives of the Emergency in Delhi*. New Delhi: Permanent Black.

Tester, Keith (ed.). 1994. *The Flâneur*. London: Routledge.

Thomas, Rosie. 1995. Melodrama and the Negotiation of Morality in Mainstream Hindi Film, in Carol Breckenridge (ed.), *Consuming Modernity: Public Culture in a South Asian World*, 157–82. Minnesota: University of Minneapolis Press.

Tiwari, Piyush. 2005. Do We Have Too Many Malls? *The Indian Express*, 26 February, p. 2.

Tölölyan, Khachig. 1991. The Nation-State and Its Others: In Lieu of a Preface. *Diaspora* (Spring): 3–7.

Trehan, Prerana. 2004. The Big Fat Indian Wedding. *The Sunday Tribune*, 29 August.

Tresidder, Richard. 1999. Tourism and Sacred Landscapes, in David Crouch (ed.), *Leisure/Tourism Geographies: Practices and Geographical Knowledge*, 137–48. London: Routledge.

Uberoi, Patricia (ed.). 1993. *Family, Kinship and Marriage in India*. New Delhi: Oxford University Press

———. 2001. A Suitable Romance? Trajectories of Courtship in Indian Popular Fiction, in Shoma Munshi (ed.), *Images of the 'Modern Woman' in Asia: Global Media, Local Meanings*, 169–86. Richmond: Curzon.

———. 2004. The Family in India, in Veena Das (ed.), *Handbook of Indian Sociology*, 275–307. New Delhi: Oxford University Press.

———. 2006. *Freedom and Destiny: Gender, Family, and Popular Culture in India*. New Delhi: Oxford University Press.

———. 2008. Aspirational Weddings: The Bridal Magazine and the Canons of 'Decent Marriage', in Christophe Jaffrelot and Peter van der Veer (eds), *Patterns of Middle Class Consumption*, 230–62. Los Angeles: Sage Publications.

UN Population Division. 2004. *World Urbanization Prospects: The 2003 Revision*. UN Report. New York: United Nations.

Urry, John. 1990. *The Tourist Gaze. Leisure and Travel in Contemporary Societies*. London: Sage Publications.

———. 2000. The Global Media and Cosmopolitanism, Department of Sociology, Lancaster University, http://www.comp.lancs.ac.uk/sociology/papers/Urry-Global-Media.pdf (accessed 30 October 2009).

van der Veer, Peter. 2002. Cosmopolitan Options. *Etnografica* VI(1): 15–26.

———. 2004. Transnational Religion; Hindu and Muslim Movements. *Journal for the Study of Religions and Ideologies* 7: 4–18.

Varma, Pavan K. 1998. *The Great Indian Middle Class*. New Delhi: Penguin.

———. 2001. Learning to Belong. *Seminar* 515 (First City: A Symposium on Remembering Delhi).

Varma, Rashmi. 2004. Provincializing the Global City: From Bombay to Mumbai. *Social Text-81* 22(4): 65–89.

Veblen, Thorstein. 1994 (1899). *The Theory of the Leisure Class*. New York: Dover Publications.

Verma, Jayant. 2006. Property Watch. *India Today Buyer's Guide*, July–September, pp. 8–14.

Vertovec, Steven. 2000. *The Hindu Diaspora: Comparative Patterns*. London: Routledge.

Vertovec, Steven and Robin Cohen. 2002. Conceiving Cosmopolitanism, in Steven Vertovec and Robin Cohen (eds), *Conceiving Cosmopolitanism: Theory, Context and Practice*, 1–24. Oxford: Oxford University Press.

Virilio, Paul. 1997. *Open Sky*. London: Verso.

Waghorne, Joanne P. 2004. *Diaspora of the Gods: Modern Hindu Temples in an Urban Middle-Class World*. New York: Oxford University Press.

Warrier, Maya. 2005. *Hindu Selves in a Modern World: Guru Faith in the Mata Amritanandamayi Mission*. London: Routledge.

Wayne, Leslie. 2004. Sikh Group Finds Calling in Homeland Security. *New York Times*, 28 September.

Weber, Max. 2006. Class, Status, Party, in David Grusky and Szonja Szelényi (eds), *Inequality: Classic Readings in Race, Class, and Gender*, 37–54. Boulder, Colorado: Westview Press.

Werbner, Pnina. 2006. Vernacular Cosmopolitanism. *Theory, Culture & Society* 23(2–3): 496–98.

Wessel, Margit van. 2004. Talking About Consumption: How an Indian Middle Class Dissociates from Middle-Class Life. *Cultural Dynamics* 16(1): 93–116.

Williams, Raymond B. 2001. *An Introduction to Swaminarayan Hinduism*. Cambridge: Cambridge University Press.

Wilson, Rob and Wimal Dissanayake (eds). 1996. *Global/Local: Cultural Production and the Transnational Imaginary*. Durham and London: Duke University Press.

Wöhler, Karlheinz (ed.). 2005. *Erlebniswelten: Herstellung und nutzung touristischer welten* [Event Worlds: Production and Use of Tourist Worlds]. Münster: LIT Verlag.

Young, Ken. 1999. Consumption, Social Differentiation and Self-Definition of the New Rich in Industrialising Southeast Asia, in Michael Pinches (ed.), *Culture and Privilege in Capitalist Asia*, 56–85. London: Routledge.

Young, Terence and Robert Riley (eds). 2002. *Theme Park Landscapes: Antecedents and Variations*. Washington, DC: Dumharton Oaks Research Library and Collection.

Zhang, Li. 2002. Spatiality and Urban Citizenship in Late Socialist China. *Public Culture* 14(2): 311–34.

Zhang, Xudong. 2000. Shanghai Nostalgia: Postrevolutionary Allegories in Wang Anyi's Literary Production in the 1990s. *Positions: East Asia Cultures Critique* 8(2): 349–87.

———. 2002. Shanghai Image: Critical Iconography, Minor Literature, and the Un-Making of a Modern Chinese Mythology. *New Literary History* 33(1): 137–67.

Zukin, Sharon. 2005 (1995). Whose Culture? Whose City? in Jan Lin and Christopher Mele (eds), *The Urban Sociology Reader*, 281–89. London: Routledge.

ABOUT THE AUTHOR

ṏ

Christiane Brosius is Professor of Visual and Media Anthropology at the Cluster of Excellence 'Asia and Europe in a Global Context: Shifting Asymmetries in Cultural Flows', Heidelberg University. She is one of the founding members of Tasveer Ghar ('House of Pictures'): A Digital Network of South Asian Popular Visual Culture, a transnational network dedicated to researching, archiving and publishing visual popular culture. Her research projects range from ritual performances of the Hindu Right in India and abroad to the representation of the Pacific Islands in early western films (1900–29). Her interests are anthropology of visual culture and media technologies in South Asia, globalisation and migration, diaspora, ritual and performance studies, urban lifestyle, consumption and nationalist movements. She is the author of *Empowering Visions: The Politics of Representation in Hindu Nationalism* (2005), and has co-edited *Visual Homes, Image Worlds: Essays from Tasveer Ghar, the House of Pictures* (forthcoming, with Sumathi Ramaswamy and Yousuf Saeed), *Ritual, Heritage and Identity* (2011, with Karin Polit), *Ritual Matters: Dynamic Dimensions in Practice* (2010, with Ute Hüsken) and *Mumbai–Delhi–Kolkata: Approaches to India's Megacities in German* (2006, with Ravi Ahuja).

INDEX

❦